Theory and Design of Adaptive Filters

John R. Treichler
Applied Signal Technology
Sunnyvale, CA

C. Richard Johnson, Jr.
School of Electrical and Computer Engineering
Cornell University
Ithaca, NY

Michael G. Larimore
Applied Signal Technology
Sunnyvale, CA

Prentice Hall
Upper Saddle River, NJ 07458

Library of Congress Cataloging-in-Publication Data
Treichler, John R.
    Theory and design of adaptive filters / John R. Treichler, C. Richard Johnson, Jr., and
Michael G. Larimore.
        p.   cm.
    Includes bibliographical references and index.
    ISBN 0-13-040265-6
    1. Adaptive filters—Design and construction.   I. Johnson, C. Richard.   II. Larimore,
Michael G.   III. Title.
TK7872.F5 T65   2001
621.3815′324—dc21   2001018504

Vice President and Editorial Director, ECS: *Marcia J. Horton*
Publisher: *Tom Robbins*
Editorial Assistant: *Jody McDonnell*
Vice President and Director of Production and Manufacturing, ESM: *David W. Riccardi*
Executive Managing Editor: *Vince O'Brien*
Managing Editor: *David A. George*
Production Editor: *Kelly Ricci*
Director of Creative Services: *Paul Belfanti*
Creative Director: *Carole Anson*
Art Director: *Jayne Conte*
Art Editor: *Adam Velthaus*
Cover Designer: *Bruce Kenselaar*
Manufacturing Manager: *Trudy Pisciotti*
Marketing Manager: *Holly Stark*
Marketing Assistant: *Karen Moon*

 © 2001 by Prentice Hall, Inc.
Upper Saddle River, New Jersey 07458

Printed in the United States of America

10   9   8   7   6   5   4   3   2   1

ISBN 0-13-040265-6

PRENTICE-HALL INTERNATIONAL (UK) LIMITED, *London*
PRENTICE-HALL OF AUSTRALIA PTY. LIMITED, *Sydney*
PRENTICE-HALL CANADA INC., *Toronto*
PRENTICE-HALL HISPANICAMERICANA, S.A., *Mexico*
PRENTICE-HALL OF INDIA PRIVATE LIMITED, *New Delhi*
PRENTICE-HALL OF JAPAN, INC., *Tokyo*
PEARSON EDUCATION ASIA PTE. LTD., *Singapore*
EDITORA PRENTICE-HALL DO BRASIL, LTDS., *Rio de Janeiro*

To Sally, Betty, and Mary Anne

Contents

Preface

Theory and Design of Adaptive Filters is a pedagogical compilation of fundamental adaptive filtering concepts, algorithm forms, behavioral insights, and application guidelines. The analysis and design of three basic classes of adaptive filters are presented: (1) adaptive finite-impulse-response (FIR) filters, (2) adaptive infinite-impulse-response (IIR) filters, and (3) adaptive property-restoral filters.

For the widely studied and utilized class of adaptive FIR filters, we develop the most popular analytical tools and distill a tutorial collection of insightful design guidelines of proven utility. In contrast, for more recently developed adaptive IIR and adaptive property-restoral filters, we focus on algorithm fabrication and behavioral insights and suggested applications. The text is framed by motivating problem statements given in Chapter 1 and by corresponding design detail in the closing chapters. This provides a sampling of successful adaptive filtering applications that are currently the subject of industrial development and deployment activity. The intertwining of theory and design is further emphasized in this book by inclusion of a comprehensive chapter on adaptive filter implementation fundamentals. Thus, both practicing engineers interested in designing appropriate adaptive filters for various applications and graduate students interested in acquiring a cohesive pedagogy for initiation of basic research in adaptive filter theory can benefit from this book.

Chapter 1 contains detailed description of the purpose and motivation of adaptive filtering in four practical signal processing problems. Basically, this chapter is for readers who do not yet know of the practical need for and utility of adaptive filters. An understanding of nonadaptive digital signal processing is assumed of the reader. More specifically, this book was written with the expectation that the reader would have a rudimentary understanding of digital filter theory (e.g., discrete Fourier transform, analog-to-digital filter transformation, and frequency-response shaping techniques of FIR and IIR digital filter design), stochastic processes (e.g., correlation functions), linear algebra (e.g., eigenvalues and eigenvectors), and systems theory (e.g., state representations, z-transforms, transfer functions, and stability theory). If the reader does not possess such a background, the following texts are recommended as possible sources: B. P. Lathi, *Linear Systems and Signals*, (Berkeley-Cambridge Press, 1992), A. V. Oppenheim and A. S. Willsky, *Signals and Systems* (Prentice-Hall, 1983), and L. R. Rabiner and B. Gold, *Theory and Application of Digital Signal Processing*, (Prentice-Hall, 1975). Given such a background, the reader should find this book a self-contained primer and reference source on adaptive filtering.

Chapter 2 provides an illustration of the basic principles underlying the conversion of (mis) performance information into digital filter adaptation. A set of number guessing games with logically obvious algorithmic solutions is examined and recognized to strongly parallel digital filter adaptation where the filter parameters are effectively the numbers being guessed. These examples of adaptation are simple enough to be understood through the use of basic algebra, yet complex enough to illustrate several of the basic attributes of adaptive filters. The reader will also find these number guessing games helpful in interpreting the purpose and usefulness of algorithmic elaborations that are introduced in subsequent chapters. Essentially, Chapter 2 is intended for those readers who believe adaptive filters are useful but do not yet have a firm idea as to the recursive form of filter parameter adaption.

Chapters 3, 4, 5, and 6 present the fundamentals of adaptive filter theory forming the core of a typical first-year graduate or advanced senior level course in adaptive filtering. Chapters 3 and 4 focus on adaptive FIR filters, which have been widely analyzed and applied since their conception in the late 1950s. Chapter 3 develops popular adaptive filter analysis tools for dynamic parameter estimate moment analysis. Chapter 4 is based on selections of fundamental material from the large body of useful work on adaptive FIR filter design. Chapters 3 and 4 are widely acknowledged as the traditional domain of adaptive filtering. Chapters 5 and 6 provide descriptions of fundamental behavior theory and proposed applications of more recently "discovered" adaptive filter algorithms. Adaptive IIR filters, first proposed in the open literature in the mid 1970s, are examined in Chapter 5 from the two conceptually distinct approaches of gradient descent minimization and stability theory. The resulting algorithm forms are interpreted as logical extensions on the basic adaptive FIR filter algorithm. The pedagogy of adaptive IIR filters is still in its youth. Chapter 6 introduces the class of adaptive property-restoral filters, initially formulated in the early 1980s. This property-restoral class is a conceptual enlargement of the basis of the adaptive FIR and IIR filters of Chapters 4 and 5. Property-restoral adaptive filters adjust their coefficients to restore some known property of the desired output sequence without (necessarily) requiring a full sample-by-sample description of the desired output sequence, as do the more traditional adaptive filter algorithms of Chapters 4 and 5. Application of the property-restoral concept has proceeded faster than development of an appropriate comprehensive theory. Chapter 6 focuses more on the particular engineering successes of this concept rather than its abstract theoretical analysis.

Where Chapters 4 through 6 focus on theoretically derived algorithms valid under certain idealizations, practice dictates certain modifications to help insure cost-effective, robust performance in the more harsh environment of real applications. Such issues and related implementation concerns are summarized in Chapter 7. Since the study of adaptive filters is driven by the need for and success of their use, Chapters 8 to 11 return one-by-one to the four applications cited in Chapter 1, specifically hum removal via noise cancelling, multipath correction via channel equalization, channel modeling via impulse response coefficient estimation, and antenna array beam steering via linear combining, as illustrations of the use of the adaptive filter algorithms studied in the intervening chapters. Chapters 1 to 6 have served the authors in their graduate teaching efforts as the foundation of a semester-long course. Course projects are often stimulated by Chapters 7 to 11.

We stress the fundamentals. Admittedly, those selected are a reflection of the biases of the authors. The possible tunnel vision imposed by such a procedure is mitigated by the citation of references examining more advanced issues.

Another feature is the inclusion in Appendix A of MATLAB® listings of some basic algorithms. One of the major hurdles for new "students" of adaptive filtering is the conversion of algorithm equations into implementable code. In fact, our teaching experience indicates that the construction of such code is a major learning experience. The listings included are intended to aid, but not to replace, this effort. We have chosen only the simpler versions of the algorithms examined due to their pedagogical clarity. The high data rate and minimal computation cost objectives of the majority of adaptive filtering applications support this focus on the simplest of algorithms with proven attractive properties. However, as is apparent from Chapter 7, high-level language code is still somewhat removed from the coding (and hardware) necessities of actual applications.

A number of people deserve our thanks for their part in the preparation of this book. In the mid-1980s Sid Burrus and Tom Parks, both at Rice University at the time, suggested this project to us as the second entry in a series of books on topics in digital signal processing sponsored by Texas Instruments. Gene Frantz of Texas Instruments receives our gratitude for his arrangement, a decade later, of the return of the rights to us that stimulated this revision.

Additional thanks go to Tom Endres and Raul Casas of NxtWave Communications, Jim Zeidler of University of California at San Diego, and Nick H. Younan of Mississippi State University for their comments and suggestions on the manuscript. Thanks also go to Ray Herring of KGO-DTV for his support of signal collection operations used in Chapter 10.

This culmination of our collaborations in adaptive filter research began under the tutelage of Doc Widrow in the office we shared, fondly known then as *The Zoo*, while we were all struggling toward Ph.D.s (all received on the same day in 1977). In the intervening years our interaction through Applied Signal Technology

(Sunnyvale, CA) proved indispensable to our combined understanding of the design (and pertinent theory) aspects of adaptive filters.

It is the widespread success of adaptive filter applications that makes this book possible. We acknowledge our indebtedness to the efforts of the community of adaptive filtering theorists and practitioners who are responsible for these successes.

John Treichler, Rick Johnson, and Mike Larimore

1

The Need for Adaptive Filtering

- *Precis: Many practical signal-processing applications call for an analog or digital filter whose characteristics can be automatically modified to accommodate incomplete knowledge or time variation in the nature of the input signals.*

An *adaptive filter* is very generally defined as a filter whose characteristics can be modified to achieve some end or objective, and is usually assumed to accomplish this modification (or "adaptation") automatically, without the need for substantial intervention by the user. While not necessarily required, it is also usually assumed that the time scale of the modification is very slow compared to the bandwidth of the signal being filtered. Implicit in this assumption is that the system designer could (over any particular substantial time window) in fact use a time-invariant, nonadaptive filter if only the designer knew enough about the input signals to design the filter before its use. This lack of knowledge may spring from true uncertainty about the characteristics of the signal when the filter is turned on, or because the characteristics of the input signal can slowly change during the filter's operation. Lacking this knowledge, the designer then turns to an "adaptive" filter, which can "learn" the signal characteristics when first turned on and thereafter can "track" slow changes in these characteristics.

As later chapters show, adaptive filters can be implemented in a variety of ways, allowing an ever wider variety of practical problems to be solved. We find that many aspects of adaptive filter design, and even the development of some of the adaptive algorithms, are governed by the nature of the applications themselves. Because of this and the desire to impart some perspective about how adaptive filters may be employed, this chapter examines four of the many possible applications. In each case, we examine no details about the adaptive filters themselves—this is done in later chapters—but instead take four practical signal-processing problems and formulate a solution for each that employs some form of "smart" filter. How to impart this "intelligence" to such a filter is discussed in Chapters 2–6. A variety of implementation issues are discussed in Chapter 7, and the four specific problems examined in this chapter form the basis for the design examples in Chapters 8–11.

1.1 REMOVAL OF POWER LINE HUM FROM MEDICAL INSTRUMENTS

We first consider the problem shown in Figure 1.1. A remote sensor is connected to an amplifier via a length of cable. The amplifier output contains not only the sensor signal, but also a 50- or 60-Hz component due to stray pickup from power mains. Pickup of this type is often associated with sensitive high-impedance sensors like microphones and electrodes. Such hum may prove to be merely bothersome in a high-fidelity sound reproduction system, but it can be overwhelming when attempting to measure very small voltages, such as are found when trying to obtain a patient's electrocardiogram (ECG). If the spectrum of the sensor signal does not include 60 Hz, then the hum component can be removed via bandpass filtering, but many applications, including ECG measurement, cannot tolerate exclusion of signal energy below 100 Hz. A very narrow notch filter might be appropriate, as long as the frequency of the electric power is steady enough to remain within the notch of the filter. Figure 1.2(a) illustrates this method.

Another approach to solving this problem is shown in Figure 1.2(b). Suppose we measure the power main itself and attempt to use that signal to eliminate the 60-Hz component entering the amplifier. Clearly, if that can be done then the amplifier input

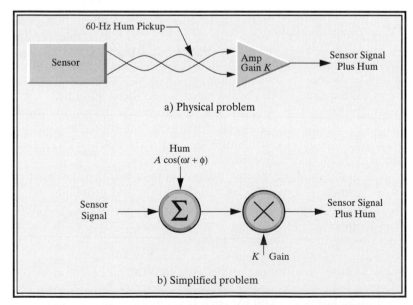

Figure 1.1   Hum pickup at the input of an instrumentation amplifier.

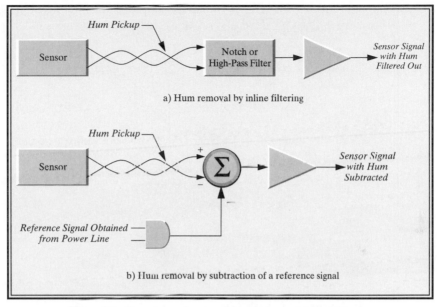

a) Hum removal by inline filtering

b) Hum removal by subtraction of a reference signal

Figure 1.2   Two approaches to solving the hum pickup problem.

and output will contain only the sensor signal. Moreover, if the power line frequency changes, then both the hum and the "reference" measurement will change together, allowing good cancellation to continue.

The problem with this cancellation approach is that the amplitude and phase of the 60-Hz reference signal must be carefully adjusted to make it accurately cancel the hum at the input of the amplifier. In some applications the required amplitude and phase settings might be determined once and then remained fixed. In most cases, however, the amount of stray 60-Hz pickup will change with the exact lead placement, the amount of power being drawn in the room, and any number of other factors that either change with time or over which the user has no control. As a practical matter, then, the gain and phase rotation applied to the reference 60-Hz waveform must be variable and some automatic technique should be available to adjust them in real time to assure good cancellation. Figure 1.3(a) shows a simplified version of how such a canceller might be designed with a variable gain G and phase ϕ. However, the variable phase shifter is difficult to implement at low frequencies like 60 Hz. The modified version of Figure 1.3(a), shown in Figure 1.3(b), is one step closer to practicality because it uses two adjustable scaling coefficients w_0 and w_1 to control the gain and phase of the filter [Widrow et al., 1975b].

What we have done here is develop an adaptive filter to solve the hum problem. The filter accepts a 60-Hz reference signal (from the wall plug) and changes its characteristics (gain and phase) to produce a signal that cancels the hum to a great extent. How to build adaptation into this filter is left to later chapters, but this example

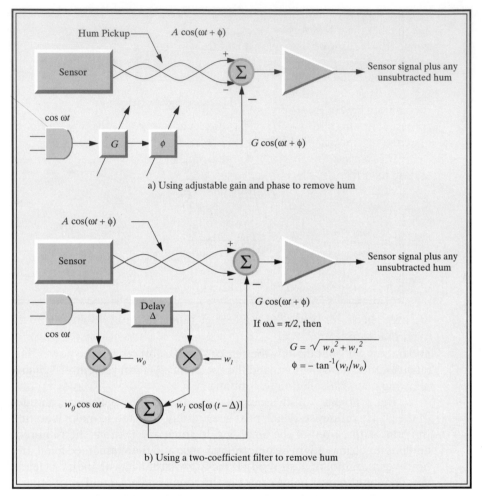

Figure 1.3 Evolutionary steps toward a practical hum canceller.

shows that an automatically adjustable or adaptive filter can be the basis of an elegant solution to the hum removal problem.

1.2 EQUALIZATION OF TROPOSCATTER COMMUNICATION SIGNALS

Many techniques exist for communicating via radio transmission over long distances. High-frequency (HF) radio and stationary line-of-sight microwave systems came into commercial use in the early 1900s for terrestrial communications and were followed by successful introduction of communications satellite systems in the 1960s. Each technique has its own merits and disadvantages, and each one has developed a niche where its mixture of economic and technical advantages makes it superior to other approaches. The technique we examine in this example is *troposcatter communications*. This technique uses a powerful transmitter (500–1000 W) and a large antenna to beam radio frequency energy toward the horizon. Some small portion of this energy is scattered toward the receiver by turbulence in the troposphere. The distance between the transmitter and receiver can be as much as 500 km, requiring no intervening repeaters or satellites. This transmission distance makes troposcatter communications systems very cost-effective for communicating across large bodies of water or otherwise inhospitable routes (e.g., the Arctic).

The economic value of a communication path usually depends on its capacity and on its reliability. In the case of troposcatter communications the scattering path limits both. A typical troposcatter link uses two transmitters and two receivers in some form of spatial and/or frequency diversity combining scheme to ensure adequate reliability. Signal capacity is also typically limited to 120 voice channels. We now explore how these limitations come about.

The effect the troposphere has on a radio signal can be modeled in a simplified fashion as shown in Figure 1.4. As a portion of the transmitted beam hits a particular region of turbulence, it is refracted because of differences in the atmosphere's refractive index. The amount of energy refracted in any given direction depends on the exact behavior of the turbulent region and cannot be reliably predicted. However, the transmitted beam illuminates many such regions, and many of those are visible at the receiver. The resulting received signal is the sum of the individual components, and depending on the exact phase relationship of these components, they

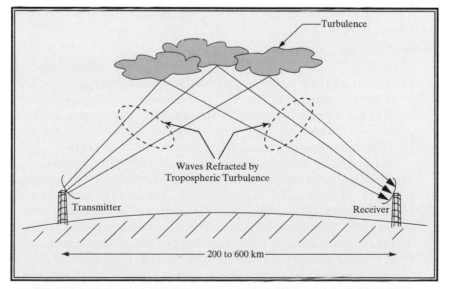

Figure 1.4 Cross-section view of an over-the-horizon communication system employing troposcatter propagation.

can add either constructively or destructively. Consequently, the instantaneous received power level is effectively a random variable. Even so, its average value can be reasonably predicted given the transmitter and receiver locations.

Using Figure 1.4 we can develop an expression for the received signal $r(t)$,

$$r(t) = \sum_{i=1}^{I} s(t - \Delta_i)g_i(t) \qquad (1.2.1)$$

where $s(t)$ is the transmitted signal, $g_i(t)$ is the gain of the propagation path through refractor i, and Δ_i is the added delay caused by taking the ith path compared to the shortest path. The received signal is effectively the sum of I delayed and scaled versions of the transmitted signal. Using the convolutional operator, the asterisk (*), we can rewrite $r(t)$ in (1.2.1) as follows:

$$r(t) = h(t, \tau) * s(t) \qquad (1.2.2)$$

with

$$h(t, \tau) = \sum_{i=1}^{I} g_i(t)\delta(t - \tau - \Delta_i), \qquad (1.2.3)$$

and $\delta(t)$ denoting the Dirac impulse function, i.e., $\delta(t)$ is infinite for $t = 0$ and 0 for $t \neq 0$. The description of $r(t)$ in (1.2.2) implies that the received signal can be written as a convolution of the transmitted signal with a time-varying impulse response $h(t, \tau)$, which represents the effect of the propagation channel. Bello [1963] and others (e.g., Rappaport, 1996) have described how after reception, down-conversion, and digitization, the received discrete-time signal can be represented by the discrete-time version of (1.2.2)

$$r(k) = h(k, n) * s(k), \qquad (1.2.4)$$

where $s(k)$ is a sampled down-converted version of the transmitted signal and $h(k, n)$ is the impulse response of a discrete-time, time-varying, finite-impulse-response filter. Such a filter is shown in Figure 1.5. The signal passes through a delay line with M taps, each separated by T seconds. Each of the M delayed versions of $s(k)$ is multiplied by a time-varying gain, and all are summed to produce $r(k)$.

The filtering that $h(k, n)$ imposes on the transmitted signal can be roughly characterized by two parameters. The first, the *delay spread* of the propagation channel, is given by M, the number of nonzero filter taps required to represent the channel. In effect, the received signal has been "spread" by MT seconds in passing through the troposphere. This delay spread is about 0.5 μsec for a typical troposcatter channel. The second parameter is called the *Doppler spread* and describes the output spectrum when a pure sinusoid (with zero bandwidth) is the input. A time-invariant filter would produce a zero bandwidth sinusoid as its output. Any spreading of the tone is caused by time variation of the filter. Thus, the Doppler spread indicates the degree to which the tap gains vary with time. A typical troposcatter channel has a Doppler spread of about 20 Hz.

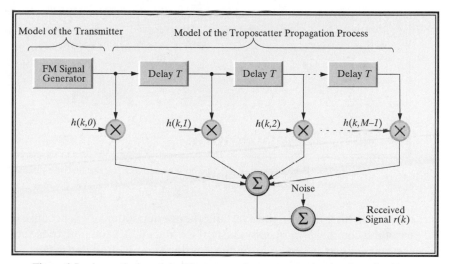

Figure 1.5   A practical model of the process that generates the signal received in a troposcatter communication system.

The impact of this time-varying filter on a transmitted signal depends on the nature of the signal itself. The effect is most easily observed for data signals. Such signals are typically composed of a train of symbols, each one of which carries one or several bits of information in its phase and (sometimes) amplitude. The first-order problem caused by the scatter channel is that each data symbol is spread into the next by an amount equal to the delay spread. If the spread is small, e.g., 10% of a symbol's interval, then little deleterious effect is noticed at the receiver. However, when more than 50% of the symbol is spread into the next, then serious degradation occurs. Thus, rates for data signals cannot exceed about 1 mega-symbols/sec if good quality is to be retained (given a spread of approximately 0.5 μsec). Analog waveforms are sent over tropo channels using frequency modulation (FM). Although not obvious, it turns out that the delay spread also adversely affects FM signals, particularly when the delay spread equals or exceeds the signal's inverse bandwidth. Practical FM tropo systems are limited to maximum bandwidths of about 1 MHz.

The power received through the troposcatter channel is usually enough to sustain low-error transmission at much higher data rates and bandwidths than the channel's delay spread will allow. Thus, we wish to develop a signal-processing technique that would allow some of that unused potential to be tapped by finding some way to reduce the delay spread seen by the receiver. Suppose we employ the scheme shown in Figure 1.6. The received signal $r(k)$, already filtered by the troposcatter channel, is passed through yet another filter before going to the demodulator. This filter has an impulse response $c(k, n)$ which is chosen so that

$$h(k, n) * c(k, n) = \delta(n - \Delta). \tag{1.2.5}$$

With (1.2.5) satisfied, the correction filter $c(k, n)$ cancels the effects of the propagation channel to the extent that the two in tandem act like only a flat delay of Δ sec. The

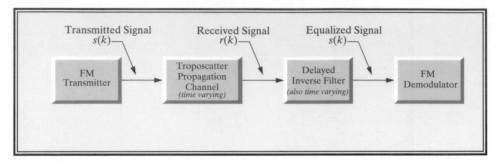

Figure 1.6 Employment of a "delayed inverse filter" to equalize the effects of the troposcatter channel on the signal.

correction filter must be time variable, hence dependent on k, because of the variability of the channel $h(k, n)$. Obviously, if we find $c(k, n)$ and plug those coefficients into the correction filter seen in Figure 1.6, then the demodulator sees the transmitted signal, delayed but not spread, and can thus attain signal quality dependent only on other factors, such as received power level.

The correction filter is usually called an *equalizer* because its function is to equalize or mitigate the effects of the propagation channel. Suppose for a moment that the channel were time invariant. It would then be possible to represent the channel by a transfer function with poles and zeros, i.e.,

$$H(z) = \frac{B(z)}{A(z)}. \tag{1.2.6}$$

The equalizer transfer function, now also time invariant, could satisfy (1.2.5) with $\Delta = 0$ by setting

$$H(z)C(z) = 1 \tag{1.2.7}$$

implying that

$$C(z) = 1/H(z) = \frac{A(z)}{B(z)}. \tag{1.2.8}$$

This equalizer would then attempt to cancel the spectral effects of the channel by placing poles on the channel's zeros and zeros on the channel's poles. Several practical considerations preclude direct use of this formula for $C(z)$. For example, if $B(z)$ has roots outside the unit circle, then the equalizer is an unstable filter. However, this time-invariant singularity cancellation approach embodied in (1.2.8) still serves to illustrate the principal objective of the equalizer, which is to compensate for the channel's effect on the signal.

The block diagram of an equalizer for troposcattered signals is shown in Figure 1.7. The received radio signal is processed to yield a form, analog or digital, suitable for filtering. The filtered signal is applied to a demodulator. The characteristics of the equalization filter are adjusted by some algorithm that attempts to gain the best possible performance. This algorithm may in fact need other signals available

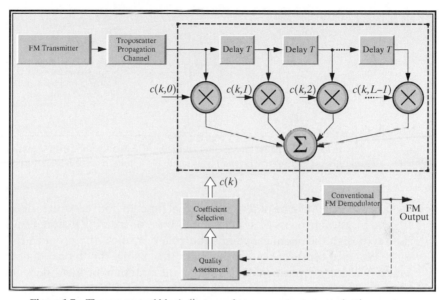

Figure 1.7   The conceptual block diagram of a troposcatter communications system employing a tapped-delay-line adaptive filter to equalize the effects of the propagation channel.

in the receiver—for example, the demodulator output—so that the quality of the equalizer can be judged.

If, as assumed earlier, the channel is time invariant, then the equalizer could be adjusted once and then left fixed. The channel impulse response does vary, however, and the equalizer must be adjusted rapidly enough and accurately enough to maintain good "cancellation" as the channel changes. The Doppler spread, about 20 Hz for tropo channels, indicates the amount of time variation to be expected and the rate at which the adaptive equalizer must track. The delay spread of the channel also has an impact on the equalizer's design. The delay spread is basically a measure of the time duration of the channel's impulse response. To equalize this, the impulse response of the equalizer must be at least as long and often many times longer. This issue is illustrated in Chapter 9.

1.3 THE MODELING OF PHYSICAL PROCESSES

There are many practical engineering circumstances in which the input–output relationship of a system or subsystem must be determined. For example, one of the very first steps in designing a controller for a chemical plant is to determine the effect of each valve setting on the volume and quality of the desired output product. Similarly, in the world of communications engineering, it is possible to apply sophisticated *forward error correction* (FEC) to a transmission system if the channel over which the

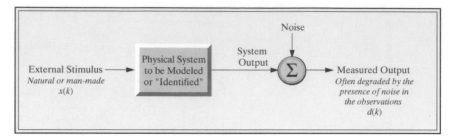

Figure 1.8 The System Identification Problem: Characterization of the input–output relationship of a system given only its input and a noisy measurement of its output.

signal propagates can be determined in real time. In both cases, it is necessary to *identify* the physical process or system in the sense of creating a model for it that can be used to design the chemical plant's controller or select the proper FEC parameters.

We can represent problems like this using the block diagram shown in Figure 1.8. Some input signal is applied to the system to be identified, and its output is observed, albeit sometimes in the presence of additive noise. Our objective is to use measurements of the input $x(k)$ and the noisy output $d(k)$, plus any side knowledge about the observation noise and the system itself, to develop a useful representation of the system. In the important case in which the input–output relationship is thought to be linear, then this representation might be the time-varying pulse response of the system, i.e., its output when a unit pulse is applied to the input. If the system can be assumed to be both linear and time invariant, then the model or representation might be a time-variant pulse response or even a transfer function.

How might such a model of the system be determined? Figure 1.9 shows how a filter with adjustable coefficients might be used for such a task. This filter is supplied with the same input signal as that applied to the system itself. The filter's output is compared with the noisy observations of the system's output. The coefficients of the adjustable filter are then selected to produce the best possible match between the system output $d(k)$ and the filter output $y(k)$. If the two can be made to match well enough, then the pulse response of the filter, or, in more generality, the coefficients describing the filter's input–output behavior, can be used as a model for the system. The better $d(k)$ and $y(k)$ match, the more accurately the filter models the system.

Note that this modeling process has many similarities with the two examples already discussed in this chapter. The input–output characteristics of the system are unknown *a priori* and may evolve with time. We presume that the system is sufficiently linear in its behavior that we can adapt the coefficients of a filter quickly enough and accurately enough to match the system's output. Again, we have not specified the form of the filter or the mechanism by which the coefficients are chosen, leaving a discussion of these options for later. One difference that is worth observing at this point, however, is that in the case of system modeling, or *identification*, as it is often called, the desired objective is the filter parameterization itself. In most adaptive filtering applications the choice of filter coefficients is not important to the user, but

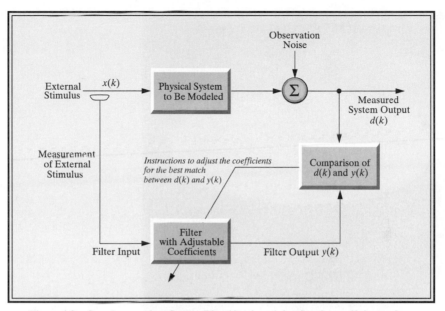

Figure 1.9   One Approach to System Identification: Adapting the coefficients of an adaptive filter to match the system's output.

the filter output $y(k)$ is. This distinction and its theoretical implications are discussed more in Chapter 10.

1.4 ENHANCING RECEPTION QUALITY USING AN ARRAY OF ANTENNAS

Many situations occur in the design of communications and sensing systems where the signal of interest to the user is available at many points and where it might be advantageous to combine a number of them to produce a system output of higher quality than any of the individual inputs. A simple example of this occurs in the field of radio astronomy. Figure 1.10 shows a photograph of a large steerable antenna of the sort used to receive microwave radio energy from space. To meet its scientific objectives, the antenna and its associated receiver must be as sensitive to radio signals as possible. This objective encourages the antenna to be as large as possible because its sensitivity is directly proportional to the surface area of the antenna's parabolic dish. Weighing against the approach of making the antenna very large, however, is the objective of making it easily steerable so that it can be pointed quickly at any part of the sky.

Thus it would appear that a radio observatory can either be very sensitive or very agile, but that it cannot be both at the same time. There is a way of resolving this conundrum, however. One could use many antennas, all pointed in the same

Figure 1.10 A 140-foot parabolic antenna operated by the National Radio Astronomy Observatory. *Photo courtesy of NRAO: www.gb.nrao.edu*

direction, and then use the right type of signal processing to combine their individual outputs coherently. An example of this approach is shown in Figure 1.11, a photograph of the Very Large Array (VLA) operated by the National Radio Astronomy Observatory (NRAO). Each antenna in this array is 25 m (81 ft) in diameter. When their outputs are combined, they have the sensitivity of a parabolic antenna 422 ft in diameter. Because the individual antennas are relatively small (by radio observatory standards), they are also easily steerable. Thus, if it were possible to coherently combine the outputs of these many antennas, it would be possible to achieve both of our objectives.

Unfortunately, it is not a simple matter to combine the outputs of the antennas. Figure 1.12 shows why this is so, using the simpler case of only two antennas in the array. When each of the two signals is received, it is amplified and then sent over a

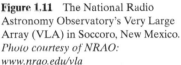

Figure 1.11 The National Radio Astronomy Observatory's Very Large Array (VLA) in Soccoro, New Mexico. *Photo courtesy of NRAO: www.nrao.edu/vla*

transmission cable to a center point, where it is combined with the other. In theory, the processing applied to the two signals is identical and they arrive at the center point ready to be simply added together. In practice, this is not true. The amplifiers do not have precisely the same gain, nor do the antennas, and the cable lengths are not the same.

The classical approach to resolving this problem, and the one used by the VLA, is to perform very careful calibration of all elements of the system and then compensate for the differences. While effective, it has the disadvantage that the calibration equipment adds more expense to the system, and usually it is not possible

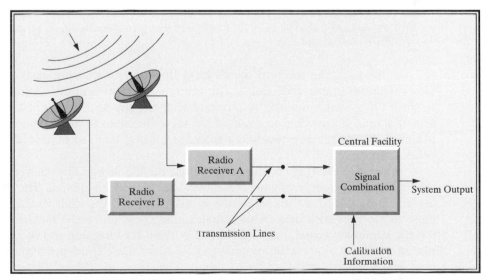

Figure 1.12 A Simpler Example: The combination of signals obtained from two antennas.

to be performing astronomic observations when the calibration is underway. Even so, this is the technique usually employed, particularly in high-bandwidth applications like radio astronomy. There is another approach, however, shown in schematic form in Figure 1.13.

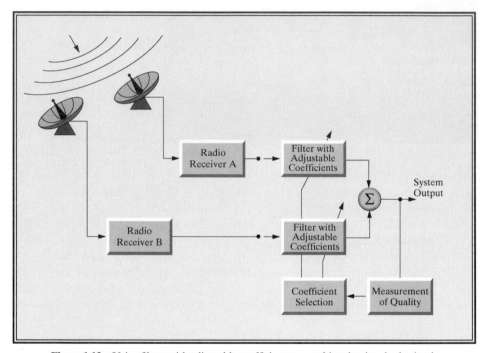

Figure 1.13   Using filters with adjustable coefficients to combine the signals obtained from two antennas.

In this case, the received signals from the two antennas are each applied to filters with adjustable coefficients. The outputs of the two filters are then added to form the system's output. By properly selecting the coefficients of the two filters, it should be possible to compensate for differences in gain, phase, and amplitude between the two received signals, permitting them to be added perfectly coherently.

Without addressing here how the coefficients should be selected, it is clear that this is another example of where adaptive filters could be applied. The appropriate *a priori* choice for the coefficients is unknown, and the right choice might be expected to vary with time. What remains, then, is to find some metric of quality for the combined signal and determine a scheme for choosing the coefficients to maximize that quality metric automatically. Both of these issues are treated in later chapters.

Before proceeding further, it should be observed that the art of combining the outputs of many sensors is a rich and interesting technical field in its own right [Liberti and Rappaport, 1999]. We examined here a single aspect, that of *aperture combination*, increasing the effective size, and therefore radio signal collection "aperture" by adding together the signals from more than one antenna. There are other reasons for processing signals from an array of sensors, however, including the following:

- **Electronic Steering**—Using the filters to steer the receiving beam of the antenna array without having to move the antennas themselves, e.g., in phased array radars
- **Spatial Diversity**—Using the filters to compensate for the propagation-induced degradation impacting each of the individually received signals, e.g., in cellular telephone base stations.
- **Interference Reduction**—Using the filters to null interference being received from a direction or at a frequency different from the one used by the desired signal while still receiving the desired signal with high quality, e.g., in sonar arrays.
- **Direction Finding**—Using the coefficients of the filters to determine the direction from which a signal is arriving.

In later chapters of this book, we find that adaptive filtering techniques have been developed to address all of these, not just the aperture combination problem.

1.5 GENERALITY AND COMMONALITY

Rather than superficially examining a more extensive list of the possible applications benefitting from adaptive filter use, we have looked at four such problems in some detail. In some ways, they seem very different. The bandwidths used in removing hum from ECG waveforms are only a few hundred Hertz, while a troposcatter communications signal can have a bandwidth of greater than a megahertz. The best filter configuration for the system identification problem might be a digital IIR form, while the troposcatter equalizer might be best realized with an analog tapped-delay-line filter, the parameters of which are only periodically adjusted. Even so, all four examples have a few common attributes:

1. In each case, the problem at hand could be solved by a circuit employing just the right filter. For example, in hum removal, a reference 60-Hz waveform is provided, but it must be scaled and phase-shifted properly to allow effective subtraction of the hum from the amplifier input.
2. In all cases, the proper choice of filter characteristics (e.g., in hum removal the desired amplitude and phase at 60 Hz) is unknown when the system is initialized.
3. In all cases the proper choice of coefficients changes with time, usually due to changes occurring in some physical process.

4. In most cases, the system into which the adaptive filter was embedded had one or more points at which the general performance of the adaptive filter could be judged. In the system identification case, for example, the creation of a perfect prediction model is indicated when the difference between the system output and the filter output is zero.

As we shall see, these common features happen to also be shared by the myriad of other applications of adaptive filters. Even so, it leaves open a wide variety of important issues, such as:

(a) How can some measure of signal quality be turned into beneficial adjustment of the coefficients of an adaptive filter?

(b) What sort of filter should be used? For example, analog or digital? If digital, which structure? For example, tapped-delay-line, lattice, or direct-form infinite-impulse-response (IIR)?

(c) How can the performance of a particular adaptive filter be analyzed or predicted and thus enhanced by designer choices in particular applications?

(d) How can adaptive filtering concepts be applied to new problems?

Each of these questions is addressed in later chapters. In the next chapter, we begin by looking at the first one: How can one develop rules (or algorithms) for adjusting the coefficients of a filter in response to feedback about how well the filter is performing.

1.6 PROBLEMS

1. Consider the hum cancelling scenario shown in Figure 1.3. Suppose that we used a fixed estimate of the hum signal to cancel the objectionable interference. Specifically, the amplitude is essentially correct, but the frequency ω is in error by a small amount $\delta\omega$. Derive an expression for the resulting interference as a function of $\delta\omega$. For clarity, assume that the phase offset is zero.

2. The following MATLAB[1] script excerpt generates a 1-sec record of a synthetic signal (a triangular pulse) disrupted by a hum interferer and a small broadband noise. The sampling rate is 500 Hz. Note that the hum interference has amplitude of 100 in comparison to the pulse amplitude of 5; its frequency is 60.06 Hz. In this exercise, we explore interference reduction with traditional filtering techniques.

```
%
%    Set up pulse cycle of 1 sec at 500 Hz
%
cycle=zeros(1,500);
x=[1 2 3 4 5 6 7 8 9 10 9 8 7 6 5 4 3 2 1 0]/2; %Triangular segment
cycle(240:259)=x; %Place pulse in 1-sec cycle


%
%    Set up 1 sec of 60.06-cycle hum
%
t=[1:500]/500;
inter=100*cos(2*pi*60.06*t)+randn(1,500);


%
%    Corrupted signal
%
y=inter+cycle;
```

   (a) Design a second-order digital filter with a notch response eliminating 60 Hz. The simplest approach is to place a conjugate pair of zeros on the unit circle, and a complementary pair of poles at the same angular position and at radial distance ρ, slightly inside the unit circle. For $\rho = 0.95$, plot the magnitude of its frequency response on a dB scale.
   (b) Apply the filter to the data record, and plot the result. Note that because the interference does not fall at the notch frequency, it is attentuated but still present.
   (c) Repeat the filter design first with a wider notch and then with a narrower notch. What do you conclude about the visibility and integrity of the pulse signal as a function of the notch?

3. In Figure 1.7, the linear equalizer filters the received signal $r(k)$ via

$$y(kT) = \sum_{i=0}^{L-1} c(kT, i)r((k-i)T). \tag{1.6.1}$$

---

[1]MATLAB is a registered trademark of The MathWorks, Inc.

(a) Rewrite $y(kT)$ as a vector inner product rather than in the summation notation of (1.6.1); i.e., compose

$$y(kT) = \mathbf{r}'(kT)\mathbf{c}(kT) \qquad (1.6.2)$$

by defining the entries of each of the column vectors $\mathbf{r}(\cdot)$ and $\mathbf{c}(\cdot)$. (*Syntax Alert*: In using the "prime" operator in MATLAB, the expression a' produces the complex conjugate transpose of a, while a prime with a period, $a.'$, delivers a transpose without conjugation.)

(b) Consider concatenating successive versions of (1.6.2) as

$$\begin{bmatrix} y(kT) \\ y((k+1)T) \\ \vdots \\ y((k+p-1)T) \end{bmatrix} = \begin{bmatrix} \mathbf{r}'(kT)\mathbf{c}(kT) \\ \mathbf{r}'((k+1)T)\mathbf{c}((k+1)T) \\ \vdots \\ \mathbf{r}'((k+p-1)T)\mathbf{c}((k+p-1)T) \end{bmatrix}. \qquad (1.6.3)$$

For a fixed equalizer parameterization, such that $\mathbf{c}(kT)$ is a constant $\mathbf{c}$ for all k, (1.6.3) can be rewritten as

$$\begin{bmatrix} y(kT) \\ y((k+1)T) \\ \vdots \\ y((k+p-1)T) \end{bmatrix} = R\mathbf{c}. \qquad (1.6.4)$$

For $L = 2$, $k = 2$, $p = 3$, and the observed received sequence

$$\{r(0),\ r(T),\ \ldots,\ r(4T)\} = \{0.8,\ 1.48,\ -0.11,\ -1.07,\ 0.36\} \qquad (1.6.5)$$

compose the 3×2 R matrix.

(c) With the objective of the the equalizer as described in (1.2.5) to match $y(kT)$ to the delayed source signal $s((k - D)T)$, we wish to minimize some measure of the vector of errors

$$\begin{bmatrix} e(kT) \\ e((k+1)T) \\ \vdots \\ e((k+p-1)T) \end{bmatrix} = \begin{bmatrix} s((k-\Delta)T) \\ s((k+1-\Delta)T) \\ \vdots \\ s((k+p-1-\Delta)T) \end{bmatrix} - \begin{bmatrix} y(kT) \\ y((k+1)T) \\ \vdots \\ y((k+p-1)T) \end{bmatrix} \qquad (1.6.6)$$

or

$$E = S_\Delta - Y = S_\Delta - R\mathbf{c}. \qquad (1.6.7)$$

Given the binary source sequence

$$\{s(0),\ s(1),\ \ldots,\ s(4)\} = \{1,\ -1,\ -1,\ 1,\ -1\}. \qquad (1.6.8)$$

synchronized with the received sequence of part (b), compose S_Δ for $\Delta = 0, 1$, and 2.

(d) A commonly used performance measure is $\sum_{j=0}^{p-1} e^2((k+j)T) = E'E$. For (1.6.7), the solution that minimizes $E'E$ is [Noble and Daniel, 1977]

$$\mathbf{c}_\Delta = (R'R)^{-1}R'S_\Delta. \qquad (1.6.9)$$

(Hint: In MATLAB, type *help slash*.) For the R of part (b) and the various S_Δ of part (c), determine the associated $\mathbf{c}_\Delta$ for $\Delta = 0, 1$, and 2.

(e) By forming $E'_\Delta E_\Delta$ for $\Delta = 0, 1$, and 2, determine the "optimum" delay associated with the minimum summed squared error equalizer.

(f) By reversing the role of the received signal and the source signal, so that the source signal is seen as the input to the channel model and the received signal as its output, reformulate the equalizer design problem as a channel identification problem. The error vector corresponding to (1.6.7) is a vector of the values $r(kT) - y(kT)$ to $r(k + p - 1) - y(k - p + 1)$, (1.6.3) has $\mathbf{r}(kT)$ replaced by a vector of $s(kT)$ and $s((k-l)T)$, and $\mathbf{c}$ now represents the impulse response coefficients of the channel model. Compose the corresponding numerical version of (1.2.4) and solve it using the counterpart of (1.6.9). Comment on why a separate delay variable does not appear in the channel identification formulation relative to the equalizer design formulation.

4. An array of multiple sensors offers a spatial sensitivity to incoming signals, and allows the ability to select based on angle of arrival. With proper arrangement of sensors and combination of their signal, the look direction of the array can be shifted virtually at will. In this exercise, we explore the concept of the *array pattern*, i.e., a graphic depiction of angular response.

Suppose that the two sensors depicted in Figure 1.14 are separated by a distance L. The direction at right angles to their axis is called the *boresight direction*. If the sensor outputs are simply added, any signal on the boresight coherently combines to double its amplitude, independent of frequency. However, a signal off-angle arrives at the two sensors with a slight time offset, which gives rise to a degree of destruction in the composite output.

Quantifying the effect can be done using elementary geometric relationships. Consider a sinusoidal signal with frequency f_c, traveling at propagation speed c, and arriving from angle θ off boresight, as shown in Figure 1.14. The differential time delay between sensors

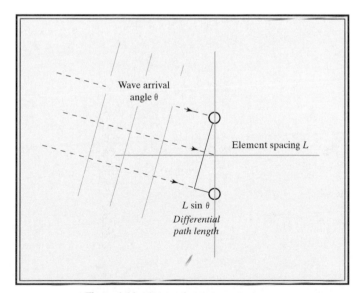

Figure 1.14   A two-element sensor array.

is then $\tau = (L/c) \sin \theta$. Note that the quantity L/c is the sensor separation in seconds. Expressed in wavelengths the separation is $L f_c / c$.

(a) If the sensors are simply added, show that the amplitude of the result is a function $g(f_c, \theta) = 2 \cos(2\pi f_c (L/2c) \sin \theta)$, i.e. dependent on frequency and angle of arrival. (Suggestion: Make the input a complex sinusoid $e^{j2\pi f_c t}$ for simplicity.)

(b) For a separation of $f_c L/c = 1$ wavelength, plot the function g in a polar format over the full 2π range. Note that at this separation, we get perfect constructive combining for both the boresight angle as well as the end arrival angle. However, the shaping is somewhat less selective for signals arriving along the array axis.

(c) Show that a perfect null response for this case falls at the $30°$ angle.

(d) Try increasing the sensor spacing $f_c L/c$ to 2, 3, 4, and 10. Note the trend of wider spacing gives narrower beamwidths, but also introduces spurious look angles.

2

Basic Principles of Adaptive Filtering

- *Precis: The correction term common to adaptive filter parameter update algorithms has an intuitively reasonable form: (a bounded step size) multiplied by (a function of the signal multiplying the corresponding parameter in the adaptive filter output computation) multiplied by (a function of the measured quality of the adaptive filter output).*

The practical examples in Chapter 1 all suggest the need for an adaptive filter that can alter its frequency (and, therefore, impulse) response as required by the particular application. The basic structure of such an adaptive filter is shown in Figure 2.1. The input signal is filtered to produce an output that is typically passed on for subsequent processing. The output of this filter is also observed by a circuit that assesses the quality of the output with regard to the objective of its particular application. This measure of quality, or some function of it, is then passed on to a circuit that uses it to decide how to modify the parameters of the filter to improve the quality of the output. In principle, this processing loop continues to operate until the parameters of the filter are adjusted so that the quality of the filter output is as good as possible. Also, in principle, if the characteristics of the input signal or quality assessment change with time, then this assessment/adjustment loop should readjust the filter's parameters until the new "optimum" output quality is attained.

The functional blocks in Figure 2.1 are quite general and can be chosen in different ways to solve different practical problems. The filter, for example, could be implemented in analog or digital form and could have a tapped-delay-line, pole-zero, or lattice structure. The parameters available for adjustment might be the impulse–response sequence values or more complicated functions of the filter's frequency response. Similarly, the circuit that assesses the quality of the filter output can take several forms, depending on the adaptive filter's application. The way in which the quality assessment is converted into parameter adjustments, which we term the *adaptive algorithm*, can also vary. Variations in the filter structure, the quality assessment mechanism, and the adaptive update are commonly used to catalog the behavior characteristics, and thus applicability, of various adaptive filters. In fact,

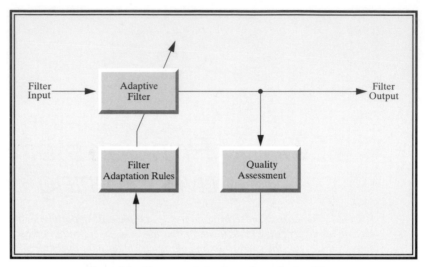

Figure 2.1   The general structure of an adaptive filter.

these distinctions can be used to characterize the coverage of the following chapters of this book.

The purpose of this chapter is to focus on the adaptive algorithm portion of the adaptive filter, given a particular generic combination of filter structure and quality assessment. We develop logical, simple algorithms that display significant features shared by the range of adaptive algorithms examined in this book. Thus, while the generality of Figure 2.1 is desirable and is exploited in later chapters, we focus now on the adaptive filter shown in Figure 2.2.

2.1 THE FIR LINEAR COMBINER

The filter in Figure 2.2 has a discrete-time, finite-impulse-response (FIR) structure, based on a tapped-delay-line and a set of N adjustable gain coefficients w_0 through w_{N-1}. The filter output $y(k)$ is simply the sum of delayed and scaled inputs, given by

$$y(k) = \sum_{i=0}^{N-1} w_i x(k - i). \tag{2.1.1}$$

For convenience, $y(k)$ can also be written as the dot (or inner) product of two vectors, i.e.,

$$y(k) = \mathbf{X}^t(k)\mathbf{W} = \mathbf{W}^t\mathbf{X}(k) \tag{2.1.2}$$

where

$$\mathbf{W} = [w_0 \ \ w_1 \ \ w_2 \ \cdots \ w_{N-1}]^t \tag{2.1.3}$$

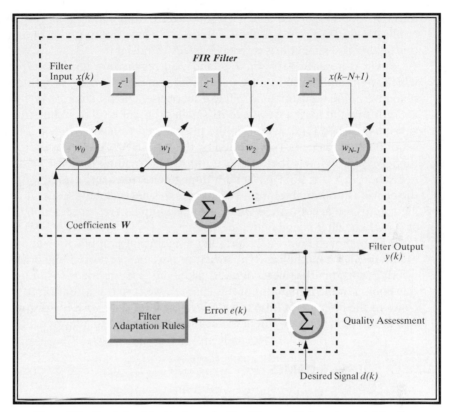

Figure 2.2   Specialized form of an adaptive filter employing a tapped-delay-line finite-impulse-response (FIR) realization and a reference matching quality assessment.

and

$$\mathbf{X}(k) = [x(k) \ \ x(k - 1) \ \ \cdots \ \ x(k - N + 1)]^{t}. \qquad (2.1.4)$$

This digital filter structure is one of the simplest. It is stable (for any bounded $\mathbf{W}$) and the impulse response is given directly by the elements of the vector $\mathbf{W}$.

The adaptive filter shown in Figure 2.2 also uses a simple form of quality assessment. The filter output $y(k)$ is compared directly to a desired waveform $d(k)$, and any difference between the two constitutes an error and hence indicates a degradation in quality. The waveform $d(k)$ is sometimes called the *desired signal*, the *reference*, or the *template waveform*. The objective in choosing the coefficients of the adaptive filter is to force $y(k)$ to equal $d(k)$ exactly. One might question why $d(k)$, rather than $y(k)$, is not simply passed on to the next stage of processing, because $d(k)$ is the desired filter output. For now, we cite two circumstances where transmission of $d(k)$ rather than $y(k)$ is infeasible. In certain applications, $d(k)$ is only available during a "training" phase in conjunction with a preselected x sequence. In such cases, adaption is ceased during processing of the actual x sequence for which $d(k)$ is unavailable. In other applications $d(k)$ is "measurable" only after we have computed $y(k)$. In other words, our quality assessment arises from "perfect" hindsight.

Any difference between $d(k)$ and $y(k)$ results in a nonzero error signal $e(k)$, which we intend to use in filter parameter adaptation rules. As we have noted, the objective of this adjustment is to find a set of coefficients, a vector $\mathbf{W}^o$, which reduces $e(k)$ (or some function of $e(k)$) to its smallest possible value. When this parameterization is reached (and retained), the filter is said to have *converged* to the optimal set of filter coefficients, represented by the vector $\mathbf{W}^o$. Note that if $d(k) = \mathbf{X}^t(k)\mathbf{W}^o$, then $\mathbf{W} = \mathbf{W}^o$ implies that $e(k) = 0$ for all k, providing the best possible match of $d(k)$ and $y(k)$. Our filter parameter adjustment rules are termed *adaptive* if, when the previously optimal solution $\mathbf{W}^o$ changes to a new value, $\mathbf{W}$ tracks it. Such adaptive algorithms are necessarily recursive. As new inputs are processed and their quality assessed, the filter is updated, if necessary.

Even though Figure 2.2 represents a significant simplification and specialization of Figure 2.1, it nonetheless is the structure assumed for most of the practical adaptive filtering work that has been done to date, and it is the focus for more than half of this book. For the remainder of this chapter, we turn our attention to the block that contains the filter adaptation rules. Given each $e(k)$, we wish to appropriately revise our choice of $\mathbf{W}$. Development of such rules is the key to adaptive filtering.

2.2 NUMBER GUESSING GAMES

To illustrate an intuitive basis for the development of adaptive parameter estimation algorithms applicable to Figure 2.2, we play a succession of number guessing games. Although at first only vaguely related to the task of Figure 2.2, our number guessing games are progressively elaborated, along with our respective adaptive algorithm solutions, until the problem structure matches that of Figure 2.2. We are then in a position to note certain general features of adaptive filter algorithms that are elaborated on in subsequent chapters.

2.2.1 Single Integer Guessing Games

We begin with a trivial integer guessing game with an obvious solution. We pick an integer between -100 and 100 that you are to guess. The only information we give you for improving your guess is whether it is high or low. Your strategy is immediate. If your guess is too high, you decrease it; if it is too low, you increase your guess. A typical "game" might begin with our picking, unknown to you, 38 as the magic number. You respond by guessing -74, which we indicate is too low. You would simply increase your guess, perhaps cautiously at first. After guessing -65, -30, 0, and 15, you jump to 50 and the sign of your error changes. Ultimately, you would converge on the correct value of 38.

Let us complicate the rules of the game. Again, we pick an integer that we label n^o, between -100 and 100. But this time we construct a more elaborate procedure for providing you with an indication of the error in your guess. After you indicate your latest (kth) guess, labeled $n(k)$, we pick another integer, $x(k)$, but we only tell you if $x(k)$ is positive or negative. We form the product

$$d(k) = n^o x(k). \qquad (2.2.1)$$

We also compute

$$y(k) = n(k)x(k), \qquad (2.2.2)$$

using your guess $n(k)$, and

$$e(k) = d(k) - y(k) = [n^o - n(k)]x(k) \qquad (2.2.3)$$

and then tell you whether e is positive or negative, i.e., whether your estimate of d is too low or too high. If e is positive, this indicates that d is greater than y, i.e.,

$$e(k) = d(k) - y(k) > 0 \Rightarrow d(k) > y(k). \qquad (2.2.4)$$

Similarly, if e is negative, then d is less than y. The objective of this game is the same as the preceding one: to ultimately guess the value n^o. You must choose a strategy that updates $n(k)$ for the next "time" to $n(k+1)$, using the correction information suggested by the sign of $e(k)$ and the sign of $x(k)$. With a successful strategy, your guesses $n(k)$ converge to n^o as k increases. Mathematically, the task is to choose the function f such that

$$n(k+1) = f(n(k), \operatorname{sgn}[e(k)], \operatorname{sgn}[x(k)]) \qquad (2.2.5)$$

causes

$$n(k) \to n^o \quad \text{as } k \to \infty, \qquad (2.2.6)$$

where

$$\operatorname{sgn}[x] = \begin{cases} 1 & \text{if } x > 0 \\ 0 & \text{if } x = 0 \\ -1 & \text{if } x < 0 \end{cases} . \qquad (2.2.7)$$

Now, (2.2.5)–(2.2.7) may seem unreasonably abstract for such a simple game. But these equations precisely describe how your kth guess $n(k)$ is "improved" to your next guess $n(k+1)$, given the signs of $e(k)$ and $x(k)$.

   A reasonable strategy is relatively easy to formulate. To begin developing an intuitive strategy that is quite similar to that of the previous integer guessing game, imagine that $\operatorname{sgn}[e(k)] = 1$. In other words, you have been told that $e(k)$ is positive, or, from (2.2.4), that $d(k)$ is greater than $y(k)$. Your natural response is to update n so that y is increased. How this is accomplished depends on the sign of $x(k)$. If $x(k)$ is positive, then increasing n increases $y(k)$ in (2.2.2). Conversely, if $x(k)$ is negative, then decreasing n increases $y(k)$ in (2.2.2). So if e is positive, a reasonable strategy is to increase n when x is positive or decrease n when x is negative. Similarly, if e is negative, y is greater than d and n should be corrected to decrease y. So, if e is negative, you should decrease n if x is positive or increase n if x is negative.

To summarize, we want to develop an f for (2.2.5) such that

$$
\begin{array}{lll}
e > 0 & \text{and} & x > 0 \rightarrow \text{ increase } n \\
e > 0 & \text{and} & x < 0 \rightarrow \text{ decrease } n \\
e < 0 & \text{and} & x > 0 \rightarrow \text{ decrease } n \\
e < 0 & \text{and} & x < 0 \rightarrow \text{ increase } n
\end{array} \tag{2.2.8}
$$

Note that if $e > 0$ and $x > 0$, then $\text{sgn}[e]$ times $\text{sgn}[x]$ is positive. If we want to increase n as indicated in (2.2.8), then we want to add a positive quantity to n. For the first line in (2.2.8) we could use

$$
n(k+1) = n(k) + \text{sgn}[e(k)] \cdot \text{sgn}[x(k)]. \tag{2.2.9}
$$

Note that (2.2.9) works for all of the other lines of (2.2.8). Essentially, if e and x have the same sign, from (2.2.8) we want to increase n. In (2.2.9), we have chosen to increase n by the addition of $+1$, that is $\text{sgn}[e(k)] = \text{sgn}[x(k)]$ results in $\text{sgn}[e(k)] \cdot \text{sgn}[x(k)] = 1$. Conversely, if e and x have opposite signs, then from (2.2.8) we want to decrease n, which (2.2.9) accomplishes by subtracting 1. Note that if $x = 0$, then $e = 0$ from (2.2.3) despite the difference between n^o and n. The strategy in (2.2.9) indicates that we appropriately leave our guess for n unchanged because we have not received any indication via e of the error in n. If $n(k) = n^o$, then from (2.2.3) $e(k) = 0$ and (2.2.9) appropriately retains $n(k+1) = n(k) = n^o$. Thus, once the correct value is obtained, it is retained.

Now, let's play a sample game. We secretly pick $n^o = -2$. Your initial guess $n(1) = 0$ is conservative. With $x(1) = 2$, $d(1) = -4$, $y(1) = 0$, and $e(1) = -4$. So, you are told that $\text{sgn}[x(1)] = 1$ and $\text{sgn}[e(1)] = -1$. Using (2.2.9), you correct $n(1)$ to $n(2) = -1$. Now, $x(2)$ is selected as -3 and, thus, $d(2) = 6$, $y(2) = 3$, and $e(2) = 3$. So, you are told that $\text{sgn}[x(2)] = -1$ and $\text{sgn}[e(2)] = 1$. Again, using (2.2.9), you decrease n by 1 to $n(3) = -2$. With three iterations the strategy of (2.2.9) has converged to the correct answer.

2.2.2 Multiple Integer Guessing Games

Once again, we increase the complexity of the game. You are now simultaneously guessing two integers. We pick two integers, n_1^o and n_2^o, and form

$$
d(k) = n_1^o x_1(k) + n_2^o x_2(k) \tag{2.2.10}
$$

given two "inputs" $x_1(k)$ and $x_2(k)$ to this linear combination of terms such as on the right of (2.2.1). Similarly, the prediction of d based on your guesses n_1 and n_2 is formed via

$$
y(k) = n_1(k)x_1(k) + n_2(k)x_2(k) \tag{2.2.11}
$$

in order to compute the prediction error

$$
e(k) = d(k) - y(k). \tag{2.2.12}
$$

You are told only the sign of e, the sign of x_1, and the sign of x_2. You should update your estimates n_1 and n_2 so that eventually $n_1 \rightarrow n_1^o$ and $n_2 \rightarrow n_2^o$. Note that the basic

TABLE 2.1 TWO INTEGER GUESSING
GAME EXAMPLE ($n_1^o = 3$, $n_2^o = -1$)

k	$n_1(k)$	$n_2(k)$	$x_1(k)$	$x_2(k)$	$e(k)$
1	0	0	1	−1	4
2	1	−1	2	−1	4
3	2	−2	−1	−2	−3
4	3	−1	0	0	0

parameter estimate correction strategy of the preceding "game" still makes sense: Change n_1 and n_2 to make y closer to d. Thus, the strategy in (2.2.9) could be applied term by term because (2.2.10) simply sums these effects. Consider the following case. Assume $e > 0$, so that you wish to increase y. If x_1 is positive, increasing n_1 will increase y. Similarly, if x_2 is positive, increasing n_2 will also increase y. Repeating all of the cases examined with the preceding game yields the following update candidate for each n_i:

$$n_i(k+1) = n_i(k) + \text{sgn}[e(k)] \cdot \text{sgn}[x_i(k)], \quad \text{for } i = 1, 2. \tag{2.2.13}$$

To gain some confidence that (2.2.13) is a reasonable strategy, we consider a sample game as summarized in Table 2.1. The path taken by the sequence of number guesses (or parameter estimates) in the space formed by Cartesian coordinates n_1 and n_2 is shown in Figure 2.3. As we shall discover, a useful translation (actually a rotation and a translation) of Figure 2.4 considers the path of successive estimates drawn

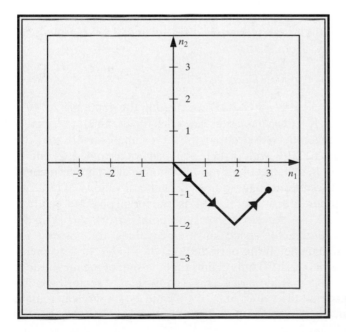

Figure 2.3 Estimate path in parameter space (of Table 2.1 example).

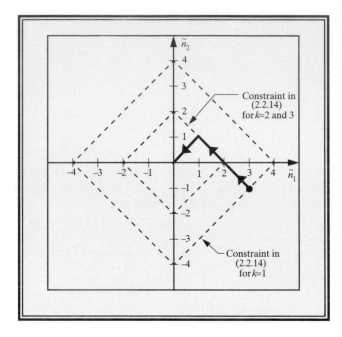

Figure 2.4 Estimate path in parameter error space (of Table 2.1 example).

instead in the parameter error space with coordinates $\tilde{n}_1 = n_1^o - n_1$ and $\tilde{n}_2 = n_2^o - n_2$. Thus, the origin in parameter estimate error space corresponds to $\tilde{n}_1 = \tilde{n}_2 = 0$ or $n_1 = n_1^o$ and $n_2 = n_2^o$. In other words, once the path in parameter estimate error space reaches the origin, the number guessing game has been successfully concluded. Therefore, if we could verify the property that the strategy in (2.2.13) never moves the estimate error point "away" from the origin, e.g.,

$$|\tilde{n}_1(k+1)| + |\tilde{n}_2(k+1)| \le |\tilde{n}_1(k)| + |\tilde{n}_2(k)|, \tag{2.2.14}$$

we would be encouraged to recommend (2.2.13) for playing the game of (2.2.10)–(2.2.12). The inequality in (2.2.14) describes a sense in which the parameter estimator of (2.2.13) never degrades the collective accuracy of the estimates. Note that the example in Table 2.1 satisfies (2.2.14) with $|\tilde{n}_1(k)| + |\tilde{n}_2(k)|$ equal to 4, 2, 2, and 0, respectively, for $k = 1, 2, 3, 4$. In fact, our observation of numerous sample "games" is likely to have been the source of our suggestion of the general validity of (2.2.14). Fortunately, we can prove rather directly that (2.2.14) is true for all possible "games."

To help us validate (2.2.14), note that from any point $(n_1(k), n_2(k))$ in the two-integer guessing game parameter space, only nine values are possible for $(n_1(k+1), n_2(k+1))$. These include all the permutations of $+1$, -1, or zero increment in each n_1 and n_2. Note that (2.2.14) only claims that the sum of the magnitudes of the errors in each parameter never increases. This is equivalent to requiring in the two-dimensional error space that the values of $\tilde{n}_1(k+1)$ and $\tilde{n}_2(k+1)$ must remain within a diamond determined by the error in the "initial" guess $(\tilde{n}_1(k), \tilde{n}_2(k))$. For the

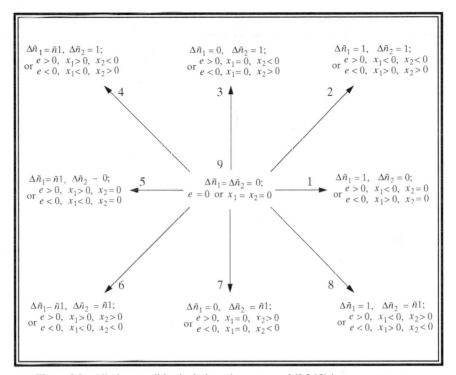

Figure 2.5 All nine possible single-iteration moves of (2.2.13) in parameter error space and their cause (in terms of e and x_i).

example in Table 2.1, this diamond is drawn for each k with a dashed line in Figure 2.4. Recognize that of the nine possible moves from any $(\tilde{n}_1(k), \tilde{n}_2(k))$, where both are nonzero, only three are forbidden in order to satisfy (2.2.14). The particular three moves that are forbidden depend on the quadrant in which $(\tilde{n}_1(k), \tilde{n}_2(k))$ is located. When one of the two parameter errors is zero, only four of the nine moves are possible in order for (2.2.14) to be satisfied.

Refer to Figure 2.5, where, with $\tilde{n}_i = n_i^o - n_i$ and (2.2.13),

$$\Delta \tilde{n}_i(k) \equiv \tilde{n}_i(k+1) - \tilde{n}_i(k) = n_i(k) - n_i(k+1)$$

$$= -\text{sgn}[e(k)] \cdot \text{sgn}[x_i(k)]. \tag{2.2.15}$$

For example, if $(\tilde{n}_1, \tilde{n}_2)$ exists in the first quadrant, i.e., both $\tilde{n}_1$ and $\tilde{n}_2$ are positive, then moves 1 through 3 should be impossible if (2.2.14) is true. Recall from (2.2.10)–(2.2.12) that

$$e(k) = \tilde{n}_1(k)x_1(k) + \tilde{n}_2(k)x_2(k). \tag{2.2.16}$$

Thus, if $\tilde{n}_1(k) > 0$ and $\tilde{n}_2(k) > 0$, for $e(k)$ to be positive, at least one of $x_1(k)$ or $x_2(k)$ must be positive. Similarly, for $e(k)$ to be negative, at least one of $x_1(k)$ or $x_2(k)$ must be negative. Note that these requirements are excluded from moves 1–3. In other words, the three moves forbidden by (2.2.14) for positive $\tilde{n}_1(k)$ and $\tilde{n}_2(k)$ are, in fact, not possible in (2.2.13). Such an examination could be continued for the other three quadrants, and points on the axes, with the same result. Thus, we have proved (2.2.14) to be valid.

At this stage some observations are pertinent. To begin, note that because (2.2.14) is not a strict inequality, the sum of the absolute values of the parameter errors ($|\tilde{n}_1| + |\tilde{n}_2|$) need not decrease at every iteration. In fact, the equality implies that the parameter estimator may be stuck at some "distance" and not move any closer to the correct parameter values. Such a failure to further reduce the "distance" to the correct parameters n_i is due to the (unsatisfactory) character of the "inputs" x_i. One possibility is that all of the $x_i(k)$ are zero, such that $n_i(k+1) = n_i(k)$ from (2.2.13). In this case $d(k)$ and $y(k)$ in (2.2.10) and (2.2.11), respectively, are also zero and $e(k)$ in (2.2.12) is zero. In other words, the prediction error measure of our parameter estimator accuracy is zero despite a nonzero parameter error. The use of zero $x_i(k)$ for all k is foolish in terms of the stated game. But such a stall could be encountered in a less obvious manner due to a peculiar input sequence. Note from (2.2.16) that for the game in Table 2.1, the prediction error is

$$e = (3 - n_1)x_1 - (1 + n_2)x_2. \tag{2.2.17}$$

For example, consider a sequence of $x_i(k)$ such that $x_1(k) = -x_2(k) \neq 0$. Thus, the prediction error in (2.2.17) is zeroed, i.e.,

$$(3 - n_1) + (1 + n_2) = 0, \tag{2.2.18}$$

by any parameter estimates that satisfy the solution of (2.2.18) as

$$n_1 - n_2 = 4. \tag{2.2.19}$$

With e zeroed, the parameter estimates are not corrected by (2.2.13), despite their possible inaccuracy. For example, with the inaccurate guesses $n_1 = -n_2 = 2$ for the game in Table 2.1, the sum of the absolute values of the parameter errors is $|3 - 2| + |-1 + 2| = 2$. With $x_1 = -x_2$, it remains at this value indefinitely while satisfying (2.2.14). To verify this stall due to $e = 0$ despite nonzero $\tilde{n}_i$, form (2.2.17) with n_1 and n_2 satisfying (2.2.19) and any $x_1 = -x_2 \neq 0$. However, if the objective of the "game" is really to zero the prediction error (rather than the parameter estimate error), as is true in the typical adaptive filtering application, this stall is acceptable.

Unfortunately, the freezing of the parameter estimates, despite their inaccuracy, due to the zeroing of the prediction error is not the only way a peculiar x_i sequence can cause (2.2.14) to remain an equality with both sides nonzero. Consider the sequence shown in Table 2.2 and the corresponding parameter error space trajectory shown in Figure 2.6. Note that the sum of the absolute values of the parameter errors is always unity and the prediction error is nonzero. Actually, in Table 2.2 any values for x_i with the signs shown would cause the counterclockwise rotation about the origin. Changing the signs on the x_i that are not associated with nonzero $\tilde{n}_i$ would alter the direction of the rotation to clockwise. The conclusion is that "peculiar" sequences

TABLE 2.2 TWO INTEGER GUESSING
GAME EXAMPLE ($n_1^o = 3$, $n_2^o = -1$)

k	$n_1(k)$	$n_2(k)$	$x_1(k)$	$x_2(k)$	$e(k)$
1	4	-1	-1	$+1$	$+1$
2	3	0	-1	-1	$+1$
3	2	-1	$+1$	-1	$+1$
4	3	-2	$+1$	$+1$	$+1$
5	4	-1	$-$	$-$	$-$

of the x_i can result in nonzero, nondecreasing summed parameter error magnitudes, i.e., equality in (2.2.14), even with nonzero prediction error. In order to successfully conclude the number guessing game, such x_i sequences must be avoided.

One might be tempted to conclude that, because the summed absolute parameter error $\sum_{i=1}^{N} |\tilde{n}_i|$ of the integer guessing game is never-increasing for $N = 2$, the same would be true for $N > 2$. Such an assertion would be false. Consider the three-integer guessing game where $n_1^o = n_2^o - n_3^o = 1$, $x_1(1) = 3$, $x_2(1) = x_3(1) = -1$, and $x_1(k + 1) = x_3(k)$, $x_2(k + 1) = x_1(k)$, $x_3(k + 1) = x_2(k)$ for $k > 0$. With the initial guess of $n_1(0) = n_2(0) = n_3(0) = 0$, the progression of $(n_1(k), n_2(k), n_3(k))$ is $(1, -1, -1), (0, 0, -2), (-1, -1, -1)$ for $k = 1, 2, 3$, respectively. Thus, $\sum_{i=1}^{3} |\tilde{n}_i(3)| = 6$, while $\sum_{i=1}^{3} |\tilde{n}_i(0)| = 3$. Continuing shows that every third iteration $n_i(k) = -k/3$ and $\sum_{i=1}^{3} |\tilde{n}_i(k)| = k$ for $k = 3, 6, 9, \dots$. Thus, the summed absolute parameter error is diverging as the parameter estimates diverge. However, for the same situation but

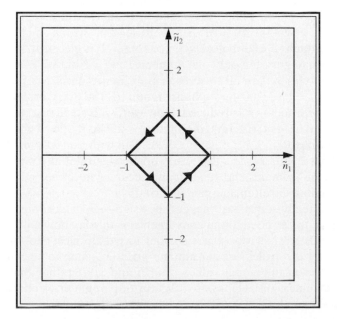

Figure 2.6 Nonzero prediction error limit cycle (of Table 2.2 example).

with different initial x_i, that is, $x_1(1) = 1$ and $x_2(1) = x_3(1) = -1$, after three itera-
tions $n_i(3) = n_i^o$ and $\sum_{i=1}^{3} |\tilde{n}_i(k)| = 0$ for $k \geq 3$. Thus, with a different x_i sequence,
convergence rather than divergence results. This again emphasizes the importance
of avoiding certain x_i sequences to attain acceptable behavior.

This (false) conjecture of the nondivergence of multiple (three or more) integer
guessing via (2.2.13) due to the nondivergence of (2.2.13) in guessing two integers
also serves as a warning against overextending algorithm behavior predictions from
a set of examples. Unfortunately, this tendency is all too common when dealing
with complicated time-varying (and often nonlinear) adaptive algorithms that defy
analysis. Consider yourself warned.

2.2.3 Multiple Real Numbers Guessing Games

Again, we alter the rules of the number guessing game. We no longer limit n_i^o (or x_i)
to be integers. Instead, they can be any real numbers. Consider using the adaptive
algorithm in (2.2.13). Because the correction term, $\text{sgn}[e(k)] \cdot \text{sgn}[x_i(k)]$, can be only
$+1, 0$, or -1, successive n_i can only be different from your initial guess by an integer
value. In other words we can only hope, at best, to cause each n_i to converge to the
integer nearest n_i^o. If we want to allow n_i to move closer to n_i^o, we must use a smaller
step size on each pass through (2.2.13). Consider

$$n_i(k + 1) = n_i(k) + \mu_i\{\text{sgn}[e(k)] \cdot \text{sgn}[x_i(k)]\}, \tag{2.2.20}$$

where all of the μ_i are positive. In (2.2.13), μ_i is unity. To permit a closer ultimate
fit to any real number, we should choose a μ_i smaller than unity. For example, if
$\mu_i = 0.01$ for both $i = 1$ and 2, we would hope to be able to ultimately improve the
n_i such that they are accurate to within ± 0.01. It is easy to see that with a smaller
μ_i it takes more iterations through (2.2.20) before we "converge." It is easiest to see
this if we return, momentarily, to guessing only one number. If $n^o = 2$ but we guess
$n(1) = 0$, then with $\mu = 1$ and $x(k) \neq 0$ for all k we reach $n = 2$ in two iterations, i.e.,
$n(k) = 2$ for $k \geq 3$. If instead, $\mu = 0.01$, 200 iterations are required. Thus, we can state
that the convergence rate is reduced as μ is reduced. However, with smaller μ, the
steady-state error is decreased, in general. Imagine that $n^o = 2.346$. If $\mu = 1$, then
the sequence of $n(k)$ (with $x(k) \neq 0$) is $0, 1, 2, 3, 2, 3, 2, 3, \ldots$. But with $\mu = 0.01, n(k)$
follows $0, 0.01, 0.02, \ldots, 2.34, 2.35, 2.34, \ldots$. This trade-off between initially rapid
improvement in the parameter estimates and steady-state accuracy in the selection
of step size μ repeatedly manifests itself in adaptive algorithms.

One way to reduce the steady-state coarseness of the "sign–sign" algorithm in
(2.2.20) while retaining larger μ_i to speed initial convergence is to somehow adjust
the correction term magnitude so that it becomes smaller as we are closer to the
correct answer. We again alter the "rules" of our number guessing game to permit
this possibility. We now give you the actual values of $e(k)$ and $x_i(k)$ rather than
just their signs. Using the smallness of $|e(k)|$ as an indicator of parameter estimate
"closeness" to the desired parameters, we wish to reduce our adjustment of $n_i(k)$

when $|e(k)|$ is small. This suggests modifying (2.2.20) to the form of

$$n_i(k+1) = n_i(k) + \mu_i\{\text{sgn}[x_i(k)]\}e(k). \qquad (2.2.21)$$

As $e(k)$ decreases toward zero, the magnitude of the adjustment of $n_i(k)$ decreases to zero.

What (2.2.21) does not exploit is the information we have available in the magnitude of each x_i. Exploiting this allows us to broaden the classes of x_i sequences for which we can achieve successful (i.e., nondiverging) recursive number guessing strategies. Recall our objective in formulating (2.2.9), and subsequently (2.2.21), of adjusting each n_i so it changes y so as to reduce the magnitude of e. Thus, the n_i associated with the smaller x_i should receive less correction due to their less significant effect on y, and thus e, for the same absolute change in the parameter estimate. This suggests considering

$$n_i(k+1) = n_i(k) + \mu_i x_i(k)e(k). \qquad (2.2.22)$$

Smaller $e(k)$ reduces the change in all n_i. The n_i receiving the least change, with all μ_i the same, is the one in, e.g., (2.2.11) associated with the smallest x_i. We can actually prove that (2.2.22) has the property that the "distance" to the parameter estimate error space origin is never increased. This property is analogous to that of (2.2.14) for (2.2.13). In the case of (2.2.22), we find that

$$\sum_{i=1}^{N} \tilde{n}_i^2(k+1)/\mu_i \le \sum_{i=1}^{N} \tilde{n}_i^2(k)/\mu_i \qquad (2.2.23)$$

and not (2.2.14) measures this nonincreasing distance. Furthermore, (2.2.23) applies for all $N \ge 1$ with the only restriction on classes of x_i sequences being that no $|x_i(k)|$ is too large relative to its μ_i.

To directly verify (2.2.23) for (2.2.22), we begin by subtracting both sides of (2.2.22) from n_i^o to form

$$\tilde{n}_i(k+1) = \tilde{n}_i(k) - \mu_i x_i(k)e(k). \qquad (2.2.24)$$

Using (2.2.22) and (2.2.24), we can rewrite the left side of (2.2.23) as

$$\sum_{i=1}^{N} \tilde{n}_i^2(k+1)/\mu_i = \sum_{i=1}^{N}\{[\tilde{n}_i(k) - \mu_i x_i(k)e(k)]^2/\mu_i\}$$

$$= \sum_{i=1}^{N}\{\tilde{n}_i^2(k)/\mu_i - 2\tilde{n}_i(k)x_i(k)e(k) + \mu_i x_i^2(k)e^2(k)\}.$$

$$(2.2.25)$$

Recall (2.2.16), written as $e(k) = \sum_{i=1}^{N}\tilde{n}_i(k)x_i(k)$, which allows (2.2.25) to be rewritten as

$$\sum_{i=1}^{N} \tilde{n}_i^2(k+1)/\mu_i = \sum_{i=1}^{N}\{\tilde{n}_i^2(k)/\mu_i\} - e^2(k)\left[2 - \sum_{i=1}^{N}\mu_i x_i^2(k)\right]. \qquad (2.2.26)$$

With all of the μ_i positive, (2.2.23) is satisfied if the last term on the right side of (2.2.26), that is, $-e^2(k)[2 - \sum_{i=1}^{N} \mu_i x_i^2(k)]$, is nonpositive. This is true, due to the nonnegativity of $e^2(k)$, if

$$2 \geq \sum_{i=1}^{N} \mu_i x_i^2(k), \quad \text{for all } k. \tag{2.2.27}$$

If we knew that the $|x_i(k)|$ were bounded by some value, say β_i, for all k, then we could choose each μ_i to satisfy

$$2/N\beta_i^2 > \mu_i \tag{2.2.28}$$

and thereby verify the satisfaction of (2.2.23) by (2.2.22).

   Conversely, if the μ_i were selected too large (or the x_i were larger than expected) such that (2.2.27) was dissatisfied for all k, then the inequality opposite that in (2.2.23) would be established. Thus, the weighted summed squared parameter error would increase with each iteration. The parameter estimates would progressively worsen; they would diverge. (Construct such an example, if you doubt this conclusion.)

   A significant consequence of the satisfaction of (2.2.23) is that it establishes that $e^2(k) \to 0$. To confirm this point, we first note for a finite initial guess $n_i(0)$, a finite correct answer n_i^o, and the definition $\tilde{n}_i(0) = n_i^o - n_i(0)$ that each initial squared parameter error $\tilde{n}_i^2(0)$ is finite. With $\mu_i > 0$ for all i, the initial weighted sum of the squared parameter errors $\sum_{i=1}^{N} \tilde{n}_i^2(0)/\mu_i$ is also finite. With satisfaction of (2.2.23) as an inequality, the summed weighted squared parameter error is decreased. Due to the finiteness of the initial summed weighted squared parameter error, ultimately there is no further summed weighted squared parameter error to take away. This means that subsequent satisfaction of (2.2.23) must be as an equality. Admittedly, (2.2.23) can be satisfied as an equality before all of the initial summed weighted squared parameter error has been depleted. In any event, ultimately the change in the summed weighted squared parameter error at each iteration must reach zero as $k \to \infty$. From (2.2.26), this establishes that

$$e^2(k)\left[2 - \sum_{i=1}^{N} \mu_i x_i^2(k)\right] \to 0. \tag{2.2.29}$$

With $x_i^2(k) < \beta_i^2 < \infty$ for all k and the positive μ_i chosen to satisfy the upper bound in (2.2.28), the bracketed term in (2.2.29) is always positive and therefore nonzero. Thus, for (2.2.29) to be satisfied, $e^2(k)$ must converge to zero as claimed. Be aware that this does not imply that the summed weighted squared parameter error in our number guessing game has reached zero. Indeed, for "peculiar" $x_i(k)$ sequences, (2.2.23) can be satisfied as an equality for a nonzero $\sum \tilde{n}_i^2(k)/\mu_i$ that does not decrease between times k and $k+1$. (For example, imagine that $x_i(k) = 0$ for all i and k.) However, in the adaptive filtering configuration of Figure 2.2, the zeroing of the prediction error $e = d - y$ is often the practical objective.

To avoid the magnitude constraints on "satisfactory" x_i for a particular μ_i in (2.2.22), modify (2.2.22) to

$$n_i(k+1) = n_i(k) + \left[\mu_i / \left(1 + \sum_i x_i^2(k) \right) \right] x_i(k) e(k). \qquad (2.2.30)$$

The algorithm of (2.2.30) adds a step size normalization absent in (2.2.22). It can be proved that (2.2.30) satisfies (2.2.23) for $0 < \mu_i < 1$ for all i, which is far less restrictive on μ_i selection (and related $\{x_i\}$ constraints) than (2.2.28) for large β_i. A disadvantage with (2.2.30) is the extra computation, including division, relative to (2.2.22).

2.3 ADAPTIVE FILTER ALGORITHM INTERPRETATION

A perusal of (2.2.13), (2.2.22), and (2.2.30) suggests a general form for parameter adaption

$$\begin{bmatrix} \text{new} \\ \text{parameter} \\ \text{estimate} \end{bmatrix} = \begin{bmatrix} \text{old} \\ \text{parameter} \\ \text{estimate} \end{bmatrix} + \begin{bmatrix} \text{bounded} \\ \text{step} \\ \text{size} \end{bmatrix} \cdot \begin{bmatrix} \text{function} \\ \text{of} \\ \text{input} \end{bmatrix} \cdot \begin{bmatrix} \text{function} \\ \text{of} \\ \text{error} \end{bmatrix}.$$

$$(2.3.1)$$

In (2.2.13), the step size is bounded by unity to allow capture of all possible integer values for the parameters. The "input" is x_i and the function used is the sign function. The prediction error e is also passed through the sign function. For (2.2.22), (2.2.27) bounds the step size multipliers μ_i, and the functions of x_i and e are simply identity functions. In (2.2.30), the functions of x_i and e remain identity functions, while the step size multipliers are the time-varying $\mu_i / (1 + \sum_i x_i^2(k))$, which are bounded with satisfaction of (2.2.28). We discover that (2.3.1) is an apt description of the structure of all of the adaptive algorithms we encounter. In fact, the principal distinctions between various algorithms come in the form of the step size specification and the various functions applied to the input and the prediction error for adaption via (2.3.1). These distinctions provide more than a mere cataloging index. As we have seen in these number guessing games and observe with their translation to adaptive filter algorithms, the distinctions in the various elements of (2.3.1) are related to differences in performance and thus applicability.

    We can now turn our number guessing game solutions into adaptive filter algorithms. Note that associating the w_i in (2.1.1) with the n_i in (2.2.11) and the $x(k - i)$ with the $x_i(k)$ equates (2.2.11) and the FIR linear combiner of (2.1.1). We could now repeat the preceding heuristic development in this signal-processing setting with the appropriate redefinitions and show that (2.3.1) applies to adaptive algorithms for the filter parameterization of (2.1.1) (or, more generically, (2.1.2)). Instead, in the following chapters we develop strategies for adaption of the w_i in a more direct association with signal-processing objectives. This approach eventually brings us to an algorithm similar to (2.2.22), among others. However, based on our number guessing game observations, we can summarize four characteristics we should look for in the adaptive filter algorithms to be developed:

  (i) The generic form of (2.3.1) should emerge with the step size appropriately bounded to insure convergence.

 (ii) Distinctions due to different realizations of (2.3.1) can be related to differences in performance and applicability.

(iii) The character of the input sequence $\{x(k)\}$ will determine whether (and how) the parameter estimates converge to their desired values.

(iv) Step size selection represents a compromise between convergence speed and steady-state coarseness (especially when the problem does not yield $e = 0$ for $\mathbf{W} = \mathbf{W}^o$). Appropriate compromise is crucial to the ability to adequately track time-varying $\mathbf{W}^o$; in other words, to successfully adapt.

2.4 PROBLEMS

1. The next to last paragraph of Section 2.2.2 indicates that the extension of (2.2.13) to three integers can suffer divergence for particular input sequences $\{x_i(k)\}$, but that not all input sequences result in divergence. For the example given in the next to last paragraph of Section 2.2.2, the only thing that changes is the value of $x_1(1)$. For $x_1(1) = 3$, divergence results. For $x_1(1) = 1$, convergence results. Find the boundary value of $x_1(1)$ above which divergence results and below which convergence results. Is this boundary value the same for different initial guesses $n_1(0), n_2(0)$, and $n_3(0)$ where $n_1(0) = n_2(0) = n_3(0) \neq 1$? Where $n_1(0) \neq n_2(0) \neq n_3(0)$?

2. An alternative to the integer guessing game algorithm of (2.2.13) is

$$n_i(k+1) = n_i(k) + \mu_i \, sgn[e(k)] \cdot x_i(k). \tag{2.4.1}$$

Prove that with $\mu_i = 1$ for all i, this algorithm converges for $i > 2$ according to the appropriate extension of (2.2.14), i.e.,

$$\sum_i |\tilde{n}_i(k+1)| \leq \sum_i |\tilde{n}_i(k)| \tag{2.4.2}$$

for any integer input sequences $\{x_i(k)\}$. Check this on the scenario of the example given in the next to last paragraph of Section 2.2.2.

3. Although, as described in the example of the next to last paragraph of Section 2.2.2, the algorithm of (2.2.13) diverged in adapting a three-integer guess with the period-3 input $\{\ldots, 3, -1, -1, 3, -1, -1, \ldots\}$, theory suggests that (2.2.22) does not, given satisfaction of (2.2.27) or (2.2.28).
   (a) Determine the range of positive μ satisfying (2.2.27) and (2.2.28).
   (b) For a μ satisfying both (2.2.27) and (2.2.28), propagate the guesses from (2.2.22) and establish convergence for a variety of initial errors $\tilde{n}_i(0)$ and confirm (2.2.29) and $e^2(k) \to 0$.
   (c) By starting from different sets of initial settings for the $\tilde{n}_i(0)$ having the same $\sum_{i=1}^{N} \tilde{n}_i^2(0)$, demonstrate that convergence time τ to a reduction of $\sum_{i=1}^{N} \tilde{n}_i^2(\tau)$ to less than $\gamma \sum_{i=1}^{N} \tilde{n}_i^2(0)$ where $1 > \gamma > 0$ depends on the initialization. Approximate the upper and lower exponential bounds on this convergence behavior.

4. The upper bound on step size in (2.2.27) for the algorithm in (2.2.22) for the multiple real numbers guessing game assures monotonic nonincreasing summed squared parameter estimate error, as specified in (2.2.23).
   (a) As stated in the paragraph below (2.2.27), a step size so large that it causes dissatisfaction of (2.2.27) at every iteration leads to divergence of the summed squared parameter estimate error. Generate such an example.
   (b) A step size that does not satsify (2.2.27) at every iteration but also does not dissatisfy (2.2.27) at every iteration does not necessarily lead to divergence. Indeed, a step size causing occasional violation of (2.2.27) can cause the summed squared parameter error to grow on some iterations but to shrink by a greater factor over subsequent iterations such that the overall behavior is convergent. Generate such an example.

5. The algorithm in (2.2.30) normalizes the step size so as to avoid the need for constraining the μ_i by an upper bound dependent on the magnitudes of the inputs x_i. Prove, in a manner similar to that for the algorithm in (2.2.22), that the algorithm in (2.2.30) for the multiple real number guessing game satisfies (2.2.23). This normalized algorithm does not

necessarily cause $e^2(k) \to 0$ as established for the unnormalized algorithm around (2.2.29). Instead, the normalized algorithm results in a normalized version of $e^2(k)$ converging to zero. Confirm this. Observe that this normalized squared prediction error can decay to zero while the unnormalized squared prediction error does not, if the normalization term dividing $e^2(k)$ grows faster than $e^2(k)$. Fortunately, if we know in advance that x_i is bounded, this undesirable situation cannot occur and convergence to zero of both the normalized and unnormalized squared prediction errors can be assured by (2.2.30) even without prior knowledge of the value of that upper bound on $x_i(k)$ for all k.

6. Consider the situation where the selector of the "unknown" numbers n_i^o to be guessed unscrupulously alters them without informing you.

   (a) Via simulation, show that the algorithm of (2.2.22) can track this change as long as the prediction error e is fairly computed.

   (b) Vary the step size and confirm that the speed with which a step change in the "unknown" numbers n_i^o is tracked is increased with an increase in algorithm step size.

7. Consider elaborating the multiple real number guessing game by adding an uncorrelated, white, zero-mean noise $w(k)$ (such as that provided by *randn* in MATLAB) to the error, as in

$$e(k) = \sum_i [\tilde{n}_i(k)x_i(k)] + w(k). \qquad (2.4.3)$$

   (a) Show via simulation for sufficiently small μ_i that the algorithm of (2.2.22) still converges to the vicinity of the correct answer for $\{x_i(k)\}$ sequences that result in convergence of the summed squared parameter error to zero in the absence of prediction error measurement noise, i.e., $\{w(k)\} = 0$.

   (b) Illustrate the tradeoff between speed of convergence and asymptotic coarseness in this noisy situation with the selection of the step size.

   (c) For the same input sequence and the same noise sequence, select the step sizes in (2.2.22) and (2.4.1) so the steady-state coarseness is the same, and ascertain which algorithm converges more rapidly from a variety of parameter error initializations. Is this ranking retained for a variety of different pairings of input and noise sequences with the same applied to both algorithms?

3

An Analytical Framework for Developing Adaptive Algorithms

- *Precis: In many cases the best adaptive filter impulse response can be determined by solving the appropriate multivariable optimization problem. Careful examination of the underlying optimization problem provides both the adaptive algorithms themselves and a formal structure for evaluating their performance.*

3.1 BACKGROUND AND DIRECTION

In Chapter 1, we saw that several practical problems could be solved if one had available a filter that could somehow be adjusted to produce just the right transfer function at the right time. In Chapter 2, we chose a fairly simple type of filter, a tapped-delay-line FIR filter, and heuristically developed techniques for updating the impulse response vector. Given the filter input and a measurement of how good or bad the resulting filter output is, a "guessing game" algorithm can be used in an attempt to improve (or at least not worsen) the estimate of the proper impulse response vector.

In this chapter, we take a different, more formal approach. We still use a tapped-delay-line FIR filter and still measure the error between our desired version of the filter output and the one we actually formed. The difference here is that we develop techniques for finding impulse-response vectors that minimize some average measurement of the error. As we shall see, this requires us to make more mathematical assumptions, but this increase in analytical formalism reveals methods for analyzing the performance of the adaptive algorithms we develop and leads to the development of additional algorithms with various performance improvements. The analytical structure and methods are introduced in this chapter, while the actual adaptive algorithms are presented in Chapter 4.

The mathematical notation used in this chapter is basically the same as before. An input waveform $x(k)$ is applied to an FIR filter to produce an output waveform

$y(k)$ according to the convolution sum

$$y(k) = \sum_{\ell=0}^{N-1} x(k-\ell)w_\ell \tag{3.1.1}$$

where $\{w_\ell\}$ is the filter impulse response. Since the filter is assumed to have a finite duration, causal impulse response, w_ℓ equals zero for ℓ less than zero and ℓ greater than $N-1$. To facilitate our development it is useful to define an input data vector $\mathbf{X}(k)$ and the impulse response vector $\mathbf{W}$ according to the following expressions[1]

$$\mathbf{X}(k) = [x(k) \quad x(k-1) \quad x(k-2) \quad \cdots \quad x(k-N+1)]^t \tag{3.1.2}$$

and

$$\mathbf{W} = [w_0 \quad w_1 \quad \cdots \quad w_{N-1}]^t. \tag{3.1.3}$$

The data vector contains the contents of the delay line, that is, the current input sample and the $N-1$ most recent past inputs. The impulse response vector, also often called the coefficient or weight vector, contains the nonzero portion of the impulse response. This vector notation allows a certain compactness of expression. Equation (3.1.1), for example, can be written as

$$y(k) = \mathbf{W}^t\mathbf{X}(k). \tag{3.1.4}$$

The waveforms $x(k)$, $y(k)$, and $d(k)$, the template or "desired" waveform, are in general complex valued. The weight vector $\mathbf{W}$ can also be complex, but for many problems a real-valued vector is adequate.

3.2 THE LEAST SQUARES PROBLEM

3.2.1 Basic Formulation

We begin by assuming that we have L samples of the input sequence, $x(0)$ through $x(L-1)$, where $L > N$. Reviewing the definition of $\mathbf{X}(k)$ in (3.1.2), this means we have the delay line vectors $\mathbf{X}(N-1)$ to $\mathbf{X}(L-1)$. Earlier values of $\mathbf{X}(k)$ such as $\mathbf{X}(0)$ are not defined because we do not know about $x(k)$ before $k=0$. Therefore, output $y(k)$ is also defined only for k between $N-1$ and $L-1$.

We also assume that we are provided the reference signal $d(k)$ for k ranging from $k=0$ to $k=L-1$. Our objective is to find the "best" impulse response vector $\mathbf{W}$, which we call $\mathbf{W}^o$. In this section, we define *best* to mean the choice of $\mathbf{W}$ that makes the summed squared difference between $d(k)$ and $y(k)$, the filter output, as

---

[1]We use the superscript t to indicate transposition and the superscript h to indicate Hermitian, i.e., the complex conjugate transpose.

small as possible. In mathematical terms, we want to find $\mathbf{W}^o$ such that

$$J_{ss} = \sum_{k=N-1}^{L-1} |d(k) - y(k)|^2 \tag{3.2.1}$$

is minimized. The resulting vector $\mathbf{W}^o$ is termed the *optimum choice* in the sense of "least squares." The variable J_{ss} is the sum of the squared errors and is called the *performance function*. It is obviously a function of $d(k)$ and also $\mathbf{X}(k)$ and $\mathbf{W}$ because they determine $y(k)$. For a given sequence of vectors $\{\mathbf{X}(k)\}$ and scalars $\{d(k)\}$, J_{ss} is a function of $\mathbf{W}$ only, and therefore J_{ss} is a measure of how well $\mathbf{W}$ performs as a filter impulse response to produce an output $y(k)$ that matches the reference sequence $d(k)$.

The choice of $\mathbf{W}$ that minimizes J_{ss} is that value that has the best performance. In this case, J_{ss} is the sum of the squared error $e(k) = d(k) - y(k)$ over all values of k where $\mathbf{X}(k)$ and hence $y(k)$ are defined. The best that J_{ss} can attain is zero, which occurs if $\mathbf{W}$ can be chosen so that

$$\mathbf{W}^t \mathbf{X}(k) \stackrel{\Delta}{=} y(k) = d(k) \quad \text{for all valid } k, \tag{3.2.2}$$

that is, $N - 1 \le k \le L - 1$. If so, then each term of the sum is zero and so is the sum itself. There is no smaller value of J_{ss} because J_{ss} cannot be made negative by any choice of $\mathbf{W}$. Note that J_{ss} is not bounded and can be made arbitrarily large with some choice of $\mathbf{W}$.

3.2.2 Reduction to the Normal Equations

To find the best value of $\mathbf{W}$, we first expand (3.2.1) as

$$J_{ss} = \sum_{k=N-1}^{L-1} [d(k) - y(k)][d^*(k) - y^*(k)]$$

$$= \sum_{k=N-1}^{L-1} |d(k)|^2 - \sum_{k=N-1}^{L-1} y(k)d^*(k)$$

$$- \sum_{k=N-1}^{L-1} d(k)y^*(k) + \sum_{k=N-1}^{L-1} |y(k)|^2, \tag{3.2.3}$$

where the asterisk ($*$) denotes conjugation of a complex variable or vector. Using the fact that

$$y(k) = \mathbf{X}^t(k)\mathbf{W} = \mathbf{W}^t\mathbf{X}(k) \tag{3.2.4}$$

the performance function in (3.2.3) can be written as four terms

$$J_{ss} = \sum_{k=N-1}^{L-1} |d(k)|^2 - \sum_{k=N-1}^{L-1} \mathbf{W}^t\mathbf{X}(k)d^*(k)$$

$$- \sum_{k=N-1}^{L-1} d(k)\mathbf{X}^h(k)\mathbf{W}^* + \sum_{k=N-1}^{L-1} \mathbf{W}^t\mathbf{X}(k)\mathbf{X}^h(k)\mathbf{W}^*, \tag{3.2.5}$$

where h denotes the conjugate transpose of a vector or matrix. Because $\mathbf{W}$ is assumed here to be a constant vector and not a function of k,

$$J_{ss} = \sum_{k=N-1}^{L-1} |d(k)|^2 - \mathbf{W}^t \left\{ \sum_{k=N-1}^{L-1} \mathbf{X}(k)d^*(k) \right\}$$

$$- \left\{ \sum_{k=N-1}^{L-1} d(k)\mathbf{X}^h(k) \right\} \mathbf{W}^* + \mathbf{W}^t \left\{ \sum_{k=N-1}^{L-1} \mathbf{X}(k)\mathbf{X}^h(k) \right\} \mathbf{W}^*. \qquad (3.2.6)$$

To simplify J_{ss} further we can define the following terms

$$D_{ss} \triangleq \sum_{k=N-1}^{L-1} |d(k)|^2 \qquad \text{(scalar)} \qquad (3.2.7)$$

$$\mathbf{P}_{ss} \triangleq \sum_{k=N-1}^{L-1} \mathbf{X}(k)d^*(k) \qquad \text{(vector)} \qquad (3.2.8)$$

and

$$R_{ss} \triangleq \sum_{k=N-1}^{L-1} \mathbf{X}(k)\mathbf{X}^h(k). \qquad \text{(square matrix)} \qquad (3.2.9)$$

With these definitions, J_{ss} can be written as

$$J_{ss}(\mathbf{W}) = D_{ss} - \mathbf{W}^t \mathbf{P}_{ss} - \mathbf{P}_{ss}^h \mathbf{W}^* + \mathbf{W}^t R_{ss} \mathbf{W}^*$$

$$= D_{ss} - \mathbf{W}^t \mathbf{P}_{ss} - (\mathbf{W}^t \mathbf{P}_{ss})^* + \mathbf{W}^t R_{ss} \mathbf{W}^*$$

$$= D_{ss} - 2\text{Re}(\mathbf{W}^t \mathbf{P}_{ss}) + \mathbf{W}^t R_{ss} \mathbf{W}^*. \qquad (3.2.10)$$

If both $x(k)$ and $d(k)$ are real valued instead of complex, then $\mathbf{W}$, $\mathbf{X}(k)$, $\mathbf{P}_{ss}$, and R_{ss} are also real valued, and (3.2.10) becomes

$$J_{ss}(W) = D_{ss} - 2\mathbf{W}^t \mathbf{P}_{ss} + \mathbf{W}^t R_{ss} \mathbf{W}. \qquad (3.2.11)$$

We now face the problem of how to find the vector $\mathbf{W}$ that minimizes J_{ss}. We do this by using the result from vector calculus [Noble and Daniel, 1977] that states that $\mathbf{W}_{ss}^o$ is the unique value of $\mathbf{W}$ that minimizes J_{ss} if and only if two conditions are satisfied:

$$\nabla_{\mathbf{W}} J_{ss}\big|_{\mathbf{W}=\mathbf{W}_{ss}^o} = \mathbf{0} \qquad (3.2.12)$$

and

$$\mathcal{H}_{\mathbf{W}} J_{ss} \text{ is positive definite,} \qquad (3.2.13)$$

where $\nabla_{\mathbf{W}} J_{ss}$ is the gradient of J_{ss} with respect to the elements of $\mathbf{W}$ and $\mathcal{H}_{\mathbf{W}} J_{ss}$ is the Hessian matrix of J_{ss} with respect to the elements of $\mathbf{W}$.

Taking the gradient of J_{ss} with respect to the elements of $\mathbf{W}$ is the same as forming a vector of the partial derivatives of J_{ss} with respect to each of the impulse-response coefficients. Thus, (3.2.12) can be written as

$$\frac{\partial J}{\partial w_j}\bigg|_{\mathbf{W}=\mathbf{W}^o_{ss}} = 0, \quad 0 \leq j \leq N-1, \tag{3.2.14}$$

i.e., the first derivative of J_{ss} with respect to each of the impulse response coefficients is zero when the derivative is evaluated at $\mathbf{W} = \mathbf{W}^o_{ss}$. The Hessian of J_{ss}, i.e., $\mathcal{H}_{\mathbf{W}} J_{ss}$, is the matrix of second derivatives. The (i, j)th element of the matrix is

$$[\mathcal{H}_{\mathbf{W}} J_{ss}]_{ij} = h_{ij} = \frac{\partial^2 J_{ss}}{\partial w_i \partial w_j}, \tag{3.2.15}$$

i.e., the second derivative with respect to element w_i and element w_j. The test described in (3.2.13) is satisfied if, for any nonzero vector $\mathbf{V}$,

$$\mathbf{V}^t \{\mathcal{H}_{\mathbf{W}} J_{ss}\} \mathbf{V} > 0. \tag{3.2.16}$$

Any matrix that satisfies this condition is called *positive definite*.

The intuitive meanings of conditions (3.2.12) and (3.2.13) are revealed by considering the one-dimensional case where $\mathbf{W} = w$. When this is true, w^o is optimum when

$$\frac{\partial J}{\partial w}\bigg|_{w=w^o} = 0 \tag{3.2.17}$$

and

$$\frac{\partial^2 J}{\partial w^2}\bigg|_{w=w^o} > 0. \tag{3.2.18}$$

These are the conditions used in functional analysis to find the local minimum of a curve. In particular,

- (3.2.17) states that the slope at the optimum point must equal zero
- (3.2.18) requires that the curvature at the optimum point must be positive, meaning the function curves upward in both directions from the optimum point.

Equations (3.2.12) and (3.2.13) are the N-dimensional versions of (3.2.17) and (3.2.18). Equation (3.2.12) requires the first derivative with respect to each weight to equal zero, setting all slopes to zero. Equation (3.2.13) ensures that the curvature is upward in all directions, which allows us to say that $\mathbf{W}^o_{ss}$ specifies a local minimum point for J_{ss}.

We can now employ the tests (3.2.12) and (3.2.13) to find necessary conditions for $\mathbf{W}^o_{ss}$. First, we evaluate the gradient of J_{ss}. Using (3.2.11), we find that

$$\nabla_{\mathbf{W}} J = \nabla_{\mathbf{W}} D_{ss} - 2\nabla_{\mathbf{W}}(\mathbf{W}^t \mathbf{P}_{ss}) + \nabla_{\mathbf{W}}(\mathbf{W}^t R_{ss} \mathbf{W}). \tag{3.2.19}$$

Because D_{ss} is a constant and not a function of $\mathbf{W}$, its gradient is zero. The gradient of $\mathbf{W}^t \mathbf{P}_{ss}$ can be found directly by evaluating each partial derivative

$$\frac{\partial}{\partial w_j}(\mathbf{W}^t \mathbf{P}_{ss}) = \frac{\partial}{\partial w_j}\left\{\sum_{n=0}^{N-1} w_n p_n\right\} = p_j, \quad 0 \le j \le N-1. \tag{3.2.20}$$

Thus,

$$\nabla_{\mathbf{W}}\{\mathbf{W}^t \mathbf{P}_{ss}\} = \mathbf{P}_{ss}. \tag{3.2.21}$$

Using the same approach, $\nabla_{\mathbf{W}}\{\mathbf{W}^t R_{ss} \mathbf{W}\}$ can be evaluated as

$$\frac{\partial}{\partial w_\ell}\{\mathbf{W}^t R_{ss} \mathbf{W}\} = \sum_{i=0}^{N-1}\sum_{j=0}^{N-1} \frac{\partial}{\partial w_\ell}\{w_i r_{ij} w_j\}$$

$$= 2\sum_{j=0}^{N-1} r_{\ell j} w_j, \tag{3.2.22}$$

which implies that

$$\nabla_{\mathbf{W}}\{\mathbf{W}^t R_{ss} \mathbf{W}\} = 2 R_{ss} \mathbf{W}. \tag{3.2.23}$$

Combining (3.2.21) and (3.2.23) with (3.2.19), the gradient of J_{ss} becomes

$$\nabla_{\mathbf{W}} J_{ss} = -2\mathbf{P}_{ss} + 2 R_{ss} \mathbf{W}. \tag{3.2.24}$$

Thus the first necessary condition for optimality, i.e., finding $\mathbf{W}_{ss}^o$ such that the gradient is zero, becomes

$$\mathbf{0} = -\mathbf{P}_{ss} + R_{ss} \mathbf{W}_{ss}^o \tag{3.2.25}$$

or

$$R_{ss} \mathbf{W}_{ss}^o = \mathbf{P}_{ss}. \tag{3.2.26}$$

The set of N linear simultaneous equations described by the matrix equation are called the *normal equations*. Their satisfaction is a requirement for $\mathbf{W}_{ss}^o$ to be considered the optimal solution.

The second condition, described by (3.2.13), is that the matrix of second derivatives be positive definite. We evaluate this matrix by evaluating each term h_{ij} of $\mathcal{H}_{\mathbf{W}} J_{ss}$

$$h_{ij} = \frac{\partial^2 J_{ss}}{\partial w_i \partial w_j}$$

$$= \frac{\partial^2}{\partial w_i \partial w_j}\{D_{ss}\} - 2\frac{\partial^2}{\partial w_i \partial w_j}\{\mathbf{W}^t \mathbf{P}_{ss}\} + \frac{\partial^2}{\partial w_i \partial w_j}\{\mathbf{W}^t R_{ss} \mathbf{W}\}. \tag{3.2.27}$$

Because the first derivative of the constant D_{ss} is zero, so is the second derivative. Because the elements of $\mathbf{P}_{ss}$ are constants, it follows that the middle term (which is linear in w_j) yields

$$\frac{\partial^2}{\partial w_i \partial w_j} \left\{ \sum_{m=0}^{N-1} w_m p_m \right\} = \frac{\partial}{\partial w_i} \{p_j\} \equiv 0, \quad 0 \le i \le N-1. \quad (3.2.28)$$

Thus, the second term is also zero. The third term can be simplified as follows

$$\frac{\partial^2}{\partial w_i \partial w_j} \left\{ \sum_{\ell=0}^{N-1} \sum_{m=0}^{N-1} w_\ell r_{\ell m} w_m \right\} = \frac{\partial}{\partial w_i} \left\{ \sum_{\ell=0}^{N-1} \sum_{m=0}^{N-1} \frac{\partial}{\partial w_j} \{w_\ell r_{\ell m} w_m\} \right\}$$

$$= \frac{\partial}{\partial w_i} \left\{ 2 \sum_{m=0}^{N-1} r_{mj} w_m \right\}$$

$$= 2r_{ij}, \quad 0 \le i, j \le N-1. \quad (3.2.29)$$

Because $h_{ij} = 2r_{ij}$, for all possible indices i and j, this means that the Hessian matrix, which describes the curvature of J_{ss} at $\mathbf{W} = \mathbf{W}_{ss}^o$, is exactly

$$\mathcal{H}_{\mathbf{W}} J_{ss} = 2R_{ss}, \quad (3.2.30)$$

i.e., twice the matrix R_{ss}. Thus, the two conditions for $\mathbf{W}_{ss}^o$ to be optimum are

$$R_{ss} \mathbf{W}_{ss}^o = \mathbf{P}_{ss} \quad (3.2.31)$$

and

$$R_{ss} > 0, \quad (3.2.32)$$

that is, R_{ss} is positive definite.

3.2.3 Direct Solution for the Optimal Vector $\mathbf{W}_{ss}^o$

If the matrix R_{ss} can be inverted, then the normal equations (3.2.31) can be used to find $\mathbf{W}_{ss}^o$, that is, if R_{ss}^{-1} exists, then

$$\mathbf{W}_{ss}^o = R_{ss}^{-1} \mathbf{P}_{ss}. \quad (3.2.33)$$

From vector calculus [Noble and Daniel, 1977], it is known that R_{ss}^{-1} exists if R_{ss} is positive definite. Thus, if R_{ss} is positive definite, then condition (3.2.32) is satisfied, meaning that the solution $\mathbf{W}_{ss}^o$ is unique and (3.2.31) can be used to produce $\mathbf{W}_{ss}^o$ according to (3.2.33).

From this analysis, we conclude that given real $\mathbf{X}(k)$ and $d(k)$, for $k = N-1$ to $k = L-1$, we can find the optimum least squares solution $\mathbf{W}_{ss}^o$ using the following steps:

(a) Use $x(k)$ to form $\mathbf{X}(k)$ and hence $R_{ss} = \sum_{k=N-1}^{L-1} \mathbf{X}(k) \mathbf{X}^t(k)$.

(b) Use $\mathbf{X}(k)$ and $d(k)$ to form $\mathbf{P}_{ss} = \sum_{k=N-1}^{L-1} \mathbf{X}(k) d(k)$.

(c) If R_{ss} is positive definite, use R_{ss} and $\mathbf{P}_{ss}$ to form $\mathbf{W}_{ss}^o$ using (3.2.33).

3.2.4 The Meaning of P$_{ss}$ and R$_{ss}$

We turn now to trying to determine exactly what $\mathbf{P}_{ss}$ and R_{ss} are and why it is reasonable that they control the optimal value of the impulse-response vector. We start with R_{ss}.

Referring back to its definition in (3.2.9), we see that r_{ij}, the (i, j)th term of R_{ss}, is given by

$$r_{ij} = \sum_{k=N-1}^{L-1} \{\mathbf{X}(k)\mathbf{X}^h(k)\}_{i,j}$$

$$= \sum_{k=N-1}^{L-1} \{\mathbf{X}(k)\}_{\text{row } i} \cdot \{\mathbf{X}^h(k)\}_{\text{column } j}$$

$$= \sum_{k=N-1}^{L-1} x(k - i) \cdot x^*(k - j). \tag{3.2.34}$$

When $x(k)$ is a real-valued rather than a complex-valued process, then

$$r_{ij} = \sum_{k=N-1}^{L-1} x(k - i) \cdot x(k - j). \tag{3.2.35}$$

On the main diagonal of R, i equals j and the (i, i)th element is

$$r_{ii} = \sum_{k=N-1}^{L-1} x^2(k - i), \tag{3.2.36}$$

which is the energy of waveform $x(k)$ measured over the interval from $k = N - 1 - i$ to $k = L - 1 - i$. Thus, the main diagonal elements of R_{ss} measure the energy in windowed portions of the waveform $x(k)$. In general, we expect these entries to be different because the instantaneous power of practical signals varies and so, therefore, does a windowed estimate of its energy.

The off-diagonal elements measure the "cross-energy" between $L - N + 1$ points of the waveform $x(k - i)$ and the same number of points of the time-shifted waveform $x(k - j)$. In general, if $x(k - j)$ closely resembles the waveshape of $x(k - i)$, then the cross-energy r_{ij} is very close to the energy of $x(k - i)$ or $x(k - j)$ with itself. If so, $x(k - j)$ is said to be "highly correlated" with $x(k - i)$. If the shifted waveforms bear little resemblance to one another, then the cross-energy r_{ij} will be much smaller than r_{ii} or r_{jj} and the waveforms are said to be relatively uncorrelated for shifts i and j.

We see now that the matrix R_{ss} contains energy measurements over an $L - N + 1$ point window for all possible shifted versions of $x(k)$. The term r_{ij} indicates the amount of correlation between shifted versions of $x(k)$ and itself. Because it measures the internal correlation properties of one signal sequence $\{x(k)\}$, R_{ss} is called the *autocorrelation matrix* for the sequence $\{x(k)\}$. Because the $\{r_{ij}\}$ are based on time averages, R_{ss} is sometimes referred to as the *time-averaged autocorrelation function*.

We progress in the same way with the vector $\mathbf{P}_{ss}$. From (3.2.8), and assuming the waveform $d(k)$ to be real, the ith element of $\mathbf{P}_{ss}$ is

$$p_i = \sum_{k=N-1}^{L-1} x(k-i)d(k), \quad 0 \le i \le N-1. \tag{3.2.37}$$

From the previous discussion, it is clear that p_i is a measurement of the cross-energy of the reference waveform $d(k)$ and a shifted version of $x(k)$. The magnitude of p_i would be expected to be high when $x(k-i)$ and $d(k)$ closely resemble each other and to be small when they differ. As a result, $\mathbf{P}_{ss}$ is referred to as the *time-averaged cross-correlation vector*, describing the correlation properties of $d(k)$ and $x(k)$ over an N-point choice of shifts.

Thus, we see that the optimal filter solution $\mathbf{W}_{ss}^o$ is just a function of the correlation properties of the input $x(k)$ and the cross-properties between $x(k)$ and the reference waveform $d(k)$. The implications of this are revealed as we continue, but one is obvious here. Suppose that $x(k-i)$ and $d(k)$ have no substantial cross energy for shifts $i = 0$ to $N-1$; if this is true, then $p_i = 0$, $0 \le i \le N-1$, and hence

$$\mathbf{P}_{ss} = \mathbf{0}. \tag{3.2.38}$$

Assuming R_{ss}^{-1} exists, we find that $\mathbf{W}_{ss}^o$ is also zero, meaning that choosing the all-zero filter (that is, $\mathbf{W} = \mathbf{0}$) is the best filter. In light of the unrelated nature of $d(k)$ and $X(k)$, this is intuitively reasonable. The filter output $y(k)$ consists of scaled versions of $x(k-i)$, for shifts $i = 0$ to $N-1$. The error $d(k) - y(k)$ is reduced when some or several past versions of $x(k)$ can be scaled and then subtracted from $d(k)$. If no delayed version $x(k-i)$ resembles (i.e., is correlated with) $d(k)$, then none can be used to reduce the error. When this is the case, all the scaling terms w_i^o should be set to zero.

3.2.5 Examples

We now consider two simple examples.

Example 1: Matching a Pure Delay

First, suppose we have an N-point FIR filter and desire to choose $\mathbf{W}$, the impulse response vector, to minimize the summed squared error J_{ss}. Suppose further that $x(k)$ and $d(k)$ are simple impulsive sequences, given as

$$x(k) = A\delta(k - k_o), \qquad N - 1 \le k \le L - 1, \quad 0 \le k_o \le N - 1 \tag{3.2.39}$$

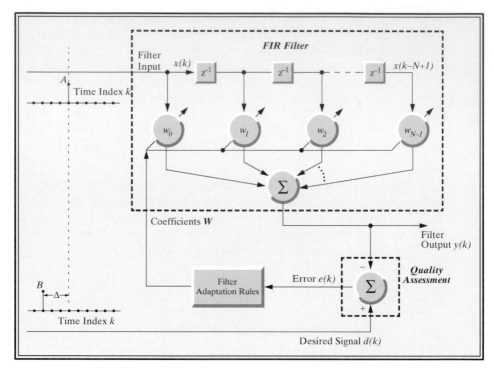

Figure 3.1   Matching a pure delay.

and

$$d(k) = B\delta(k - k_o - \Delta), \quad N - 1 \leq k \leq L - 1, \quad 0 \leq \Delta \leq N - 1, \qquad (3.2.40)$$

where $\delta(k)$ is used here to denote the unit pulse function. This set of conditions is shown in Figure 3.1. To find $\mathbf{W}_{ss}^o$, we first determine the autocorrelation matrix R_{ss} and the cross-correlation vector $\mathbf{P}_{ss}$. From (3.2.9) and (3.2.35),

$$r_{ij} = \sum_{k=N-1}^{L-1} x(k - i) \cdot x(k - j), \quad 0 \leq i, j \leq N - 1$$

$$= A^2 \sum_{k=N-1}^{L-1} \delta(k - k_o - i) \cdot \delta(k - k_o - j), \quad 0 \leq i, j \leq N - 1$$

$$= A^2 \cdot \delta(i - j), \qquad (3.2.41)$$

that is, all diagonal elements are equal and all off-diagonal elements are zero. Thus,

$$R_{ss} = A^2 \cdot I_N, \qquad (3.2.42)$$

where I_N is the $N \times N$ identity matrix. Next, from (3.2.8),

$$p_i = \sum_{k=N-1}^{L-1} x(k-i) \cdot d(k)$$

$$= \sum_{k=N-1}^{L-1} A \cdot \delta(k - k_o - i) \cdot B \cdot \delta(k - k_o - \Delta)$$

$$= AB \sum_{k=N-1}^{L-1} \delta(k - k_o - i) \cdot \delta(k - k_o - \Delta). \qquad (3.2.43)$$

Just as with R_{ss}, it can be verified that the product of the two delta functions equals zero unless their two arguments are identical, which occurs in this case when $i = \Delta$. Thus,

$$p_i = AB \cdot \delta(i - \Delta), \quad 0 \le i \le N - 1 \qquad (3.2.44)$$

or

$$\mathbf{P}_{ss} = AB \cdot \mathbf{e}_\Delta, \qquad (3.2.45)$$

where $\mathbf{e}_\Delta$ is an N-element column vector with all zeros except for a one in the Δth element. This $\mathbf{P}$ vector tells us that only $x(k - \Delta)$ is correlated with $d(k)$.

    Equations (3.2.31) and (3.2.32) are used to find the optimal solution. As long as A is nonzero, R_{ss} is positive definite, R_{ss} is therefore invertible, and a unique solution $\mathbf{W}_{ss}^o$ exists. Thus, with $A \ne 0$,

$$\mathbf{W}_{ss}^o = R_{ss}^{-1}\mathbf{P}_{ss} = \frac{1}{A^2}I_N \cdot AB \cdot \mathbf{e}_\Delta = \frac{B}{A}\mathbf{e}_\Delta. \qquad (3.2.46)$$

The optimal impulse response $\mathbf{W}_{ss}^o$ has only one nonzero coefficient; that is, the Δth component is

$$w_\Delta^o = \frac{B}{A} \qquad (3.2.47)$$

It can be confirmed by examining Figure 3.1 that this choice of impulse response delays the input $x(k)$ by Δ time steps and scales it by B/A. Doing this makes the output $y(k)$ identical to $d(k)$ and makes the output error $d(k) - y(k)$ identically equal to zero. One can do no better, in that making other filter coefficients differ from zero or making the Δth coefficient differ from B/A all increase the error.

Example 2: Matching a Rotating Phasor

Now suppose that $x(k)$ is a complex-valued sinusoid described by

$$x(k) = Ae^{j\omega_o kT} \qquad (3.2.48)$$

where ω_o is the radian frequency and T is the sampling interval. Suppose further that $d(k)$ is given by another complex waveform having the same frequency

$$d(k) = Be^{j\omega_o(k-\Delta)T} \qquad (3.2.49)$$

The FIR filter has N complex coefficients and we desire to find the optimal (possibly complex) impulse response $\mathbf{W}_{ss}^o$.

A comparison of this problem with the previous one of matching a pure delay shows a great similarity, and in fact it can be quickly confirmed that

$$\mathbf{W} = \frac{B}{A}\mathbf{e}_\Delta \qquad (3.2.50)$$

results in a zero output error when used in this situation. We press ahead with the analytic solution in any case.

First, we find R_{ss}:

$$r_{\ell m} = \sum_{k=N-1}^{L-1} x(k-\ell)\cdot x^*(k-m)$$

$$= A^2 \sum_{k=N-1}^{L-1} e^{j\omega_o T(k-\ell)}e^{-j\omega_o T(k-m)}$$

$$= A^2 \sum_{k=N-1}^{L-1} e^{j\omega_o T(m-\ell)}$$

$$= A^2(L-N+1)e^{j\omega_o T(m-\ell)}. \qquad (3.2.51)$$

Similarly, for $\mathbf{P}_{ss}$

$$p_\ell = \sum_{k=N-1}^{L-1} x(k-\ell)\cdot d^*(k)$$

$$= AB \sum_{k=N-1}^{L-1} e^{j\omega_o T(k-\ell)}e^{-j\omega_o T(k-\Delta)}$$

$$= AB \cdot (L-N+1)\cdot e^{j\omega_o T(\Delta-\ell)}. \qquad (3.2.52)$$

Given these expressions for R_{ss} and $\mathbf{P}_{ss}$, we set out to determine $\mathbf{W}_{ss}^o$. As before, the first step is to confirm that R_{ss} is positive definite and then to invert it. Here we run into trouble. Consider the almost trivial case, where $N=2$ and

$$R_{ss} = A^2(L-1)\cdot \begin{bmatrix} 1 & e^{jT\omega_o} \\ e^{-jT\omega_o} & 1 \end{bmatrix}. \qquad (3.2.53)$$

The determinant of the matrix is

$$1\cdot 1 - e^{j\omega_o T}\cdot e^{-j\omega_o T} \equiv 0. \qquad (3.2.54)$$

Therefore, R_{ss} does not have full rank, is not positive definite, and cannot be inverted. Thus, while (3.2.31) is still true, for $N=2$, the other condition for a unique solution (3.2.32) is not. Does this mean there is no optimal solution? No, it means there are many. To see why, we now try again with $N=1$.

If $N=1$, then $R_{ss} = A^2 L$ and $\mathbf{P}_{ss} = A\cdot B\cdot L\cdot e^{j\omega_o T\Delta}$. Because R_{ss} is a positive scalar, it is certainly positive definite and invertible. The optimum and unique solution $\mathbf{W}_{ss}^o$ is then the scalar

$$w_{ss}^o = \frac{ABLe^{-j\omega_o T\Delta}}{A^2 L}$$

$$= \frac{B}{A}e^{-j\omega_o T\Delta}. \qquad (3.2.55)$$

This can be confirmed to be a good solution because

$$y(k) = x(k) \cdot w_{ss}^o = Ae^{j\omega_o kT} \cdot \frac{B}{A}e^{-j\omega_o \Delta T}$$

$$= Be^{j\omega_o T(k-\Delta)}$$

$$\equiv d(k). \tag{3.2.56}$$

We see that the optimal filter inserts a gain of B/A and a phase rotation of $-\omega_o T \Delta$ radians. This phase rotation exactly compensates for the apparent delay in $d(k)$.

Why, then, are the second- and higher-order filter solutions not unique? The answer is this: There are too many degrees of freedom in the impulse response to uniquely specify its value. All the optimal filter need do is provide a gain of B/A and a phase shift of $-\omega_o T \Delta$ radians at frequency ω_o. Any number of filters with $N = 2$ can do that, and all satisfy (3.2.31). Obviously, for $N = 3$ and above, multiple solutions are possible, including (3.2.46).

What we find here is that solutions are available, but there may not be just one for any given N. The source of this nonuniqueness is the character of the input. Clearly something is different about the input in (3.2.39) compared to the complex sinusoidal input in (3.2.48). The effect of the character of the input on the uniqueness of the solution was also noted in the number guessing games in Chapter 2. This important issue and its impact on the performance of adaptive filters is revisited in Section 3.4.

3.2.6 Two Solution Techniques

Suppose we have followed the procedure outlined earlier to solve for the optimal impulse response $\mathbf{W}_{ss}^o$. We collected L samples of $x(k)$, $L - N + 1$ samples of $d(k)$, computed R_{ss} and $\mathbf{P}_{ss}$, and confirmed the invertibility of R_{ss}, and now desire to compute $\mathbf{W}_{ss}^o$. We examine two techniques here; neither is commonly used in practice; however, both are theoretically sound and serve as benchmarks by which we can measure other methods.

Direct inversion.   The most straightforward approach to solving (3.2.33) is the direct inversion of R_{ss} followed by its multiplication with the vector $\mathbf{P}_{ss}$. Because R_{ss} is of dimension N by N, this inversion requires approximately N^3 multiplications, a roughly equal number of additions, and a smaller number of divisions, if done with the classical Gaussian elimination technique. Multiplication of R_{ss}^{-1} by $\mathbf{P}_{ss}$ requires an additional N^2 multiply-adds. The net complexity is said to be "order N^3," or $\mathcal{O}(N^3)$.

Iterative approximation.   Suppose now that we try to iteratively determine $\mathbf{W}_{ss}^o$ by using the following scheme. Given R_{ss} and $\mathbf{P}_{ss}$, we form an estimate $\mathbf{W}(\ell)$ and try to improve the estimate according to the following rule

$$\mathbf{W}(\ell + 1) = (I - \mu R_{ss}) \cdot \mathbf{W}(\ell) + \mu \mathbf{P}_{ss}, \quad \mathbf{W}(0) = \mathbf{0}, \tag{3.2.57}$$

where μ is a small positive constant and ℓ is allowed to increase by one after computation of each $\mathbf{W}(\ell + 1)$ until $\mathbf{W}(\ell)$ approximates $\mathbf{W}_{ss}^o$ well enough

Does this scheme work? We can show that

$$\mathbf{W}(1) = (1 - \mu R_{ss}) \cdot \mathbf{W}(0) + \mu \mathbf{P}_{ss} = \mu \mathbf{P}_{ss}$$

$$\mathbf{W}(2) = \mu(I - \mu R_{ss})\mathbf{P}_{ss} + \mu \mathbf{P}_{ss}$$

or after k steps

$$\mathbf{W}(k) = \mu \left[\sum_{m=0}^{k-1}(I - \mu R_{ss})^m \right] \mathbf{P}_{ss}. \qquad (3.2.58)$$

Recall from the study of power series [Knopp, 1956] that for a scalar constant α

$$\sum_{m=0}^{k-1}|\alpha|^m = \frac{1 - |\alpha|^k}{1 - |\alpha|} \qquad (3.2.59)$$

and, if α has magnitude less than 1, then

$$\lim_{k \to \infty} \sum_{m=0}^{k-1}|\alpha|^m = \frac{1}{1 - |\alpha|}. \qquad (3.2.60)$$

Similarly, if we think of the matrix $I - \mu R_{ss}$ as "less than one" in the sense that multiplying any vector $\mathbf{V}$ by $I - \mu R_{ss}$ decreases its length or magnitude, such that $\|(I - \mu R_{ss})\mathbf{V}\| < \|\mathbf{V}\|$, then it can be shown that the summation in (3.2.58) is expressible as

$$\mathbf{W}(k) = \mu\{[I - (I - \mu R_{ss})^k] \cdot [I - (I - \mu R_{ss})]^{-1}\}\mathbf{P}_{ss}$$

$$= \{I - (I - \mu R_{ss})^k\}R_{ss}^{-1}\mathbf{P}_{ss}. \qquad (3.2.61)$$

If, as assumed, repeated multiplication of $(I - \mu R_{ss})$ by itself shrinks the product, then

$$\lim_{k \to \infty} (I - \mu R_{ss})^k \to \mathbf{0}, \qquad (3.2.62)$$

and (3.2.61) becomes

$$\lim_{k \to \infty} \mathbf{W}(k) = R_{ss}^{-1}\mathbf{P}_{ss} = \mathbf{W}_{ss}^o. \qquad (3.2.63)$$

Thus, by making μ small enough to make $I - \mu R$ "less than 1," we see that repeated iteration of (3.2.57) forces $\mathbf{W}(\ell)$ toward the optimal vector $\mathbf{W}_{ss}^o$.

The number of mathematical operations needed to determine $\mathbf{W}_{ss}^o$ in this way is more difficult to specify clearly than with the direct inversion method. Neglecting the calculations needed to initialize the iterative procedure, each iteration requires N^2 multiply-adds, where N is the filter length. What is harder to specify is how many iterations are required to make $\mathbf{W}(\ell)$ close enough to $\mathbf{W}_{ss}^o$. By iteration K, $K \cdot N^2$ multiply-adds have been done.

Computational comparisons.   At this point, it is interesting to examine these two methods in terms of the computation required in terms of their general philosophies.

First, we count computations. Both require the availability of R_{ss} and $\mathbf{P}_{ss}$, and thus share their computation load. Assuming that $x(k)$ and $d(k)$ are real-valued functions for the moment, it can be confirmed that each vector outer product $\mathbf{X}(k) \cdot \mathbf{X}^t(k)$ requires N^2 multiplications and therefore that composing R_{ss} requires

$$C_R = (L - N + 1) \cdot N^2 \text{ multiply} - \text{adds.} \tag{3.2.64}$$

Similarly, computing $\mathbf{P}_{ss}$ requires

$$C_P = (L - N + 1) \cdot N \text{ multiply} - \text{adds.} \tag{3.2.65}$$

Computing $\mathbf{W}_{ss}^o$ with the direct inversion method uses an additional

$$C_D = N^3 + N^2 \text{ operations,} \tag{3.2.66}$$

while the iterative matrix inversion technique uses

$$C_I = K \cdot N^2, \tag{3.2.67}$$

where K is the number of iterations considered to be sufficient to approximate $\mathbf{W}_{ss}^o$ well enough. Combining these terms, we see that

$$C_{\text{direct inversion}} = C_R + C_P + C_D = (L - N + 1) \cdot (N^2 + N) + N^3 + N^2 \tag{3.2.68}$$

and

$$C_{\text{iterative inversion}} = C_R + C_P + C_I = (L - N + 1) \cdot (N^2 + N) + K \cdot N^2. \tag{3.2.69}$$

In most practical problems, K must be significantly larger than N to attain adequate approximation of $\mathbf{W}(k)$ to $\mathbf{W}_{ss}^o$. On the surface, then, the direct method almost always uses fewer computations than the iterative techniques. Even here, however, several factors make the issue harder to decide:

(a) In most practical problems, the amount of data L is much longer than the filter length N. When this is true, C_R, the computation required to compute the correlation matrix R_{ss}, overwhelms C_P, C_D, and C_I. When this is true, the difference between C_D and C_I may be irrelevant compared to the total computation required.

(b) If R_{ss} does not have full rank, then R_{ss} cannot be inverted and no value of $\mathbf{W}_{ss}^o$ can be found by the direct method. As we shall see, (3.2.57) can still be used in this case to find a solution to the normal equations. Such a solution is not necessarily unique, but does minimize the summed squared performance function.

(c) The iterative technique is less sensitive to numerical problems such as roundoff errors.

In reality, none of these techniques is used very often for adaptive filters because substantially more efficient techniques of computing $\mathbf{W}_{ss}^o$ have been developed, as we show in Chapter 4. It is useful to go through the exercise, however, because the issues examined here will arise later. In particular, some algorithms yield an exact solution for $\mathbf{W}_{ss}^o$ while others approximate it. Some algorithms take a predictable number of computations to reach their solutions, while the computation time for others may depend on the vagaries of the data itself. Properties of the data may in fact preclude any solution at all for some techniques.

3.2.7 Consolidation

In Chapter 2 we developed an iterative algorithm that accepts a data vector $\mathbf{X}(k)$ and a reference sample $d(k)$ at each time k and uses it to improve (or at least not degrade) the weight vector $\mathbf{W}(k)$. In this chapter, we have taken an alternative approach; we form an objective or performance function that describes how good a choice $\mathbf{W}$ is, and then we develop procedures for finding the best possible choice.

In particular, Section 3.2 focuses on the least squares problem, where the performance function J_{ss} is the sum of the squared difference between the filter output $\mathbf{W}^t\mathbf{X}(k)$ and the reference waveform $d(k)$. We showed that this best choice of the impulse response vector $\mathbf{W}$ satisfies the "normal equations"

$$R_{ss}\mathbf{W}_{ss}^o = \mathbf{P}_{ss}, \tag{3.2.70}$$

where the time-averaged autocorrelation matrix R_{ss} and the time-averaged cross-correlation vector $\mathbf{P}_{ss}$ are computed directly from the input data vectors $\mathbf{X}(k)$ and the reference waveform $d(k)$. If the number of data vectors $\mathbf{X}(k)$ exceeds the filter order N, and if the input $x(k)$ has the right properties, then R_{ss} is positive definite and invertible. When this is true (as it usually is in practice), the solution for the best impulse response vector is unique and is given by

$$\mathbf{W}_{ss}^o = R_{ss}^{-1}\mathbf{P}_{ss}. \tag{3.2.71}$$

Given this expression, we examined two techniques for computing $\mathbf{W}_{ss}^o$. The first was a brute force technique, computing R_{ss} and $\mathbf{P}_{ss}$ directly, inverting R_{ss}, and then multiplying by $\mathbf{P}_{ss}$. The second was a iterative technique based on repeating a simple matrix formula.

This effort shows that it is possible to state a performance function and then find a closed-form expression for the best weight vector. It also illustrates that even though the closed-form solution can be written, one might want to compute the expression by some technique other than the most obvious one.

We have bypassed some important aspects of the behavior of the optimum sum squared error solution, such as how the input process $x(k)$ affects the rank of R_{ss} and hence the uniqueness of $\mathbf{W}_{ss}^o$. We do address this in Section 3.4, but only after we develop a class of optimal filters based on a different averaging technique.

3.3 THE LEAST MEAN SQUARES PROBLEM

3.3.1 Formulation

The least squares technique described in the last section forms the basis for most practical adaptive filtering algorithms. Even so, learning about its properties is difficult simply because the input $x(k)$ can be any bounded sequence. Given L points of input $x(k)$ and the reference waveform $d(k)$, the exact optimum impulse-response vector can be found. Given another set of L points, however, there is no guarantee that the resulting optimum vector $\mathbf{W}_{ss}^o$ is at all close to, or even related to, the first solution. Intuitively, we expect the impulse response vector to be essentially constant for different sections of the same waveform if the "properties" of the waveform do not change. Unfortunately, it is difficult to translate these concepts into mathematical definitions for the least squares problem. To do so, we adopt a different analytical direction and develop another way of representing the signals and their averages.

Suppose that the input sequence $x(k)$ is now defined over all time instead of just from $k = 0$ to $k = L - 1$, and that it is a stochastic process. The desired or reference waveform $d(k)$ is also defined for all time and is assumed to be a stochastic process as well. We define the data vector $\mathbf{X}(k)$ and the filter output $y(k)$ as before, but now they also exist for all time because $x(k)$ does. The error $e(k)$ is defined by

$$e(k) = d(k) - y(k), \tag{3.3.1}$$

and is also a stochastic process because $x(k)$ and $d(k)$ are.

With these differences in the pertinent signals, we now define a new performance function called J_{ms}, the mean squared error, by the expression

$$J_{ms} = \mathrm{E}\{e^2(k)\}, \tag{3.3.2}$$

where $\mathrm{E}\{\cdot\}$ denotes the expectation operator. To properly interpret this expression and the ensuing analysis, we digress temporarily to discuss the nature of stochastic processes and some of the associated definitions.

3.3.2 A Brief Review of Stochastic Processes

Working definition of a stochastic process[2].   The signals we dealt with in Section 3.2 were functions of only the time index k. In its simplest form, the stochastic process $f(k, q)$ is a function of two variables, the time index k and the "realization index" q. As discussed, k ranges from $-\infty$ to ∞. The index q selects one of Q "realizations" of the signal time waveform. The number of realizations can in principle be finite or infinite. For each choice of index q, say q_o, there is exactly one deterministic function $f(k, q_o)$, which is defined for all time. Randomness is introduced into $f(k, q)$ by making q a random variable. We assume that q is chosen

---

[2]In Section 3.3.2, we make frequent use of material from Melsa and Sage [1973].

randomly and that a particular value of q is chosen with a probability of $p(q)$. As usual with probability functions,

$$0 \le p(q = q_o) \le 1, \quad \text{for all } q, \tag{3.3.3}$$

and

$$\sum_{\text{all } q} p(q) = 1. \tag{3.3.4}$$

This implies that if we randomly pick a realization of the stochastic process f, then the probability of it being $f(k, q_o)$ is given by $p(q = q_o)$. The set of all possible realizations of $f(k, q)$ is called the *ensemble of functions* and has a total of Q members.

Ensemble averages.   The procedures developed in Section 3.2 assumed the existence of two finite-duration signals $x(k)$ and $d(k)$ and used those to find a single optimal impulse-response vector $\mathbf{W}_{ss}^o$. Our goal in this section is to extend this approach across other function pairs (x, d) within a particular class and find the impulse response that is the best over all such pairs. To do this, we must develop some tools that allow us to perform averages within the class (or ensemble) of function pairs (x, d).

Consider the function g dependent on the realization $f(k, q)$. Given the ensemble of Q realizations indexed by q, we can compute the "ensemble average" of g, denoted $\bar{g}$, by

$$\bar{g}(k) = \sum_{i=1}^{Q} p(q = q_i) \cdot g(f(k, q_i)). \tag{3.3.5}$$

Here, g is computed for each realization of f and weighted by its probability of occurrence, and then all are summed to produce the ensemble average $\bar{g}$ of g. When Q becomes infinite or uncountable, this expression gracefully turns into an infinite sum or an integral.

This ensemble average is also sometimes called the *mean* of g or the *expected value* of g, that is, $\mathrm{E}\{g\}$. Because the probability weighting sums to unity, the sum in (3.3.5) always exists if $g(\cdot)$ is bounded. We should also observe that $\bar{g}$ is in general a function of k because the averaging is done over the realization index only.

We now make some useful definitions.

Mean of $f(k, q)$.   Suppose that

$$g(f(k, q)) \equiv f(k, q), \tag{3.3.6}$$

that is, g is just f itself. The mean of g, hence f, is

$$\bar{g} = \bar{f}(k) = \sum_{i=1}^{Q} p(q = q_i) \cdot f(k, q_i), \tag{3.3.7}$$

simply a weighted average of $f(k, q)$ over all realizations. Notice that $\bar{f}$ is in fact a function of time.

Average Power of $f(k, q)$.   Suppose now that

$$g(f(k, q)) \equiv |f(k, q)|^2. \tag{3.3.8}$$

The ensemble average of g is then

$$\bar{g} = \overline{f^2}(k) = \sum_{i=1}^{Q} p(q = q_i)|f(k, q_i)|^2. \tag{3.3.9}$$

Because $|f(k, q)|^2$ is the instantaneous power of realization q at time k, $\overline{f^2}$ is the (ensemble) average power of f at time k.

Autocorrelation of $f(k, q)$.   Define $g(k, \Delta, q)$ by the expression

$$g(k, \Delta, q) \equiv f(k + \Delta, q) \cdot f^*(k, q), \tag{3.3.10}$$

the product of f and a time shifted version of itself. The ensemble average of this function g is

$$\bar{g} \equiv r(k, \Delta) = \sum_{i=1}^{Q} p(q = q_i) \cdot f(k + \Delta, q_i) \cdot f^*(k, q_i). \tag{3.3.11}$$

This average is called the *ensemble average autocorrelation function* of f and indicates on the average how much f resembles (i.e., is "correlated" with) a time-shifted version of itself. We note that for zero shift, $r(k, \Delta)$ is just the average power

$$r(k, 0) = \overline{f^2}(k). \tag{3.3.12}$$

Cross-Correlation of $f_1(k, q)$ and $f_2(k, q)$.   Suppose now that we have two distinct ensembles, $f_1(k, q)$ and $f_2(k, q)$, both with the same number of members Q and both using the same realization index q. Clearly the mean, average power, and autocorrelation function for either f_1 or f_2 can be computed as described previously. Here, we desire to measure the degree of correlation or statistical dependence between realizations of the two stochastic processes. We do this by defining g as

$$g(k, \Delta, q,) = f_1(k + \Delta, q) \cdot f_2^*(k, q). \tag{3.3.13}$$

The average of $\bar{g}$ across the two ensembles is called the cross-correlation function of f_1 and f_2, and is defined by

$$c(k, \Delta) \equiv \bar{g}(k, \Delta)$$

$$= \sum_{i=1}^{Q} p(q = q_i) \cdot f_1(k + \Delta, q) \cdot f_2^*(k, q). \tag{3.3.14}$$

In general, we expect $c(k, \Delta)$ to be near zero if $f_1(k + \Delta, q)$ and $f_2^*(k, q)$ do not resemble each other on the (ensemble) average and to be nonzero if they do.

An Example

Suppose we define an ensemble of functions by the expression

$$f(k, q) = A \cos(\omega kT + 2\pi q/Q), \quad 1 \le q \le Q, \quad (3.3.15)$$

where the amplitude A, the radian frequency ω, and the sampling interval T are constant. The index realization q affects only the "starting phase" of the cosine, i.e., the phase of the cosine's argument when k equals zero. Suppose further that the probability of occurrence of any specific value of q, say q_o, is given by

$$p(q = q_o) = \frac{1}{Q}, \quad (3.3.16)$$

for all choices of q_o between 1 and Q. Thus, any value of q is equally likely, and the realization f has a uniformly likely starting phase.

Following (3.3.7), the mean value of $f(k, q)$ is

$$\bar{f}(k) = \sum_{i=1}^{Q} A \cos(\omega kT + 2\pi q_i/Q) \cdot p(q = q_i)$$

$$= \frac{A}{Q} \cdot \sum_{i=1}^{Q} \cos(\omega kT + 2\pi q_i/Q)$$

$$= \frac{A}{Q} \cos \omega kT \cdot \sum_{i=1}^{Q} \cos 2\pi q_i/Q - \frac{A}{Q} \sin \omega kT \cdot \sum_{i=1}^{Q} \sin 2\pi q_i/Q,$$

$$= 0, \quad (3.3.17)$$

because both sums equal zero. Note again that this calculation is distinct from the average over a time interval, even though the values are both zero.

Similarly, we determine the average power by using (3.3.9)

$$\overline{f^2}(k) = A^2 \sum_{i=1}^{Q} p(q = q_i) \cdot |\cos(\omega kT + 2\pi q_i/Q)|^2$$

$$= \frac{A^2}{Q} \cdot \sum_{i=1}^{Q} \left(\frac{1}{2} + \frac{1}{2} \cos 4\pi q_i/Q \right)$$

$$= \frac{A^2}{Q} \left\{ \frac{Q}{2} + \frac{1}{2} \cdot \sum_{i=1}^{Q} \cos 4\pi q_i/Q \right\}$$

$$= \frac{A^2}{2}. \quad (3.3.18)$$

As in the calculation of the mean, the fact that phases $180°$ apart are equally likely causes the sum in the next to last line of (3.3.18) to equal zero. A different probability distribution $p(q)$ might ruin this symmetry. Because of the uniform $p(q)$, however, neither the mean nor the average power are functions of the time index k.

The autocorrelation function of $f(k, q)$ is determined using (3.3.11) and various sine/cosine identities:

$$r(k, \Delta) = A^2 \sum_{i=1}^{Q} p(q = q_i) \cdot \cos(\omega(k + \Delta)T + 2\pi q_i/Q) \cdot \cos(\omega kT + 2\pi q_i/Q)$$

$$= \frac{A^2}{Q} \sum_{i=1}^{Q} \left\{ \frac{1}{2} \cos[\omega(k + \Delta)T + 2\pi q_i/Q - \omega kT - 2\pi q_i/Q] \right.$$

$$\left. + \frac{1}{2} \cos[\omega(k + \Delta)T + 2\pi q_i/Q + \omega kT + 2\pi q_i/Q] \right\}$$

$$= \frac{A^2}{2Q} \cdot \sum_{i=1}^{Q} \left\{ \cos(\omega \Delta T) + \cos(2\omega kT + \Delta \omega T + 4\pi q_i/Q) \right\}$$

$$= \frac{A^2}{2} \cdot \cos \omega \Delta T. \tag{3.3.19}$$

Again, the portion of the final sum containing q_i disappears because a full rotation of the cosine sums to zero. Two other points:

(a) Because $r(k, \Delta)$ turns out to have no dependence on k, it may be written as $r(\Delta)$, i.e., a function only of the time *difference* between the two waveforms.
(b) Note that, in accordance with (3.3.12), at a zero shift ($\Delta = 0$), the autocorrelation of $f(k, q)$ equals its average power, that is, $r(k, 0) = \overline{f^2}(k)$.

Finally, to provide an example of the cross-correlation function, as well as of the complex arithmetic version of these formulas, define $f_1(k, q)$ and $f_2(k, q)$ by the following

$$f_1(k, q) = Ae^{j(\omega kT + 2\pi q/Q)} \tag{3.3.20}$$

and

$$f_2(k, q) = Be^{j(\omega kT + \theta + 2\pi q/Q)}, \tag{3.3.21}$$

where A, B, ω, T and θ are constants. Note that f_1 and f_2 have the same frequency, but are offset in phase, and differ in amplitude. The Q realizations of both f_1 and f_2 are indexed by q and each is assumed to be equally likely with probability $1/Q$. The cross-correlation function $c(k, \Delta)$ is given by

$$c(k, \Delta) = \sum_{i=1}^{Q} p(q = q_i) \cdot f_1(k + \Delta, q) \cdot f_2^*(k, q)$$

$$= \frac{AB}{Q} \cdot \sum_{i=1}^{Q} e^{j(\omega(k+\Delta)T + 2\pi q_i/Q)} \cdot e^{-j(\omega kT + 2\pi q_i/Q + \theta)}$$

$$= ABe^{j(\omega \Delta T - \theta)}. \tag{3.3.22}$$

Again, $c(k, \Delta)$ is not a function of time, but is directly affected by the phase offset θ that appears in f_2.

This example has been considered assuming that the realization was chosen from a finite set of Q functions. In fact, the reader should verify that these examples are easily carried over to the countably infinite and uncountably infinite cases. For example, suppose $f(k, \theta)$ is complex sinusoid of the form

$$f(k, \theta) = Ae^{j(\omega kT + \theta)}, \tag{3.3.23}$$

where θ is chosen from the continuous interval $(-\pi, \pi]$ with a uniform probability density of

$$p_\theta(\theta = \theta_o) = \frac{1}{2\pi}. \tag{3.3.24}$$

If so,

$$\textbf{(a) } \bar{f}(k, \theta) = \int_{-\pi}^{\pi} p_\theta(\theta = \theta_o) \cdot Ae^{j(\omega kT + \theta)} d\theta = 0 \tag{3.3.25}$$

$$\textbf{(b) } \overline{f^2}(k) = \overline{f^2} = A^2 \tag{3.3.26}$$

$$\textbf{(c) } r(k, \Delta) = r(\Delta) = A^2 e^{j\omega\Delta T}. \tag{3.3.27}$$

Stationarity.   A stochastic process is *strictly stationary* if $f(k)$ and $f(k + \Delta)$ have the same statistics, that is, the mean power, variance, and all other statistics must be invariant with time. This further implies that the probability density and distribution functions of all orders must be invariant under any time translation.

A *wide-sense stationary* (WSS) process is one for which the first- and second-order statistics (mean and correlation) are time-invariant. This is a much relaxed version of stationarity but is adequate for most of the purposes of this book. We note that from (3.3.25) to (3.3.27), the stochastic process (3.3.23) can be proclaimed WSS because $\bar{f}$, $\overline{f^2}$, and $r(\Delta)$ are all time-invariant.

The concept of white noise.   The concept of white noise is widely used for both analysis and as a practical benchmark for testing systems and algorithms. For reasons to be immediately seen, it is also sometimes called *uncorrelated noise*.

Suppose we construct a discrete-time stochastic process by allowing each sample $x(k)$ to be a random variable with zero mean. The probability distribution of each of these variables is not too important, but we do assume that each random variable is statistically independent of all others. Suppose α and β are two such variables and they are assigned to $x(k_1)$ and $x(k_2)$. Because α and β are statistically independent, their joint probability distribution is just the product of their individual ones, that is

$$p_{\alpha\beta}(\alpha = \alpha_o, \beta = \beta_o) = p_\alpha(\alpha = \alpha_o) \cdot p_\beta(\beta = \beta_o). \tag{3.3.28}$$

Consider the statistics of $x(k)$:

(a) Mean:

$$\bar{x}(k_1) = \bar{\alpha} = \int_\alpha p_\alpha(\alpha = \alpha_o) \cdot \alpha = 0, \tag{3.3.29}$$

because all variables were assumed to have zero mean.

(b) Variance:

$$\overline{x^2}(k_1) = \overline{\alpha^2} = \int_\alpha p_\alpha(\alpha = \alpha_o) \cdot (\alpha_o - \bar{\alpha})^2, \qquad (3.3.30)$$

where the exact value depends on the distribution p_α.

(c) Correlation between $x(k_1)$ and $x(k_2)$:

$$\overline{x(k_1) \cdot x(k_2)} = \int_{\alpha,\beta} p_{\alpha,\beta}(\alpha = \alpha_o, \beta = \beta_o) \cdot \alpha \cdot \beta$$

$$= \int_\alpha p_\alpha(\alpha = \alpha_o) \cdot \alpha \cdot \int_\beta p_\beta(\beta = \beta_o) \cdot \beta$$

$$= \bar{\alpha} \cdot \bar{\beta} = 0 \cdot 0 = 0 \qquad (3.3.31)$$

unless $k_1 = k_2$, so that $x(k_1) = x(k_2) = \alpha = \beta$. If so,

$$\overline{x(k_1) \cdot x(k_2)} = \overline{\alpha^2}. \qquad (3.3.32)$$

From (c) we observe that because the process is zero mean and because each sample of $x(k)$ is independent of all others, then the autocorrelation function has the simple form of

$$r(k, \Delta) = \overline{x^2(k)} \cdot \delta(\Delta), \qquad (3.3.33)$$

that is, at time k, the autocorrelation function is a pulse function, zero for all Δ other than zero.

We note that this process is not stationary because the power and the autocorrelation function depend on exactly which random variable is used for each value of $x(k)$. It is common to make the white noise process better behaved by assuming that all values of $x(k)$ are chosen from the same probability distribution, that is, that they are independent and identically distributed (i.i.d.). If so, the power is the same for each value of k, and

$$r(k, \Delta) = r(\Delta) = \overline{x^2} \cdot \delta(\Delta). \qquad (3.3.34)$$

Now the white noise process is also wide-sense stationary. It is also common, but not necessary, to assume that the random variables are chosen from a particular type of probability distribution, such as Gaussian or Poisson. For the remainder of Section 3.3, we assume that the samples of the stochastic process are i.i.d., but we make no assumption about the distribution itself.

A process such as $x(k)$ is termed a *white noise process*. To see this, we use the Wiener–Khinchine relationship, which states that the power spectrum of a WSS stochastic process is given by the Fourier transform of the process's autocorrelation function [Melsa and Sage, 1973], i.e.,

$$S(\omega) \triangleq \sum_{\Delta=-\infty}^{\infty} r(\Delta)e^{-j\omega\Delta T}, \qquad -\frac{\pi}{T} \leq \omega < \frac{\pi}{T}. \qquad (3.3.35)$$

Using the autocorrelation function specified in (3.3.34), the power spectrum of $x(k)$ is

$$S_x(\omega) = \sum_{\Delta=-\infty}^{\infty} \overline{x^2} \cdot \delta(\Delta)e^{-j\omega\Delta T} = \overline{x^2}, \quad \text{for all } \omega. \qquad (3.3.36)$$

Note that the process has a uniform power density of $\overline{x^2}$ at all frequencies. Because all frequencies are equally represented, like white light, the process is termed *white*. Any correlation between samples "colors" the process and destroys the spectral uniformity.

3.3.3 Development of the Normal Equations

We return now to (3.3.2) and set out to find an impulse response vector $\mathbf{W}^o_{ms}$ that minimizes this new objective function J_{ms}, the expected value of the squared error. As we shall see, much of the analysis parallels that of Section 3.2, except that ensemble instead of time averaging is employed. We begin by assuming that $x(k)$ and $d(k)$ are stochastic processes. As the development proceeds, we add a few other conditions.

Using the definition of $e(k)$ in (3.3.1), we first expand J_{ms} in (3.3.2) as

$$J_{ms} = \mathrm{E}\{e^2(k)\} = \mathrm{E}\{d(k) - y(k)\}^2$$
$$= \mathrm{E}\{d^2(k)\} - 2 \cdot \mathrm{E}\{d(k) \cdot y(k)\} + \mathrm{E}\{y^2(k)\}. \qquad (3.3.37)$$

Because $y(k) \overset{\Delta}{=} \mathbf{X}^t(k)\mathbf{W}$, J_{ms} becomes

$$J_{ms} = \mathrm{E}\{d^2(k)\} - 2 \cdot \mathbf{W}^t \cdot \mathrm{E}\{d(k)\mathbf{X}(k)\} + \mathbf{W}^t \cdot \mathrm{E}\{\mathbf{X}(k)\mathbf{X}^t(k)\} \cdot \mathbf{W}^*. \qquad (3.3.38)$$

For convenience we make the following definitions:

(a) The expected power of $d(k)$:

$$D_{ms} \overset{\Delta}{=} \mathrm{E}\{d^2(k)\}. \qquad (3.3.39)$$

(b) The ensemble autocorrelation matrix of $x(k)$

$$R_{ms} \overset{\Delta}{=} \mathrm{E}\{\mathbf{X}(k)\mathbf{X}^t(k)\}. \qquad (3.3.40)$$

(c) The ensemble average cross-correlation vector

$$\mathbf{P}_{ms} \overset{\Delta}{=} \mathrm{E}\{d(k)\mathbf{X}(k)\}. \qquad (3.3.41)$$

To make D, $\mathbf{P}$, and R time-invariant, we must assume that $d(k)$ and $x(k)$ are at least wide-sense stationary. Then, for real-valued processes J_{ms} can be written compactly as

$$J_{ms}(\mathbf{W}) = D_{ms} - 2\mathbf{W}^t \mathbf{P}_{ms} + \mathbf{W}^t R_{ms} \mathbf{W}. \qquad (3.3.42)$$

Note the similarity between this expression and J_{ss} in (3.2.11).

To find that choice of $\mathbf{W}$ that minimizes J_{ms}, we follow the same steps as those used to minimize J_{ss}. We find the gradient of J_{ms} with respect to $\mathbf{W}$ and find the value of $\mathbf{W}$ that sets it to zero. This leads to the normal equations,

$$R_{ms}\mathbf{W}^o = \mathbf{P}_{ms}. \tag{3.3.43}$$

We determine the uniqueness of this solution by evaluating the Hessian matrix of J_{ms} and checking it for positive definiteness. Exactly the same analysis that led to (3.2.30) shows us that

$$\mathcal{H}_{\mathbf{W}} J_{ms} = 2R_{ms}; \tag{3.3.44}$$

the Hessian matrix is just twice the autocorrelation matrix. If this matrix has full rank, then the solution is unique, R_{ms} is invertible, and

$$\mathbf{W}^o_{ms} = R^{-1}_{ms}\mathbf{P}_{ms}. \tag{3.3.45}$$

We obtain this result promptly because, once $\mathbf{P}_{ms}$ and R_{ms} are defined, the solution for $\mathbf{W}^o_{ms}$ comes directly from vector analysis of the quadratic form of the performance function. We now look at the meaning of $\mathbf{P}_{ms}$ and R_{ms}, as a start towards understanding the relationship between J_{ss} in (3.2.1) and J_{ms} in (3.3.2).

3.3.4 The Ensemble Average Auto- and Cross-Correlation Functions

We turn first to the autocorrelation matrix R_{ms}. The (i, j)th term of R_{ms} is given by

$$r_{ij} = \mathrm{E}\{x(k - i) \cdot x(k - j)\}. \tag{3.3.46}$$

Because we have assumed $x(k)$ to be WSS, the statistic r_{ij} should be invariant to a time shift. Thus,

$$r_{ij} = \mathrm{E}\{x(k + (j - i)) \cdot x(k)\}. \tag{3.3.47}$$

For real-valued $x(k)$, this is just the definition of $r(\Delta)$ from (3.3.11). Therefore,

$$r_{ij} = r(j - i) \tag{3.3.48}$$

and the matrix R_{ms} is built up completely with values of $r(\Delta)$. Because $0 \leq i, j \leq N - 1$, we can note a few things about R_{ms}:

(a) It is Toeplitz or "banded." All terms in the main diagonal or in the same off-diagonal have the same value of $j - i$, and hence the same value $r(j - i)$.

(b) For real-valued $x(k)$,

$$r(j - i) = r(i - j). \tag{3.3.49}$$

Thus R_{ms} is symmetric and symmetrically banded. If $x(k)$ is complex valued, the R becomes conjugate symmetric (sometimes called *Hermitian*).

(c) The average power appears N times on the main diagonal.

(d) The highest value of shift Δ employed from $r(\Delta)$ to build R_{ms} is $\pm(N-1)$, because $\Delta = j - i$ and both i and j are limited to $N - 1$. Thus only a $2N - 1$ point window of the whole autocorrelation function is needed to build R_{ms}.

The cross-correlation vector $\mathbf{P}_{ms}$ is given by components

$$p_i = E\{d(k) \cdot x(k - i)\}. \tag{3.3.50}$$

Again, following the cross-correlation definition in (3.3.14) and invoking the assumed stationarity of d and x,

$$p_i = E\{d(k + i) \cdot x(k)\}$$
$$= c(i), \quad 0 \le i \le N - 1, \tag{3.3.51}$$

where $c(i)$ is just the cross-correlation function of $d(k)$ and $x(k)$. The cross-correlation vector is built directly from an N-point window of the cross-correlation function.

3.3.5 Examples

To show how (3.3.45) can be used to develop the optimal filter in the mean square sense, we do three examples, two of which are closely related to the examples in Section 3.2.5. The key difference is that the stochastic framework is used here.

Matching a pure delay with white noise excitation

Suppose we have an N-point FIR filter and desire to choose $\mathbf{W}$, the impulse response vector, to minimize the ensemble average of the squared error, that is, J_{ms}. Suppose further that $x(k)$ and $d(k)$ are given as

$$x(k) = An(k), \quad -\infty < k < \infty, \tag{3.3.52}$$

where $n(k)$ is a zero mean white process with average power σ^2, and

$$d(k) = Bn(k - \tau), \quad 0 \le \tau \le N - 1, \tag{3.3.53}$$

that is, $d(k)$ is a scaled and delayed version of the filter input $x(k)$.

To determine R_{ms} and $\mathbf{P}_{ms}$, we must first find $r(\Delta)$ and $c(\Delta)$. Because $n(k)$ has been defined as white, with power σ^2 and zero mean, the autocorrelation function for $x(k)$ is

$$r(\Delta) = A^2 \sigma^2 \delta(\Delta). \tag{3.3.54}$$

Because $r_{ij} = r(j - i)$, the autocorrelation matrix R_{ms} has $A^2\sigma^2$ on the main diagonal (where $j - i = 0$) and zero on all other diagonals since $j - i \ne 0$ there. Therefore,

$$R_{ms} = \sigma^2 A^2 I_N, \tag{3.3.55}$$

where I_N is the N-dimensional identity matrix.

We find $c(\Delta)$ as follows

$$c(\Delta) \triangleq \mathrm{E}\{d(k) \cdot x(k - \Delta)\}$$

$$= \mathrm{E}\{Bn(k - \tau) \cdot A \cdot n(k - \Delta)\}$$

$$= A \cdot B \cdot \mathrm{E}\{n(k - \tau + \Delta) \cdot n(k)\}$$

$$= A \cdot B \cdot \sigma^2 \delta(\Delta - \tau) \qquad (3.3.56)$$

Thus $c(\Delta)$ equals $AB \cdot \sigma^2$ when $\Delta = \tau$ but is zero otherwise. The vector $\mathbf{P}_{ms}$ is then

$$\mathbf{P}_{ms} = A \cdot B \cdot \sigma^2 \mathbf{e}_\tau, \qquad (3.3.57)$$

where $\mathbf{e}_\tau$ has zeros in all locations except for the τth entry, which is unity.

The optimal vector $\mathbf{W}_{ms}^o$ is found using (3.3.45). Because A^2 and σ^2 are positive, R_{ms} is invertible and

$$\mathbf{W}_{ms}^o = R_{ms}^{-1} \mathbf{P}_{ms} = (A^2 \sigma^2 I_N)^{-1} AB \cdot \sigma^2 \mathbf{e}_\tau = \frac{B}{A} \mathbf{e}_\tau. \qquad (3.3.58)$$

It can be confirmed that the impulse response vector $\mathbf{e}_\tau$ simply delays the filter input by τ samples. Thus, the optimal filter scales the input by B/A and delays it by τ samples.

Matching a rotating phasor

Now suppose that $x(k)$ is a complex-valued sinusoid with random starting phase,

$$x(k) = Ae^{j(\omega kT + \theta)}, \qquad (3.3.59)$$

where ω and T are constants and θ is a random variable chosen from a uniform distribution over $(-\pi, \pi]$. Suppose further that $d(k)$ is given by another complex waveform

$$d(k) = Be^{j(\omega(k-\tau)T + \theta)}. \qquad (3.3.60)$$

The autocorrelation function $r(\Delta)$ can be determined by reference to (3.3.27) as

$$r(\Delta) = A^2 e^{j\omega \Delta T} \qquad (3.3.61)$$

and $c(\Delta)$ can easily be found to be

$$c(\Delta) = ABe^{j\omega(\Delta - \tau)T}. \qquad (3.3.62)$$

At this point, the correlation functions, plus R and $\mathbf{P}$, are identical to the time-average correlation functions used in Section 3.2.5, except for a constant scaling factor. As a result, the same solution holds. Recall that only for $N = 1$ is the solution unique,

$$w^o = \frac{B}{A} e^{-j\omega \tau T}, \qquad (3.3.63)$$

and that for high-order filters there are an infinite number of choices for $\mathbf{W}_{ms}^o$ that minimize J_{ms}.

Filtering a noisy sinusoid

We now consider a problem that represents a simplified form of many practical situations. We assume that the filter input $x(k)$ is the sum of two components, one a complex-valued zero-mean white noise process $An(k)$ and the other a complex sinusoid $Be^{j(\omega_o kT+\theta)}$. Because $n(k)$ is white, we know that each time sample is statistically independent of all others, but here we also assume that θ, the random starting phase of the sinusoid, is independent of all samples of $n(k)$. As in (3.3.59), we further assume that the starting phase θ is uniformly distributed over the interval $(-\pi, \pi]$. For this example, the desired signal $d(k)$ is given by

$$d(k) = Se^{j(\omega_o(k-\tau)T+\theta)}, \tag{3.3.64}$$

which is a delayed and scaled version of the sinusoidal component present at the input. The amplitudes A, B, and S are constants and the variance of $n(k)$, its power, is given by σ^2. The filter input is a complex sinusoid plus broadband noise, and the desired output is the sinusoid only. Intuitively, then, it seems that the optimal filter should have a bandpass response that selects the sinusoid and suppresses the noise. To see if this is true, we solve for the optimal impulse response vector $\mathbf{W}_{ms}^o$.

Because θ and $n(k)$ are statistically independent, the autocorrelation function of $x(k)$, denoted as $r_x(\Delta)$, is just the sum of the autocorrelation functions of $n(k)$ and the sinusoid. Using (3.3.54) and (3.3.61), we can write

$$r_x(\Delta) = A^2\sigma^2\delta(\Delta) + B^2e^{j\omega_o\Delta T}, \tag{3.3.65}$$

and the elements of the autocorrelation matrix as

$$r_{i\ell} = r_x(\ell - i) = A^2\sigma^2\,\delta(\ell - i) + B^2e^{j\omega_o T(\ell-i)}. \tag{3.3.66}$$

The results of the two previous sections can also be used to determine the cross-correlation function $c(\Delta)$. By definition,

$$\begin{aligned}
c_{xd}(\Delta) &= \mathrm{E}\{x(k)d(k+\Delta)\} = \mathrm{E}\{d(k)x(k-\Delta)\} \\
&= \mathrm{E}\{d(k)[A\,n(k-\Delta) + Be^{j\omega_o(k-\Delta)T+\theta}]\} \\
&= c_{nd}(\Delta) + c_{sd}(\Delta), \tag{3.3.67}
\end{aligned}$$

which is the sum of the cross-correlation functions of $d(k)$ with the two components of $x(k)$. But θ has been assumed to be independent of $n(k)$, thereby making c_{nd} equal to zero for any value of Δ. Thus, reusing (3.3.62),

$$c_{xd}(\Delta) = c_{sd}(\Delta) = BSe^{j\omega_o(\Delta-\tau)T}. \tag{3.3.68}$$

Now that we have $r_x(\Delta)$ and $c_{xd}(\Delta)$ we could simply plug values into R_{ms} and $\mathbf{P}_{ms}$ and solve, but first we find convenient forms for R and $\mathbf{P}$. Suppose we define the complex N-vector $\mathbf{\Gamma}(\omega)$ as

$$\mathbf{\Gamma}(\omega_o) = \begin{bmatrix} 1\,e^{j\omega_o T} & \cdots & e^{j\omega_o(N-1)T} \end{bmatrix}^t. \tag{3.3.69}$$

If we evaluate the (i, ℓ)th term of $\mathbf{\Gamma}(\omega_o)\, \mathbf{\Gamma}^h(\omega_o)$, we find it to be

$$\{\mathbf{\Gamma}(\omega_o)\mathbf{\Gamma}^h(\omega_o)\}_{i,\ell} = e^{j\omega_o iT} \cdot e^{-j\omega_o \ell T}$$
$$= e^{j\omega_o (i-\ell)T}. \tag{3.3.70}$$

Comparing this with the second term of (3.3.66), we see that R_{ms}, the autocorrelation matrix of $x(k)$, can be written as the sum of a scaled identity matrix (the noise component) and an outer product of two vectors (the sinusoidal component)

$$R_{ms} = A^2\sigma^2 I_N + B^2 \mathbf{\Gamma}(\omega_o)\mathbf{\Gamma}^h(\omega_o). \tag{3.3.71}$$

The cross-correlation vector can also be expressed in terms of $\mathbf{\Gamma}(\omega_o)$ because

$$\{\mathbf{P}\}_i = c_{xd}(\Delta - i) = BSe^{j\omega_o(i-\Delta)T} = BSe^{-j\omega_o\Delta T} \cdot e^{j\omega_o iT} \tag{3.3.72}$$

or

$$\mathbf{P} = BS \cdot \{e^{j\omega_o \tau T}\} \cdot \left[1, e^{j\omega_o T}, \ldots, e^{j\omega_o(N-1)T}\right]'$$
$$= BS\{e^{-j\omega_o \tau T}\} \cdot \mathbf{\Gamma}(\omega_o). \tag{3.3.73}$$

Now that we have R_{ms} and $\mathbf{P}_{ms}$, we can solve for $\mathbf{W}_{ms}^o$. As we show in a later section, an autocorrelation matrix of this form always has full rank if σ^2, the power of the noise process, is not zero. It is easily confirmed that the inverse of R_{ms} is given by

$$R_{ms}^{-1} = \frac{1}{A^2\sigma^2}\left\{I_N - \frac{B^2}{A^2\sigma^2 + NB^2}\mathbf{\Gamma}(\omega_o)\mathbf{\Gamma}^h(\omega_o)\right\}. \tag{3.3.74}$$

Multiplying by $\mathbf{P}_{ms}$ yields

$$\mathbf{W}_{ms}^o = \frac{1}{A^2\sigma^2}\left\{I_N - \frac{NB^2}{A^2\sigma^2 + B^2 N}\right\} \cdot \{BS \cdot e^{-j\omega_o \tau T}\mathbf{\Gamma}(\omega_o)\}$$
$$= \frac{BS}{A^2\sigma^2 + B^2 N} \cdot e^{-j\omega_o \tau T} \cdot \mathbf{\Gamma}(\omega_o); \tag{3.3.75}$$

thus the optimal coefficient vector $\mathbf{W}_{ms}^o$ is simply a scaled version of the vector $\mathbf{\Gamma}(\omega_o)$.

The implications of this result become clearer when we determine the frequency response of the filter with the parameter vector in (3.3.75). Transforming the optimal weight vector yields

$$W(\omega) = \sum_{i=0}^{N-1} w_i^o e^{-j\omega iT}$$
$$= \frac{BS}{A^2\sigma^2 + B^2 N} e^{-j\omega_o \tau T}\left\{\sum_{i=0}^{N-1} e^{j\omega_o iT} e^{-j\omega iT}\right\}$$
$$= \begin{cases} \frac{BS}{A^2\sigma^2 + B^2 N} \cdot e^{-j\omega_o \tau T}\left\{\frac{1 - e^{jN(\omega_o - \omega)T}}{1 - e^{j(\omega_o - \omega)T}}\right\}, & \omega \neq \omega_o \\[2ex] \frac{NBS}{A^2\sigma^2 + B^2 N} \cdot e^{-j\omega_o \tau T}, & \omega = \omega_o. \end{cases} \tag{3.3.76}$$

A plot of this frequency response is shown in Figure 3.2, where $\omega_o = 0$ rad/sec, $N = 25$, and the DC gain of the filter is unity. The optimal filter clearly has a bandpass response just as intuition predicted. The maximum gain is attained at the frequency of the complex sinusoid, and the noise is suppressed over the remainder of the band.

What may be unexpected, however, is the scaling factor of the optimal filter. Reviewing the problem statement again, we see that a filter gain of S/B is required to scale the sinusoidal input component so that it precisely cancels template waveform $d(k)$. In light of that, we ask when $W(\omega_o)$ can attain this value. Rewriting $W(\omega_o)$, we see that

$$|W(\omega_o)| = \frac{S}{B} \left\{ \frac{B^2 N}{A^2 \sigma^2 + B^2 N} \right\} \triangleq \frac{S}{B} \left\{ \frac{N\rho}{1 + N \cdot \rho} \right\} \qquad (3.3.77)$$

where $\rho = (B^2)/(A^2 \sigma^2)$ is the signal-to-noise power ratio. Thus if ρ, the ratio of the tone-to-noise power at the input, is very high, then the gain approaches S/B asymptotically. If, however, ρ is very low compared to $1/N$, then the gain falls. If ρ equals zero, then so do the gain and the optimal vector $\mathbf{W}_{ms}^o$. The analytical explanation for this behavior is developed in the next section, but an intuitive one can be offered already. The error signal consists of two components, the uncancelled portion of the sinusoid and any noise that is able to pass through the filter. If the tone-to-noise ratio is very high, then there is only a small amount of noise to pass through the filter, so the overall error power is minimized by cancelling the tone well. When ρ is very low, however, the filter input is mostly noise, and minimizing the error power is done best by "turning off" the filter, that is, reducing its gain to zero as ρ goes to zero. For moderate levels of tone and noise amplitude, the optimal solution is a compromise between the two extremes.

3.3.6 Consolidation

In this section, we phrased a new problem in a stochastic optimization context. The objective was still to find the filter impulse response that minimizes the error $e(k)$, but by averaging over an ensemble of possible waveforms instead of averaging over a finite time segment of one waveform.

We find that much of the mathematics is shared by the summed squared error and the mean squared error formulations. In both cases the average squared error can be written in terms of the auto- and cross-correlation functions of the signals $x(k)$ and $d(k)$. The only difference in the formulations is in the way these correlation functions are defined. Given those functions, hence R_{ms} and $\mathbf{P}_{ms}$, vector calculus techniques are used to find the impulse response vector(s) that minimize the solution itself, and even methods of computing the solution are identical, once given R_{ms} and $\mathbf{P}_{ms}$.

What, then, is different, and why should we pursue the analysis of the mean square solution? Consider again the sum-of-squares criterion of Section 3.2. If the data window from $k = 1$ to $k = L$ is used instead of the window from $k = 0$ to $L - 1$, there is no guarantee that the two associated optimal impulse response vectors will be close to each other at all. This comes simply from the fact that we do not have any

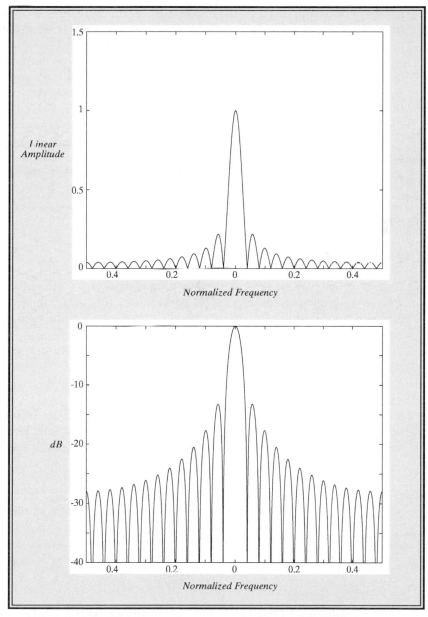

Figure 3.2   Linear and log magnitude frequency response of an FIR filter with an impulse response length *N* of 25.

good way of quantifying the similarity of two deterministic waveforms. The stochastic framework allows us to do this, however. The degree of waveform "similarity" is a more formal concept in the stochastic context.

The paradox, then, is this: In the real world we have only one realization, and therefore can really only consider the summed squared solution. It is virtually impossible to generalize this solution to neighboring situations. As a result, we create the analytical artifice of a stochastic process, one realization of which is our observed sequence. With these stochastic process definitions, however, we can predict the optimal solution over a broad class of possible realizations, including the one actually observed. Broadly speaking, we prove theorems about the mean square problem, but in practice actually solve the sum-of-squares problem.

3.4 PROPERTIES OF THE SOLUTION

3.4.1 Evaluation of the Performance Function

In this section, we use the solutions developed earlier for the optimal impulse response to find new expressions for the performance function J. In all cases, the intent is to add some intuitive insight into what J means and how the optimal solution $\mathbf{W}^o$ depends on the characteristics of $x(k)$ and $d(k)$.

We know from Sections 3.2 and 3.3 that both the summed square and mean square performance functions can be written as

$$J = D - 2\mathbf{W}^t\mathbf{P} + \mathbf{W}^t R\mathbf{W} \qquad (3.4.1)$$

where D, $\mathbf{P}$, and R are computed with the appropriate averaging technique. For convenience, we also assume $x(k)$ and $d(k)$ to be real-valued functions. Both summed and mean square problems yield an optimal solution that satisfies the normal equations

$$R\mathbf{W}^o = \mathbf{P}, \qquad (3.4.2)$$

regardless of whether $\mathbf{W}^o$ is unique. We can then evaluate J_{min}, the minimum value of J, as the value of J achieved when $\mathbf{W}$ satisfies the normal equations

$$\begin{aligned}
J_{min} &= D - 2\mathbf{W}^{ot}\mathbf{P} + \mathbf{W}^{ot} R\mathbf{W}^o \\
&= D - 2\mathbf{W}^{ot}\mathbf{P} + \mathbf{W}^{ot}\mathbf{P} \\
&= D - \mathbf{W}^{ot}\mathbf{P}.
\end{aligned} \qquad (3.4.3)$$

Thus, the minimum value of J depends on the energy of $d(k)$, called D, on the optimal weight vector $\mathbf{W}^o$, and on the cross-correlation between $\mathbf{X}(k)$ and $d(k)$, called $\mathbf{P}$.

Given this minimum value, it is interesting to know how large a price in performance is paid by not using the optimal vector. In particular, let $\mathbf{W}$, the actual weight vector, be defined by

$$\mathbf{W} = \mathbf{W}^o + \mathbf{V}, \qquad (3.4.4)$$

where $\mathbf{V}$ is an N-dimensional deviation vector representing the difference between W and $\mathbf{W}^o$. Substituting this value of $\mathbf{W}$ in (3.4.1), we find that

$$J = D - 2(\mathbf{W}^{ot} + \mathbf{V}^t)\mathbf{P} + \{\mathbf{W}^{ot} + \mathbf{V}^t\}R\{\mathbf{W}^o + \mathbf{V}\}$$
$$= D - 2\mathbf{W}^{ot}\mathbf{P} + \mathbf{W}^{ot}R\mathbf{W}^o - 2\mathbf{V}^t\mathbf{P} + \mathbf{W}^{ot}R\mathbf{V} + \mathbf{V}^t R\mathbf{W}^o + \mathbf{V}^t R\mathbf{V}.$$
$$(3.4.5)$$

We recognize the first three terms to be J_{min}. Using the normal equations again and the fact that R is a symmetric matrix for real signals, we can write J as

$$J = J_{min} - 2\mathbf{V}^t\mathbf{P} + \mathbf{P}^t\mathbf{V} + \mathbf{V}^t\mathbf{P} + \mathbf{V}^t R\mathbf{V}$$
$$= J_{min} + \mathbf{V}^t R\mathbf{V}. \qquad (3.4.6)$$

Thus, ΔJ, the excess average squared error, is expressible as

$$\Delta J \triangleq J - J_{min} = \mathbf{V}^t R\mathbf{V}. \qquad (3.4.7)$$

This is a key result and forms the basis for much intuition about optimal squared error filters. It states that any excess squared error is a quadratic function of the difference between the actual weight vector $\mathbf{W}$ and the optimal one $\mathbf{W}^o$. We assumed earlier, and shortly prove, that R is positive semidefinite, meaning that

$$\mathbf{V}^t R\mathbf{V} \geq 0 \qquad (3.4.8)$$

for any nonzero vector $\mathbf{V}$ (that is, $\mathbf{V}^t\mathbf{V} \neq 0$). Because $\mathbf{V}^t R\mathbf{V}$ is never negative, J_{min} is in fact the minimum attainable value. For most well-behaved problems $\mathbf{V}^t R\mathbf{V}$ is always positive for nonzero $\mathbf{V}$, meaning that any difference between $\mathbf{W}$ and $\mathbf{W}^o$, hence nonzero $\mathbf{V}$, results in J being greater than the minimum possible value. We notice that ΔJ, the penalty for poor choice of $\mathbf{W}$, depends only on the input process $x(k)$ and not on the desired template waveform $d(k)$. Thus, once again the character of the filter input affects the nature of the solution.

The quadratic penalty for nonoptimal choices of $\mathbf{W}$ has many implications, including the idea of iteratively choosing $\mathbf{W}$ in such a way as to reduce J each time, thus ultimately reaching J_{min} and $\mathbf{W}^o$. We return to the expression for ΔJ first, however, and try to determine under what circumstances a nonzero difference vector $\mathbf{V}$ leads to no performance penalty.

3.4.2 The Positivity of R

If the correlation matrix R is positive definite, i.e., (3.4.8) is satisfied with a strict inequality, then several related facts are implied:

(a) $\Delta J > 0$ for any $\mathbf{V} \neq 0$; that is, any difference between $\mathbf{W}$ and $\mathbf{W}^o$ leads to a performance penalty;

(b) R has full rank;

(c) R is invertible;

(d) The normal equations have a unique solution; and

(e) $\mathbf{W}^o = R^{-1}\mathbf{P}$.

One might ask when R is in fact positive definite. To answer this enquiry, we return to the definition of R

$$R = \text{Avrg}\{\mathbf{X}(k)\mathbf{X}^t(k)\}, \tag{3.4.9}$$

where $\text{Avrg}\{\cdot\}$ denotes the appropriate form of averaging. The quadratic form $\mathbf{V}^t R \mathbf{V}$ then becomes

$$\mathbf{V}^t R \mathbf{V} = \mathbf{V}^t [\text{Avrg}\{\mathbf{X}(k)\mathbf{X}^t(k)\}] \cdot \mathbf{V}$$

$$= \text{Avrg}\{\mathbf{V}^t\mathbf{X}(k)\mathbf{X}^t(k)\mathbf{V}\}. \tag{3.4.10}$$

Including constant $\mathbf{V}^t$ and $\mathbf{V}$ inside the averaging operator is possible for any linear averaging technique. Now suppose we write $\mathbf{V}^t\mathbf{X}(k)$ as

$$\mathbf{V}^t\mathbf{X}(k) = s(k). \tag{3.4.11}$$

Notice that $s(k)$ is just the output of an N-tap FIR filter whose impulse-response vector is $\mathbf{V}$ and whose input is $x(k)$. Thus, $s(k)$ is the output of a fictitious "difference filter." If $\mathbf{V}$ equals zero, then $s(k)$ also equals zero for any input $x(k)$, and hence for any state vector $\mathbf{X}(k)$. Using this output $s(k)$, we see that, since $\mathbf{V}^t\mathbf{X}(k) = s(k) = \mathbf{X}^t(k)\mathbf{V}$; the quadratic form is just

$$\mathbf{V}^t R \mathbf{V} = \text{Avrg}\{s^2(k)\}. \tag{3.4.12}$$

But $s^2(k)$ is never negative, and therefore no time or ensemble average of it can be. Therefore, we have proved that $\mathbf{V}^t R \mathbf{V}$ is never less than zero.

Under what conditions can it equal zero? Looking back, it is clear that $\text{Avrg}\{s^2(k)\}$ equals zero only if $s(k)$ equals zero identically for every term in the average. For a time average, it means $\text{Avrg}\{s^2(k)\}$ equals zero for all appropriate k; for the ensemble average, it means that $\text{Avrg}\{s^2(k)\}$ equals zero for every realization (or strictly speaking, for all except a set of measure zero). In other words, $\mathbf{V}^t R \mathbf{V}$ can equal zero if there is some value of $\mathbf{V}$ for which $\mathbf{V}^t\mathbf{X}(k) = s(k) = 0$ for all possible choices of $\mathbf{X}(k)$, over an ensemble or over time. If, for all possible $x(k)$, there is some choice of $\mathbf{V}$, call it $\mathbf{V}_o$, that makes $s(k) \equiv 0$, then R is not positive definite. If there is no such $\mathbf{V}_o$, then R is called *strictly positive definite*, any nonzero difference $\mathbf{V}$ is sensed by ΔJ, and a unique solution exists for $\mathbf{W}^o$.

What is the intuitive meaning of this? Suppose there is some vector $\mathbf{V}_o$ that makes the difference filter output $s(k)$ equal to zero. If so, then any amount of this difference vector can be added to $\mathbf{W}^o$ without increasing the output $y(k)$, without having an impact on the error $e(k)$, and therefore without influencing the performance function J. Thus the performance function J is blind to a difference between $\mathbf{W}^o$ and $\mathbf{W}^o + \alpha \cdot \mathbf{V}_o$, where α is any scalar. When this is true, the optimal solution is definitely not unique. If we want filters with unique solutions, we want to avoid situations where there exists some $\mathbf{V}_o$ that is unobservable in the output. A general way of analyzing this is presented the next section, but for now it is useful to show one example of where this nonuniqueness can happen.

Suppose $x(k)$, the filter input, is a sinusoid given by

$$x(k) = B\cos(2\pi nk/N + \theta), \quad 0 < n < N/2, \tag{3.4.13}$$

where N is the filter length, n is an integer, and θ is an unknown (or random) phase. We can quickly show that if $\mathbf{V}_o$ is given by $\mathbf{V}_o = [1\ 1\ \cdots\ 1]^t$, then $\mathbf{X}^t(k)\mathbf{V}_o \equiv 0$. Why is this nonzero $\mathbf{V}_o$ allowed with no output error $s(k)$ from (3.4.11)? One answer is that the frequency response of the filter given by $\mathbf{V}_o$ has a transmission peak at $f = 0$ and zeros at all nonzero multiples of $f = 1/N$ including n/N and $-n/N$. Thus, $\mathbf{V}_o$ has spectral nulls at exactly the frequency of the input, making the output zero in spite of any change in the magnitude of $\mathbf{V}_o$.

As it happens, there are many other choices of $\mathbf{V}_o$ for which $s(k) \equiv 0$, but all of them share the property that they have zero gain at the frequency of the input sinusoid. A more complete analytical answer is developed in the next section, but as a practical matter, the nonpositivity of R almost always stems from some form of spectral imbalance of the input signal. If the input signal does not have any energy in some band of frequencies, then the filter's solution may not be unique with respect to that region. Even if lack of uniqueness does not bother the designer, the associated fact that R is not invertible may be a cause for concern, depending on how $\mathbf{W}^o$ is to be determined.

3.4.3 Examples Revisited

Matching a pure delay with noise excitation

Continuing from Section 3.3.5, recall that

$$R = \sigma^2 A^2 I_N, \qquad \mathbf{P} = AB\sigma^2 \mathbf{e}_\tau, \qquad \text{and} \quad \mathbf{W}_{ms}^o = \frac{B}{A}\mathbf{e}_\tau. \tag{3.4.14}$$

We find that J_{min} is given by (3.4.3) as

$$J_{min} = D - \mathbf{P}^t \mathbf{W}^o = B^2\sigma^2 - AB\sigma^2 \mathbf{e}_\tau^t \cdot \frac{B}{A}\mathbf{e}_\tau$$

$$= B^2\sigma^2 - B^2\sigma^2 \equiv 0, \tag{3.4.15}$$

and thus there is no residual error. The excess error ΔJ is given by

$$\Delta J = J - J_{min} = \mathbf{V}^t R \mathbf{V} = \sigma^2 A^2 \mathbf{V}^t \mathbf{V} = \sigma^2 A^2 |\mathbf{V}|^2. \tag{3.4.16}$$

Thus every component of the difference vector can cause excess error, which is consistent with an invertible R and the uniqueness of $\mathbf{W}^o$.

Filtering a noisy sinusoid

Again continuing from Section 3.3.5, we have

$$R_{ms} = A^2\sigma^2 I_N + B^2\mathbf{\Gamma}(\omega_o)\mathbf{\Gamma}^h(\omega_o) \tag{3.4.17}$$

and

$$\mathbf{P}_{ms} = BS\{e^{-j\omega_o\tau T}\}\mathbf{\Gamma}(\omega_o). \tag{3.4.18}$$

The optimal solution yields a minimum performance penalty of

$$J_{min} = D - \mathbf{P}^h\mathbf{W}^o = B^2 - BSe^{j\omega_o\tau T}\mathbf{\Gamma}^h(\omega_o) \cdot \frac{B}{S}\left(\frac{\rho}{1+N\rho}\right)\{e^{-j\omega_o\tau T}\}\mathbf{\Gamma}(\omega_o)$$

$$= B^2 - B^2\left(\frac{N\rho}{1+N\rho}\right) = B^2\left(\frac{1}{1+N\rho}\right), \quad \text{where} \quad \rho = \frac{B^2}{A^2\sigma^2}. \tag{3.4.19}$$

If ρ, the SNR, is very high, then $J_{min} \to 0$. If the SNR is very low, then $\mathbf{W}^o \to 0$ and $J_{min} = B^2$, the power of the template signal alone.

The excess performance penalty is given by

$$\Delta J = \mathbf{V}^t R\mathbf{V} = A^2\sigma^2|\mathbf{V}|^2 + B^2\{\mathbf{V}^t\mathbf{\Gamma}(\omega_o)\}^2. \tag{3.4.20}$$

The first term on the right of (3.4.20) is always positive if $\mathbf{V}$ has any nonzero component and σ^2 is not zero. However, the size of the second term depends on the frequency response of the filter described by $\mathbf{V}$ at frequency ω_o.

3.4.4 Decompositions Based on the Eigensystem of *R*

Each of the examples in Section 3.4.3 has in common the fact that the associated autocorrelation matrix *R* could be presented in some simplified form. In every case, the simplicity sprang from the assumed form of the input $x(k)$. With a more general (and realistic) input signal, *R* cannot be so tidily decomposed. Even so, such a decomposition does exist and it can be exploited to understand both the convergence and transient behavior of important adaptive filtering algorithms.

To provide the background tools for the decomposition and exploitation of *R*, we quickly review the linear algebra concepts of eigenvalues, eigenvectors, and the modal matrix. This modal matrix permits a rotation of the coordinate system used to describe *R*, **W**, and **P**. In this rotated coordinate system, both the optimal filter impulse response and revealing properties of the adaptive algorithms can be written in a simplified manner.

Suppose we have an *N*-by-*N* matrix *A* and some *N*-element vector **V**. The vector **V** has a certain length, called the norm $\|\mathbf{V}\|$, and points in some specific direction in *N*-space. This direction is that established by associating each entry in **V** with a different coordinate location and drawing a vector from the origin to this point. The multiplication of **V** by the matrix *A* generally has the effect of changing (e.g., rotating) the direction of **V** and changing its length. For some matrices there are special vectors, called *eigenvectors*, that have the special property that they are not rotated when multiplied by A. When this is true, multiplying $\mathbf{V}$ by A results in a vector pointed in the same direction as $\mathbf{V}$ but perhaps of a different length. We write this condition as

$$AV = \lambda V, \tag{3.4.21}$$

where $\mathbf{V}$ is an eigenvector and λ is a scalar, called the *eigenvalue*, which accounts for a change in length introduced by multiplication with A. As far as the vector $\mathbf{V}$ is concerned, multiplication by A is accomplished by a simple scalar multiplication with λ. There can be as many as N unique eigenvector–eigenvalue combinations for a given N-by-N matrix A, but these combinations are important to us because, as we see later, we can use the eigenvectors to decompose A in a special way.

We turn our attention now to the autocorrelation matrix R. We have already shown that R has some special properties. In particular,

(a) R is symmetric for real input data, and conjugate symmetric in the case of complex input data; that is, $r_{ij} = r_{ji}^*$, $1 \le i, j \le N$.

(b) R is positive semidefinite; that is, $\mathbf{V}^h R \mathbf{V} \ge 0$, if $\mathbf{V}^h \mathbf{V} \ne 0$.

Because of these properties, the eigenvalues and eigenvectors of R have special properties as well [Noble and Daniel, 1977], including:

(a) R has N linearly independent eigenvectors. We call them $\mathbf{U}_1$ through $\mathbf{U}_N$. Because their length is arbitrary, we define them to be unit length vectors; that is,

$$\mathbf{U}_i^h \mathbf{U}_i = ||\mathbf{U}_i|| = 1, \quad \text{for } 1 \le i \le N. \tag{3.4.22}$$

(b) The N eigenvectors of R are orthogonal; that is,

$$\mathbf{U}_i^h \mathbf{U}_j = 0, \quad \text{for } 1 \le i, j \le N \quad \text{and} \quad i \ne j, \tag{3.4.23}$$

(c) Because the eigenvectors are orthogonal and normalized to unit length, we call them *orthonormal* and write their inner products using the Kronecker delta δ_{ij},

$$\mathbf{U}_i^h \mathbf{U}_j = \delta_{ij} = \begin{cases} 1, & i = j \\ 0, & i \ne j. \end{cases} \tag{3.4.24}$$

(d) If the input $x(k)$ is real-valued, then N real eigenvectors can be found. If $x(k)$ is complex, then the eigenvectors are in general complex-valued.

We exploit the special nature of the "eigensystem" of R by using it to decompose the various expressions that depend on R. The key to this decomposition is the formation of the so-called modal matrix Q, composed of the eigenvectors of R;

that is,

$$Q = [\mathbf{U}_1 \cdots \mathbf{U}_N]. \tag{3.4.25}$$

Because the vectors are orthonormal, the product $Q^h Q$ is simply

$$Q^h Q = I_N, \tag{3.4.26}$$

i.e., the N-by-N identity matrix, implying that $Q^{-1} = Q^h$. It is also easy to prove that

$$Q^h R Q = \Lambda \quad \text{and} \quad Q\Lambda Q^h = R, \tag{3.4.27}$$

where Λ is an N-by-N diagonal matrix whose diagonal elements are the eigenvalues of R. This relationship between R and Λ is called a *similarity transformation*. The matrix Q is called the *modal matrix* because, as we see later, it can be used to decompose various important equations into their uncoupled "modes."

Given Q, suppose we now define a coordination transformation of the impulse response vector $\mathbf{W}$ as

$$\mathbf{W} = Q\mathbf{W}' \quad \text{or} \quad Q^h \mathbf{W} = \mathbf{W}', \tag{3.4.28}$$

where $\mathbf{W}'$ is the transformed weight vector. This transformation changes the direction but not the length of the weight vector. This is proved by

$$||\mathbf{W}||^2 = \mathbf{W}^h \mathbf{W} = \mathbf{W}'^h Q^h Q \mathbf{W}' = \mathbf{W}'^h I_N \mathbf{W}' = \mathbf{W}'^h \mathbf{W}' = ||\mathbf{W}'||^2. \tag{3.4.29}$$

We use the transformation in (3.4.28) often. As an example of its usefulness, we first look at what it tells us about the normal equations. From (3.2.31) and (3.3.43), the optimal solution to either of the average squared error problems in Sections 3.2 and 3.3 is given by the matrix normal equation

$$R\mathbf{W}^o = \mathbf{P}. \tag{3.4.30}$$

If we substitute $Q\Lambda Q^h$ for R from (3.4.27) and recognize $Q^h \mathbf{W}^o$ to be $\mathbf{W}^{o'}$ from (3.4.28), we can write

$$Q\Lambda \mathbf{W}^{o'} = \mathbf{P}. \tag{3.4.31}$$

We define the transformed version of the cross-correlation vector as

$$\mathbf{P}' = Q^h \mathbf{P}. \tag{3.4.32}$$

Premultiplication of both sides of (3.4.31) by Q^h yields

$$\Lambda \mathbf{W}^{o'} = \mathbf{P}'. \tag{3.4.33}$$

What makes this new form so useful is that Λ is a diagonal matrix. The whole set of N equations can be written as

$$\lambda_i w_i^{o'} = p_i', \quad 1 \le i \le N, \tag{3.4.34}$$

where w_i' and p_i' are the ith scalar entries of $\mathbf{W}^{o'}$ and $\mathbf{P}'$, respectively.

Each uncoupled weight w_i' can be written in terms of its own eigenvalue λ_i and its uncoupled cross-correlation term p_i'. Clearly, if $\lambda_i \neq 0$, then

$$w_i^{o'} = \frac{p_i'}{\lambda_i}, \quad 1 \leq i \leq N, \tag{3.4.35}$$

and, if λ_i does equal zero, then the value of w_i' is indeterminate. It is this zero eigenvalue case that results in a lack of uniqueness in the solution for the optimal weight vector.

Other useful matrix formulas developed in Section 3.4 can also be decoupled into scalar equations. The minimum average squared error becomes

$$\begin{aligned} J_{min} &= D - \mathbf{P}^h \mathbf{W}^o \\ &= D - (\mathbf{P'}^h Q^h)(Q\mathbf{W}^{o'}) = D - \mathbf{P'}^h \mathbf{W}^{o'} \\ &= D - \sum_{i=1}^{N} p_i' w_i^{o'} = D - \sum_{i=1}^{N} |p_i'|^2/\lambda_i. \end{aligned} \tag{3.4.36}$$

If we define the uncoupled difference vector $\mathbf{V}'$ by the expression

$$\mathbf{V} \triangleq \mathbf{W} - \mathbf{W}^o = Q\mathbf{V}', \tag{3.4.37}$$

we can write the excess average squared error as

$$\begin{aligned} \Delta J = J - J_{min} &= \mathbf{V}^h R \mathbf{V} \\ &= \mathbf{V'}^h \Lambda \mathbf{V}' = \sum_{i=1}^{N} \lambda_i |v_i'|^2. \end{aligned} \tag{3.4.38}$$

Thus the excess squared error is quadratic with each uncoupled difference term v_i' and the eigenvalue determines the degree of penalty. A high value of λ_i means that a small change in v_i' makes a big difference in ΔJ. No change in ΔJ is observed for any change in the uncoupled weight if $\lambda_i = 0$.

3.4.5 A Geometrical View of the Squared-Error Performance Function

A picture is often worth many equations. This is definitely true when first learning about adaptive filters and squared-error performance functions. In this section we review some of the analytical results we obtained in the previous sections and find that, for small enough filter orders, it is possible to express those results in simple drawings. As we progress through the book, we find that this additional perspective is useful another important way—it suggests how one might invent "adaptive algorithms", ones which can automatically search the performance function, or an estimate of it, to find its minimum, thus identifying the coefficients which optimize the filter's performance.

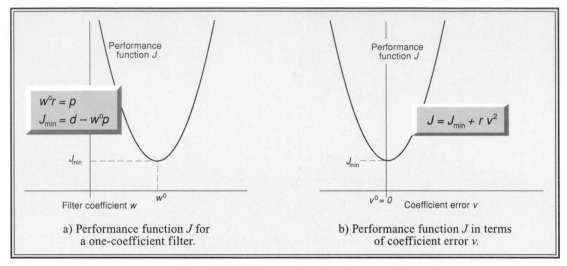

$w^{o}r = p$

$J_{min} = d - w^{o}p$

$J = J_{min} + r\,v^{2}$

a) Performance function J for
a one-coefficient filter.

b) Performance function J in terms
of coefficient error v.

Figure 3.3 Performance function of a one-coefficient filter.

Let us first consider the formulas for the squared-error performance function J which we developed in Section 3.4.1. Figure 3.3(a) shows the performance function J for a simple adaptive filter which has only one coefficient. When the filter is reduced to one coefficient, J can be plotted versus that one coefficient. From (3.4.2) we know that the minimum value of J is obtained when the coefficient w satisfies the equation $rw = p$. From (3.4.3) we know that J obtains its lowest value there, given by $J_{min} = D - w^{o}p$, and from (3.4.7) we know that the performance function rises parabolically at a rate determined by r from both sides of the optimum point w^{o}. Summarizing, the performance function in this simple case is a parabola which attains its minimum value of J_{min} where $w = w^{o}$.

It is also common to redraw Figure 3.3(a) in terms of the coefficient errors, defined by (3.4.4). The parabola is of course the same, but the abcissa is now the coefficient error $v = w - w^{o}$, and the parabola's minimum is found where $v = 0$, that is, where $w = w^{o}$. Centering the performance function curve at $v = 0$ permits a very simple form for the performance function itself. Drawing from (3.4.6) and (3.4.7) we find in this one-dimensional case that the y-intercept of the performance function is J_{min} and that it rises parabolically on both sides at a rate determined by r. We can also see that the "steepness" of the parabola's growth is directly related to r.

Figures 3.4(a) and (b) correspond to Figures 3.3(a) and 3.3(b) in the case where the adaptive filter is permitted to have two coefficients, not just one. We must now choose w_1 and w_2 so that the squared-error performance function J is minimized. In examining Figure 3.4(a) we see that it is just an extension of Figure 3.3(a). The parabola is now a paraboloid which obtains its minimum value of J_{min} where w_1 and w_2 equal their optimum values of w_1^o and w_2^o, as given by the solutions of (3.4.2). If Figure 3.4(a) is replotted as a function of the coefficient errors v_1 and v_2, then

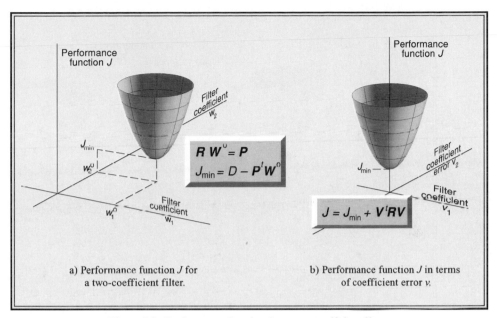

a) Performance function J for a two-coefficient filter.

b) Performance function J in terms of coefficient error v.

Figure 3.4   Performance function for a two-coefficient filter.

Figure 3.4(b) results. The two-dimensional paraboloid corresponding to the performance function is now centered at $(v_1, v_2) = (0, 0)$ and it rises in all directions as determined by the correlation matrix R.

While the conceptional move from one to two (or more) dimensions is apparently quite straightforward, a new issue does arise. In reexamining the paraboloids in Figure 3.4 we see that they were drawn to have circular cross-sections. By this we mean that all points on the paraboloid corresponding to a constant value of J lie on a circle centered at the optimum values of the coefficients. This implies that the performance function grows equally in all directions leading away from the optimum point W^o. The only time that this is true is when the autocorrelation matrix R is the positively scaled version of the identity matrix I. This is rarely true in practice and therefore Figures 3.4(a) and 3.4(b) are idealized to some degree. What happens more typically is illustrated in the transition from Figure 3.5(a) to 3.5(b). Figure 3.5(a) shows a performance function with circular cross-sections, just as those seen in Figure 3.4. Figure 3.5(b) shows the performance function for a two-coefficient adaptive filter when the input correlation function R is not the scaled identity matrix I. A typical cross-section of the performance function J is shown in the upper right. It is generally elliptical, not circular, and its semimajor and semiminor axis are not usually aligned with the coefficient axes w_1 and w_2.

The character of these ellipses can be neatly described using the eigenanalysis just described in Section 3.4.4. To see this we must first observe that each of the elliptic cross-sections corresponds to those points on the paraboloid which are

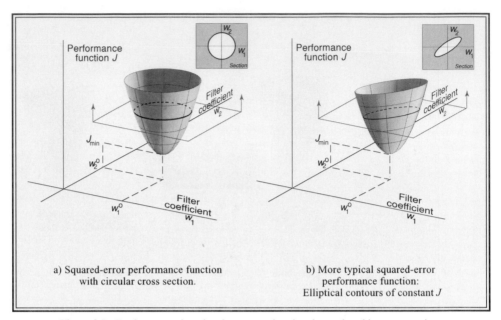

a) Squared-error performance function
with circular cross section.

b) More typical squared-error
performance function:
Elliptical contours of constant J

Figure 3.5 Performance function for uncorrelated and correlated input scenarios.

some constant value above the minimum point J_{min}. For convenience, let us recall that we defined ΔJ with the expression $\Delta J = J - J_{min}$. Each cross-sectional ellipse then corresponds to some positive value of ΔJ.

As a part of the eigenanalysis of squared-error performance function in Section 3.4.4, we saw that ΔJ can be simply written as

$$\Delta J = \sum_{i=1}^{N} \lambda_i |v_i'|^2. \tag{3.4.39}$$

This implies that the shape and orientation of the ellipses of constant ΔJ are defined completely by the eigensystem of the autocorrelation matrix R.

For our simple two-coefficient adaptive filter, these results permit us to characterize the ellipses of constant ΔJ as shown in Figure 3.6. By choosing a positive value for ΔJ and then allowing each of the v_i' to be the only non-zero normalized error coefficient in (3.4.39), we find that the ellipse extends to $\sqrt{\frac{\Delta J}{\lambda_i}}$ in the normalized direction defined by λ_i and its corresponding eigenvector $\mathbf{Q}_i$. This is shown graphically in Figure 3.6. The ellipse seen in the upper right of Figure 3.5(b) is now expanded in Figure 3.6 and appropriately annotated. Just as in Figure 3.5(b), the ellipse is centered on the optimum choice of filter coefficients w_1^o and w_2^o. It is oriented in the directions defined by the eigenvectors of R, and its maximum extent in each direction is determined by the chosen value of ΔJ and the eigenvalue corresponding to that direction. In the two-dimensional case being discussed here, the semimajor axis of the ellipse is determined by the smaller of the two eigenvalues and the semiminor axis is

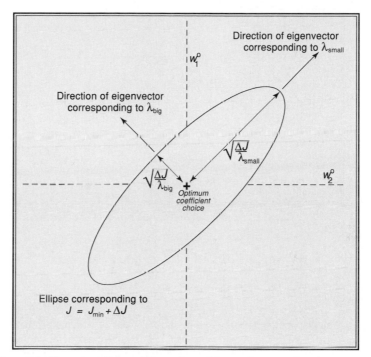

Figure 3.6   The orientation and dimensions of the performance function contours are determined by the eigenvectors and eigenvalues of the autocorrelation matrix R.

determined by the larger of the two eigenvalues. By comparing the paraboloids with the contours, it can be seen that the paraboloids are "steeper" in the direction defined by the larger eigenvalue and "shallower" in the direction defined by the smaller one.

Example Contour

For a real-valued signal, for which R is the autocorrelation matrix, R is symmetric. Accordingly, for the two-dimensional example of Figures 3.5 and 3.6, consider the symmetric matrix

$$R = \begin{bmatrix} 1 & \beta \\ \beta & 1 \end{bmatrix}. \tag{3.4.40}$$

From (3.4.4) and (3.4.7),

$$\Delta J = (\mathbf{W} - \mathbf{W}^o)^t R (\mathbf{W} - \mathbf{W}^o). \tag{3.4.41}$$

We will now evaluate ΔJ for eight particular deviations about $\mathbf{W}^o$:

- $\mathbf{W} - \mathbf{W}^o = \pm \begin{bmatrix} 0 & 1 \end{bmatrix}^t$ Choice A
- $\mathbf{W} - \mathbf{W}^o = \pm \begin{bmatrix} 1 & 0 \end{bmatrix}^t$ Choice B

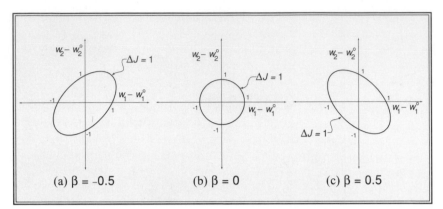

Figure 3.7 Sample eigenstructure contours of constant performance.

- $\mathbf{W} - \mathbf{W}^o = \dfrac{\pm 1}{\left(\sqrt{2(1+\beta)}\right)}[1 \quad 1]^t$ Choice C

- $\mathbf{W} - \mathbf{W}^o = \dfrac{\pm 1}{\left(\sqrt{2(1-\beta)}\right)}[-1 \quad 1]^t$ Choice D

The curious feature of all eight choices (four of which are functions of the off-diagonal term in R) is that in every case $\Delta J = 1$. Thus, for a specific choice for β, we can use these eight points to sketch the unity ΔJ contour, as is done in Figure 3.7 for $\beta = -0.5,\ 0,$ and 0.5. For $\beta = 0$ and R diagonal, the ΔJ contour is circular. For $\beta \neq 0$ the ΔJ contour is elliptical. For $\beta < 0\ (>0)$, the ellipse tilts to the right (left) with its longer, semimajor axis at $45°\ (-45°)$. Scaling the eight parameter error locations by γ can be used to draw the contour for $\Delta J = \gamma^2$. The eigenvalues and unit-normalized eigenvectors of R are

$$\lambda_1 = 1 + \beta, \qquad \mathbf{v}_1 = [1/\sqrt{2} \quad 1/\sqrt{2}]^t \tag{3.4.42}$$

and

$$\lambda_2 = 1 - \beta, \qquad \mathbf{v}_2 = [1/\sqrt{2} \quad -1/\sqrt{2}]^t. \tag{3.4.43}$$

Confirm this by checking their satisfaction of $\lambda_i \mathbf{v}_i = \bar{R}\mathbf{v}_i$ and $\mathbf{v}_i^t \mathbf{v}_i$. Note that the Choice C and D test points are aligned with the eigenvector directions away from $\mathbf{W}^o$. With the semimajor axis of the ellipse the elongated one corresponding to the smallest eigenvalue of R, this eigenanalysis suggests that the $\beta = -0.5\ (0.5)$ choice should be elongated along the direction of $\mathbf{v}_1\ (\mathbf{v}_2)$, i.e. a $45°\ (-45°)$ line, from the optimal parameterization, as in Figure 3.7.

These concepts carry over directly to the performance functions for filters with more than two coefficients, even though they are much more difficult to draw. In these cases the performance functions are "hyperparaboloids" and the cross-sections of constant ΔJ are "hyperellipses". Virtually all other points extend directly, however:

- The hyperellipses are rarely "circular," but rather have semiaxes of differing lengths.
- The hyperellipses are centered at the optimum choice of filter coefficients W^o.
- Their orientation and maximum dimensions are determined by the eigenvectors and eigenvalues, respectively, of the autocorrelation function R.
- The semimajor axis is determined by the smallest eigenvalue of R and corresponds to the "shallowest" approach to the optimum point W^o
- Conversely, the semiminor axis is determined by the largest eigenvalue and corresponds to the "steepest" approach the optimum point.

What appears academic here will turn out to have significant importance in Chapters 4, 5, and 6. But we must wait until then to say why!

3.4.6 Another Useful View—Spectral Decomposition of the Filter Input

Before leaving this chapter, we examine one more view of the optimal filter solution, one based on the spectrum of the input signal $x(k)$. We find in later chapters that this view point helps us understand some of the dynamic behavior of adaptive filtering algorithms. It also suggests some computationally efficient ways of implementing adaptive filters.

We begin with some mathematics. Suppose we define the matrix F as

$$F = \frac{1}{\sqrt{N}} \left\{ \Gamma(0) \ \Gamma\left(\frac{2\pi}{NT}\right) \cdots \Gamma\left(\frac{2(N-1)\pi}{NT}\right) \right\}, \tag{3.4.44}$$

where $\Gamma(\omega)$ is as defined in (3.3.69) Note that F is its own conjugate inverse; that is,

$$F^t F^* = I_N, \quad \text{the } N \times N \text{ identity matrix.} \tag{3.4.45}$$

Now we define what we call $\bar{\mathbf{X}}(k)$, the "spectrally decomposed" version of the input data vector $\mathbf{X}(k)$, with the expression

$$\bar{\mathbf{X}}(k) = F^t \, \mathbf{X}(\mathbf{k}). \tag{3.4.46}$$

Similarly, we can define a decomposed version of the filter coefficient vector $\mathbf{W}$ as $\bar{\mathbf{W}}$ using the expression

$$\bar{\mathbf{W}} = F^h \, \mathbf{W}. \tag{3.4.47}$$

It is easy to show that in the spectrally decomposed space defined by F, the filter output is given by

$$\bar{\mathbf{X}}^t(k)\bar{\mathbf{W}} = \mathbf{X}^t(k) \, F \, F^h \, \mathbf{W} = \mathbf{X}(k)^t \, \mathbf{W} = y(k), \tag{3.4.48}$$

the output in the undecomposed space.

To gain some insight into this decomposition we can examine more carefully the expression for $\bar{x}_n(k)$, the nth element of $\bar{\mathbf{X}}(k)$.

$$\bar{x}_n(k) = \frac{1}{\sqrt{N}} \mathbf{\Gamma}^t \left(\frac{2\pi n}{NT} \right) \mathbf{X}(k)$$

$$= \frac{1}{\sqrt{N}} \sum_{\ell=0}^{N-1} x(k-\ell) \cdot e^{j\left(\frac{2\pi n}{NT}\right)\ell T}$$

$$= \frac{1}{\sqrt{N}} \sum_{\ell=0}^{N-1} x(k-\ell) \cdot e^{j\frac{2\pi \ell n}{N}} \qquad (3.4.49)$$

Thus $\bar{x}_n(k)$ is the FIR-filtered version of the input signal $x(k)$ using the pulse response

$$h_n(\ell) = \frac{1}{\sqrt{N}} e^{j\frac{2\pi \ell n}{N}}, \quad \text{for } 0 \le \ell \le N-1. \qquad (3.4.50)$$

Using this view, we can show the formation of $\bar{x}_n(k)$ and $y(k)$ using the block diagram shown in Figure 3.8. The input $x(k)$ is applied to a bank of N FIR filters, where the pulse response of the nth filter is given by $h_n(\ell)$ in (3.4.50). The filter output $y(k)$ is obtained by scaling the filter outputs $\bar{x}_n(k)$ using $\bar{w}_n$ and summing them up.

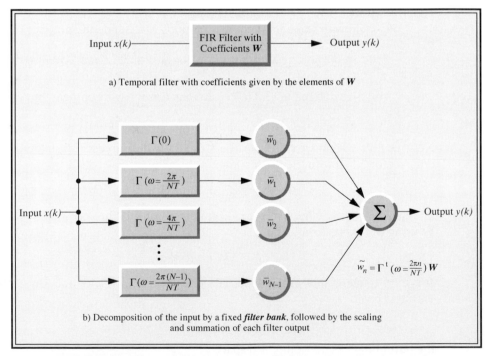

Figure 3.8 Two theoretically equivalent ways to obtain a filter with pulse response given by **W**.

What then are the spectral characteristics of the filters in this filter bank? We can determine this by computing the transfer function of the nth filter's pulse response using the Fourier transform.

$$H_n(\omega) = \sum_{\ell=0}^{N-1} h_n(\ell) \cdot e^{-j\omega\ell T}$$

$$= \sum_{\ell=0}^{N-1} \frac{1}{\sqrt{N}} e^{j\frac{2\pi\ell n}{N}} \cdot e^{-j\omega\ell T}$$

$$= \frac{(-1)^n}{\sqrt{N}} \cdot e^{-j\frac{\omega(N-1)T}{2}} \cdot \frac{\sin\left[\frac{N\omega T}{2}\right]}{\sin\left[\frac{\omega T}{2} - \frac{\pi n}{N}\right]}. \qquad (3.4.51)$$

The magnitude of this transfer function is plotted in Figure 3.9 for each of the N pulse responses in the filter bank. (For the purposes of the figure, the value of N is arbitrarily set to 17.) It can quickly be observed that each filter has the characteristics of a bandpass filter and that the particular choice of F that was made in (3.4.44) is tantamount to the creation of a set of bandpass filters spanning the complete spectral range from $\omega = \frac{-\pi}{T}$ to $\omega = \frac{\pi}{T}$ radians/second. The transformation defined by F and (3.4.46) can therefore be seen to be separating the input $x(k)$ into N "spectral bins," i.e., decomposing $x(k)$ into its spectral components. Equation (3.4.47)

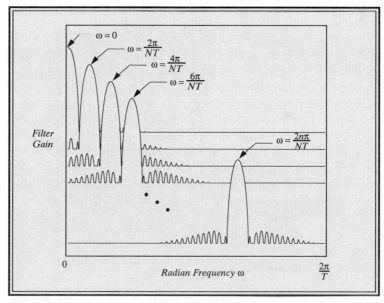

Figure 3.9   Frequency response characteristics of filters with pulse response given by $\Gamma(\omega = \frac{2\pi n}{NT})$.

is the corresponding spectral decomposition of the FIR filter coefficents given by the weight vector $\mathbf{W}$.

The amount of computation required to directly implement an FIR filter using the "filter bank" approach suggested in (3.4.46)–(3.4.48) is actually substantially higher (because premultiplying $\mathbf{X}(k)$ by F^t requires N^2 multiplications) than doing it in the conventional way, making it unattractive from a practical point of view. We present it here, however, for three important reasons:

- In Chapter 7, it is shown that by using the *fast Fourier transform (FFT)* in various ways it is possible to reduce the computation required to implement this "spectral decomposition" approach to substantially less than that needed for the direct computation of the dot product $\mathbf{X}^t(k)\,\mathbf{W}$.

- In Chapter 7, it is also shown that the performance of some adaptive algorithms is superior when the filter itself is implemented using this filter bank approach.

- In Chapter 4, we find that the spectral decomposition of an input signal $x(k)$ permits important insights to be gained about the dynamic and steady-state performance of some practically important adaptive algorithms. These insights provide a great deal of intuition about the actual practical behavior that can be expected of these algorithms.

A last comment: The "spectral decomposition" matrix F (which in fact computes the *discrete Fourier transform* of whatever it operates on) and the "modal matrix" Q discussed earlier in Section 3.4 are not the same. They can both be used to decompose signal vectors and correlation matrices, but F is fixed for a given value of N, and Q depends on the actual characteristics of the input signal $x(k)$ as embodied in the autocorrelation matrix R. Specifically, the matrix F is not capable of "orthogonalizing" R for general values of filter length N and for any input signal. Even so, an interesting analytic result contained in Gray [1972] proves useful in the following chapters. Gray [1972] showed that as the filter order N gets large, and under a reasonable set of conditions levied on the input signal, then F becomes arbitrarily close to the modal matrix Q. Thus, as the filter order gets large, F can be used as proxy for Q, the matrix of eigenvectors, and further the magnitude squared of the *discrete Fourier transform* (DFT) of the input signal $x(k)$ can be used as an accurate proxy for the eigenvalues of R. In this limit, then, the spectral decomposition accomplished with F can be used, both theoretically and practically, to link the theoretical construct of eigensystems to the real world.

3.5 SUMMARY AND PERSPECTIVE

This chapter presents a structure for developing adaptive filtering algorithms based on the idea of optimizing some function of the data waveforms provided to the filter.

While the formal structure discussed here (and the algorithms seen in Chapter 4) are the basis of most adaptive filters in current use, it is useful to remember that this chapter considers a very specific and quite limited problem. We assume that the filter has a discrete-time finite impulse response and is implemented with a tapped-delay-line (transversal) structure. The filter's performance is judged based on some template or reference waveform also provided to the algorithm.

Given these choices for the filter structure and the manner in which the quality of the filter output would be judged, we then turned to the third aspect of adaptive filter design: the development of the methods to be used to choose the filter impulse response. In Chapter 2, we did this by developing an intuitively reasonable set of rules for updating an estimate of the desired impulse response in such a way as to improve the match between the filter output and the reference or template waveform. In this chapter, a more rigorous approach was used. We define a performance function based on an average of the squared output error; that is, the difference between the filter output and the reference, and then develop methodical procedures that allow us to determine the impulse response that provides the best performance.

In addition to the optimal impulse responses themselves, we also develop a set of tools in this chapter that allow us to study some of the properties of the algorithms developed in the next few chapters. We did this by putting the filter input and reference waveforms in a stochastic framework and then defining a new performance function based on the ensemble average of the squared error. Because this ensemble average reflects the behavior of the sum-squared error over all possible signal waveforms, analysis of the properties of this performance function allows us to judge the general or average behavior of adaptive algorithms. Using this framework, we characterized the performance function itself, examined the effects of input signals that do not fully "excite" the filter, and are able to estimate the convergence rates of several important adaptive algorithms. These tools are used in later chapters to both suggest new algorithms and provide means to analyze them.

3.6 PROBLEMS

1. Consider the doubly-infinite, zero-mean sequence

$$\{\ldots, \; x(0), \; x(1), \ldots, \; x(10), \ldots\} = \{\ldots, \; 2, \; 1, \; -1, \; -2, \; -1, \; 1, \; 2, \; 1, \; -1, \; -2, \; -1, \ldots\} \tag{3.6.1}$$

with a period of 6 samples.

(a) For a 3-tap FIR filter with weight vector $\mathbf{W} = [1 \; 1 \; 1]'$, compute the output $y(k)$ from (3.1.4) for $k = 0, 1, \ldots, 10$. $\{y\}$ is periodic. What is the period? For $\mathbf{W} = [1 \; 1 \; 1 \; 1]'$ what is the period of $\{y\}$? Is the period the same as that for $\mathbf{W} = [1 \; 1 \; 1]'$?

(b) For $L = 10, 14$, and 18, compute R_{ss} from (3.2.9) for $N = 1, 2, 3$, and 4.

(c) For the period-6 desired sequence

$$\{\ldots, \; d_a(0), \; d_a(1), \ldots, \; d_a(10), \ldots\}$$

$$= \{\ldots, \; 4, \; -4, \; -8, \; -4, \; 4, \; 8, \; 4, \; -4, \; -8, \; -4, \; 4, \ldots\} \tag{3.6.2}$$

compute $\mathbf{P}_{ss}$ from (3.2.8) for $N = 1, 2, 3$, and 4.

(d) For $\{d_a(k)\}$, a parameter vector $\mathbf{W}$ from (3.1.3) with $N = 4$ or less offers a perfect fit, i.e. $d(k) - y(k) = 0$ for all k. Find such a perfect $\mathbf{W}$ by inspection.

(e) Using the direct inversion formula of (3.2.33), compute the optimal (least squares) $\mathbf{W}_{ss}^o$ for $N = 1, 2, 3$, and 4 and $L = 10, 14$, and 18. Is the answer for a particular N the same across all L? Explain any differences.

(f) For the L among the choices $10, 14$, and 18 providing the best match of the $\mathbf{W}_{ss}^o$ of part (e) to the perfect answer of part (d), compute J_{ss} from (3.2.11) with $\mathbf{W} = \mathbf{W}_{ss}^o$ for $N = 1, 2, 3, 4$.

(g) Using the iterative approximation procedure of (3.2.57), approximate the optimal (least squares) $\mathbf{W}_{ss}^o$ for $N = 1, 2, 3$, and 4. How many iterations are needed to have each entry of the iterative solution vector within $\pm 1\%$ of the solution to part (e)? How many iterations are needed to have the corresponding J_{ss} (from (3.2.11)) to less than 1% of the difference between its initial value (with $\mathbf{W} = 0$) and its optimal value from part (f)?

(h) Repeat parts (c)–(g) for

$$\{\ldots, \; d_b(0), \; d_b(1), \ldots, \; d_b(10), \ldots\} = \{\ldots, \; 1, \; 1, \; 1, \; 1, \; 1, \; 1, \; 1, \; 1, \; 1, \; 1, \; 1, \ldots\}. \tag{3.6.3}$$

(i) Repeat parts (c)–(g) for

$$\{\ldots, \; d_c(0), \; d_c(1), \ldots, \; d_c(10), \ldots\}$$

$$= \{\ldots, \; -1, \; -1, \; 1, \; 1, \; -1, \; -1, \; 1, \; 1, \; -1, \; -1, \; 1, \ldots\}. \tag{3.6.4}$$

(j) Repeat parts (c)–(g) for

$$\{\ldots, \; d_d(0), \; d_d(1), \ldots, \; d_d(10), \ldots\}$$

$$= \{\ldots, \; -6, \; -3, \; 3, \; 6, \; 3, \; -3, \; -6, \; -3, \; 3, \; 6, \; 3, \ldots\}. \tag{3.6.5}$$

2. Consider the signal $x(k) = \sum_{i=1}^{4} g_i \sin(\omega_i k T)$ with $g_1 = 1$, $g_2 = 0.5$, $g_3 = 0.2$, $g_4 = 0.3$, $\omega_1 = \frac{\pi}{6}, \omega_2 = \frac{\pi}{4}, \omega_3 = \frac{\pi}{3}$, and $\omega_4 = \frac{\pi}{2}$.

(a) For $L = 12 + N$ compute R_{ss} of (3.2.9) with $X(k)$ defined as in (3.1.2) for $N = 1$ to 10.

(b) Plot the minimum eigenvalue of R_{ss} as a function of N.

(c) What is the largest N for which this minimum eigenvalue of R_{ss} is not (near) zero? Is this largest N retaining nonsignular R_{ss} effected by alterations in the g_i (with none less than 0.1)?

(d) Repeat parts (a) and (b) with $g_4 = 0$. What is the largest N for which the minimum eigenvalue of the resulting R_{ss} is not (near) zero? Does it change from the answer in part (c)? Do your examples support the claim that a sum of m sinusoids of frequencies less than π and greater than zero radians/sample results in a nonsingular R_{ss} for $N \leq 2m$?

3. Consider a two-tap real-valued FIR filter

$$y(k) = w_0 x(k) + w_1 x(k-1) \tag{3.6.6}$$

with regressor vector $\mathbf{X}(k) = [x(k) \ x(k-1)]^t$.

(a) Demonstrate that in steady-state the average regressor outer product for the sum of two similar amplitude sinusoids is proportional to the identity matrix if the frequency of one sinusoid is displaced $\frac{\pi}{2} \pm i\pi$ radians/sample from the frequency of the other one.

(b) Does the result of part (a) extend to a three-tap FIR filter with a three entry regressor $\mathbf{X}(k) = [x(k) \ x(k-1) \ x(k-2)]^t$ for $\{x\}$ a sum of three sinusoids with frequencies $\frac{\pi}{3} \pm i\pi$ from each other? Explain your answer.

(c) Show that, for a finite length $n \times 1$ regressor, an input composed of a sum of substantially more than n equi-amplitude sinusoids at evenly spaced frequencies results in an average regressor outer product approximately proportional to identity.

4. Consider the operating scenario with $\{x\} = \{\ldots, 1, 1, 1, \ldots\}$ and $\{d\} = \{\ldots, 5, 5, 5, \ldots\}$ for the two-tap FIR filter

$$y(k) = w_0 x(k) + w_1 x(k-1). \tag{3.6.7}$$

(a) In the (w_0, w_1) plane, plot all of the points that result in a perfect match of $y(k)$ to $d(k)$.

(b) For the initial setting of $(w_0(0), w_1(0)) = (7, 2)$, plot the successive "answers" for $\mathbf{W}(k)$ for $k > 0$ from the iterative solution of (3.2.57) in the (w_0, w_1) plane.

(c) Repeat part (b) for $(w_0(0), w_1(0)) = (-1, 2)$.

(d) Do the asymptotic "answers" from parts (b) and (c) match? Explain your answer in terms of the eigenstructure of R_{ss}.

5. Consider extending the task of filtering a noisy sinusoid in Section 3.3.5 to include a sinusoidal interferer in the desired signal. The filter input remains

$$x(k) = An(k) + Be^{j(\omega_0 kT + \theta)} \tag{3.6.8}$$

where $n(k)$ is a complex-valued, zero-mean, white noise process and the starting phase θ of the sinusoid is uniformly distributed over the interval $(-\pi, \pi]$. However, the desired signal, instead of as in (3.3.64), is

$$d(k) = S_0 e^{j(\omega_0(k-\tau)T + \theta)} + S_1 e^{j(\omega_1 kT)}. \tag{3.6.9}$$

(a) Evaluate R_{ms} and compare the result to (3.4.17).

(b) Evaluate $\mathbf{P}_{ms}$ and compare the result to (3.4.18).

(c) Evaluate J_{min} and compare the result to (3.4.19).

(d) Describe in words (without equations) the shift in minimum mean squared error (MMSE) filter performance due to a narrowband disturbance in the measurement of the desired signal. Speculate on what the effect would be with the addition of further sinusoidal interferers to d at frequencies within $(0, \pi]$ different from all other components of d.

6. Consider extending the task of filtering a noisy sinusoid in Section 3.3.5 to include a si-nusoidal interferer in the input signal not reflected in the desired signal. The filter input becomes

$$x(k) = An(k) + B_0 e^{j(\omega_0 kT + \theta)} + B_1 e^{j(\omega_1 kT)} \tag{3.6.10}$$

where $n(k)$ is a complex-valued, zero-mean, white noise process, the starting phase θ of the sinusoid is uniformly distributed over the interval $(-\pi, \pi]$, and $\omega_0 \neq \omega_1$. The desired signal remains as in (3.3.64).
  (a) Evaluate R_{ms} and compare the result to (3.4.17).
  (b) Evaluate $\mathbf{P}_{ms}$ and compare the result to (3.4.18).
  (c) Evaluate J_{min} and compare the result to (3.4.19).
  (d) Describe in words (without equations) the shift in MMSE filter performance due to an extra narrowband component in the input signal not reflected in d. Speculate on what the effect would be with the addition of further sinusoidal interferers to x at frequencies within $(0, \pi]$ different from all other sinusoidal components of x.

7. Consider the 3-tap FIR filter with output

$$y(k) = w_0 x(k) + w_1 x(k-1) + w_2 x(k-2). \tag{3.6.11}$$

The symmetric, Toeplitz, nonnegative-definite, average outer product $\mathbf{R}$ of the associated regressor $X(k) = [x(k) \ x(k-1) \ x(k-2)]^t$ has the generic form

$$R = \begin{bmatrix} 1 & a & b \\ a & 1 & a \\ b & a & 1 \end{bmatrix}. \tag{3.6.12}$$

  (a) For $a = 0.7$ and $b = 0.3$, compute the eigenvalues, eigenvectors, and condition number of R.
  (b) For $a = 0.7$ and $b = 0.3$, find the parameter error vector $\mathbf{V} (= \mathbf{W}^o - \mathbf{W})$ of unit length (i.e., $\mathbf{V}^T \mathbf{V} = 1$) that results in the maximum excess average squared prediction error ΔJ in (3.4.7) and (3.4.38).
  (c) For $a = 0.7$ and $b = 0.3$, find the parameter error vector $\mathbf{V} (= \mathbf{W}^o - \mathbf{W})$ of unit length (i.e., $\mathbf{V}^T \mathbf{V} = 1$) that results in the minimum excess average squared prediction error ΔJ in (3.4.7) and (3.4.38).
  (d) Repeat parts (a)–(c) for $a = 0.3$ and $b = 0.7$.

8. Using the modal matrix Q of (3.4.25) and its properties in (3.4.26)–(3.4.27), orthogonalize the iterative solution of (3.2.57) by rewriting it in terms of the transformed weight vector in (3.4.28) as the decoupled transformed weight dynamics

$$w_i'(\ell + 1) = [1 - \mu \lambda_i] \cdot w_i'(\ell) + \mu p_{i,ss}' \tag{3.6.13}$$

where λ_i is the ith eigenvalue of R_{ss}, w_i' is the ith entry of the transformed weight vector, and $p_{i,ss}'$ is the ith entry of the transformed cross-correlation vector as in (3.4.32). Which of the transformed weight vector entries converges the fastest? Which converges the slowest? Explain your answers.

4

Algorithms for Adapting FIR Filters

- *Precis: Once the adaptive filtering problem is expressed in terms of multivariable minimum average squared error optimization problem, two basic types of adaptive algorithms emerge: simple but somewhat inefficient techniques that search for the optimum solution, and more elegant, but complicated, techniques that maintain optimality with each new input sample.*

4.1 INTRODUCTION

We now turn our attention to developing procedures, or algorithms, for finding the optimal weight vector $\mathbf{W}^o$. In principle, this is simple. Given a record of data $\{x(k), d(k)\}$, one computes R_{ss} and $\mathbf{P}_{ss}$, and, inversion permitted, determines $\mathbf{W}^o_{ss}$ according to the equation $\mathbf{W}^o_{ss} = R^{-1}_{ss}\mathbf{P}_{ss}$ of (3.2.33). Even so, we often choose to compute $\mathbf{W}^o$ in other ways. Some reasons for this include the following:

(a) R_{ss} may not be invertible.

(b) Even if R_{ss} were theoretically invertible, the numerical precision required to invert R_{ss} properly may be beyond the capabilities of the hardware or computer used in implementing the filter.

(c) There may be more efficient ways to calculate $\mathbf{W}^o$ than the direct path that has been discussed.

In this chapter, we examine two different methodologies for developing adaptive filtering algorithms. The first class is based on so-called search techniques, which have the advantage of being simple to implement, but at the price of some inaccuracy in the final estimate of the optimal solution. In Section 4.3, we examine techniques that compute $\mathbf{W}^o$ exactly, but at the expense of more complicated algorithms.

4.2 SEARCH TECHNIQUES

Our goal is to find $\mathbf{W}^o$, that particular choice of the weight vector for which the performance function J is minimized. One relatively straightforward way of finding $\mathbf{W}^o$ is to search over the function J to find its minimum. This might be done by computing J for all possible values of $\mathbf{W}$ and then picking the smallest, or it might be done by randomly picking values of $\mathbf{W}$, computing J, and seeing if it is smaller than those seen already [Widrow and McCool, 1976]. A better approach yet is to develop an orderly search procedure that leads one methodically from a starting point to the value of $\mathbf{W}$ that minimizes J.

4.2.1 The Gradient Search Approach

From Section 3.4, we recall several facts that can be used to develop search procedures. If we presume that R_{ss} has full rank, they include

(a) The optimal solution $\mathbf{W}^o$ is a unique choice of $\mathbf{W}$;

(b) Any difference between the actual weight vector $\mathbf{W}$ and the optimal one $\mathbf{W}^o$ leads to an increase in the performance function; that is, $\Delta J = \mathbf{V}^t R \mathbf{V}$, where $\mathbf{V} = \mathbf{W}^o - \mathbf{W}$; and

(c) $\Delta J > 0$ for $\mathbf{V} \neq 0$.

Suppose now that we iteratively estimate $\mathbf{W}^o$; that is, we start with some initial choice of $\mathbf{W}$, called $\mathbf{W}(0)$, and then choose a new value $\mathbf{W}(1)$ in some way that leads us closer to the optimal value. The points made above suggest how to do this. Unless $\mathbf{W}(0)$ equals $\mathbf{W}^o$, the value of J at $\mathbf{W}(0)$ is greater than J_{min}. Suppose we choose $\mathbf{W}(1)$ in such a way that ΔJ and hence J is reduced by some amount. If ΔJ is still greater than zero, an improvement is made but $\mathbf{W}(1)$ is not $\mathbf{W}^o$. Suppose we take additional steps, $\mathbf{W}(2)$, $\mathbf{W}(3)$, etc., and each time are able to reduce ΔJ by some amount. If this can be done every time, then ultimately ΔJ will approach zero and $\mathbf{W}(\ell)$ will approach $\mathbf{W}^o$. The fact that $\mathbf{W}^o$ is unique and minimizes J guarantees that if a search procedure finds the minimum of the performance function, then it has also found $\mathbf{W}^o$.

How, then, should we move from $\mathbf{W}(\ell)$ to $\mathbf{W}(\ell + 1)$? One good technique is to use the gradient function to select the direction. The basic idea is shown in the one-dimensional example in Figure 4.1. The performance function J has a clear minimum, at $w = w^o$, and has a quadratic shape. At $w(\ell)$, ΔJ exceeds zero, indicating that $w(\ell) \neq w^o$. If we desire to improve $w(\ell)$, we want to move in the direction toward w^o. Without direct solution we do not know where w^o is, but, by evaluating the derivative of J at $w(\ell)$, we can get a clue. By evaluating the derivative we determine the first-order change in J caused by a small change in w. Suppose, as shown, that dJ/dw is positive. Therefore, increasing w makes J increase. Our goal, however, is to decrease J, and this may be done by taking a step in the negative direction. This

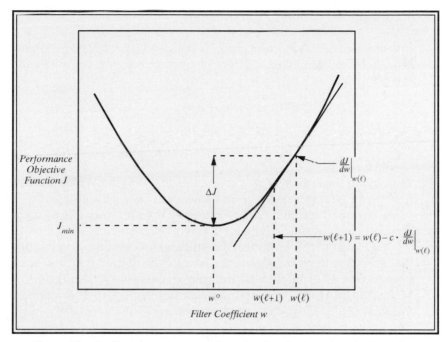

Figure 4.1 Gradient descent on one-dimensional projection of quadratic performance function.

rule can be reduced to an equation as follows:

$$w(\ell + 1) = w(\ell) - c \cdot \left.\frac{dJ}{dw}\right|_{w(\ell)} , \qquad (4.2.1)$$

where c is a small positive constant. Thus whenever the derivative is positive, $w(\ell)$ is decreased to yield $w(\ell + 1)$, and if dJ/dw is negative, $w(\ell)$ is increased. Reference again to Figure 4.1 shows that repeated application of this rule causes $w(\ell)$ to take steps down the parabola and to finally come to rest at the minimum point of J. This is exactly the intended behavior, and at that point $w(\ell)$ equals w^o.

This derivative-based search is extended to the N-dimensional adaptive filter by using the gradient function, the vector of first derivatives of J with respect to the coefficients of the impulse response vector. This updating rule then becomes

$$\mathbf{W}(\ell + 1) = \mathbf{W}(\ell) - c \cdot \nabla_{\mathbf{W}} J|_{\mathbf{W}=\mathbf{W}(\ell)}, \quad \ell \geq 0, \qquad (4.2.2)$$

where c, as before, is a small positive constant. For each estimate $\mathbf{W}(\ell)$, the gradient is computed and a small step proportional to that gradient is taken, leading to a small reduction in the performance function J. Continuation of this procedure would, in theory, reduce J until it attained its minimum value.

4.2.2 Approximation of the Gradient

The gradient of J with respect to the impulse response vector $\mathbf{W}$ can be estimated directly from the input data $\{x, d\}$. Suppose we compute the gradient of the squared error, that is,

$$
\begin{aligned}
\mathbf{G}(k) = \nabla_{\mathbf{W}}[e^2(k)] &= 2e(k) \cdot \nabla_{\mathbf{W}}e(k) \\
&= 2e(k)\nabla_{\mathbf{W}}\{d(k) - \mathbf{W}^t\mathbf{X}(k)\} \\
&= -2e(k)\nabla_{\mathbf{W}}\{\mathbf{W}^t\mathbf{X}(k)\} = -2e(k)\mathbf{X}(k).
\end{aligned} \tag{4.2.3}
$$

The next to the last step relies on the fact that $d(k)$ is not affected by changes in $\mathbf{W}$. This vector $\mathbf{G}(k)$ is termed the *instantaneous gradient* because it is based only on the value of e and $\mathbf{X}$ at time k. The vector $\mathbf{G}(k)$ can be ensemble averaged to yield the gradient of J_{ms} or time-averaged to produce the gradient of J_{ss}.

We can use this instantaneous gradient to form an adaptive filtering algorithm that approximates a true gradient search of the desired performance function. Suppose we use $\mathbf{G}(k)$ in place of the true gradient in (4.2.2). The result is the Least Mean Square (LMS) algorithm popularized by Widrow [Widrow and Hoff, 1960] [Widrow et al., 1976], which can be stated as

$$
\begin{aligned}
\mathbf{W}(\ell + 1) = \mathbf{W}(\ell) - c\mathbf{G}(\ell), \quad \ell > 0 \\
= \mathbf{W}(\ell) + \mu e(\ell)\mathbf{X}(\ell), \quad \ell > 0,
\end{aligned} \tag{4.2.4}
$$

where μ is a small positive constant.

Usually, but not always, the coefficient vector estimate $\mathbf{W}(\ell)$ is updated for every input sample. When this is true, $\ell = k$ and the complete LMS algorithm is written as three equations

- LMS:

$$
y(k) = \mathbf{W}^t(k)\mathbf{X}(k): \quad \text{filter output} \tag{4.2.5}
$$

$$
e(k) = d(k) - y(k): \quad \text{error formation} \tag{4.2.6}
$$

$$
\mathbf{W}(k + 1) = \mathbf{W}(k) + \mu e(k)\mathbf{X}(k): \quad \text{weight vector update} \tag{4.2.7}
$$

This is a straightforward algorithm and has served as the cornerstone for most of the adaptive filtering field. Referring back to Chapter 2, we find that this LMS algorithm is of exactly the same form as those heuristically developed there. The new parameter estimate is based on the old one plus a term that is the product of a bounded step size (μ), a function of the input state ($\mathbf{X}(\mathbf{k})$), and a function of the prediction error ($e(k)$). Even though the form is exactly the same, we developed it here in a very different way from the number guessing game logic of Chapter 2. In particular, to arrive at the LMS algorithm in (4.2.5)–(4.2.7), we did the following:

(a) developed an analytical performance function based on averaging the squared error,

(b) developed a search procedure for finding that value of weight vector that minimizes the performance function, and

(c) developed an approximation for the required gradient function that can be computed directly from the data.

The fact that the algorithms are the same provides a certain confidence in the formulation. What is new, however, is that the analytical structure built up in Chapter 3 can now be used to predict the performance of this adaptive algorithm.

4.2.3 The Average Convergence Properties of LMS

The LMS algorithm stated in (4.2.5)–(4.2.7) can be analyzed in a number of different ways to determine where and how fast it converges. We choose here to model the LMS adaptation as if it had actually used the true gradient function instead of the approximate one. While not perfectly accurate, it provides many of the answers we seek. Moreover, in the limit of small adaptation constant μ, the approximation is quite good [Widrow et al., 1976] [Benveniste et al., 1990] [Macchi, 1995] [Solo and Kong, 1995].

From Sections 3.2, 3.3, and 3.4, we know that the gradient of a squared error function is given by (3.2.24) as

$$\nabla_{\mathbf{W}} J = -2\mathbf{P} + 2R\mathbf{W}. \tag{4.2.8}$$

Evaluating $\nabla_{\mathbf{W}} J$ at $\mathbf{W} = \mathbf{W}(\ell)$ yields

$$\nabla_{\mathbf{W}} J |_{\mathbf{W}(\ell)} = -2\mathbf{P} + 2R\mathbf{W}(\ell). \tag{4.2.9}$$

Combining this expression with (4.2.2) produces the expression

$$\mathbf{W}(\ell+1) = \mathbf{W}(\ell) - \mu(-\mathbf{P} + R\mathbf{W}(\ell))$$
$$= (I - \mu R) \cdot \mathbf{W}(\ell) + \mu\mathbf{P}, \quad \ell > 0. \tag{4.2.10}$$

This recursion expression might be recalled from Section 3.2.6, where it was shown that as $\ell \to \infty$, $\mathbf{W}(\ell)$ converges to the optimum weight vector $\mathbf{W}^o$ if μ is small enough. To gain some additional insight, however, we use the eigenvector decomposition developed in Section 3.4 to examine this recursion.

We start by defining $\mathbf{W}'(\ell)$ by the expression

$$\mathbf{W}(\ell) = Q\mathbf{W}'(\ell), \tag{4.2.11}$$

where Q is the N-by-N matrix formed by the eigenvectors of R. Similarly, we define in Section 3.4.4

$$R = Q\Lambda Q^h, \quad \Lambda = Q^h R Q, \quad \text{and} \quad \mathbf{P}' = Q^h \mathbf{P}, \tag{4.2.12}$$

where Λ is the diagonal matrix of eigenvalues of R. Applying these expressions to (4.2.10) and noting $QQ^h = I$ leads to the expression

$$\mathbf{W}'(\ell+1) = (I - \mu\Lambda) \cdot \mathbf{W}'(\ell) + \mu\mathbf{P}', \quad \ell \geq 0. \tag{4.2.13}$$

While it looks very much like (4.2.10), this expression is much simpler to analyze because Λ is a diagonal matrix. Each of the N equations in the matrix recursion is now uncoupled and can be written separately as

$$w_i'(\ell+1) = [1 - \mu\lambda_i] \cdot w_i'(\ell) + \mu p_i', \quad 1 \leq i \leq N. \tag{4.2.14}$$

In this simple scalar form we can determine several interesting aspects of the algorithm's behavior.

Convergence points.   The scalar equation can be solved to yield a closed-form expression for $w_i'(\ell)$. It becomes

$$w_i'(\ell) = \left\{ \mu \sum_{n=0}^{\ell-1} (1 - \mu\lambda_i)^{\ell-n} \cdot p_i' \right\} + (1 - \mu\lambda_i)^\ell w_i'(0). \tag{4.2.15}$$

If we choose μ to be small enough to assure that

$$|1 - \mu\lambda_i| < 1, \tag{4.2.16}$$

then using (3.2.59) and (3.2.60),

$$\sum_{n=0}^{\ell-1} (1 - \mu\lambda_i)^n = \frac{1 - (1 - \mu\lambda_i)^\ell}{1 - (1 - \mu\lambda_i)}. \tag{4.2.17}$$

Because

$$\lim_{\ell\to\infty} (1 - \mu\lambda_i)^\ell = 0 \tag{4.2.18}$$

then

$$\lim_{\ell\to\infty} \frac{1 - (1 - \mu\lambda_i)^\ell}{1 - (1 - \mu\lambda_i)} = \frac{1}{\mu\lambda_i}. \tag{4.2.19}$$

In this case, $w_i'(\ell)$ converges to

$$\lim_{\ell\to\infty} w_i'(\ell) = \frac{1}{\mu\lambda_i} \cdot \mu p_i' = \frac{p_i'}{\lambda_i} \equiv w_i'^o. \tag{4.2.20}$$

Reference to (3.4.35) confirms that p_i'/λ_i equals the ith uncoupled optimal weight. Thus, each uncoupled coefficient converges to the proper point as $\ell \to \infty$.

Bounds on the adaptive constant μ.   To obtain a closed-form solution for $w_i'(\ell)$, we assumed that $|1 - \mu\lambda_i|$ was less than 1. In fact, we have to choose μ so that this condition is attained for all N uncoupled weights. This leads to the following condition on the selection of μ:

$$|1 - \mu\lambda_i| < 1, \quad \text{for } 1 \le i \le N, \quad \Rightarrow \quad 0 < \mu < \frac{2}{\lambda_{max}}, \tag{4.2.21}$$

where λ_{max} is the maximum of the N eigenvalues of R. As a practical matter, it is found in most applications of the LMS algorithm that μ should be chosen to be substantially smaller than the upper bound. It is not unusual to use a value of μ two orders of magnitude smaller than μ_{max} to obtain smooth convergence.

Adaptive time constants.   Because the uncoupled weights $w'_i(\ell)$ obey a first-order recursion expression, it is possible to describe their behavior in terms of a time constant, that is, the time required for any transient to decay to $1/e$ ($\approx 37\%$) of its initial value. We can determine this time duration by looking again at (4.2.15), assuming p'_i to equal zero, and asking how many iterations are required for $w'_i(\ell)$ to decay from $w'_i(0)$ to $w'_i(0)/e$. Suppose this number is τ_i. It can be found by taking the natural logarithm of both sides of the expression

$$\ln\left\{\frac{w'_i(0)}{e}\right\} = \ln\{(1 - \mu\lambda_i)^{\tau_i} w'_i(0)\} \tag{4.2.22}$$

or, after eliminating the initial value $w'_i(0)$,

$$-1 = \tau_i \cdot \ln(1 - \mu\lambda_i). \tag{4.2.23}$$

When x is small compared to unity, $\ln(1+x) \approx x$. If μ is small enough so that $0 < \mu\lambda_i \ll 1$ (the "small μ" assumption made above), then

$$-1 \approx \tau_i \cdot (-\mu\lambda_i) \tag{4.2.24}$$

and the time constant of the ith uncoupled coefficient is

$$\tau_i \approx \frac{1}{\mu\lambda_i}. \tag{4.2.25}$$

Note that the time constants τ_i are different, in general, for the various i because the eigenvalues λ_i are typically not equal. Note also that τ_i depends only on the nature of the input signal $x(k)$ as manifested in the autocorrelation matrix R, and not on the desired signal $d(k)$.

Algorithm convergence time.   The implication of (4.2.25) is that each un-coupled adaptive mode has its own time constant that is determined by the overall adaptation constant μ and the eigenvalue λ_i associated with that mode. Because the actual observed weight vector $\mathbf{W}(\ell)$ is a linear function of these uncoupled weights, it is clear that $\mathbf{W}(\ell)$ does not converge until all of the uncoupled weights do, and therefore that $\mathbf{W}(\ell)$ converges no faster than the slowest mode. We define the "time constant" of $\mathbf{W}(\ell)$, called τ, by its worst case bound

$$\tau = \max_i \left\{ \frac{1}{\mu\lambda_i} \right\} = \frac{1}{\mu \cdot \min_i \lambda_i} \equiv \frac{1}{\mu\lambda_{min}}. \qquad (4.2.26)$$

Thus the mode with the smallest eigenvalue determines the overall convergence time of the algorithm.

The dependence of LMS's convergence time on the eigenstructure of the R can be demonstrated further. Suppose we define the normalized step size α by the expressions

$$\alpha = \frac{\mu\lambda_{max}}{2}, \quad \text{or, equivalently,} \quad \mu = \frac{2\alpha}{\lambda_{max}}. \qquad (4.2.27)$$

From (4.2.21) we know that for convergence α must be bounded by $0 < \alpha < 1$. Substituting (4.2.27) into (4.2.26), we see that the convergence time τ is expressible as

$$\tau = \frac{1}{2\alpha} \cdot \frac{\lambda_{max}}{\lambda_{min}}. \qquad (4.2.28)$$

For any given value of the normalized adaptation constant α, the ratio of maximum to minimum eigenvalues (sometimes called the *eigenvalue disparity* or *condition number of R*) determines the speed of convergence of $\mathbf{W}(\ell)$.

4.2.4 The Effects of a Singular Autocorrelation Matrix

So far, our analysis assumes that the input process $x(k)$ is well-enough behaved so that the autocorrelation matrix R is nonsingular. This in turn implies that $\mathbf{W}^o$ is unique and that a search procedure can be guaranteed to find the optimum value of the impulse response vector. Suppose now that R is singular. To examine the effects of this, we revisit some of the points made in the previous section.

When R is singular, it can be shown that at least one of its eigenvalues is zero. Furthermore, it can be shown that if $\lambda_i = 0$, then so does the associated uncoupled cross-correlation term p_i'. The uncoupled weight recursion (4.2.14) becomes

$$w_i'(\ell + 1) = (1 - \mu\lambda_i) \cdot w_i'(\ell) + \mu p_i'$$
$$= (1 - 0) \cdot w_i'(\ell) + 0 = w_i'(\ell). \qquad (4.2.29)$$

In other words, the associated uncoupled coefficient is undriven and undamped. It does not decay, nor does it grow. It remains unchanged at its initial value. All uncoupled weights with nonzero eigenvalues converge as before.

Because $\lambda_i = 0$, initial conditions in $w_i'(\ell)$ cannot decay and the time constant is infinite. This in turn implies that the weight vector $\mathbf{W}(\ell)$ never converges. While strictly speaking this is true, it does not necessarily mean that the algorithm will not produce a useful solution. This apparent paradox can be resolved as follows.

Suppose there is one zero eigenvalue in R and that $\mathbf{U}$ is its associated eigen-vector. This implies that

$$R \cdot \{\gamma \mathbf{U}\} = \gamma R \mathbf{U} = 0 \qquad (4.2.30)$$

for any scalar γ. Because of this property, $\mathbf{U}$ is said to be the *null space* of R. Now consider the problem of finding $\mathbf{W}^o$ so that the "normal equations" are satisfied; that is,

$$R \mathbf{W}^o = \mathbf{P}. \qquad (4.2.31)$$

Suppose that instead of $\mathbf{W}^o$, we substitute $\mathbf{W}^o + \gamma \mathbf{U}$. Surprisingly, the normal equations are still satisfied; i.e.,

$$R(\mathbf{W}^o + \gamma \mathbf{U}) = R \mathbf{W}^o + \gamma R \mathbf{U} = \mathbf{P} + 0 = \mathbf{P}. \qquad (4.2.32)$$

Thus if R is singular, then any vector or combination of vectors from the null space of R can be added to $\mathbf{W}^o$ without disturbing the satisfaction of the normal equations. This has two key implications. The first, already obvious, is that $\mathbf{W}^o$ is not unique. The second, however, is that the convergence of the "null space modes," i.e., those for which $\lambda_i = 0$, is irrelevant if the goal is only to find any solution, as opposed to the unique solution, of the normal equations. When null space modes are present, the bound on convergence time of the algorithm should be based on the smallest nonzero eigenvalue. In this case, the expression for τ becomes

$$\tau = \frac{1}{2\alpha} \frac{\lambda_{max}}{\lambda^*_{min}}, \quad \lambda^*_{min} = \min_i \{\lambda_i\} \quad \text{such that } \lambda_i \neq 0. \qquad (4.2.33)$$

However, in certain applications where convergence of the weight vector to $\mathbf{W}^o$ is the goal, as opposed to minimizing J, the infinite time constant correctly reflects the fact that this algorithm (or any other) cannot attain that value if R is singular.

4.2.5 Using the Input Signal Spectrum to Predict the Performance of an LMS-Adapted FIR Filter

Sections 4.2.3 and 4.2.4 used the modal decomposition to analyze the transient and convergent behavior of an FIR digital filter being adapted using the LMS algorithm. While theoretically accurate, this approach has the disadvantage that the eigenvalues and eigenvectors of the input signal's autocorrelation matrix are rarely known, and therefore the analytical results derived in those sections can rarely be quantified in practice. In a great many cases, however, this shortcoming can be successfully addressed using the spectral decomposition discussed in Section 3.4.6. We pursue that in this section, and use it to restate succinctly many of the results seen earlier.

In Section 3.4.6 it was shown that any FIR filter of length N can be written as a bank of N bandpass filters whose outputs are scaled by N coefficients and then summed together. The pulse responses of the N filters are defined by the columns of the matrix F and the scaling coefficients $\overline{w}_n$ are obtained by transforming the filter coefficients $\mathbf{W}$ by multiplying them by F. A result attributed to Gray [1972] shows that for a suitably well-behaved input $x(k)$ and as the filter order N gets larger, the matrix F comes to closely approximate the modal matrix Q and the eigenvalues of R are well approximated by

$$\lambda_n \approx \text{Avrg}\left|\Gamma_n^t X(k)\right|^2 = \text{Avrg}|\text{DFT}\{X(k)\}|^2 = S_n, \quad 1 \le n \le N. \tag{4.2.34}$$

Thus the time-averaged power spectrum of the input signal $x(k)$, denoted S_n, closely approximates the eigenvalues of R when N is large and $x(k)$ is statistically stationary and ergodic.

The close association of the eigensystem and the spectral decomposition defined by the matrix F can be made even more intuitive by reexamining Figure 3.8. Recall that the outputs of the bank of filters were denoted as $\bar{x}_n(k)$. It can easily be shown that by the definition of S_n that $S_n = \text{Avrg } |\bar{x}_n(k)|^2$, the power present at the output of the nth bandpass filter. This in turn implies that when the equivalence of the modal and spectral decompositions applies, then

$$\text{Avrg}|\bar{x}_n(k)|^2 = S_n \approx \lambda_{n+1}, \quad 0 \le n \le N - 1, \tag{4.2.35}$$

that is, each eigenvalue of R indicates the power present at the output of the corresponding filter in the filter bank. Note that a zero-valued eigenvalue implies that the corresponding bandpass filter output is zero, and therefore that the input signal $x(k)$ has no energy in that spectral band.

The correspondence of the modal and spectral transformation permits intuitive interpretation of many of the theoretical results derived in Sections 4.2.3 and 4.2.4.

Bounds on the adaptation constant μ.   The close approximation of the eigenvalues of R to the power spectrum $\{S_n\}$, $0 \le n \le N - 1$, permits equation (4.2.21), which defines the upper bound on the adaptive update constant μ, to be written as

$$0 < \mu < \frac{2}{\lambda_{max}} \approx \frac{2}{\max S_n} = \frac{2}{S_{max}}, \tag{4.2.36}$$

where S_{max} is the maximum value of the input power spectrum.

Adaptive time constants.   Similarly, using equation (4.2.25), the time constant for each uncoupled adaptive mode can be closely approximated as

$$\tau_{i+1} \approx \frac{1}{\mu\lambda_{i+1}} \approx \frac{1}{\mu S_i}, \quad 0 \le i \le N - 1. \tag{4.2.37}$$

Algorithm convergence time.   The convergence time for the LMS was found in Section 4.2.3 to be proportional to the ratio of the maximum to the minimum eigenvalues of the input signal's autocorrelation matrix. From the spectral viewpoint, this relationship becomes

$$\text{Convergence time constant } \tau = \frac{1}{2\alpha} \cdot \frac{S_{max}}{S_{min}}, \tag{4.2.38}$$

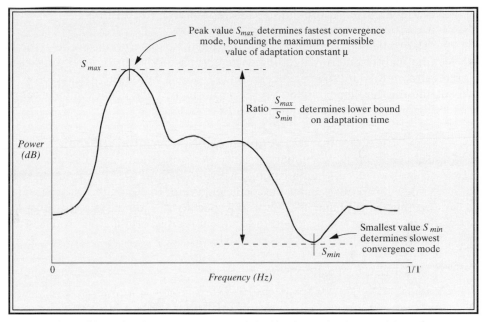

Figure 4.2 Using the power spectrum of the filter input signal as a guide to the behavior of the LMS adaptive algorithm.

where S_{min} is the minimum value of the input signal's power spectrum and α is the normalized adaptation constant defined in (4.2.27).

The effect of R's singularity.   From this spectral viewpoint, the singularity of R can be seen to be equivalent to the existence of spectral bands in which the input signal has no energy. The filter coefficients associated with these adaptive modes are "undriven" and drift aimlessly.

The implications of some of these observations can be seen by examining Figure 4.2. This figure shows the average power spectrum of a hypothetical filter input signal. Some important points are explicitly marked. The maximum power level in the spectrum determines the maximum allowable value of the adaptation constant μ. The lowest point determines the time constant for the slowest adaptation mode. The ratio of the highest to the lowest power levels defines the minimum overall limit convergence time for the adaptive algorithm. If the power level is as low as zero for any significant frequency range, then at least one eigenvalue equals zero and at least one uncoupled adaptive mode is undriven by the input.

As noted earlier, this spectral decomposition only applies with great accuracy in the limit of very large filter orders. Even so, the trends it indicates are usually true for much lower orders as well, and as a result, the filter input's power spectrum is commonly used by practitioners to predict of the behavior of an LMS-driven adaptive filter.

4.2.6 Related Approximate Gradient Search Algorithms

The LMS algorithm described in Section 4.2.2 serves as the cornerstone for most of the adaptive filtering algorithms actually in use today. Its simplicity makes it relatively straightforward to implement, while its close relationship to the theory of optimum filtering has appeal in terms of its performance. We now examine a set of adaptive algorithms that are all direct variants of LMS.

The Complex LMS Algorithm[1] [Widrow et al., 1975a].   When the input sequence $x(k)$, the output sequence $y(k)$, and the desired sequence $d(k)$ are all complex-valued, then a complex version of the LMS algorithm must be used. It is developed by assuming the coefficient vector to be complex as well and then determining the gradient of $|e(k)|^2$ with respect to that complex vector. Incorporating this instantaneous gradient into the gradient search formulation produces the complex LMS algorithm.

- Complex LMS:

$$y(k) = \mathbf{X}^t(k)\mathbf{W}(k)$$

$$e(k) = d(k) - y(k) \qquad (4.2.39)$$

$$\mathbf{W}(k+1) = \mathbf{W}(k) + \mu e(k)\mathbf{X}^*(k).$$

The asterisk ($*$) denotes complex conjugation.

Normalized LMS [Albert and Gardner, 1967].   All forms of the LMS algorithm examined so far use the adaptation constant μ, a small constant that determines, among other things, the speed of convergence of the algorithm. Various issues associated with the choice of μ are discussed in Chapter 7, but one practical problem often confronted is that of finding some way to ensure that μ does not become large enough to impact algorithm stability. The theoretical limit to stability is provided in (4.2.21); i.e., the largest possible value of μ is determined by the largest eigenvalue of R. This result is of limited practical use because R is usually not available, and even if it were, computing its eigenvalues is an undesirable chore. A more reasonable approach is to find some bounds for the largest of the eigenvalues. To this end, it can be shown that

$$\text{Avrg}\{\mathbf{X}^t(k)\mathbf{X}(k)\} = \sum_{i=1}^{N}\lambda_i, \qquad (4.2.40)$$

[1]Discussed further in Section 7.4.3.

that is, the average value of the dot product of the data vector with itself equals the sum of the eigenvalues of R. Because all eigenvalues are nonnegative,

$$\text{Avrg}\{\mathbf{X}^t(k)\mathbf{X}(k)\} = \sum_{i=1}^{N} \lambda_i \geq \lambda_{max}, \qquad (4.2.41)$$

meaning that the average value of the inner product is an upper bound to λ_{max}. This suggests defining μ as

$$\mu(k) = \frac{\alpha}{\mathbf{X}^t(k)\mathbf{X}(k)}, \qquad (4.2.42)$$

where α is a positive constant chosen to be between 0 and 2. It can be seen that on the average, $\mu\lambda_{max}$ abides by (4.2.21). Another insightful interpretation of (4.2.42), this one based on projection concepts, is presented in Goodwin and Sin [1984].

Using this form for μ results in the following.

- Normalized LMS:

$$y(k) = \mathbf{W}^t(k)\mathbf{X}(k)$$

$$e(k) = d(k) - y(k) \qquad (4.2.43)$$

$$\mathbf{W}(k+1) = \mathbf{W}(k) + \frac{\alpha e(k)\mathbf{X}(k)}{\gamma + \mathbf{X}^t(k)\mathbf{X}(k)}.$$

The term α is the new "normalized" adaptation constant, while γ is a small positive term included to ensure that the update term does not become excessively large should $\mathbf{X}^t(k)\mathbf{X}(k)$ temporarily become small.

It first appears that the inclusion of $\mathbf{X}^t(k)\mathbf{X}(k)$ in the denominator increases the computation requirement by another N multiplications and additions, but this can be avoided if N extra storage locations are available. At time k, $\mathbf{X}^t(k)\mathbf{X}(k)$ is given by

$$\mathbf{X}^t(k)\mathbf{X}(k) = \sum_{i=0}^{N-1} x^2(k-i). \qquad (4.2.44)$$

The term $\mathbf{X}^t(k+1)\mathbf{X}(k+1)$ can be computed by adding in $x^2(k+1)$ and subtracting $x^2(k-N+1)$. By storing the intermediate values of $x^2(\cdot)$, the computation required to update the inner product is reduced to a squaring, an addition, and a subtraction. A division operation is still needed, however.

Normalized LMS with recursive power estimation.   A closer examination of (4.2.42) shows the data vector inner product to be an N-point arithmetic average of the input signal power. Therefore, the normalized LMS algorithm gains its stability by normalizing the weight vector update with an estimate of the signal power. Another way of obtaining this normalization is by computing a recursive estimate of the signal power, called $\pi(k)$. This algorithm has the following form:

- Normalized LMS with Recursive Power Estimation:

$$y(k) = \mathbf{X}^t(k)\mathbf{W}(k)$$
$$e(k) = d(k) - y(k)$$
$$\pi(k) = (1 - \beta) \cdot \pi(k-1) + N\beta x^2(k) \tag{4.2.45}$$
$$\mathbf{W}(k+1) = \mathbf{W}(k) + \frac{\alpha e(k)\mathbf{X}(k)}{\gamma + \pi(k)}.$$

Instead of N locations of extra storage to compute $\mathbf{X}^t(k)\mathbf{X}(k)$, this algorithm uses one location. The positive constant β is used to control the averaging time constant. If β is chosen according to the rule

$$\beta = \frac{1}{N}, \tag{4.2.46}$$

then the exponential power averaging has a time constant of approximately N samples (for $N > 10$), and when β is chosen this way, (4.2.45) exhibits roughly the same performance as the normalized LMS algorithm in (4.2.43).

Accelerated algorithms. The approximate gradient search algorithms examined so far are often called *steepest descent* algorithms because, by following the gradient, each adaptation step moves down the gradient slope, i.e., in the direction of the steepest slope, not necessarily directly toward the minimum of the performance function. By changing the direction of the adaptation, it is theoretically possible to force the adaptation steps to lead more directly to the minimum of the performance function and thereby converge faster. Many of these algorithms take the form

$$y(k) = \mathbf{X}^t(k)\mathbf{W}(k)$$
$$e(k) = d(k) - y(k) \tag{4.2.47}$$
$$\mathbf{W}(k+1) = \mathbf{W}(k) + \mu e(k)C\mathbf{X}(k).$$

The matrix C is chosen based on some *a priori* knowledge to improve the convergence performance. In particular, if C can be chosen to approximate R^{-1}, then the convergence time of the algorithm can be reduced substantially in cases of high eigenvalue disparity; that is, $\lambda_{max} \gg \lambda_{min}$. As a practical matter, these algorithms have limited utility, however. The reasons for this include:

(a) The proper choice of the accelerating matrix C is dependent on R and hence on the properties of the data $x(k)$. Choosing C without knowing the characteristics of the data can be counterproductive.

(b) The matrix C is in general an N-by-N matrix, and computing $C\mathbf{X}(k)$ requires N^2 multiplications and $N(N-1)$ additions. This overwhelms the computational requirements for LMS itself (about $2N$ multiplications), and this in itself usually precludes the use of accelerated algorithms, except under the most demanding convergence requirements.

Griffiths' algorithm [Griffiths, 1967].   All of the algorithms described so far have assumed that the reference waveform $d(k)$ is available. While this assumption is valid in some cases (see Chapter 6 for examples), there are practical situations where adaptive filtering would be useful but no reference waveform can be provided. The absence of the reference implies that the prediction error $e(k)$ cannot be formed and therefore that algorithms such as LMS cannot be used directly. Griffiths developed an algorithm that can be used in applications in which $d(k)$ is not directly available, but the correlation function between $d(k)$ and the data vector $\mathbf{X}(k)$ is. First we rewrite the LMS update (4.2.7) as

$$\begin{aligned} \mathbf{W}(k+1) &= \mathbf{W}(k) + \mu e(k)\mathbf{X}(k) \\ &= \mathbf{W}(k) - \mu y(k)\mathbf{X}(k) + \mu d(k)\mathbf{X}(k). \end{aligned} \tag{4.2.48}$$

The average behavior of this update equation can be evaluated by determining the ensemble average of both sides of the equation

$$E\{\mathbf{W}(k+1)\} = E\{\mathbf{W}(k)\} - \mu \cdot E\{y(k)\mathbf{X}(k)\} + \mu \cdot E\{d(k)\mathbf{X}(k)\}. \tag{4.2.49}$$

Substituting (3.3.41) for the last term, (4.2.49) can be rewritten as

$$E\{\mathbf{W}(k+1)\} = E\{\mathbf{W}(k)\} - \mu E\{y(k)\mathbf{X}(k)\} + \mu \mathbf{P}_{ms}. \tag{4.2.50}$$

Based on this expression, Griffiths suggested the algorithm variously known as "Griffiths' algorithm," the "**P**-vector algorithm," and the "steering vector algorithm."

- Griffiths' algorithm:

$$y(k) = \mathbf{X}^t(k)\mathbf{W}(k) \tag{4.2.51}$$

$$\mathbf{W}(k+1) = \mathbf{W}(k) - \mu y(k)\mathbf{X}(k) + \mu \mathbf{P}_{ms}. \tag{4.2.52}$$

The basic idea of this approach is to substitute the expected average behavior of $d(k)\mathbf{X}(k)$ for the vector itself and thus avoid needing $d(k)$.

In general, $\mathbf{P}_{ms}$ is not known *a priori*, and more powerful techniques, such as those in Chapter 6, are required to circumvent the need for $d(k)$. However, Griffiths' algorithm does have practical application. An example is the case where the input $x(k)$ consists of a signal with known correlation characteristics and interference that is statistically uncorrelated with the signal. Suppose $x(k)$ is given by

$$x(k) = s(k) + i(k), \tag{4.2.53}$$

where $s(k)$ and $i(k)$ are the signal of interest and the interference, respectively. If $s(k)$ were available, we might employ it as the template waveform $d(k)$ to adapt an LMS-based adaptive filter. If so, the cross-correlation vector $\mathbf{P}_{ms}$ is given by

$$E\{d(k)\mathbf{X}(k)\} = E\{s(k)\mathbf{S}(k)\} + E\{s(k)\mathbf{I}(k)\}$$

$$= \mathbf{P}_s + \mathbf{0} = \mathbf{P}_s, \qquad (4.2.54)$$

where $s(k) = d(k)$, $\mathbf{S}(k)$ and $\mathbf{I}(k)$ are the vectors of current and $N - 1$ past values of $s(k)$ and $i(k)$, respectively, and $\mathbf{P}_s$ is the cross-correlation of $s(k)$ with delayed versions of itself. The use of $\mathbf{P}_s$ in Griffiths' algorithm allows the filter to adapt to suppress the interference and pass the desired signal with the same average effectiveness as an LMS-based adaptive filter would have.

This same basic algorithm was suggested by Kaczmerz [1937] to iteratively invert matrices and forms the basis for the Algebraic Reconstruction Technique (ART) used for computerized axial tomography (CAT) scanners. It was developed in the signal-processing context by Griffiths in 1967 to adapt antenna arrays so as to reject interference based on arrival angle.

4.2.7 Simplified and Modified Versions of the LMS Algorithm

The previous section examined several algorithms which extended the basic gradient search approach along some analytically motivated line. This section examines several more, but in this case the motivation for each is some practical consideration, such as simplicity in implementation or robustness in operation.

Sign-Error LMS [Gersho, 1984].   Looking again at the real arithmetic version of the LMS, it can be seen that it requires almost exactly $2N$ real multiplications and additions to compute $y(k)$ and the update $\mathbf{W}(k)$ for each iteration, where N is the length of the filter impulse response. While this amount of computation is lower than required for many more complicated adaptive algorithms (e.g., see Section 4.3), even this level of computational cost has motivated efforts to simplify the algorithm and reduce the number of multiplications required. One such simplified algorithm employs only the sign of the error.

- Sign-error LMS:

$$y(k) = \mathbf{X}^t(k)\mathbf{W}(k)$$

$$\bar{e}(k) = \text{sgn}\{d(k) - y(k)\} = \begin{cases} 1 & \text{if} \quad d(k) - y(k) > 0 \\ 0 & \text{if} \quad d(k) - y(k) = 0 \\ -1 & \text{if} \quad d(k) - y(k) < 0 \end{cases} \qquad (4.2.55)$$

$$\mathbf{W}(k+1) = \mathbf{W}(k) + \mu\bar{e}(k)\mathbf{X}(k).$$

Computation of each output $y(k)$ still requires N multiplications and $N - 1$ additions, but the weight update equation is much simpler. If μ is chosen to be a power of 2, then each term of the update $w_i(k)$ can be done by shifting $x(k - i)$ to accomplish the

μ multiplication, followed by adding or subtracting it with $w_i(k)$ to obtain $w_i(k+1)$. Thus, the update is done with N shifts and adds rather than N multiplications and adds. Depending on the relative execution times for multiplications and additions, this algorithm can provide a significant speed improvement over the normal LMS algorithm. This reduction in computation comes at the expense of performance, how-ever. The sign-error algorithm effectively uses a noisy estimate of the instantaneous gradient as its basis for searching for the minimum of the squared error performance function. The noisy estimate is reflected into noisy estimates of the optimal weight vector. Obtaining the same estimate quality as LMS generally requires using a smaller value of the adaptation constant, thus slowing down the adaptation of the algorithm. This effect is examined more in Section 4.2.8.

An alternate method can be used to reduce the number of multiplications required for each update of the LMS algorithm. Instead of using the sign of the error $e(k)$, one can use the sign of the elements of $\mathbf{X}(k)$. This algorithm is described by the following equations.

- Sign-data LMS:

$$y(k) = \mathbf{X}^t(k)\mathbf{W}(k)$$

$$e(k) = d(k) - y(k) \tag{4.2.56}$$

$$w_i(k+1) = w_i(k) + \mu e(k) \cdot \text{sgn}\{x(k-i)\}, \quad 0 \le i \le N-1.$$

Just as with the sign-error algorithm, this technique does not change the number of multiply-adds required for the filtering operation, but does reduce the computation needed for the updating to just N shifts and additions. This algorithm also shares another attribute of the sign-error technique. Because both use a simplified version of the gradient to update the impulse response vector, this estimate is noisier than it would be were the actual instantaneous gradient employed.

Neither technique mimics the LMS algorithm closely. The sign-data algorithm actually modifies the direction of the update vector of LMS, while the sign-error algorithm scales it differently. Indeed, the directional alteration by the sign-data LMS algorithm can lead it to diverge for certain input sequences that result in conver-gence by (unsigned) LMS [Sethares et al., 1988]. With sign-error LMS only rescaling each update, thereby leaving the correction direction in parameter space intact, the potential for divergence for certain input sequences by sign-data LMS is not shared by sign-error LMS [Sethares and Johnson, 1989].

Note that the sign-error and sign-data use can be combined to generate a sign-sign algorithm.

- Sign-sign LMS:

$$y(k) = \mathbf{X}^t(k)\mathbf{W}(k)$$

$$e(k) = d(k) - y(k) \tag{4.2.57}$$

$$w_i(k+1) = w_i(k) + \mu \cdot \text{sgn}[e(k)] \cdot \text{sgn}[x(k-i)].$$

The popularity of this sign-sign algorithm is based on the fact that no multiplication at all is required for the updating equation. Even though this method uses a very "noisy" gradient estimate, its implementation ease has led to its frequent use; for example, in the ITU standard for ADPCM transmission [Jayant and Noll, 1984]. Even so, the sign-sign algorithm is not as well-behaved as the full LMS algorithm and, similar to the update direction-altering sign-data algorithm, can even be shown to diverge in situations where LMS would not [Dasgupta and Johnson, 1986].

Coefficient leakage. In Section 4.2.4 it was shown that the convergence of approximate gradient search algorithms such as LMS can be problematical when the input process $x(k)$ does not fully excite all the modes of the adaptive algorithm. When the autocorrelation matrix associated with the input process has one or more zero eigenvalues, then the associated modes of the adaptive algorithm are undriven and undamped. (From the spectral decomposition perspective discussed in Section 4.2.5, the presence of zero-valued eigenvalues is commonly associated with an input power spectrum devoid of energy over a nontrivial portion of the frequency band.) This can lead to several undesirable situations:

(a) The adaptive filter will not converge to a unique solution;
(b) The uncoupled modes do not converge; and, worse,
(c) The uncoupled modes can be driven by second-order terms, such as those resulting from an imperfect implementation of the filter and/or algorithm. It is not uncommon in this third situation for the uncoupled coefficients to grow without bound until hardware overflow or underflow occurs, with the usual catastrophic results.

To deal with problems such as this, several solutions have been proposed, including the injection of a small amount of white noise into the filter input to "quiet" the coefficients [Zahm, 1973]. A related, and preferred, method is that of using coefficient leakage. Using LMS as an example, the "leaky" algorithm can be written as

$$\mathbf{W}(k+1) = (1 - \mu\gamma) \cdot \mathbf{W}(k) - \mu\hat{\nabla}(k)$$
$$= (1 - \mu\gamma) \cdot \mathbf{W}(k) + \mu e(k)\mathbf{X}(k). \tag{4.2.58}$$

As before, the adaptation constant μ is a small positive value. The leakage coefficient γ is also a small positive number. Obviously, with conventional LMS, $\gamma = 0$.

Because μ and γ are both small compared to 1 and positive in sign, the factor $1 - \mu\gamma$ is slightly less than 1. The first-order effect of this term can be seen by assuming for the moment that the gradient estimate $e(k)\mathbf{X}(k)$ equals zero. If so,

$$\mathbf{W}(k+1) = (1 - \mu\gamma)\mathbf{W}(k), \tag{4.2.59}$$

which exhibits exponential behavior over time

$$\mathbf{W}(k + m) = (1 - \mu\gamma)^m \mathbf{W}(k) \qquad (4.2.60)$$

such that

$$\lim_{m \to \infty} \mathbf{W}(k + m) = \mathbf{0}, \qquad (4.2.61)$$

because $1 - \mu\gamma$ is slightly less than unity. Thus, in the absence of the driving term $e(k)\mathbf{X}(k)$, the filter coefficients $\mathbf{W}(k)$ tend to decay or "leak" to zero, thereby emulating the behavior of a leaky capacitor.

The effect of this leakiness can be evaluated directly by using the modal decomposition of the coefficient update equation developed in Section 4.2.3. With the introduction of coefficient leakage, the uncoupled weight vector $\mathbf{W}'(k)$ is given by

$$\begin{aligned}
\mathbf{W}'(k + 1) &= (1 - \mu\gamma) \cdot \mathbf{W}'(k) - \mu(-\mathbf{P}' + \Lambda\mathbf{W}'(k)) \\
&= (I - \mu\gamma I - \mu\Lambda)\mathbf{W}'(k) + \mu\mathbf{P}' \\
&= \{I - \mu(\gamma I + \Lambda)\} \cdot \mathbf{W}'(k) + \mu\mathbf{P}'.
\end{aligned} \qquad (4.2.62)$$

From this equation and analysis of the type used in Section 4.2.3, we draw the following conclusions:

(a) Leakage has the effect of modifying the correlation matrix of the input process. In particular,

$$R_{new} = \gamma I + R_{old} \qquad (4.2.63)$$

$$\Lambda_{new} = \gamma I + \Lambda_{old} \qquad (4.2.64)$$

and

$$\lambda_{i,new} = \gamma + \lambda_{i,old}, \quad 1 \le i \le N. \qquad (4.2.65)$$

(b) If $\gamma > 0$, then all eigenvalues of the update process are positive, even if some of the "old" input eigenvalues equal zero.

(c) The positivity of all eigenvalues implies a unique solution and bounded time constants for all uncoupled weights.

(d) Because all time constants are bounded, the overall algorithm always converges with a time constant of less than or equal to

$$\tau_{max} = \frac{1}{\mu\lambda_{new,min}} \le \frac{1}{\mu\gamma}. \qquad (4.2.66)$$

Thus the introduction of coefficient leakage leads to convergence in a finite interval to a unique solution. The price of leakage, however, is some added complexity in the updating equation and the introduction of some bias into the convergent solution.

This bias is introduced because the weight vector $\mathbf{W}$ converges to the solution

$$\lim_{k \to \infty} \mathbf{W}(k) = (R + \gamma I)^{-1} \mathbf{P}, \tag{4.2.67}$$

which is not in general the solution of

$$R\mathbf{W} = \mathbf{P}. \tag{4.2.68}$$

As a practical matter, designers use the amount of leakage that just suffices to mask the offending noise source or second-order effect. The choice of γ thus represents a compromise between biasing the convergence weight vector away from the optimum and "quieting" undriven filter modes. Even though it must be applied carefully, coefficient leakage is an important part of algorithms that must operate with band-limited signals. It has been employed successfully in fractionally spaced adaptive equalizers for telephone data modems [Gitlin et al., 1982], in ADPCM [Jayant and Noll, 1984], and in adaptive interference suppressors.

4.2.8 Gradient Noise, Weight Noise, and the Concept of Misadjustment

Central to the concept of the gradient search methods is the idea of iteratively stepping down the squared error performance function until the minimum point of the function is reached. At that point the gradient equals zero, and therefore no change is made to the weight vector estimate $\mathbf{W}(k)$. Because the minimum has been so attained, the weight vector would then equal the optimal weight vector. As soon as we choose to employ an approximation of the gradient, instead of the gradient itself, then various imperfections in this procedure begin to appear. In this section, we briefly examine their causes and effects.

The cause of these problems are termed here *gradient noise,* the vector difference between the theoretical gradient and the instantaneous estimate employed in its place. If we term this vector $\mathbf{N}(k)$, it is given by

$$\mathbf{N}(k) = \hat{\nabla} - \nabla_{\mathbf{W}} J. \tag{4.2.69}$$

In the particular case of the LMS algorithm, it is given by

$$\mathbf{N}(k) = -e(k)\mathbf{X}(k) - (R\mathbf{W}(k) - \mathbf{P}). \tag{4.2.70}$$

The effect of gradient noise is most obvious when adaptation has progressed far enough that $\mathbf{W}(k)$ is very close to the optimal value $\mathbf{W}^o$. At this point the true gradient is very nearly equal to zero, and therefore any extra component in the gradient estimate tends to push the weight estimate away from the optimal choice. Because of this gradient noise, the weight estimate $\mathbf{W}(k)$ obtains a noise component, again most obvious near convergence. The weights of approximate gradient algorithms are often said to "rattle" near convergence. The magnitude of this weight noise and its effect on the output $y(k)$ depend on many signal- and application-related factors, but in almost every case it depends directly on the adaptation constant μ. In general, a reduction in μ reduces the weight noise because it reduces the amount the weights can be adapted in response to a noise component in the gradient estimate.

Because the filter output $y(k)$ depends on $\mathbf{W}(k)$, one can expect $y(k)$ to contain a small extraneous component $s(k)$ that is attributable to weight noise. In particular, if $\mathbf{W}(k)$ is written as

$$\mathbf{W}(k) = \mathbf{W}^o + \mathbf{V}(k), \tag{4.2.71}$$

then the filter output can be written as

$$y(k) = \mathbf{X}^t(k)\mathbf{W}^o + \mathbf{X}^t(k)\mathbf{V}(k) \equiv y^o(k) + s(k), \tag{4.2.72}$$

where $y^o(k)$ is the output expected if the optimal filter were used. The term $s(k)$ results directly from the weight noise, and its presence degrades the quality of the adaptive filter's output. Its effect is quantified by defining the so-called misadjustment, the increase in the average squared error induced by $s(k)$. The exact theoretical form of the misadjustment depends on the exact algorithm employed and input signal characteristics, but it is usually proportional to both μ and the filter order N. For an example, see Widrow et al. [1976]. Decreasing μ decreases the weight noise, while decreasing N reduces the number of noisy weights acting on the data vector $\mathbf{X}(k)$. Simplifications in the gradient estimate, such as those discussed in Section 4.2.7, also increase the misadjustment.

It is common to make comparisons of algorithm convergence rate while holding some measure of steady-state performance constant. Misadjustment is often used as that measure.

4.2.9 The Effect of the Adaptation Constant on Tracking Performance

In Chapter 1 we found that adaptive filters offer two significant practical advantages over the use of deterministically chosen "fixed" filters—their ability to learn a new signal environment and their ability to alter their characteristics in response to any changes in the signal environment. This latter capability is often referred to as *tracking*. In the earlier sections of this chapter, we developed a number of algorithms for adapting filter coefficients and analyzed the behavior of a few of them when operating in the first mode—that is, when attempting to learn in a new, but stationary, signal environment. Here we examine the tracking problem and attempt to determine what sort of performance might be expected in that case.

Two principal factors limit the degree to which the tracking problem can be carefully analyzed. The first is the wide variation in the ways in which a signal's characteristics can change in a practical environment. The second is the mathematical difficulty encountered when attempting to analyze a nonlinear adaptive algorithm in the presence of nonstationary input signals. As a practical matter, then, the study of tracking behavior in adaptive filters has historically been performed using computer simulations or even laboratory and field experiments with actual hardware. To give the reader some intuition, however, we examine an example used by Widrow et al.

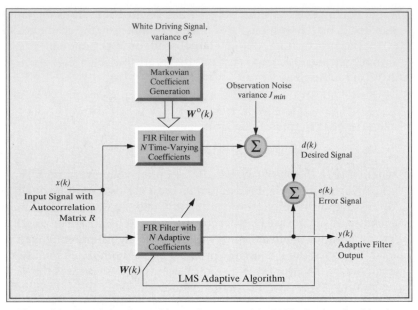

Figure 4.3 Examining the tracking performance of the LMS adaptive algorithm for a particular form of nonstationary signal.

[1976] to illustrate the effects of filter order N and the adaptation constant μ on the tracking behavior of the LMS adaptive algorithm.

Consider the situation shown in Figure 4.3. A stationary input signal $x(k)$ with autocorrelation matrix R is applied to two Nth-order FIR adaptive filters. The upper FIR filter has coefficients that vary with time. The coefficients of the lower FIR filter are adjusted by the LMS adaptive algorithm. Widrow et al. [1976] assumed that the coefficients of the time-varying filter were selected randomly and in accordance with a first-order Markovian process. Because of this time variation, the top filter's output is nonstationary even though the filter's input is stationary. This filter's output is further combined with white additive "observation noise" to form the "desired signal" $d(k)$.

In a fashion very similar to the type of analysis discussed in Section 4.2.8, Widrow et al. [1976] determined the component of the error $e(k) = d(k) - y(k)$ that accrues from the adaptive filter's lag behind the upper filter's current state $\mathbf{W}^o(k)$. Squaring and averaging this "lag component" in the error allows the additional mean squared error to be quantified as well as the misadjustment component that is suffered owing to the filter's inability to perfectly tracking the randomly varying "target."

Under the set of analytical conditions imposed by Widrow et al. [1976], they found that the lag-induced additional mean squared error was given by

$$\text{Lag} - \text{induced } \Delta MSE = \frac{N\sigma^2}{\mu} \ . \tag{4.2.73}$$

This expression implies that the additional error power is proportional to the number of filter coefficients, just as it was for the filter misadjustment discussed in Section 4.2.8, and to the variance of the target coefficient variation σ^2, but inversely proportion to the adaptation constant μ. This implies that as μ is increased and the ability of the filter to respond to changes grows, the noise induced by lagging the target coefficients declines.

It is instructive to compare this result with the one in the previous section. There it was shown that the excess mean squared error induced by using a gradient descent algorithm to estimate a fixed target $\mathbf{W}^o$ is proportional to μ, implying that making μ as small as possible is the best thing to do. Equation (4.2.73) indicates that making μ small is a bad thing to do if the filter's objective is to track a changing environment. Widrow et al. [1976] pursued this point analytically by determining the optimum choice of μ to make the two excess MSE contributions the same. This was made possible by the fact that their problem statement permitted an analytical solution and therefore the determination of a theoretically optimum compromise choice of μ. It has been shown in practice, however, that this result applies quite generally. These two trends exist in virtually every application and for every approximate-gradient descent algorithm—making μ smaller improves performance in stationary environments while making μ larger improves the algorithm's ability to track changes. The best overall performance is obtained by choosing a compromise value of μ or by performing "gain scheduling," that is, using some external quality indicator to choose the value of μ most appropriate at each stage of the adaptive filter's operation.

4.2.10 The Concept of the Adaptive Learning Curve

The concept of the *adaptive learning curve* was developed early in the history of adaptive filtering and has proved to be very useful in both the analysis and application of systems employing adaptive algorithms. The general form of such a curve is shown in Figure 4.4. The ordinate of the curve is the performance function which is being minimized by the chosen adaptive algorithm. The abcissa is the iteration number ℓ indicating how many times the adaptive algorithm has been performed. Since it is very common to iterate the adaptive algorithm with every new incoming data sample, it is common to use the sample index k as the abcissa because, in that case, $\ell = k$.

The learning curve shown in Figure 4.4 begins at the upper left at the performance functions's initial value, and then declines with iteration number ℓ (or k) toward an asymptote. For a perfect adaptive algorithm, the descent of the curve would be abrupt, indicating quick convergence, and the asymptote would be J_{min}, the lowest value of J attainable. Practical algorithms, however, deviate from this model in three ways. First, they take some time to learn what they must from the incoming data, resulting in slower convergence. Secondly, the vagaries of real data often drive J upward for short intervals instead of proceeding monotonically downward. The third deviation is that some adaptive algorithms cannot actually

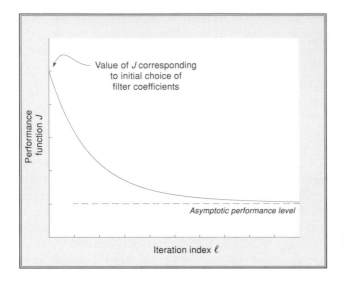

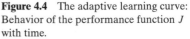

Figure 4.4 The adaptive learning curve: Behavior of the performance function J with time.

achieve the theoretical minimum. An important example is the LMS algorithm. From Section 4.2.8 we recall that gradient-descent algorithms such as LMS never fully converge and instead "rattle around" the optimum coefficient choice $\mathbf{W}^o$. This so-called "misadjustment" reflects itself in random errors in the coefficients themselves and in an increase in the squared error seen at the filter output. The presence of this extra squared error means that the learning curve for an LMS-directed adaptive filter reaches an asymptote which is always greater than the theoretical minimum of J.

Once the learning curve has been defined in this way, it must be quickly declared that there are many variations on the theme. For theoretical analyses, the ordinate is usually the linear or logarithmically scaled version of the performance function. In computer simulation work and in actual implementations, the vertical axis is usually an estimate of J obtained by taking a short time average of the instantaneous kernel of the performance function, $|e(k)|^2$, for example. In other cases it is sometimes chosen to be a surrogate for J, such as the squared norm of the coefficient errors $\mathbf{V}^h\mathbf{V}$. The abcissa is variously chosen to be the iteration number ℓ, the input sample number k, the absolute time t, or the number of operations.

The shape of the learning curve will not necessarily be of the form shown in Figure 4.4. In fact the shape depends on many considerations, including the particular performance function that has been chosen for use, the choice of adaptive algorithm, the length of the filter, the choice of parameters used in the adaptation algorithm (e.g., μ in the LMS algorithm), and the nature of the input signals themselves. The "sum of weighted exponential" form of the learning shown in Figure 4.4 is in fact typical of simple stochastic-gradient-descent algorithms like LMS in descending a unimodal, quadratic surface, but other performance criteria and other adaptive algorithms can provide very different curves. (We will see such examples in Chapter 6.)

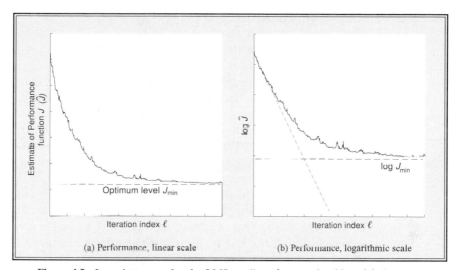

Figure 4.5 Learning curve for the LMS gradient descent algorithm. (a) Average of the instantaneous performance function $|e(k)|^2$, on a linear scale. (b) Same data, logarithmic vertical scale.

Figure 4.5 shows two views of the learning curve for a digital filter adapted with the LMS algorithm. The view in Figure 4.5(a) plots an estimate of the performance function linearly on the vertical scale. In this case the estimate is a time-averaged version of $|e(k)|^2$. The abcissa is the time index k. We note that the performance function estimate begins to decline immediately as the adaptive filter's operation begins, but is not perfectly monotonic. It declines to the vicinity, but not exactly to, the asymptote defined by the observation noise present in the system. The difference between the filter's asymptote and J_{min}, the theoretical limit defined by the observation noise, is the "misadjustment" discussed above and in Section 4.2.8.

Figure 4.5(b) is the same except that the performance function estimate is plotted on a logarithmic scale. This particular view is useful since it allows the presence of "exponential relaxation" in the learning curve to be easily detected. This behavior is very typical of simple gradient descent algorithms such as LMS. It is revealed in this figure by the fact that the "curve" is essentially straight until the point that it bends to approach its asymptote. The appearance of straight lines in logarithmically plotted data indicates that the learning curve is dominated by exponential decay modes. The presence of exponential decay should not be surprising to the reader, since error decay modes of this type were the exact basis of the convergence analysis done in Section 4.2.3. Conversely, the occurrence of learning curves composed of straight lines (e.g., Figure 6.8(c) and 6.8(d)) is an immediate clue to the presence of a simple gradient-descent algorithm whose convergence is dominated by a single adaptive mode.

4.3 RECURSIVE SOLUTION TECHNIQUES

4.3.1 The Motivation for Recursive Algorithms

Section 4.2 shows how adaptive algorithms can be developed by employing the concept of a search. The available data are used in an algorithm that attempts to move the current estimate of the impulse response vector to the optimum value. The algorithms that result from this approach have the advantage of being quite simple to implement, but carry with them the disadvantages that they can be slow to approach the optimal weight vector and, once close to it, usually "rattle around" the optimal vector rather than actually converge to it, due to the effects of approximations made in the estimate of the performance function gradient.

To overcome those difficulties we examine another approach in this section. Here we develop algorithms that use the input data $\{x, d\}$ in such a way as to ensure optimality at each step. If this can be done, then clearly the result of the algorithm for the last data point is the overall optimal weight vector.

We now make this more precise. Suppose that we redefine the sum squared performance function J_{ss} by the expression

$$J_k = \sum_{\ell=N-1}^{k-1} |y(\ell) - d(\ell)|^2, \quad N - 1 \le k \le L - 1. \tag{4.3.1}$$

This form of J simply reflects how much data have been used so far. Clearly, J_L uses all the available data from $k = 0$ to $k = L - 1$ and has exactly the same form as J_{ss} in (3.2.1). Suppose we define $\mathbf{W}_k^o$ as the impulse response vector that minimizes J_k. By this definition, $\mathbf{W}_{L-1}^o$ equals $\mathbf{W}_{ss}^o$, the optimal impulse vector over all the data.

The motivation for developing "recursive-in-time" algorithms can be seen as follows. Suppose $x(\ell)$ and $d(\ell)$ have been received for time up through $k - 1$ and that $\mathbf{W}_k^o$ has been computed. Now suppose that $x(k)$ and $d(k)$ are received, allowing us to form

$$J_{k+1} = \sum_{\ell=N-1}^{k} |y(\ell) - d(\ell)|^2 \triangleq J_k + |y(k) - d(k)|^2. \tag{4.3.2}$$

We desire to find some procedure by which $\mathbf{W}_k^o$ can be updated to produce $\mathbf{W}_{k+1}^o$, the new optimal vector. If we can develop such a procedure, then we can build up the optimal weight vector step by step until the final pair of data points $x(L - 1)$ and $d(L - 1)$ are received. With these points, $\mathbf{W}_{L-1}^o$ can be computed, which, by definition, is the global optimum vector $\mathbf{W}_{ss}^o$.

4.3.2 Recursive Least Squares (RLS)

The update formula.　　The simplest approach to updating $\mathbf{W}_k^o$ is the following procedure:

(a) Update R_{ss} via

$$R_{ss,k+1} = R_{ss,k} + \mathbf{X}(k)\mathbf{X}^t(k).$$ (4.3.3)

(b) Update $\mathbf{P}_{ss}$ via

$$\mathbf{P}_{ss,k+1} = \mathbf{P}_{ss,k} + d(k)\mathbf{X}(k).$$ (4.3.4)

(c) Invert $R_{ss,k+1}$.

(d) Compute $\mathbf{W}_{k+1}^o$ via

$$\mathbf{W}_{k+1}^o = R_{ss,k+1}^{-1}\mathbf{P}_{ss,k+1}.$$ (4.3.5)

The autocorrelation matrix and the cross-correlation vectors are updated and then used to compute $\mathbf{W}_{k+1}^o$. While direct, this technique is computationally wasteful. Approximately $N^3 + 2N^2 + N$ multiplications is required at each update, where N is the impulse response length, and of that N^3 are required for the matrix inversion if done with the classical Gaussian elimination technique.

In an effort to reduce the computational requirement for this algorithm, we focus first on this inversion. We notice that Gaussian elimination makes no use whatsoever of the special form of $R_{ss,k}$ or of the special form of the update from $R_{ss,k}$ to $R_{ss,k+1}$. We now set out to take advantage of it. We do so by employing the well-known matrix inversion lemma [Kailath, 1980], also sometimes called the *ABCD* lemma,

$$(A + BCD)^{-1} = A^{-1} - A^{-1}B(DA^{-1}B + C^{-1})^{-1}DA^{-1}.$$ (4.3.6)

We use this lemma by making the following associations:

$$
\begin{aligned}
A &= R_k \\
B &= \mathbf{X}(k) \\
C &= 1 \\
D &= \mathbf{X}^t(k).
\end{aligned}
$$ (4.3.7)

With these associations, R_{k+1} can be represented as

$$R_{k+1} = R_k + \mathbf{X}(k)\mathbf{X}^t(k) = A + BCD$$ (4.3.8)

and R_{k+1}^{-1} is given by

$$R_{k+1}^{-1} = R_k^{-1} - \frac{R_k^{-1}\mathbf{X}(k)\mathbf{X}^t(k)R_k^{-1}}{1 + \mathbf{X}^t(k)R_k^{-1}\mathbf{X}(k)}.$$ (4.3.9)

Thus, given R_k^{-1} and a new input $x(k)$, hence $\mathbf{X}(k)$, we can compute R_{k+1}^{-1} directly. We never compute R_{k+1}, nor do we invert it directly.

The optimal weight vector $\mathbf{W}_{k+1}^o$ is given by

$$\mathbf{W}_{k+1}^o = R_{k+1}^{-1}\mathbf{P}_{k+1},$$ (4.3.10)

which can be obtained by combining (4.3.9) with (4.3.4)

$$\mathbf{W}_{k+1}^o = \left\{ R_k^{-1} - \frac{R_k^{-1}\mathbf{X}(k)\mathbf{X}^t(k)R_k^{-1}}{1 + \mathbf{X}^t(k)R_k^{-1}\mathbf{X}(k)} \right\} \cdot \{\mathbf{P}_k + d(k)\mathbf{X}(k)\}$$

$$= R_k^{-1}\mathbf{P}_k - \frac{R_k^{-1}\mathbf{X}(k)\mathbf{X}^t(k)R_k^{-1}\mathbf{P}_k}{1 + \mathbf{X}^t(k)R_k^{-1}\mathbf{X}(k)}$$

$$+ d(k)R_k^{-1}\mathbf{X}(k) - \frac{d(k) \cdot R_k^{-1}\mathbf{X}(k)\mathbf{X}^t(k)R_k^{-1}\mathbf{X}(k)}{1 + \mathbf{X}^t(k)R_k^{-1}\mathbf{X}(k)}. \qquad (4.3.11)$$

To simplify this result, we make the following associations and definitions. The kth optimal weight vector:

$$R_k^{-1}\mathbf{P}_k = \mathbf{W}_k^o. \qquad (4.3.12)$$

The filtered information vector:

$$\mathbf{Z}_k \overset{\Delta}{=} R_k^{-1}\mathbf{X}(k). \qquad (4.3.13)$$

The *a priori* output:

$$y_o(k) \overset{\Delta}{=} \mathbf{X}^t(k)\mathbf{W}_k^o. \qquad (4.3.14)$$

The normalized input power:

$$q = \mathbf{X}^t(k)\mathbf{Z}_k = \mathbf{X}^t(k)R_k^{-1}\mathbf{X}(k). \qquad (4.3.15)$$

With these expressions, the optimal weight vector $\mathbf{W}_{k+1}^o$ becomes

$$\mathbf{W}_{k+1}^o = \mathbf{W}_k^o - \frac{\mathbf{Z}_k\mathbf{X}^t(k)\mathbf{W}_k^o}{1 + \mathbf{X}^t(k)\mathbf{Z}_k} + d(k)\mathbf{Z}_k - \frac{d(k)\mathbf{Z}_k\mathbf{X}^t(k)\mathbf{Z}_k}{1 + \mathbf{X}^t(k)\mathbf{Z}_k}$$

$$= \mathbf{W}_k^o - \frac{\mathbf{Z}_k y_o(k)}{1 + q} + d(k)\mathbf{Z}_k - \frac{d(k)q\mathbf{Z}_k}{1 + q}$$

$$= \mathbf{W}_k^o - \frac{\mathbf{Z}_k y_o(k)}{1 + q} + \frac{d(k)\mathbf{Z}_k}{1 + q}$$

$$= \mathbf{W}_k^o + \frac{\{d(k) - y_o(k)\} \cdot \mathbf{Z}_k}{1 + q}. \qquad (4.3.16)$$

Equations (4.3.9) and (4.3.12)–(4.3.16) comprise the *recursive least squares* (RLS) algorithm.

Interpretation of the update equations.   We now examine (4.3.16) and interpret it in terms of the quantities named in (4.3.12)–(4.3.15). The update equation for $\mathbf{W}_{k+1}^o$ is based on starting with $\mathbf{W}_k^o$, and then adding a correction term that depends on $x(k)$ and $d(k)$. This dependence comes in three ways. The first factor is the *a priori* error,

$$e_o(k) = d(k) - y_o(k), \tag{4.3.17}$$

which is the difference between the new template sample $d(k)$ and the *a priori* output $y_o(k)$. This name for y_o comes from the timing relationships implied by (4.3.12)–(4.3.16). That is, when $x(k)$ is received, the new data vector $\mathbf{X}(k)$ is formed. The output $y_o(k)$ is formed by using the best filter available at time $k - 1$, called $\mathbf{W}_k^o$, but with the new vector of data $\mathbf{X}(k)$. Therefore, $y_o(k)$ is the output estimate *before* $x(k)$ is used to update $\mathbf{W}$; that is, it is a prediction of the optimal filter output given $\mathbf{X}(k)$ but with the old impulse response $\mathbf{W}_k$. Because $y_o(k)$ is computed before $\mathbf{W}_{k+1}^o$ is computed, y_o is called the *a priori output*, and $e_o(k)$ is called the *a priori error*. It is also sometimes called the *a priori prediction error*.

The dependence of the update on $e_o(k)$ is also clear. If the old filter $\mathbf{W}_k^o$ allows $d(k)$ to be perfectly predicted, that is, $y_o(k) = d(k)$, then no update is needed, i.e., $e_o(k) = 0$, so no update is added on. If they do indeed differ, such that $e_o \neq 0$, a refining adjustment is made.

The term $\mathbf{Z}_k$ is called the *filtered information vector* because R_k^{-1} acts to influence or "filter" the direction and length of the data (information) vector. The importance of this vector emerges later.

The term q is a measure of the input signal power, just as $\mathbf{X}^t(k)\mathbf{X}(k)$ would be, but with a normalization introduced by R_k^{-1}. The effect of this normalization is to make q have an average value of N rather than being proportional to the actual signal level. Instantaneously, however, q combines with $\mathbf{Z}_k$ and e_o to produce exactly the optimal weight update. Because R_k is nonnegative definite, $1 + q$ always equals or exceeds 1.

Related gradient descent algorithms.   The adaptive updating algorithm shown in (4.3.9), (4.3.13), and (4.3.16) was developed based on the concept of updating the optimal vector $\mathbf{W}_k^o$ by just the right amount to generate the optimal vector $\mathbf{W}_{k+1}^o$. This differs from the approach used in Section 4.2 based on searching a performance surface. Even so, the form of (4.3.16) closely resembles some of the gradient descent algorithms cataloged in Section 4.2.6. To gain some perspective, we briefly examine two such algorithms.

Accelerated LMS.   The accelerated LMS update equation can be written as

$$\mathbf{W}_{k+1} = \mathbf{W}_k + \mu e(k) C \mathbf{X}(k), \tag{4.3.18}$$

where μ is the adaptation constant and C is a matrix chosen to improve the algorithm rate of convergence by acting on the information vector $\mathbf{X}(k)$ to change its direction or its length. Using (4.3.16) and (4.3.18), we can write the Recursive Least Squares (RLS) update as

$$\mathbf{W}_{k+1}^o = \mathbf{W}_k^o + \frac{1}{1+q} \cdot e_o(k) \cdot R_k^{-1} \mathbf{X}(k). \tag{4.3.19}$$

By making the following "equivalences,"

$$\mu \Leftrightarrow \frac{1}{1+q} = \frac{1}{1 + \mathbf{X}^t(k)R_k^{-1}\mathbf{X}(k)} \qquad (4.3.20)$$

and

$$C \Leftrightarrow R_k^{-1}, \qquad (4.3.21)$$

the accelerated LMS algorithm becomes the RLS algorithm, which is in some sense the ultimate in algorithm convergence acceleration. The RLS algorithm defines just the right step size and the right direction to retain optimality over each time sample.

Normalized LMS. The normalized LMS algorithm uses a time-varying adaptation constant of the form

$$\mu(k) = \frac{\alpha}{\gamma + \mathbf{X}^t(k)\mathbf{X}(k)}, \quad 0 < \alpha < 2. \qquad (4.3.22)$$

This form was developed using a simple bound for the maximum eigenvalue of R_k. The term γ was introduced heuristically just to avoid the possibility of a zero denominator. Clearly, the RLS derivation shows that γ is a theoretically important part of the update. It also shows that the time-varying gain concept is closer to the optimal updating technique than is conventional LMS with its fixed gain.

The RLS algorithm. With the analytical derivation we have developed, we can now write down a step-by-step procedure for updating $\mathbf{W}_k^o$. This set of steps is efficient in the sense that no unneeded variable is computed and that no needed variable is computed twice. We do, however, need assurance that R_k^{-1} exists. The procedure then goes as follows:

(i) Accept new samples $x(k), d(k)$.
(ii) Form $\mathbf{X}(k)$ by shifting $x(k)$ into the information vector.
(iii) Compute the *a priori* output $y_o(k)$:

$$y_o(k) = \mathbf{W}_k^{ot}\mathbf{X}(k). \qquad (4.3.23)$$

(iv) Compute the *a priori* error $e_o(k)$:

$$e_o(k) = d(k) - y_o(k). \qquad (4.3.24)$$

(v) Compute the filtered information vector $\mathbf{Z}_k$:

$$\mathbf{Z}_k = R_k^{-1}\mathbf{X}(k). \qquad (4.3.25)$$

(vi) Compute the normalized error power q:

$$q = \mathbf{X}^t(k)\mathbf{Z}_k. \qquad (4.3.26)$$

(vii) Compute the gain constant v:

$$v = \frac{1}{1+q}. \tag{4.3.27}$$

(viii) Compute the normalized filtered information vector $\tilde{\mathbf{Z}}_k$:

$$\tilde{\mathbf{Z}}_k = v \cdot \mathbf{Z}_k. \tag{4.3.28}$$

(ix) Update the optimal weight vector $\mathbf{W}_k^o$ to $\mathbf{W}_{k+1}^o$:

$$\mathbf{W}_{k+1}^o = \mathbf{W}_k^o + e_o(k)\tilde{\mathbf{Z}}_k. \tag{4.3.29}$$

(x) Update the inverse correlation matrix R_k^{-1} to R_{k+1}^{-1} in preparation for the next iteration:

$$R_{k+1}^{-1} = R_k^{-1} - \tilde{\mathbf{Z}}_k \mathbf{Z}_k^t. \tag{4.3.30}$$

This procedure assumes that R_k^{-1} exists at the initial time in the recursion. As a result, two initialization procedures are commonly used. The first is to build up R_k and $\mathbf{P}_k$ according to (4.3.3) and (4.3.4) until R has full rank, i.e., at least N input vectors $\mathbf{X}(k)$ are acquired. At this point R_k^{-1} is computed directly and then $\mathbf{W}_k$. Given these, the recursion can proceed as described above indefinitely or until $k = L - 1$. The advantage of this first technique is that optimality is preserved at each step. The major price paid is that about N^3 computations are required once to perform that initial inversion.

A second, much simpler approach is also commonly used. In this case R_{N-1}^{-1} is initialized as

$$\hat{R}_{N-1}^{-1} = \eta I_N, \tag{4.3.31}$$

where η is a large positive constant and I_N is the N-by-N identity matrix. Since R_{N-1}^{-1} almost certainly will not equal ηI_N, this inaccuracy will influence the final estimate of R_k and hence $\mathbf{W}_k$. As a practical matter, however, η can usually be made large enough to avoid significant impact on $\mathbf{W}_{L-1}^o$ while still making R_{N-1} invertible. Because of the simplicity and the low computational cost, the second approach is the one most commonly used. It becomes even more theoretically justifiable when used with the exponentially weighted RLS algorithm to be discussed shortly.

The computational cost for the RLS algorithm.   As a prelude to developing even more efficient adaptive algorithms, we first should determine how much computation is required to execute the RLS algorithm laid out in the previous section.

We find that the 10 steps in the procedure can be grouped by their computational complexity:

(a) Order 1: Steps (iv) and (vii) require only a few simple operations, such as a subtraction or an addition and division. These are termed *order 1* and denoted

$\mathcal{O}(1)$ because the amount of computation required is not related to the filter order.

(b) Order N: Steps (iii), (vi), (viii), and (ix) each require a vector dot product, a scalar-vector product, or a vector scale and sum operation. Each of these requires N multiplications and up to N additions for each iteration of the algorithm. The actual number of multiplications required for these steps is $4N$, but we refer to them as order N, or $\mathcal{O}(N)$, because the computation requirement is proportional to N, the length of the filter impulse response.

(c) Order N^2: Step (v), a matrix vector product, and step (x), the vector outer product, both require N^2 multiplications and approximately N^2 additions. These are termed $\mathcal{O}(N^2)$ procedures.

The total number of computations needed to execute the RLS algorithm for each input sample pair $\{x(k), d(k)\}$ is

$$2N^2 + 4N \ \text{multiplications}, \tag{4.3.32}$$

an approximately equal number of additions, and one division. Because this amount of computation is required for each sample pair, the total requirement of multiplications to process the sample window is

$$C_{RLS} = (L - N + 1) \cdot 2N^2 + (L - N + 1) \cdot 4N. \tag{4.3.33}$$

It is interesting to compare this to the number of multiplications needed to do a brute force calculation of $\mathbf{W}_{ss}^o$ after all the data are received, instead of updating with each new sample. In (3.2.68), we found this brute force method's computational requirements to be

$$C_{ss} = (L - N + 1) \cdot N^2 + (L - N + 1) \cdot N + N^3 + N. \tag{4.3.34}$$

The N^3 term in C_{ss} comes from the single matrix inversion of R_{ss}, a requirement avoided by the recursive updating scheme used with the RLS algorithm. Depending on how large N is with respect to $L - N + 1$, this inversion can be significant $(L - N + 1 < N)$ or insignificant $(L \ll N)$. We see that the RLS algorithm is more computationally expensive in the $\mathcal{O}(N)$ and $\mathcal{O}(N^2)$ terms. For example, the RLS algorithm requires $(L - N + 1) \cdot 2N^2$ multiplications compared to $(L - N + 1) \cdot N^2$ for the brute force technique. Similarly, the respective $\mathcal{O}(N)$ terms are $4N \cdot (L - N + 1)$ and $(L - N + 2) \cdot N$. Thus, avoiding the inversion with its $\mathcal{O}(N^3)$ computational requirement leads to a growth in the $\mathcal{O}(N^2)$ and $\mathcal{O}(N)$ cost.

When the length of the data record L is substantially larger than the filter length N, the cost of the one-time inversion is overwhelmed by the $\mathcal{O}(N^2)$ terms, and in this case the brute force method is computationally cheaper than the more elegant RLS procedure. Because this situation $(1 < N \ll L)$ is typical of adaptive filtering problems, one might question why the RLS method should be explored at all. There are, in fact, several reasons for exploring and using RLS techniques:

(a) RLS can be numerically better behaved than the direct inversion of R_{ss};
(b) RLS provides an optimal weight vector estimate at every sample time, while the direct method produces a weight vector estimate only at the end of the data sequence; and
(c) This recursive formulation leads the way to even lower-cost techniques.

Each of these aspects are discussed in later sections.

The RLS algorithm with exponential data weighting.   We now modify the definitions of R_k and $\mathbf{P}_k$ slightly as

$$R_k = \sum_{\ell=N-1}^{k-1} \rho^{k-1-\ell} \mathbf{X}(\ell)\mathbf{X}^t(\ell) \tag{4.3.35}$$

and

$$\mathbf{P}_k = \sum_{\ell=N-1}^{k-1} \rho^{k-1-\ell} \mathbf{X}(\ell)d(\ell), \tag{4.3.36}$$

where ρ, the averaging or "forgetting" factor, is a positive constant. It is usually chosen to be slightly less than 1, thereby diminishing the contribution of the "older" data. The exponential weighting emphasizes the most recently received data and has a time constant, or effective averaging period of $1/(1-\rho)$. Clearly, when $\rho = 1$, the expressions for R_k and $\mathbf{P}_k$ are identical to those introduced early in Section 4.3.2, and the averaging interval is infinite, implying that all data are averaged with equal weighting.

The principal motivation for introducing this type of weighting stems from the problem of data nonstationarity—that is, the situation where the input data $\{x, d\}$ changes its "character" within the record of L data points. As the examples revisited in Chapters 8–11 show, this is a common practical situation and in fact is one of the principal reasons for employing an adaptive filter. By choosing to provide an averaging interval shorter than the time interval over which the data changes character, the adaptive updating algorithm "tracks" the changes.

As shown, exponential weighting can be introduced into the RLS procedure quite easily. We start by noting that R_k and $\mathbf{P}_k$ can be recursively defined by the expressions

$$R_{k+1} = \sum_{\ell=N-1}^{k} \rho^{k-\ell} \mathbf{X}(\ell)\mathbf{X}^t(\ell) = \mathbf{X}(k)\mathbf{X}^t(k) + \sum_{\ell=N-1}^{k-1} \rho^{k-\ell} \mathbf{X}(\ell)\mathbf{X}^t(\ell)$$

$$= \rho \left\{ R_k + \frac{1}{\rho} \mathbf{X}(k)\mathbf{X}^t(k) \right\} \tag{4.3.37}$$

and

$$\mathbf{P}_{k+1} = \sum_{\ell=N-1}^{k} \rho^{k-\ell} \mathbf{X}(\ell) d(\ell)$$

$$= \left\{ \sum_{\ell=N-1}^{k-1} \rho^{k-\ell} \mathbf{X}(\ell) d(\ell) \right\} + \mathbf{X}(k) d(k)$$

$$= \rho \left\{ \mathbf{P}_k + \frac{1}{\rho} d(k) \mathbf{X}(k) \right\}. \tag{4.3.38}$$

The optimal weight vector at time step k is given by

$$\mathbf{W}_{k+1}^o = R_{k+1}^{-1} \mathbf{P}_{k+1} = \left\{ R_k + \frac{1}{\rho} \mathbf{X}(k) \mathbf{X}^t(k) \right\}^{-1} \cdot \left\{ \mathbf{P}_k + \frac{1}{\rho} d(k) \mathbf{X}(k) \right\}. \tag{4.3.39}$$

At this point the general approach used earlier in this section can be employed. The only significant difference is that C in (4.3.7) equals $1/\rho$ instead of 1. In fact, it can be easily shown that the weight vector estimate is updated according to the expression

$$\mathbf{W}_{k+1}^o = \mathbf{W}_k^o + \left\{ \frac{d(k) - y_o(k)}{\rho + q} \right\} \mathbf{Z}_k. \tag{4.3.40}$$

This leads to trivial differences in the 10-step procedure described for "unweighted" RLS. In addition to (4.3.40), the only other modification is that needed to properly update R_k^{-1} (step (x) in (4.3.30))

$$R_{k+1}^{-1} = \frac{1}{\rho} \left\{ R_k^{-1} - \frac{\mathbf{Z}(k) \mathbf{Z}^t(k)}{\rho + q} \right\}. \tag{4.3.41}$$

Note that (a) the usual RLS algorithm is attained when $\rho = 1$, (b) no change in the amount of computation is required by introducing the exponential averaging, and (c) the algorithm is almost always initialized with $R_{N-1}^{-1} = \eta I$, since the effect of this erroneous initial condition will be "forgotten" as time evolves.

4.3.3 "Fast" RLS Algorithms

Approach. The basic motivation for developing the recursive algorithms examined in the previous section was to reduce the amount of computation required at each time step. We accomplished this by exploiting a special property of R_k to obtain a computationally less expensive procedure for computing the inverse. In particular, we noticed that R_k becomes R_{k+1} with the addition of a vector outer product. We then used the $ABCD$ lemma in (4.3.6) to produce a recursive procedure for obtaining R_{k+1}^{-1} from R_k^{-1}, reducing the computational load from N^3 to $\mathcal{O}(N^2)$ per iteration. We now desire to reduce the computational cost still more, if possible to the level that only $\mathcal{O}(N)$ operations are required at each time step. Algorithms that attain this goal have been termed *fast algorithms*, and, as we shall see, they obtain the desired improvement in efficiency by exploiting another special property of the adaptive filtering problem.

We start by making two apparently unrelated observations. The first is that the vector $\mathbf{X}(k)$ evolves to $\mathbf{X}(k+1)$ with the incorporation of only one new input sample $x(k+1)$. Of the N samples in the "delay line" of the filter, the oldest is dropped out, a new one $x(k+1)$ is incorporated, and $N-1$ remains in the delay line. This property is not exploited with the RLS algorithm, and in fact, RLS works with any choices of $\mathbf{X}$ data input vectors. This is useful, for example, in the case of adaptive sensor arrays where this "shifting" property does not hold. One might expect the computational efficiency to improve if this shifting property of $\mathbf{X}$ could be exploited.

The second observation is that if $\mathbf{Z}_k$ could be simply propagated to $\mathbf{Z}_{k+1}$ in the RLS procedure, then the updating of R_k^{-1} and its multiplication by $\mathbf{X}(k)$ would not be necessary. This is very important, because these two steps are the ones that require N^2 multiplications each. If they could be avoided, then the computational load would drop to the desired level of $\mathcal{O}(N)$.

A recursive formula for $\bar{\mathbf{Z}}_k$.   In the light of these observations, we seek a procedure that allows us to exploit the shift properties of $\mathbf{X}(k)$ to produce an $\mathcal{O}(N)$ updating scheme for the filtered information vector. We start by defining the filtered information vector $\bar{\mathbf{Z}}_k$. An expression for this vector can be developed by solving for $\mathbf{V} = \mathbf{W}_{k+1}^o - \mathbf{W}_k^o$, the difference between the optimum weight vectors at times $k+1$ and k. From the left of (4.3.39) and the preceding definition of $\mathbf{V}$ emerges

$$R_{k+1}\mathbf{W}_{k+1}^o = R_{k+1}(\mathbf{W}_k^o + \mathbf{V}_k) = \mathbf{P}_{k+1}$$

$$= R_{k+1}\mathbf{W}_k^o + R_{k+1}\mathbf{V}_k = \mathbf{P}_{k+1}. \tag{4.3.42}$$

Substituting the recursive definitions of R_k and $\mathbf{P}_k$, we find that

$$\{R_k + \mathbf{X}(k)\mathbf{X}^t(k)\}\mathbf{W}_k^o + R_{k+1}\mathbf{V}_k = \mathbf{P}_k + d(k)\mathbf{X}(k). \tag{4.3.43}$$

Recall the following relationships:

$$R_k\mathbf{W}_k^o = \mathbf{P}_k \tag{4.3.44}$$

$$y_o(k) \triangleq \mathbf{X}^t(k)\mathbf{W}_k^o. \tag{4.3.45}$$

Using these, (4.3.43) becomes

$$R_{k+1}\mathbf{V}_k = \{d(k) - y_o(k)\}\mathbf{X}(k), \tag{4.3.46}$$

and because

$$e_o(k) = d(k) - y_o(k), \tag{4.3.47}$$

we have

$$\mathbf{V}_k = e_o(k) \cdot R_{k+1}^{-1}\mathbf{X}(k). \tag{4.3.48}$$

The vector $\mathbf{V}_k$ is the update to $\mathbf{W}_k^o$, which preserves optimality in the step from sample $k-1$ to k. This update depends directly on the prediction error $e_o(k)$ and the vector $\bar{\mathbf{Z}}_k$ given by

$$\bar{\mathbf{Z}}_k = R_{k+1}^{-1}\mathbf{X}(k) = \left\{ \sum_{\ell=N-1}^{k} \mathbf{X}(\ell)\mathbf{X}^t(\ell) \right\}^{-1} \mathbf{X}(k). \tag{4.3.49}$$

We see now that $\bar{\mathbf{Z}}_k$ depends on R_{k+1}^{-1} rather than R_k^{-1} as $\mathbf{Z}_k$ does. It is this vector that we endeavor to update recursively.

We note that $\bar{\mathbf{Z}}_k$ depends solely on the input sequence $x(k)$. The computationally efficient techniques for updating this vector hinge on the concept of prediction; that is, a block of N adjacent data points is used to predict the data samples immediately before and after the block. The resulting prediction errors are used to improve the predictors and, implicitly, to develop a model for the data. This model can then be used to update some function of that data, namely $\bar{\mathbf{Z}}_k$.

One procedure for computing $\bar{\mathbf{Z}}_k$ is laid out as follows. It uses the auxiliary vectors $\mathbf{A}(k)$ and $\mathbf{B}(k)$. For reasons to be seen, $\mathbf{A}$ is known as the *forward predictor* and $\mathbf{B}$ is called the *backward predictor*.

(i) Compute the *a priori* forward prediction error ϵ_o

$$\epsilon_o(k+1) = x(k+1) + \mathbf{A}^t(k)\mathbf{X}(k). \tag{4.3.50}$$

(ii) Update the forward prediction vector $\mathbf{A}$

$$\mathbf{A}(k+1) = \mathbf{A}(k) - \bar{\mathbf{Z}}_k \epsilon_o(k+1). \tag{4.3.51}$$

(iii) Compute the *a posteriori* forward prediction error ϵ

$$\epsilon(k+1) = x(k+1) + \mathbf{A}^t(k+1)\mathbf{X}(k). \tag{4.3.52}$$

(iv) Compute prediction crosspower Σ

$$\Sigma(k+1) = \Sigma(k) + \epsilon(k+1)\epsilon_o(k+1). \tag{4.3.53}$$

(v) Form the augmented vector $\mathbf{F}$

$$\mathbf{F} \triangleq \begin{bmatrix} \epsilon(k+1)/\Sigma(k+1) \\ \bar{\mathbf{Z}}(k) + \mathbf{A}(k+1)\epsilon(k+1)/\Sigma(k+1) \end{bmatrix} \begin{matrix} \text{1 element} \\ N \text{ elements} \end{matrix}. \tag{4.3.54}$$

(vi) Partition $\mathbf{F}$

$$\mathbf{F} = \begin{bmatrix} \mathbf{M}(k+1) \\ \mu(k+1) \end{bmatrix} \begin{matrix} N \text{ elements} \\ \text{1 element} \end{matrix}. \tag{4.3.55}$$

(vii) Compute the *a priori* backward prediction error η_o

$$\eta_o(k+1) = x(k-N+1) + \mathbf{B}^t(k)\mathbf{X}(k+1). \tag{4.3.56}$$

(viii) Update the backward prediction vector $\mathbf{B}$

$$\mathbf{B}(k+1) = [\mathbf{B}(k) - \mathbf{M}(k+1)\eta_o(k+1)]/[1 - \mu(k+1)\eta_o(k+1)]. \tag{4.3.57}$$

(ix) Update $\bar{\mathbf{Z}}_k$

$$\bar{\mathbf{Z}}_{k+1} = \mathbf{M}(k+1) - \mathbf{B}(k+1) \cdot \mu(k+1). \tag{4.3.58}$$

A proof of this procedure is not shown here, but it is available from several sources, e.g., Ljung et al. [1978] Most of the steps involve either predicting the waveform $x(k)$ or using those predictions to improve the predictors. The last step produces $\bar{\mathbf{Z}}_k$ as a weighted combination of the forward and backward prediction vectors. The theory on which this procedure is based is quite powerful, and allows proofs to be given and other algorithms to be developed. It is, however, beyond the scope of this book, and the interested reader is invited to pursue the topic in Ljung et al. [1978], Cioffi and Kailath [1984], Honig and Messerschmitt [1984], or Alexander [1986].

Given a method for recursively computing $\bar{\mathbf{Z}}_k$, we can now state a "fast" algorithm for recursively computing $\mathbf{W}_{k+1}^o$ from $\mathbf{W}_k^o$.

For each k:

(a) Compute the *a priori* output $y_o(k+1)$

$$y_o(k+1) = \mathbf{X}^t(k)\mathbf{W}_k^o. \tag{4.3.59}$$

(b) Form the *a priori* output prediction error $e_o(k+1)$

$$e_o(k+1) = d(k+1) - y_o(k+1). \tag{4.3.60}$$

(c) Update $\bar{\mathbf{Z}}_k$ to $\bar{\mathbf{Z}}_{k+1}$.

(d) Compute the updated impulse response vector

$$\mathbf{W}_{k+1}^o = \mathbf{W}_k^o + e_o(k+1)\bar{\mathbf{Z}}(k+1). \tag{4.3.61}$$

Here step (c) includes steps (i) through (ix) listed in (4.3.50)–(4.3.58). We note that $\bar{\mathbf{Z}}(k)$ carries most of the needed information about $x(k)$ into the weight vector update. The filter output is computed and compared to the template waveform $d(k+1)$. The vector $\bar{\mathbf{Z}}(k+1)$ carries all the directional information needed to update $\mathbf{W}_k$.

Computational issues.   The principal objective of developing these relatively complicated algorithms was to reduce the amount of computation needed to attain "exact" optimality at each time step. A review of steps (i)–(ix) and (a)–(d) shows that this objective has been met. Steps (i), (ii), (iii), (v), (vii), (viii), and (ix) involve a vector dot or scalar product and require N multiply-adds each. The conversion of $\bar{\mathbf{Z}}_{k+1}$ to $\bar{\mathbf{W}}_{k+1}$ requires two more vector operations at a cost of $2N$ multiplications and additions. Thus, if we ignore a small number of scalar operations, we see that this particular fast algorithm needs $9N$ multiply-adds, a distinct improvement over the "slow" RLS procedure.

Cioffi and Kailath [1984] analyze a large variety of fast RLS algorithms and show that all can be written as recursions on a set of transversal filters by using the generic updating formula

$$\mathbf{C}_{new} = s_1 \cdot \mathbf{C}_{old} + s_2 \cdot \mathbf{D} \qquad (4.3.62)$$

and

$$\rho = \mathbf{X}^t(k)\mathbf{E}. \qquad (4.3.63)$$

A quick comparison of (i)–(ix) and (a)–(d) with these equations shows this observation to be true for the algorithm stated in this section. Cioffi and Kailath [1984] further show, however, that the most computationally efficient algorithms attain their efficiency by making s_1 and/or s_2 equal to one as often as possible. Using this approach algorithms requiring about $7N$ multiply-adds per sample have been developed. Perversely, it appears that this efficiency is attained at the cost of numerical stability. Algorithms with good numerical stability tend to use values of s_1 and s_2 other than unity and require $11N$ to $20N$ computations per sample. The trade-off between computational efficiency and numerical stability continues to be an active research area.

4.4 AN EXAMPLE USING BOTH LMS AND RLS

To demonstrate the behavior of some of the algorithms described in earlier sections, we now examine a simple filtering problem. Consider the configuration shown in Figure 4.6. The input of the adaptive filter consists of white noise and two real-valued sinusoids of amplitudes a and b and distinct radian frequencies of ω_1 and ω_2. The filter is a real-valued N-tap FIR discrete-time tapped delay line structure. The

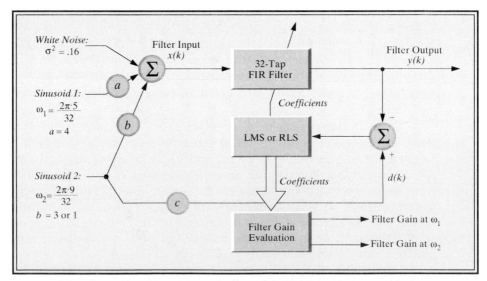

Figure 4.6   The adaptive filter configuration used for the example in Section 4.4.

error $e(k)$ is the difference between the filter output and the template waveform $d(k)$, which, for this example, is a real-valued sinusoid of amplitude c and frequency ω_2. Thus the template waveform has exactly the same frequency but possibly a different phase and amplitude than one of the two input sinusoids.

Intuitively, we would expect an adaptive filter to reduce the error of its average squared value by adjusting its impulse response to provide a gain of c/b at frequency ω_2, a gain of zero at ω_1, and a generally small gain across the band to suppress the input white noise. If this is done, then the filter removes the sinusoid at ω_1 from its output $y(k)$ and scales the sinusoid at ω_2 to match the amplitude and phase of the template waveform.

In this section, we present computer simulation examples of both the LMS algorithm and the RLS algorithm. The algorithms used are exactly those stated in Sections 4.2 and 4.3. Before discussing the simulation results, however, we first predict the filter's behavior. To simplify the mathematics, we assume that ω_1 and ω_2 are distinct integer multiples of $2\pi/N$ where N is the filter length. When the input frequencies are selected in this way, the eigenanalysis of Section 3.4 is particularly simple.

Consider the LMS algorithm first. We can predict its convergence rate and determine allowable values of the adaptation constant by determining the eigenvalues of the input data correlation matrix. Following the type of decomposition used in Section 3.4, we find the eigenvalues of R_{ms} to be given by

$$\lambda_1 = \lambda_2 = \frac{Na^2}{2} + \sigma^2 \qquad (4.4.1)$$

and

$$\lambda_3 = \lambda_4 = \frac{Nb^2}{2} + \sigma^2 \qquad (4.4.2)$$

and

$$\lambda_n = \sigma^2, \quad N \geq n \geq 5, \qquad (4.4.3)$$

assuming here that the filter length N equals or exceeds 4 and that the input noise variance is given by σ^2. From (4.2.21), the adaptive constant μ is bounded by

$$0 < \mu < \min\left(\frac{1}{\lambda_i}\right), \quad i = 1, \ldots, N \qquad (4.4.4)$$

or

$$0 < \mu < \frac{2}{N} \min\left(\frac{1}{a^2}, \frac{1}{b^2}\right), \qquad (4.4.5)$$

assuming that a^2 and b^2 considerably exceed σ^2. As long as this equation is satisfied, then LMS will theoretically converge. It is common practice, however, to use a value of μ substantially smaller than this theoretical limit simply to reduce the effects of input noise and gradient estimation error.

The convergence rate of the algorithm is determined by the time constants of the individual adaptive modes. In this case,

$$\tau_1 = \tau_2 = \frac{1}{\mu\lambda_1} \cong \frac{2}{\mu N a^2} \tag{4.4.6}$$

and

$$\tau_3 = \tau_4 = \frac{1}{\mu\lambda_3} \cong \frac{2}{\mu N b^2}. \tag{4.4.7}$$

If $N > 4$, then the remaining $N - 4$ eigenvalues all equal σ^2, making the associated time constants equal $1/\mu\sigma^2$.

The RLS algorithm converges very rapidly because it uses the inverse autocorrelation matrix to direct the weight vector update at each step. Because of this, the algorithm can be expected to converge in about N iterations. For the purpose of the example, we assume that $N = 32$ and $\sigma^2 = 0.16$. The first simulation, shown in Figure 4.7, was conducted with $a = 4, b = 3, c = 2$, and $\omega_1 = 2\pi \cdot 5/32$, and $\omega_2 = 2\pi \cdot 9/32$ rad/sec. From (4.4.5), μ must be less than 0.0078, and has been chosen to be one-tenth of that, that is, $\mu = 0.00078$. The adaptive time constants are thus

$$\tau_1 = \tau_2 = 10 \tag{4.4.8}$$

and

$$\tau_3 = \tau_4 = \left(\frac{4}{3}\right)^2 10 = 18, \tag{4.4.9}$$

meaning that the LMS algorithm should be expected to asymptotically converge with a time constant of 18 iterations, the longest of its time constants.

Figure 4.7(a) shows the actual response of the LMS algorithm. The filter gain at frequencies ω_1 and ω_2 is shown versus update iteration, and it is seen that, other than a small amount of jitter due to gradient estimation error, the filter gains converge to the values expected (i.e., zero and c/b) at the rates expected. The RLS results are shown in Figure 4.7(b), with the gains converging promptly as expected. Note the large excursions associated with the ill-conditioned startup of RLS.

Another aspect of performance can be demonstrated by keeping all parameters the same except the input level of the desired sinusoid. Suppose now that $b = 1$. Thus, instead of the two input sinusoids having roughly equivalent power, they now differ by 12 dB. Retracing our steps, we find that because a still equals 4, μ must still be less than 0.0078. As before, it is chosen to be 0.00078 and $\tau_1 = \tau_2 = 10$. Because b is so much smaller, however, $\tau_3 = \tau_4 = 160$ iterations. This result is borne out in the simulations shown in Figure 4.8. As before, the filter gains at frequencies ω_1 and ω_2 are plotted versus the iteration number in Figure 4.8(a). The gain at ω_1 again responds quickly, but the gain at ω_2 takes several hundred samples to converge to c/b. As before, the RLS technique quickly converges for both filter gains, as seen in Figure 4.8(b).

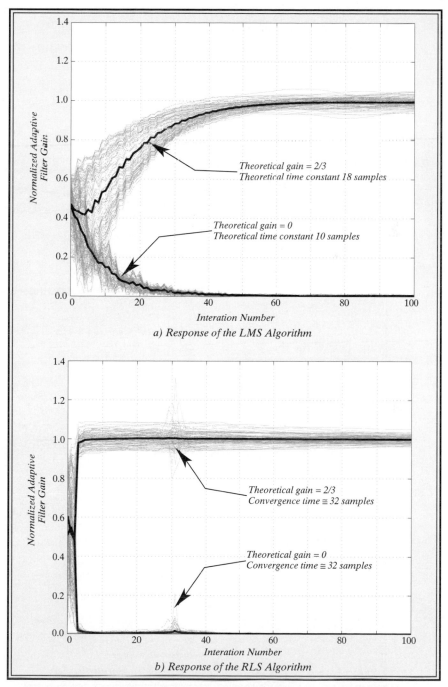

a) Response of the LMS Algorithm

b) Response of the RLS Algorithm

Figure 4.7   Comparison of the adaptation performance of the LMS and RLS algorithms where the input sinusoids are nearly matched in power.

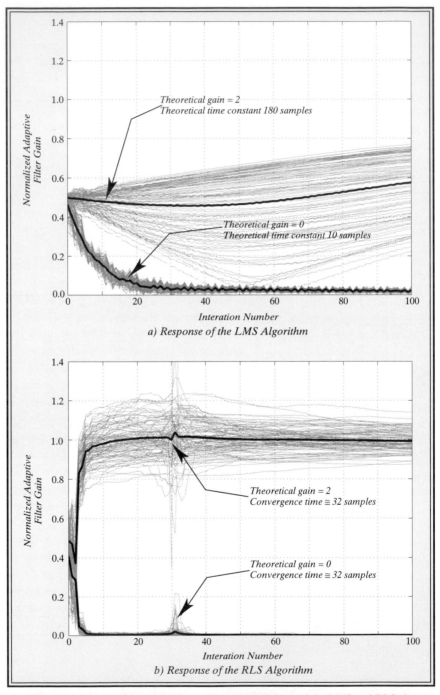

Figure 4.8   Comparison of the convergence performance of the LMS and RLS algorithms where the input sinusoids are disparate in power.

With this example, we see the algorithms do in fact converge to the expected results and that the rate can be reasonably well predicted. By conducting several trials and averaging the "ensemble," even closer adherence can be attained. For this example, it is also tempting to conclude that the RLS technique is superior to gradient search methods because of its prompt convergence. This conclusion must be made carefully, however. While it was not done here in this simple example, careful comparisons of convergence rate are usually done while holding some measure of filter quality constant. The quantity measure usually employed is the "filter misadjustment," defined in Section 4.2.8. Convergence might also be measured in "multiplications" instead of input samples, thus giving the simple gradient algorithms a large advantage. Thus, we see that selection of the "best" algorithm depends on the arithmetic precision available, the rank of the input process, the required output quality, the time-variability of the inputs, and the amount of computation that can be tolerated. In general, RLS and "fast RLS" require fewer data samples to converge, but gradient descent techniques are simpler, more robust, use less computation per iteration, and need less memory. All these issues must be weighed in selecting a filter structure and algorithm for an application.

4.5 SUMMARY AND PERSPECTIVE

This chapter develops a set of adaptive filtering algorithms based on the idea of optimizing some function of the data waveforms provided to the filter. While the algorithms discussed here are the basis of most adaptive filters in current use, it is useful to remember that Chapter 4 considers a very specific and quite limited problem. We assume that the filter has a discrete-time finite impulse response and is implemented with a tapped-delay-line (transversal) structure. The filter's performance is judged based on some template or reference waveform also provided to the algorithm.

Given these choices for the filter structure and the manner in which the quality of the filter output would be judged, we then turn to the third aspect of adaptive filter design: the development of the algorithms to be used to choose the filter impulse response. In Chapter 2, we did this by developing an intuitively reasonable set of rules for updating an estimate of the desired impulse response in such a way as to improve the match between the filter output and the reference or template waveform. In this chapter, a more rigorous approach was used. In Chapter 3 we defined a performance function based on an average of the squared output error—that is, the square of the difference between the filter output and the reference, and then in this chapter developed methodical procedures that allow us to find the impulse response that provides the best performance. We focused principally on the performance function based on the sum of the squared errors over the entire input data record.

Two types of procedures were developed. The first used estimates of the gradient of the performance function to update an estimate of the optimal impulse response. In this way, the performance function is "searched" to find the best possible operating point. The LMS algorithm and many of its variants stem from this idea. They are relatively low in their computational requirements, work adequately in a variety of signal environments, and are the basis for many existing adaptive processors, such as adaptive equalizers and telephone echo cancellers.

The second approach is based on the idea of starting with the optimal solution and then using each input sample to update the impulse response in such a way as to maintain that optimality. This approach yields the Recursive Least Squares (RLS) algorithm and a set of "fast" algorithms that maintain the optimality of the solution with a relative minimum of computation. The normal and "fast" RLS algorithms offer faster convergence than the gradient-search-type algorithms, but usually at the cost of more computation per data sample and more numerical difficulties. Adaptive filters employing the RLS approach are coming into practical use, but so far only in applications that need fast convergence, such as "fast-startup" modem equalizers and adaptive differential pulse code modulation (ADPCM) encoders.

Given this background and the set of adaptive algorithms that satisfy our limited objectives in this chapter, we expand our horizon in the next two chapters. Chapter 5 treats the case of adapting filter realizations other than a finite-impulse-response tapped-delay-line, e.g., an infinite-impulse-response filter. As shown, the presence of feedback in the filter itself complicates many aspects of the adaptive algorithm design. Chapter 6 examines yet a different problem, that is, what if there is no reference waveform to guide the algorithm's adaptation? We see there that criteria other than output prediction error can be used to define a performance function, and hence to fashion an adaptive algorithm. Thus, by the end of Chapter 6, we have probed into each aspect of the generic adaptive filter cited in the introduction of Chapter 2: filter structure, performance evaluation, and parameter updating.

4.6 PROBLEMS

1. Below are brief descriptions that each pose a signal processing scenario. For each, explain a top-level approach appropriate to satisfy the intended goal. A few sentences and a block diagram should suffice. Structure your solution in terms of a processing configuration suited to an FIR filter with its impulse response parameters adapted via LMS. Explicitly indicate how the prediction error is created for driving the adaptation.

   (a) Biomedical instruments for measuring fetal heart rate are used to monitor stress of the baby during birth. This uses an external abdominal pickup on the mother, which is likely to be corrupted by the mother's breathing and heartbeat.

   (b) Given 90-year-old recordings of the operatic tenor Enrico Caruso, restore fidelity lost to the mechanics of gramophone recording technology of the time. Assume you have access to all of the original recording equipment.

   (c) In drilling for oil and gas, it is necessary to monitor the condition of the drill's bit and the nature of the rock strata that it passes through. Traditional visual inspection requires costly suspension of operations and pulling the whole rig up the bore hole. As a possible alternative solution, consider using a very low rate digital status signal from the drill bit during actual drilling, acoustically coupled through the wet "slurry" that fills the bore hole.

   (d) To test feasibility of intratrain communication via the pressure lines of the airbrake system, the nature of the acoustic path must be characterized. You are free to design the test signal.

2. Consider the 3-weight, adaptive tapped-delay-line filter with output

$$y(k) = w_0(k)x(k) + w_1(k)x(k-1) + w_2(k)x(k-2), \qquad (4.6.1)$$

period-4, doubly infinite input sequence

$$\{\ldots, x(0), \ x(1), \ldots, \ x(7), \ldots\} = \{\ldots, \alpha, 0, 0, 0, \alpha, 0, 0, 0, \ldots\}, \qquad (4.6.2)$$

and the desired sequence

$$\{\ldots, d(0), \ d(1), \ldots, \ d(7), \ldots\} = \{\ldots, 0, 0, \beta, 0, 0, 0, \beta, 0, \ldots\}. \qquad (4.6.3)$$

A perfect match, with zero prediction error $d(k) - y(k)$ for all k, is provided by $(w_0, w_1, w_2) = (0, 0, \beta/\alpha)$. We examine the dynamics of the $w_i(k)$ for $k \geq 0$ for LMS of (4.2.5)–(4.2.7).

   (a) For $k = 0$, what are the contents of the adapted filter's tapped-delay line, i.e., $\mathbf{X}(0)$ in (4.2.5)?

   (b) Initialize the 3×1 $\mathbf{W}(0)$ as the zero vector and compute $\mathbf{W}(k)$ according to (4.2.5)–(4.2.7) for $k = 1, 2, 3, \ldots, 17$, and 18.

   (c) For $\mu = 0.1, \alpha = 2$, and $\beta = 1$, extrapolate the formulas for $\mathbf{W}(1)$ to $\mathbf{W}(18)$ from part (b) and plot $w_i(k)$ for $i = 0, 1$, and 2 for $k = 1$ to 100. Note the ascending staircase (with collapsing tread height) shape of $w_2(k)$.

   (d) With $\mathbf{W}(0) = [1 \ 0 \ 0]'$, compute $\mathbf{W}(k)$ for $k = 1, 2, 3, \ldots, 17$, and 18.

   (e) For $\mu = 0.2, \alpha = 2$, and $\beta = 1$, extrapolate the formulas for $\mathbf{W}(1)$ to $\mathbf{W}(18)$ from part (b) and plot $w_i(k)$ for $i = 1, 2$, and 3 for $k = 1$ to 100. Note the descending staircase (with collapsing tread height) shape of $w_0(k)$. Comment on the relative rates of tread height collapse in parts (c) and (e).

3. By their very nature, adaptive filters are time-varying systems. Fortunately, as pointed out in Section 4.2.3, they can be well described by their average behavior, and the dynamics underlying their average behavior can be modeled as a linear time-invariant system. Thus, we take this opportunity to examine certain properties of simple linear, time-invariant systems that prove quite useful in interpreting adaptive system behavior.

   (a) Consider the scalar, time-invariant, homogeneous, linear system described by

   $$x(k+1) = [1 - \mu a]x(k). \tag{4.6.4}$$

   With $a = 0.8$ pick a particular μ so $x^2(k) \to 0$ as $k \to \infty$ for any finite $x(0)$. Use a MATLAB simulation to confirm your answer. Determine the full range of μ for which $x^2(k) \to 0$ as $k \to \infty$ for any finite $x(0)$.

   (b) Consider the linear system

   $$x(k+1) = [I - \mu A]x(k) \tag{4.6.5}$$

   with a 2×1 vector state x and

   $$A = \begin{bmatrix} 1 & a \\ a & 1 \end{bmatrix}. \tag{4.6.6}$$

   (i) Produce a formula for $\mu(a)$ for $0 \leq |a| < 1$ that retains stability of (4.6.5), i.e. $x(k)^t x(k) \to 0$ as $k \to \infty$. Hint: Stability requires that the largest eigenvalue of $I - \mu A$ in (4.6.5) is less than unity in magnitude.

   (ii) Plot two curves on an axis set with time constant on the vertical axis and a on the horizontal axis. The first curve is the time constant of the fastest convergence rate over all possible initializations of $x(0)$ for each value of a. The other curve is the time constant of the slowest convergence rate over all possible initializations of $x(0)$ for each value of a.

   (iii) For eight initializations equally spaced around the circle defined by $x^t(0)x(0) = 2$, plot the trajectories of (4.6.5) with $\mu = 0.001$ and $a = 0.8$ in the state space plane with the horizonal coordinate the first entry of x and the vertical coordinate the second entry of x. For these eight initializations, also plot the corresponding $x^t(k)x(k)$ trajectories on one graph as functions of time.

   (c) Consider the linear system in (4.6.5) with

   $$A = \begin{bmatrix} 1 & c \\ \frac{a}{c} & b \end{bmatrix}. \tag{4.6.7}$$

   For eight initializations equally spaced around the circle defined by $x^T(0)x(0) = 2$, plot the trajectories of (4.6.5) (with $\mu = 0.001$, $c = 0.8$, and a and b chosen such that the eigenvalues of A in (4.6.7) are complex) in the state space plane with the horizonal coordinate the first entry of x and the vertical coordinate the second entry of x. If the resulting trajectories were to be viewed as the steepest descent trajectories across some three-dimensional surface, discuss the shape of this surface relative to the one underlying the similarly interpreted curves in part (iii) of part (b).

   (d) Consider the linear system in (4.6.5) with

   $$A = \begin{bmatrix} 1 & a\cos(\omega k) \\ a & 1 \end{bmatrix} \tag{4.6.8}$$

   where $\mu = 0.01$ and $a = 0.8$. Plot $x^t(k)x(k)$ for $\omega = 0.001, 0.01$, and 0.1 from various initializations. Is there a value of ω for which $x'(k)x(k)$ does not decay to zero as $k \to \infty$?

(e) Consider the linear system

$$x(k+1) = (I - \mu A)x(k) + w(k) \tag{4.6.9}$$

where A is described by (4.6.6) with $a = 0.8$ and w is drawn from a uniform distribution from -0.2 to 0.2. Establish whether the steady-state value of $E[x'(k)x(k)]$ is a linear function of μ.

4. Consider the task of equalization of the AR(1) channel

$$x(k) = ax(k-1) + d(k) \tag{4.6.10}$$

with a two-tap FIR equalizer

$$y(k) = w_0(k)x(k) + w_1(k)x(k-1) \tag{4.6.11}$$

such that $y(k)$ converges to $d(k)$ The desired (source) signal is independent, identically distributed binary (± 1) sequence. The LMS algorithm is proposed for updating the w_j as

$$w_0(k+1) = w_0(k) + \mu[d(k) - y(k)]x(k) \tag{4.6.12}$$

$$w_1(k+1) = w_1(k) + \mu[d(k) - y(k)]x(k-1). \tag{4.6.13}$$

During training, $e(k)$ $(= d(k) - y(k))$ is available for performing these adaptive updates.

(a) Confirm the utility of LMS in this case, by composing the prediction error, as for an identification setting of the linear combiner format, as an inner product of the parameter error vector

$$\mathbf{V}(k) = [1 - w_0(k) \quad -a - w_1(k)]' \tag{4.6.14}$$

and the regressor

$$\mathbf{X}(k) = [x(k) \quad x(k-1)]'. \tag{4.6.15}$$

This also establishes the desired error-zeroing solution as $w_0 = 1$ and $w_1 = -a$.

(b) As described in (4.2.10), the average behavior of the parameter estimates generated by this algorithm is governed by the average outer product of the regressor. Compute the eigenvalues of this average outer product for $a = 0.95$. Confirm that their ratio (i.e., the condition number of the average outer product of the regressor) is a factor of approximately 39.

(c) When the eigenvalues are disparate by more than a factor of 10, the resulting parameter trajectories take on the appearance of descending noticably elongated ellipsoidal contours on the average squared error surface. Plot the error surface contour, in the (w_0, w_1)-plane with $a = 0.95$.

(d) For the eigenvalues of part (b), select an appropriate range for the step size μ. Using $\mu = 0.005$, trace a few simulated $\mathbf{W}$ trajectories across the error surface drawn in part (c). These trajectories should be quite smooth and follow (4.2.10) quite closely. What fraction of the maximum allowable step size maintaining monotonic decay of the summed squared parameter error for this example does the value of $\mu = 0.005$ represent? At what fraction of the maximum do the simulated trajectories no longer look as smooth as with $\mu = 0.005$?

(e) Proposing robust, low-complexity modifications to adaptive algorithms that improve convergence speed in terms of data sample periods has been a prominent pursuit of researchers and developers since the widespread realization by the early 1970s that stochastic gradient descent schemes can be quite slow when the governing dynamics have a wide eigenspread. (Douglas et al. [1999] is one example.)

   (i) In particular, consider the accelerated algorithm of (4.2.54) with the matrix step size C chosen as equal to R^{-1}. The resulting trajectories will appear to be descending a circularly shaped cost surface. Confirm this.

  (ii) Thus, a matrix step size approximately equal to R^{-1} reduces the potential for very long convergence times to reach within some radius in parameter space about the desired answer for certain starting points on an excessively elongated error surface. Confirm this.

 (iii) Take care in approximating R^{-1}. The more elongated the surface, due to an excessive condition number for R^{-1}, the more accurately C needs to approximate R^{-1} to enjoy this convergence speed improvement benefit. Confirm this.

(f) Can the convergence speed improvement achieved in part (e) by the accelerated algorithm with an appropriately selected step size be crudely approximated by using different values for μ in the updates for w_0 and w_1? If so, provide an example. If not, explain why not.

5. Consider the desired signal y formed via

$$d(k) = w_0^o x(k) + w_1^o x(k-1) + w_2^o x(k-2) \tag{4.6.16}$$

and its estimate formed via

$$y(k) = w_0(k)x(k) + w_1(k)x(k-1) + w_2(k)x(k-2). \tag{4.6.17}$$

The desired signal and its estimate can be written as $\mathbf{X}^t(k)\mathbf{W}^o$ and $\mathbf{X}^t(k)\mathbf{W}(k)$, respectively, with

$$\mathbf{X}(k) = [x(k) \quad x(k-1) \quad x(k-2)]^t \tag{4.6.18}$$

$$\mathbf{W}^o = [w_0^o \quad w_1^o \quad w_2^o]^t \tag{4.6.19}$$

$$\mathbf{W}(k) = [\hat{w}_0(k) \quad \hat{w}_1(k) \quad \hat{w}_2(k)]^t. \tag{4.6.20}$$

Thus, the average regressor vector outer product is

$$R = \mathrm{E}[\mathbf{X}(k)\mathbf{X}^t(k)] = \mathrm{E}\begin{bmatrix} x^2(k) & x(k)x(k-1) & x(k)x(k-2) \\ x(k-1)x(k) & x^2(k-1) & x(k-1)x(k-2) \\ x(k-2)x(k) & x(k-2)x(k-1) & x^2(k-2). \end{bmatrix} \tag{4.6.21}$$

For a stationary signal,

$$\mathrm{E}[x(k)x(k-\Delta)] = \mathrm{E}[x(j)x(j-\Delta)] \ \forall k, j. \tag{4.6.22}$$

Therefore, with $\{x\}$ a stationary signal,

$$R = \mathrm{E}\begin{bmatrix} x^2(k) & x(k)x(k-1) & x(k)x(k-2) \\ x(k)x(k-1) & x^2(k) & x(k)x(k-1) \\ x(k)x(k-2) & x(k)x(k-1) & x^2(k) \end{bmatrix} = \begin{bmatrix} \alpha & \beta & \gamma \\ \beta & \alpha & \beta \\ \gamma & \beta & \alpha \end{bmatrix}, \tag{4.6.23}$$

which is symmetric and Toeplitz.

(a) Derive compact formulas for the eigenvalues and eigenvectors of R in (4.6.23) in terms of $\alpha, \delta = (\beta/\alpha)$, and $\rho = (\gamma/\alpha)$, by examining the eigenvalues and eigenvectors of $\alpha \bar{R}$ where

$$\bar{R} = \begin{bmatrix} 1 & \delta & \rho \\ \delta & 1 & \delta \\ \rho & \delta & 1 \end{bmatrix}. \tag{4.6.24}$$

Note that the eigenvalues of R are simply α times those of $\bar{R}$ and the eigenvectors of $\bar{R}$ and R are the same. Do a few numerical examples to confirm the formulas you derive.

(b) Using an $\{x\}$ that creates a full rank R with distinct eigenvalues, for the LMS algorithm

$$w_i(k+1) = w_i(k) + \mu x(k-i)[d(k) - y(k)], \tag{4.6.25}$$

simulate the trajectories of $\tilde{w}_i(k)(= w_i^o - w_i(k))$ from $\tilde{w}_i(0) \neq 0$ for $i = 1, 2$, and 3. Plot the three squared parameter errors $\tilde{w}_i^2(k)$ separately and notice that each trace is a sum of exponential decays leading to a decay curve that is not a straight line on a plot of $\log(\tilde{w}_i^2(k))$ versus k. (Hint: The trajectories are easier to distinguish if every pair from the three eigenvalues is separated by a factor of at least 2 or so.)

(c) Form the modal matrix Q of eigenvectors of R and for the previous LMS simulation, rather than plotting the three entries of $\tilde{\mathbf{W}}(k)$, plot the three trajectories of $Q^t \tilde{\mathbf{W}}(k)$. Confirm that each trace has a single exponential decay. Relate the observed time constants of the decay curves of the entries of $Q^t \tilde{\mathbf{W}}(k)$ to the eigenvalues of R.

(d) Add small amounts of white, zero-mean noise w (uncorrelated with x) to the prediction error observation so $d - y$ in the LMS algorithm of (4.6.25) is replaced by $d(k) - y(k) + w(k)$ and see if the transient behavior of the simulation in part (c) still holds (on average).

(e) With $\alpha = 1$, $\beta = 0.6$, and $\gamma = 0.2$, find (one of) the $\tilde{\mathbf{W}}(0)$ with $\tilde{\mathbf{W}}^t(0)\tilde{\mathbf{W}}(0) = 1$ that results in the slowest convergence rate by LMS of (4.6.25) of $\tilde{\mathbf{W}}^t(k)\tilde{\mathbf{W}}(k)$. What is the associated time constant (as a function of μ)?

(f) With $\alpha = 1$, $\beta = 0.6$, and $\gamma = 0.2$, find (one of) the $\tilde{\mathbf{W}}(0)$ with $\tilde{\mathbf{W}}^t(0)\tilde{\mathbf{W}}(0) = 1$ that results in the fastest convergence rate by LMS of (4.6.25) of $\tilde{\mathbf{W}}^t(k)\tilde{\mathbf{W}}(k)$. What is the associated time constant (as a function of μ)?

(g) For a $\mu = 0.01$ and an input $\{u\}$ that results in an R in (4.6.23) with $\alpha = 1$, $\beta = 0.6$, $\gamma = -0.2$, determine analytically which initialization of the two picked in parts (e) and (f) exhibits the shortest time (in number of samples) before reaching (and staying within) 1% of $\tilde{\mathbf{W}}^t(0)\tilde{\mathbf{W}}(0)$. Confirm your answer via simulation of (4.6.25).

(h) Simulate LMS of (4.6.25) for the three-parameter model of (4.6.17) with x a unit amplitude sinusoid of frequency 0.2 radians/sample. Presume that the prediction error is measured in the presence of white, zero-mean noise $w(k)$, so that $e(k) = d(k) - y(k) + w(k)$. Discuss the observed long-term behavior of the trajectory of the point $(\tilde{w}_1(k), \tilde{w}_2(k), \tilde{w}_3(k))$ in parameter error space in terms of the eigenstructure of the associated R.

6. In the operating scenario discussed in Section 4.2.9 and illustrated in Figure 4.3, both desired signal observation noise and time variations in the desired filter parameters contribute to the prediction error. In the identification format of Figure 4.3, the desire is for the update of $\mathbf{W}(k)$ to "ignore" the observation noise component and "track" the parameter variations.

A fundamental behavior theory observation is that a larger step size in the adaptive algorithm reduces error due to not keeping up with the time-varying desired parameters while it increases errors due to overreaction to measurement noise. Thus, the selection of step size becomes an application-dependent trade-off driven by the relative "strengths" of measurement noise and desired parameter time-variations. (Hint: Read Widrow et al. [1976].)

(a) Compose a four-element weight vector version of LMS. Compose the desired signal as the output of a four weight tapped-delay line with fixed weights and an input drawn from a white, zero-mean sequence of random variables with uniform distribution from -0.5 to 0.5. Confirm the appropriate operation of your adaptive filter by showing a plot of the squared prediction error (i.e., the square of the difference between the desired signal and the output of the adaptive filter), which should decay toward zero.

(b) State the maximum allowable step size for the adaptive filter in part (a). Perform experiments for step sizes ranging from 1/2 to 1/20 of this maximum value and plot the number of iterations needed to converge to 2% of the initial summed squared parameter error (i.e., the sum of the squares of the differences between the coefficients of the filter generating the desired signal and the initial settings of the corresponding coefficients of the adaptive filter).

(c) Convert the desired signal generator of part (a) to a 4-weight tapped-delay line with time-varying coefficients. These time-varying coefficients of the desired signal generator should follow a random walk, i.e., the weight of a particular tap at the next time index equals the one at the current time plus a normally distributed random variable with zero mean and variable variance. For a variance driving the random walk that produces reasonably smooth trajectories for the desired signal generator coefficients and for three step sizes across the range of those considered in part (b), plot the trajectories of the four coefficients generating the desired signal and the corresponding weights in the adaptive filter. The plots of these trajectories should extend to at least 500 iterations after the 2% settling time ascertained in part (b).

(d) Add a uniformly distributed zero-mean noise of adjustable variance to the calculation of the prediction error, i.e., the prediction error should equal the desired signal from the time-varying filter of part (c), minus the adaptive filter's output plus this uniform noise. For the same desired parameterization random walk as in part (c), plot an ensemble average trajectory of the asymptotic behavior (i.e., samples after 2% settling time) of one of the adapted parameters for each of the three step sizes used in part (c). On the same axes, plot the corresponding desired trajectory and the one standard deviation tube about the ensemble average across the ensemble. These plots should illustrate the fact that larger step size reduces the tracking lag of the ensemble mean but increases the parameter tracking error variance across the ensemble.

7. In a circumstance where (i) the desired signal is generated by an impulse response much longer than that of the adaptive filter and (ii) prediction error observation noise is present, a tradeoff exists in "optimal" adaptive filter length selection. An increase in length can decrease the achieveable mean-squared error by improving the modeling capability of the adaptive filter. However, an increase in filter length can also result in an increase in the asymptotic squared prediction error due to observation noise, as discussed in Section 4.2.8. (Furthermore, in a time-varying desired parameterization scenario, as discussed in Section 4.2.9, increased filter length increases lag-induced additional MSE.) Thus, adaptive filter length selection is an application-dependent compromise between these various cost components in the total performance measure.

As a specific example, consider the following parameter estimation task. The difference equation describing the desired signal $d(k)$ has an infinite impulse response

$$d(k) = 0.5u(k-1) - 0.4u(k-2) + 0.4d(k-1) - 0.5d(k-2). \tag{4.6.26}$$

The adaptive filter uses a direct-form FIR model with N taps

$$y(k) = \sum_{i=1}^{N} f_i(k)u(k-i). \tag{4.6.27}$$

The algorithm for updating the f_i is LMS

$$f_i(k+1) = f_i(k) + 0.04\{u(k-i)e(k)\}, \tag{4.6.28}$$

where the prediction error e is measured in the presence of a white, zero-mean noise w that is uniformly distributed between -0.15 and 0.15

$$e(k) = d(k) - y(k) + w(k). \tag{4.6.29}$$

The input u is a sum of two sinusoids plus a white component v that is uniformly distributed between -0.3 and 0.3

$$u(k) = g_1\sin(\omega_1 k) + g_2\sin(\omega_2 k) + v(k), \tag{4.6.30}$$

where $g_1 = 0.3$, $\omega_1 = 0.66$ radians/sample, $g_2 = 1.1$, and $\omega_2 = 1.4$ radians/sample. The two noises w and v are not correlated with each other.

Your task is to find the adaptive filter length N among the set $(2, 4, 8, 16, 32)$ that results in the minimum asymptotic average squared output prediction error.

8. In Figure 4.9 are four plots that correspond to "learning curves" for a hypothetical processing scenario. Assume that they represent an average of a finite ensemble of test cases, i.e., they have been smoothed by running the same case many times with different input sequences drawn from the input distribution and averaging the results. One curve is the base configuration using LMS and the other four show what happens when something in the base case is changed. *Effects are exaggerated for perceptual ease.*

For the four descriptions below, match up the number of the curve. Provide an explanation for your choice.

(a) Larger step size, same number of taps
(b) Same step size, but using more taps
(c) Recursive least squares used rather than LMS
(d) Change in input correlation, reducing smallest eigenvalue, but maintaining largest, and maintaining a fixed converged MSE.

9. Consider the prediction error of an FIR parameter-adapted filter

$$e(k) = d(k) - \mathbf{X}^t(k)\mathbf{W}(k) \tag{4.6.31}$$

and the nonnegative performance measure

$$J = \mathrm{E}\left[\frac{1}{2}\{e^2(k)\} + \alpha\{\mathbf{W}^t(k)\mathbf{W}(k)\}\right] \tag{4.6.32}$$

with its addition of the summed squared (adapted) parameters and the squared prediction error.

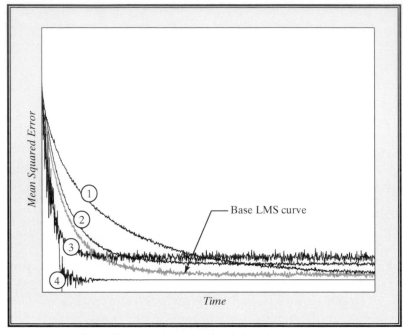

Figure 4.9   Learning curves for various circumstances.

(a) Using a stochastic gradient descent approach to adaptive algorithm creation as used in Section 4.2.2, show that the resulting algorithm is leaky LMS of (4.2.58). Specifically, relate α in (4.6.32) to the step size μ and leakage factor γ of (4.2.58).

(b) Simulate leaky LMS and confirm the following:

   (i) the formula in (4.2.58) for the maximum time constant. (Hint: Select $\mathbf{W}(0)$ away from $\mathbf{W}^o$ along the direction of the eigenvector of R_{new} with smallest eigenvalue.)

   (ii) the formula of the biased convergent weight vector of (4.2.67). (Hint: Select $\mathbf{W}(0)$ at the value in (4.2.67) and fill $\mathbf{X}(0)$ with nonzero values corresponding to R.)

10. Consider the prediction error of an FIR parameter-adapted filter

$$e(k) = d(k) - \mathbf{X}^t(k)\mathbf{W}(k) \qquad (4.6.33)$$

and the nonnegative performance measure

$$J = \mathrm{E}[|e(k)|] \qquad (4.6.34)$$

based on the magnitude of the prediction error rather than its square used for the basis of LMS.

(a) Show that using a stochastic gradient descent approach to adaptive algorithm creation, as in Section 4.2.2, to achieve the least mean absolute (LMA) prediction minimizing J in (4.6.34) results in the sign-error LMS algorithm of (4.2.55)

(b) In a comparison of sample-to-sample dynamic behavior of adaptive filters (without regard to relative computational and memory requirements) in seeking fixed desired values $\mathbf{W}^o$ from $\mathbf{W}(0) \neq \mathbf{W}^o$, the primary features are (i) convergence rate (potentially quantified as the settling time to reduction of MSE below a prespecified threshold across a set of initializations) of the transient phase and (ii) achieved steady-state performance (typically assessed as MSE) of the asymptotic (or steady-state) phase. A fair comparison equilibrates one of these indicators over the entire set of candidate adaptive filters and then ranks the algorithms in terms of the other performance indicator, as noted in the last paragraph of Section 4.2.8. Your task is to construct an experiment comparing the performance of sign-error LMS from (4.2.56) to (unsigned) LMS of (4.2.5)–(4.2.7). Select the step sizes in the two algorithms to achieve the same asymptotic MSE performance. The resulting comparison should verify the claim following (4.2.56) that sign-error LMS is subsequently slower than (unsigned) LMS. (Note that this problem echoes part (c) of Problem 7 in Chapter 2.)

5

Algorithms for Adapting IIR Filters

- *Precis:* *Relative to the FIR case, adaptive IIR filter algorithms compensate for the nonunity filtering of the signal-weighted parameter error in the measured prediction error via algorithm modifications and excitation constraints.*

5.1 INTRODUCTION

The algorithms developed in Chapter 4 provide a variety of methods for adapting finite-impulse-response (FIR) filters. To date, the overwhelming majority of adaptive filtering problems have been solved with FIR filters, primarily because these algorithms are well understood. Applications for which an infinite-impulse-response (IIR) filter appears to be more appropriate have often been dealt with by using an FIR filter that is sufficiently long to adequately model the resonances (poles) and nulls (zeros) of the desired frequency response. While this method is effective and has the advantage of relying on a background of known FIR techniques, it can lead to significant computational costs compared to using the "right" IIR filter. To emphasize the computational impact, we examine the problem of reducing the data transmission rate needed to send a speech signal over a digital telephone circuit.

5.1.1 A Justification of IIR Modeling

Adaptive digital signal processing is used routinely to transmit a speech signal with substantially less than the 12 to 13 bits per sample needed for toll-quality quantization via pulse code modulation (PCM). As shown in Figure 5.1, the basic technique of adaptive differential pulse code modulation (ADPCM) employs an adaptive filter to model the speech generation process of the speaker. This estimate is subtracted from the actual speech, and the difference, presumed to be much smaller in variance than the actual signal, is quantized and transmitted.

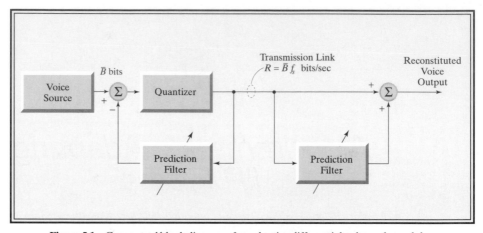

Figure 5.1 Conceptual block diagram of an adaptive differential pulse code modulation (ADPCM) communications system employing adaptive digital filters to produce the predicted voice signal.

Figure 5.2 shows a simplified model of the human speech generation process. The vocal tract is excited in one of two ways. For "voiced" sounds, the vocal cords vibrate and produce quasi-periodic excitation. For "unvoiced" sounds, air is forced through constrictions in the vocal tract, causing turbulence and a noiselike excitation [Rabiner and Schafer, 1978]. The excitation, whether "voiced" or "unvoiced" in origin, is filtered by the vocal tract, i.e., the throat, mouth, and nasal passages, to modify the spectrum of the speech waveform. The vocal tract has resonances at certain frequencies, modeled by the roots of $1 - A(z^{-1})$ (i.e., the vocal tract poles) and nulls at certain frequencies, modeled by the roots of $1 + C(z^{-1})$ (i.e., the vocal tract zeros).

Any nonzero choice of the polynomials $A(z^{-1})$ and $C(z^{-1})$ increases the variance of the output speech signal over that of the original white excitation signal entering the vocal tract. The filtering also adds correlation to the processed version of the excitation signal, making each speech sample correlated with those before and after it. This correlation and the associated increase in the variance of the speech

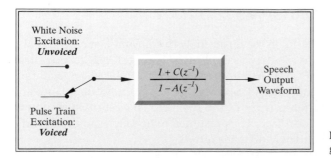

Figure 5.2 Simple model of speech generation.

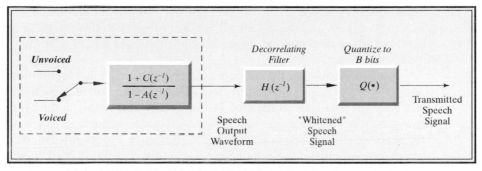

Figure 5.3   Reduction of dynamic range by decorrelating the speech signal.

waveform increase the dynamic range needed to transmit the speech signal over that needed for the excitation alone.

Figure 5.3 shows how ADPCM techniques can be used to reduce the number of bits required for each sample. By developing just the right "decorrelation filter" $H(z^{-1})$, the filtering introduced by the vocal tract can be cancelled, thereby removing the sample-to-sample correlation from the waveform and reducing its variance. The output of the decorrelation filter can then be quantized to a smaller number of bits (e.g., four) and transmitted. This filter can be viewed as a predictor of the speech waveform and may in fact be implemented with a different structure than that in Figure 5.1. In any case, the reduction in the dynamic range of the transmitted signal is obtained by "inverting" the spectral shaping introduced by the vocal tract, and thus decorrelating the speech waveform. An appropriate $H(z^{-1})$ then approximates (the magnitude of) the inverse $[1 - A(z^{-1})]/[1 + C(z^{-1})]$ of the vocal tract transfer function. To adequately capture the unpredictable time-varying character of the human vocal tract during speech, this inverse filter should be time-varying, which suggests its implementation as an adaptive filter.

The required length of the decorrelation/inverse filter impulse response can be determined from a physical analysis of the vocal tract. Such analysis [Rabiner and Schafer 1978] has shown that the desired inverse filter impulse response sequence $h(k)$ should be significantly nonzero for approximately 20 msec. Given an 8-kHz sampling frequency, which is standard for the less than 4-kHz frequency bandwidth considered adequate for reconstructed speech, 20 msec represents a vocal tract decorrelator impulse-response duration of 160 samples. Thus, a viable FIR filter should have approximately 160 taps (or delay elements and weights). For operation at 8-kHz, this results in a computation rate of 1.28 megamultiplies per second, just for filter output computation without considering the computational requirements of adaptation.

In contrast, the CCITT/ITU standard G.721 for ADPCM [Jayant and Noll 1984] uses an adaptive IIR filter to accomplish the same 4-bit quantization at 8 kHz (for a 32-kbps data transmission rate). This IIR structure uses eight weights for a two-pole, six-zero model. This results in a total of only 8 multiplications per input sample for prediction formation, or a computation rate of 0.064 megamultuples per second. This 20 : 1 ratio cannot be attained for all applications, but in this ADPCM application it certainly does motivate the search for algorithms capable of adapting IIR digital filters.

We should observe that this considerable reduction in computation comes at some cost. For example, a time-invariant FIR filter with bounded coefficients has all of its poles at the origin of the z-plane and is therefore stable in the sense that any bounded input sequence generates a bounded output sequence. This is not true for IIR filters, where it is comparatively easy to find a choice of bounded filter coefficients that leads to an unbounded output given a bounded input. Any fixed filter with a pole outside the unit circle in the z-plane can produce such an unbounded output. This stability problem is compounded with adaptation. We have already seen that adaptive FIR filter instability can result due to "parameter runaway" if the adaptive step size is chosen inappropriately relative to the character of its input. With adaptive IIR filters we must be wary of both parameter runaway (which can also happen with FIR adaptive filters) and output explosion without parameter runaway (which happens only with IIR filters).

Essentially, the same practical issues that suggest the use of nonadaptive IIR filters in place of nonadaptive FIR filters also apply to the choice of adaptive IIR filters in place of adaptive FIR filters. Furthermore, the same needs that lead to the use of adaptation in FIR filters, such as lack of adequate *a priori* information for a fixed filter design and/or the expectation of unpredictable variations over time in the desired filter parameterization, also imply the addition of adaptation to IIR implementations. The first adaptive IIR filter algorithm published in the archival literature appeared in White [1975].

5.1.2 Alternate Realizations and Altered Algorithms

The generic adaptive filter in Figure 2.1 (reproduced here as Figure 5.4) has three components

- filter realization
- performance measure
- filter adaptation rules

The filter realization used in Chapter 4 is direct-form FIR. The performance measure used is the prediction error between the adaptive filter output and its desired value. The LMS algorithm arises with the choice of a direct-form FIR filter realization, selection of the average squared prediction error as the "cost" to be minimized, and the use of the stochastic gradient descent paradigm for adaptive algorithm formulation; that is,

$$\mathbf{W}(k+1) = \mathbf{W}(k) - \mu \frac{\partial J(k)}{\partial \mathbf{W}(k)}, \tag{5.1.1}$$

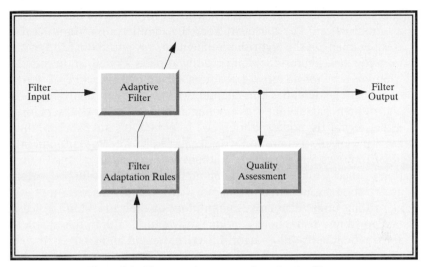

Figure 5.4   The general structure of an adaptive filter.

where J is the instantaneous (rather than averaged) cost function and $\mathbf{W}$ is the adaptive filter's parameter vector. With $y(k)$ the output of the adaptive filter, the instantaneous cost function gradient can be written using the chain rule as

$$\frac{\partial J(k)}{\partial \mathbf{W}(k)} = \frac{\partial J(k)}{\partial y(k)} \cdot \frac{\partial y(k)}{\partial \mathbf{W}(k)}. \qquad (5.1.2)$$

The first term $\partial J(k)/\partial y(k)$ on the right side of (5.1.2) depends on the relationship of the adaptive filter output to the instantaneous cost. The second term $\partial y(k)/\partial \mathbf{W}(k)$ depends on the relationship of the adaptive filter output to its parameterization.

The first term on the right side of (5.1.2) is governed by the choice made for performance measure (or cost). So far in this book, we have focused on prediction error schemes. We continue with this prediction error performance measure in this chapter. We consider alternative performance measures in the next chapter.

The second term on the right side of (5.1.2) is governed by the filter realization. Change the filter realization and you run the risk of altering the format of $\partial y/\partial \mathbf{W}$ so that the unadorned update kernel associated with LMS (i.e., the product of prediction error and the past input, as in (4.2.7)) is inadequate. In this chapter, we study the impact of altering the filter realization on adaptive algorithms with conversion from a direct-form FIR to a direct-form IIR realization.

5.1.3 Adaptive IIR Filter Algorithm Construction

A primary objective of this chapter is to give a template for adaptive IIR filter algorithm construction with an assurance of locally "good" behavior. This is accomplished by viewing various algorithm mutations as attempts to return the underlying error system behavior to that of LMS for a direct-form FIR model, at least in the vicinity of a "good answer." For clarity, we keep the adaptive algorithms in their simplest form. Besides, many of the algorithm refinements proposed for LMS to improve behavior in particular circumstances are readily applied as well to the simple algorithms we examine here for adaptive IIR filters. Given our objective of describing algorithm construction guidelines, this chapter does not provide analysis of adaptive IIR filter algorithm behavior that is as detailed as that in earlier chapters for LMS adapting a direct-form FIR model, although we refer you to sources where this is done.

In our efforts here to reveal a source and interpretation of adaptive IIR filter algorithms, we follow first the gradient descent approach to cost function minimization so successful and widely adopted in adaptive FIR filter development and characterization, as indicated in Chapter 4. We quickly discover that adaptive IIR filter algorithms utilize distinctive elaborations on their FIR counterparts. This revelation of algorithmic distinctions continues as we turn, later in this chapter, to an alternate source for adaptive filter algorithm development and analysis: the identification format and nonlinear system stability theory. The fundamental form of the adaptive algorithm will remain intact, however, as in (2.3.1); that is,

$$
\begin{bmatrix} \text{new} \\ \text{parameter} \\ \text{estimate} \end{bmatrix} = \begin{bmatrix} \text{old} \\ \text{parameter} \\ \text{estimate} \end{bmatrix} + \begin{bmatrix} \text{bounded} \\ \text{step} \\ \text{size} \end{bmatrix} \cdot \begin{bmatrix} \text{function} \\ \text{of} \\ \text{information} \\ \text{vector} \end{bmatrix} \cdot \begin{bmatrix} \text{function of} \\ \text{prediction} \\ \text{error} \end{bmatrix}.
$$

$$(5.1.3)$$

The distinct approaches of cost function gradient descent and identification-format stability theory are exploited to justify the distinct algorithm forms considered in Sections 5.2 and 5.3, respectively. Section 5.4 summarizes various direct-form IIR adaptive laws arising from these paradigms. For tutorial surveys on behavior theory for adaptive IIR filters, refer to Johnson [1984], Treichler [1985], Shynk [1989b], and Cousseau [1999]. For much deeper and broader coverage of the theory of adaptive IIR filter algorithms, refer to Regalia [1995].

Once this adaptive IIR algorithm heirarchy has been erected, we are in a position to pose adaptive IIR filter algorithm construction tasks that utilize it.

- In Section 5.5, a particular pole-zero model identification algorithm (i.e., the Steiglitz-McBride algorithm [Steiglitz and McBride, 1965]) is shown to fit in this common framework with a twist on the definition of the information vector.

- In Section 5.6, adaptive algorithms for an IIR whitener—of the same structure as the IIR predictor in the adaptive differential pulse code modulation (ADPCM) standard G.721 [Jayant and Noll, 1984] mentioned in Section 5.1.1—are composed.

- In Section 5.7, the autoregressive, moving-average, with exogenous input (or ARMAX) model common in stochastic time series modeling—and useful in signal processing applications [Friedlander, 1982]—is shown to fit the adaptive IIR filter algorithm framework.

5.2 GRADIENT DESCENT MINIMIZATION
OF SQUARED PREDICTION ERROR

Using an autoregressive, moving-average (ARMA) model, our adaptive IIR filtering task is to update the a_i and b_j parameters in

$$y(k) = \sum_{i=1}^{n} a_i(k)y(k-i) + \sum_{j=0}^{m} b_j(k)x(k-j). \qquad (5.2.1)$$

Note that (5.2.1) possesses an IIR due to its use of past output estimates in forming its current output estimate $y(k)$. Assuming that we would like to have y emulate a desired signal d in a least squares sense, our objective is to select the a_i and b_j in (5.2.1) such that

$$J(a_1, a_2, \ldots, a_n, b_0, b_1, \ldots, b_m) = \sum_{k=1}^{L} [d(k) - y(k)]^2 \qquad (5.2.2)$$

is minimized. The character of d and x and the choices of n and m strongly influence the optimal parameterization.

As with the adaptive FIR filter development in Section 4.2.2, we resort to consideration of an approximate gradient descent procedure based on evaluation of the instantaneous squared prediction error gradient rather than the gradient of its "averaged" value in (5.2.2). In other words, our chosen algorithm form is

$$a_i(k+1) = a_i(k) - \mu_i \frac{\partial(\frac{1}{2}[d(k) - y(k)]^2)}{\partial a_i(k)}, \quad \mu_i > 0 \qquad (5.2.3)$$

$$b_j(k+1) = b_j(k) - \rho_j \frac{\partial(\frac{1}{2}[d(k) - y(k)]^2)}{\partial b_j(k)}, \quad \rho_j > 0. \qquad (5.2.4)$$

Because d is not a function of a_i and b_j,

$$\frac{\partial(\frac{1}{2}[d(k) - y(k)]^2)}{\partial a_i(k)} = -[d(k) - y(k)] \frac{\partial y(k)}{\partial a_i(k)} \qquad (5.2.5)$$

and

$$\frac{\partial(\frac{1}{2}[d(k) - y(k)]^2)}{\partial b_j(k)} = -[d(k) - y(k)] \frac{\partial y(k)}{\partial b_j(k)}. \qquad (5.2.6)$$

Thus, our task is to evaluate the partial derivative of y with respect to the a_i and b_j. Focusing for the moment on the derivative with respect to a_i and utilizing (5.2.1) results in

$$\frac{\partial y(k)}{\partial a_i(k)} = y(k-i) + \sum_{s=1}^{n} a_s(k) \frac{\partial y(k-s)}{\partial a_i(k)}. \qquad (5.2.7)$$

Note that each a_i is functionally related to all previous y due to the interconnection of (5.2.3), (5.2.5), and (5.2.7) and the causal interdependence of the y in (5.2.1). This functional relationship is complex and forbidding to our ability to evaluate (5.2.7) by determining a closed-form expression for $\frac{\partial y(k-s)}{\partial a_i(k)}$. At the very least, we can assert that this partial derivative of past y with respect to more recent a_i is not to be ignored. It is not necessarily zero.

To further evaluate (5.2.7), we utilize the small step size convention common in adaptive IIR (and FIR) filter development [White, 1975], [Stearns et al., 1976], [Parikh and Ahmed, 1978], [Horvath, 1980]. The use of a sufficiently small step size μ_i in (5.1.3) causes small changes in the $a_i(k)$ over each iteration. We actually assume that each μ_i is sufficiently small such that

$$\frac{\partial y(k-s)}{\partial a_i(k)} \approx \frac{\partial y(k-s)}{\partial a_i(k-s)}, \quad \text{for } s = 1, 2, \ldots, n. \tag{5.2.8}$$

This assumption converts (5.2.7) to

$$\frac{\partial y(k)}{\partial a_i(k)} \approx y(k-i) + \sum_{s=1}^{n} a_s(k) \frac{\partial y(k-s)}{\partial a_i(k-s)}. \tag{5.2.9}$$

Note that (5.2.9) provides a recursive formula for approximating $\frac{\partial y(k)}{\partial a_i(k)}$, which was also derived in Cadzow [1976] for gradient-search-based IIR filter design. Similarly, if we assume that the ρ_j in (5.2.4) are sufficiently small such that

$$\frac{\partial y(k-s)}{\partial b_j(k)} \approx \frac{\partial y(k-s)}{\partial b_j(k-s)}, \tag{5.2.10}$$

then using (5.2.10) in (5.2.6) yields

$$\frac{\partial y(k)}{\partial b_j(k)} \approx x(k-j) + \sum_{s=1}^{n} a_s(k) \frac{\partial y(k-s)}{\partial b_j(k-s)}, \quad 0 \le j \le m. \tag{5.2.11}$$

Concatenating the $n + m + 1$ partial derivative approximations into one vector yields

$$\left[\frac{\partial y(k)}{\partial a_1(k)} \cdots \frac{\partial y(k)}{\partial a_n(k)} \frac{\partial y(k)}{\partial b_0(k)} \cdots \frac{\partial y(k)}{\partial b_m(k)} \right]$$
$$\approx [y(k-1) \cdots y(k-n) \ x(k) \cdots x(k-m)]$$
$$+ \sum_{s=1}^{n} a_s(k) \left[\frac{\partial y(k-s)}{\partial a_1(k-s)} \cdots \frac{\partial y(k-s)}{\partial a_n(k-s)} \frac{\partial y(k-s)}{\partial b_0(k-s)} \cdots \frac{\partial y(k-s)}{\partial b_m(k-s)} \right]. \tag{5.2.12}$$

Define the *information vector* (also labeled the *regressor*)

$$\mathbf{X}(k) = [y(k-1) \ \cdots \ y(k-n) \ x(k) \ \cdots \ x(k-m)]^t \tag{5.2.13}$$

and an autoregressively filtered version of $\mathbf{X}$,

$$\mathbf{\Psi}(k) = \mathbf{X}(k) + \sum_{s=1}^{n} a_s(k) \mathbf{\Psi}(k-s). \tag{5.2.14}$$

Given (5.2.12), $\mathbf{\Psi}$ can be viewed as an approximation of the partial derivative of the current output estimate $y(k)$ with respect to the parameter estimate vector composed of $a_i(k)$ and $b_j(k)$.

As a brief aside, note that this approximate gradient descent strategy could be followed for other IIR filter structures then the direct form parameterization of (5.2.1). For example Parikh et al. [1980] use the gradient descent approach to develop a centralized algorithm for IIR lattice parameter adaption that was simplified in Rodriguez-Fonollosa and Masgrau [1991] and shown to be locally stable in Williamson et al. [1991b]. Forssen [1990] and Williamson et al. [1991b] describe how to generalize the application of the gradient descent approach to the IIR lattice and other alternative-to-direct-form realizations.

Using (5.2.14) in the concatenation of (5.2.3)–(5.2.6) yields the adaptive IIR filter algorithm

$$\mathbf{W}(k+1) = \mathbf{W}(k) + \Lambda \mathbf{\Psi}(k)e(k) \qquad (5.2.15)$$

for updating the parameters in the direct form of (5.2.1), where

$$\mathbf{W}(k) = [a_1(k) \cdots a_n(k)\, b_0(k) \cdots b_m(k)]^t \qquad (5.2.16)$$

$$\Lambda = \text{diag}[\mu_1 \cdots \mu_n\, \rho_0 \cdots \rho_m], \quad \mu_i > 0,\ \forall i \ \text{ and } \ \rho_j > 0,\ \forall j, \qquad (5.2.17)$$

$$e(k) = d(k) - \mathbf{X}^t(k)\mathbf{W}(k), \qquad (5.2.18)$$

$\mathbf{X}(k)$ is given by (5.2.13), and $\mathbf{\Psi}(k)$ by (5.2.14). Note that the algorithm in (5.2.15) provides a causal method for determining y. In (5.2.15), $d(k), x(k)$ and past x (i.e., $x(k-j)$ for $j = 1, 2, \ldots, m$), past y, $\mathbf{W}(k)$, and past $\mathbf{\Psi}$ are sufficient to compute $\mathbf{W}(k+1)$.

5.2.1 A Less Expensive Gradient Approximation

The form of $\mathbf{\Psi}$ in (5.2.14) imposes a significant computational and storage burden because n past values of the full $(n + m + 1) \times 1$ $\mathbf{\Psi}$ vector must be stored and each element of $\mathbf{\Psi}$ updated independently via an nth-order regression. Recognizing that $\mathbf{X}(k)$ in (5.2.13), which drives the propagation of $\mathbf{\Psi}(k)$ in (5.2.14), is composed of successively delayed versions of y and x suggests [Söderström et al., 1978] [Horvath, 1980] a more computationally efficient approximation for $\partial y(k)/\partial \mathbf{W}(k)$. This alternate approximation uses filtered versions of y and x

$$y^F(k) = y(k) + \sum_{s=1}^{n} a_s(k)y^F(k-s) \qquad (5.2.19)$$

$$x^F(k) = x(k) + \sum_{s=1}^{n} a_s(k)x^F(k-s) \qquad (5.2.20)$$

and composes $\mathbf{\Psi}^F$ from past values of y^F and x^F

$$\mathbf{\Psi}^F(k) = [y^F(k-1) \ \cdots \ y^F(k-n) \ x^F(k) \ \cdots \ x^F(k-m)]^t. \qquad (5.2.21)$$

The updating of $\mathbf{\Psi}^F$ thus requires only two nth-order autoregression operations rather than the $n + m + 1$ for $\mathbf{\Psi}$ in (5.2.14). It also reduces the memory requirement for the $n(n + m + 1)$ entries in past Ψ needed for (5.2.14) to n past y^F in (5.2.19) and n past x^F for (5.2.20). The algorithm of (5.2.15) is unchanged except for the use of Ψ^F rather than Ψ.

That Ψ^F in (5.2.21) is not equivalent to Ψ in (5.2.14) can be noted by comparing the second entry Ψ_2 in (5.2.14)

$$\Psi_2(k) = y(k - 2) + \sum_{s=1}^{n} a_s(k)\Psi_2(k - s) \qquad (5.2.22)$$

and the second entry Ψ_2^F in (5.2.21)

$$\Psi_2^F(k) = y^F(k - 2) = y(k - 2) + \sum_{s=1}^{n} a_s(k - 2)\Psi_s^F(k - 2). \qquad (5.2.23)$$

Even if the past values $\Psi_2(k - s)$ and $\Psi_s^F(k - 2)$ were equal for $s = 1, 2, \ldots, n$, $\Psi_2(k)$ need not equal $\Psi_2^F(k) (= \Psi_1^F(k - 1))$ due to the difference in the time indices on the a_i. However, under the small μ_i assumption used to generate (5.2.8), $a_i(k) \approx a_i(k - i)$ for $i = 1, 2, \ldots, n$ and these two approximations Ψ and Ψ^F for $\partial y(k)/\partial \mathbf{W}(k)$ are essentially interchangeable.

5.2.2 Stability Check and Projection

Compare the adaptive IIR filter algorithm of (5.2.15) and the similar LMS algorithm for FIR filter adaptation in (4.2.7). An obvious difference in the adaptive IIR filter algorithm is the filtering of the information vector before forming the prediction error and filtered information vector product $\Psi(k)e(k)$. In the adaptive FIR algorithm, the unfiltered information vector $\mathbf{X}$ is used for the update kernel $\mathbf{X}(k)e(k)$. In the proof of adaptive FIR filter convergence, $\mathbf{X}$ is assumed bounded, which it is because x is bounded. Similarly, for the convergence of the adaptive IIR filter algorithm in (5.2.15), Ψ should remain bounded. Establishment of this property is not as immediate because, from (5.2.14) (or (5.2.21)), Ψ (or Ψ^F) is the output of autoregressions driven by x and y in $\mathbf{X}$ in (5.2.13). Because either parameter explosion or (5.2.1) input-output instability could result in unbounded y from bounded x, the adaptive IIR filter information vector $\mathbf{X}$ in (5.2.13) need not be bounded simply because x is bounded.

Under the assumption that the μ_i are small and that the a_i are very slowly varying, a stability test for all roots less than 1 of the polynomial

$$1 - A(q^{-1}, k + 1) = 1 - \sum_{i=1}^{n} a_i(k + 1)q^{-i}, \qquad (5.2.24)$$

where q^{-i} is the delay operator, that is, $q^{-i}\mathbf{X}(k) = \mathbf{X}(k - i)$, would be reasonable in checking the stability of Ψ generation from $\mathbf{X}$ (and y from x). (The shift operator q^{-i} is used here rather than the more familiar z-transform operator z^{-i} to allow us to distinguish the shift operator from the complex variable in the z-transform.) One way to establish the stability and convergence of adaptive IIR filter algorithms, such as (5.2.15), is to frequently perform a stability check, and if (5.2.24) is unstable, the $a_i(k+1)$ should be modified so all the roots of $1 - A(q^{-1}, k+1)$ are projected to within the stability region of the unit circle in the complex q-plane.

One concern with this need for stability check and projection is that a real-time stability test of the time-varying, autoregressive information vector filter can be a significant computational burden in many situations. Another concern is selection of a successful procedure for the associated projection requirement. Should the destabilizing update be ignored or reduced in magnitude so instability is not induced? Should the roots of the offending polynomial be shrunk radially toward the origin or should some more complicated mapping be employed? Simulations indicate that projection schemes, no matter how clever, can in certain circumstances result in a cycle of migration into instability, projection back to the stable region, and repeated migration into instability such that the adapted parameters are stalled near a setting at the instability boundary in the adapted filter parameter space [Ljung, 1977].

Without such a stability check and projection facility on the adapted regressor filter (which in different applications need not match the denominator of the adapted IIR filter transfer function), explosive algorithm failure can occur. As might be suspected, simulations have verified that when the desired roots for this information vector filter are near the unit circle, more frequent projection is required. However, other simulations indicate that in different circumstances temporary instability is not encountered and the projection mechanism is not needed.

5.3 PARAMETER IDENTIFICATION FORMAT AND STABILITY THEORY INTERPRETATION

In the preceding section, no explicit assumptions were made regarding the generation of the desired filter output $d(k)$. Implicitly, we assumed that d was generated from x in such a manner that (5.2.1), if properly parameterized, would offer a reasonable approximation. In this section, we begin by imposing the assumption that the desired signal $d(k)$ is generated by a model with the same structure as (5.2.1),

$$d(k) = \sum_{i=1}^{n} a_i^\circ d(k-i) + \sum_{j=0}^{m} b_j^\circ x(k-j). \qquad (5.3.1)$$

(To help avoid confusion between the desired a_i° of (5.3.1) and the adapted $a_i(k)$ of (5.2.1), the adapted parameters are always cited with the time index included and no superscript.)

We have focused the goal of adapting the parameters of (5.2.1) to be identifying precisely those in (5.3.1) in order to make y match d for any possible x. This places us in the domain of recursive identification [Ljung and Söderström, 1983] within the broader subject of system identification [Ljung, 1987] [Söderström and Stoica, 1989]. Clearly, with the extra structure that (5.3.1) provides to our problem statement, a more thorough theoretical understanding is possible. One result has been that a wider range of system-theoretic tools has been employed to develop and interpret adaptive algorithms than just the gradient descent approach of the preceding section. In this section, we exploit one of them: stability theory. But before we embark on our utilization of this approach, we consider some of the algebraic consequences of the precise structural match of the adaptive filter and the desired signal generator.

First, we reconsider the adaptive FIR filter

$$y(k) = \sum_{j=0}^{m} b_j(k)x(k-j) \tag{5.3.2}$$

using the LMS update

$$b_j(k+1) = b_j(k) + \mu_j x(k-j)[d(k) - y(k)]. \tag{5.3.3}$$

Assuming that the desired signal is composed similarly to (5.3.2),

$$d(k) = \sum_{j=0}^{m} b_j^\circ x(k-j), \tag{5.3.4}$$

the prediction error can be written as

$$e(k) = d(k) - y(k) = d(k) - \mathbf{X}^t(k)\mathbf{W}(k)$$
$$= \mathbf{X}^t(k)\mathbf{V}(k) \tag{5.3.5}$$

where

$$\mathbf{V}(k) = \mathbf{W}^\circ - \mathbf{W}(k) \tag{5.3.6}$$

$$\mathbf{W}^\circ = [b_0^\circ \ b_1^\circ \ \cdots \ b_m^\circ]^t \tag{5.3.7}$$

$$\mathbf{W}(k) = [b_0(k) \ b_1(k) \ \cdots \ b_m(k)]^t \tag{5.3.8}$$

and

$$\mathbf{X}(k) = [x(k) \ x(k-1) \ \cdots \ x(k-m)]^t. \tag{5.3.9}$$

The pertinent observation is that the prediction error in (5.3.5) is simply the inner product of the information vector and the parameter estimate error vector, that is, $\mathbf{X}^t\mathbf{V}$.

For an adaptive IIR filter, the output estimate is

$$y(k) = \sum_{i=1}^{n} a_i(k)y(k-i) + \sum_{j=0}^{m} b_j(k)x(k-j) = \mathbf{X}^t(k)\mathbf{W}(k), \tag{5.3.10}$$

with

$$\mathbf{X}(k) = [y(k-1) \ \cdots \ y(k-n) \ x(k) \ x(k-1) \ \cdots \ x(k-m)]^t \tag{5.3.11}$$

and

$$\mathbf{W}(k) = [a_1(k) \ \cdots \ a_n(k) \ b_0(k) \ b_1(k) \ \cdots \ b_m(k)]^t. \tag{5.3.12}$$

Subtracting (5.3.10) from (5.3.1) yields the prediction error

$$e(k) = d(k) - y(k)$$

$$= \sum_{i=1}^{n} a_i^\circ [d(k-i) - y(k-i)] + \sum_{i=1}^{n} [a_i^\circ - a_i(k)] y(k-i)$$

$$+ \sum_{j=0}^{m} [b_j^\circ - b_j(k)] x(k-j)$$

$$= \sum_{i=1}^{n} a_i^\circ e(k-i) + \mathbf{X}^t(k)\mathbf{V}(k) \tag{5.3.13}$$

or

$$[1 - A^\circ(q^{-1})]e(k) = \mathbf{X}^t(k)\mathbf{V}(k). \tag{5.3.14}$$

In (5.3.14), $\mathbf{V}$ is still the parameter error vector, as in (5.3.7) for the adaptive FIR filter. However, the definition of $\mathbf{W}^\circ$ changes from that of (5.3.8) to a vector of the parameters of (5.3.1) in correspondence with the adapted parameter vector of (5.2.16) or (5.3.12). The operator notation of $1 - A^\circ(q^{-1})$ in (5.3.14) is simply shorthand for

$$[1 - A^\circ(q^{-1})]e(k) = \left[1 - \sum_{i=1}^{n} a_i^\circ q^{-i} \right] e(k) = e(k) - \sum_{i=1}^{n} a_i^\circ e(k-i). \tag{5.3.15}$$

With inversion of the scalar operator $1 - A^\circ(q^{-1})$, (5.3.14) can be written as

$$e(k) = [1 - A(q^{-1})]^{-1} \{ \mathbf{X}^t(k)\mathbf{V}(k) \}, \tag{5.3.16}$$

which is simply shorthand for (5.3.13). Recognizing $[1 - A^\circ(q^{-1})]^{-1}$ as an autoregressive operator, the prediction error for the parameter identification formulation of adaptive IIR filtering is an autoregressively filtered version of the inner product of the information vector $\mathbf{X}$ and the parameter estimate error vector $\mathbf{V}$. Note that this autoregression is the "unknown" autoregression of the desired signal model in (5.3.1).

An obvious question is: Can we use the prediction error e of (5.3.16), with its inclusion of the filtering by $[1 - A]^{-1}$, to update the parameters of an adaptive IIR filter, much as we used e ($= d - y$) of (5.3.5) in (5.3.3) to adapt the parameters of an FIR filter? The next section develops a stability theory problem reinterpretation of this question that allows us to apply substantial analytical tools for answering it. Because we know that this works when this added operator is exactly unity, we suspect that it will work under broad operating conditions even if $[1 - A]^{-1}$ is only approximately unity.

5.3.1 Homogeneous Error System Stability Formulation

Return, once again, to the adaptive FIR filter algorithm of (5.3.3). Given (5.3.5), (5.3.8), and (5.3.9), (5.3.3) can be written in vector form as

$$\mathbf{W}(k+1) = \mathbf{W}(k) + \Lambda \mathbf{X}(k)\mathbf{X}^t(k)\mathbf{V}(k). \qquad (5.3.17)$$

Subtract both sides of (5.3.17) from $\mathbf{W}^\circ$ to yield

$$\mathbf{V}(k+1) = \mathbf{V}(k) - \Lambda \mathbf{X}(k)\mathbf{X}^t(k)\mathbf{V}(k) \qquad (5.3.18)$$

or

$$\mathbf{V}(k+1) = [I - \Lambda \mathbf{X}(k)\mathbf{X}^t(k)]^{-1}\mathbf{V}(k). \qquad (5.3.19)$$

The reformulation in (5.3.19) can be viewed as the state equation of a homogeneous (or unforced) system with state $\mathbf{V}$ and time-varying state transition matrix $[I - \Lambda \mathbf{XX}^t]^{-1}$. Our objective of parameter identification can be stated as a zero-state asymptotic stability problem. In other words, we would like for (5.3.19) to stably return an initial nonzero state to zero as $k \to \infty$. This is due to the fact that if the state $\mathbf{V}$ of (5.3.19) is zero, then from (5.3.7) $\mathbf{W} = \mathbf{W}^\circ$ (and $e = d - y = 0$) as desired. It can be proved that the "energy" of the state of the system in (5.3.19), measured as $\mathbf{V}^t\Lambda^{-1}\mathbf{V}$, is nonincreasing, such that (5.3.19) is globally asymptotically stable when Λ is finite, symmetric, and positive definite [Mendel, 1973]. In fact,

$$\mathbf{V}^t(k+1)\Lambda^{-1}\mathbf{V}(k+1) - \mathbf{V}^t(k)\Lambda^{-1}\mathbf{V}(k) = -(2 - \mathbf{X}^t(k)\Lambda\mathbf{X}(k))^{-1}e^2(k).$$

$$(5.3.20)$$

With Λ diagonal, the computation of (5.3.20) mimics that of (2.2.24)–(2.2.26) in the nondivergence proof for a number guessing strategy in Chapter 2. It can also be proved that the linear, time-varying system exhibits zero-state asymptotic stability if Λ is positive definite (i.e., all eigenvalues of Λ are greater than zero, and $\mathbf{X}$ satisfies certain richness requirements [Anderson and Johnson, 1982a]). The condition on $\mathbf{X}$ said to define $\{\mathbf{X}\}$ as persistently exciting and that yields exponentially fast convergence of $\mathbf{V}$ to zero is

$$\alpha_1 I > \sum_{k=j}^{j+S} \mathbf{X}(k)\mathbf{X}^t(k) > \alpha_2 I > 0 \qquad (5.3.21)$$

for some S and all j. As noted in Anderson and Johnson [1982a], an x, from which $\mathbf{X}$ is composed in (5.3.9), containing a sufficient number $> (m+1)/2$ of distinct sinusoids satisfies the persistent excitation condition of (5.3.21). Compare this to the existence of R^{-1} required in Section 3.2.6. If $\mathbf{X}$ does not satisfy these richness requirements, (5.3.19) is still stable but $\mathbf{V}$ need not decay to zero. In any event, (5.3.19) is stable such that $\mathbf{V}$ remains bounded and $\mathbf{X}^t\mathbf{V}(= e)$ decays to zero if $\mathbf{X}$ remains bounded. As noted before, the decay of the prediction error to zero is the sole objective in many adaptive filtering applications.

There is a significant practical consequence of (local) exponential stability of the zero state in a possibly nonlinear homogeneous system such as (5.3.19). When a suitably small bounded input is applied, and the inital state is suitably small, the resulting state will remain bounded [Anderson et al., or 1986]. With order under-modeling of $\mathbf{W}$ relative to $\mathbf{W}^\circ$ and/or time-varying $\mathbf{W}^\circ$, (5.3.19) acquires a nonzero input [Anderson and Johnson, 1982b]. For example, if $\mathbf{W}^\circ$ is not fixed but actually time-varying so that $\mathbf{V}(k) = \mathbf{W}^\circ(k) - \mathbf{W}(k)$, then subtracting both sides of (5.3.17) from $\mathbf{W}^\circ(k+1)$ yields

$$\mathbf{V}(k+1) = \mathbf{W}^\circ(k+1) - \mathbf{W}(k+1)$$
$$= \mathbf{W}^\circ(k+1) - \mathbf{W}^\circ(k) + \mathbf{W}^\circ(k) - \mathbf{W}(k) - \Lambda\mathbf{X}(k)\mathbf{X}^t(k)\mathbf{V}(k)$$
$$= [I - \mathbf{X}(k)\mathbf{X}^t(k)]\mathbf{V}(k) + \mathbf{W}^\circ(k+1) - \mathbf{W}^\circ(k) \qquad (5.3.22)$$

Thus, given persistent excitation by $\mathbf{X}$ as in (5.3.21) and sufficiently small $\mathbf{W}^\circ(k+1) - \mathbf{W}^\circ(k)$, $\mathbf{V}$ converges to settings within a suitably small region about the origin [Anderson and Johnstone, 1983] [Mareels and Polderman, 1996].

One might be tempted, as suggested in Feintuch [1976], to simply apply an adaptive FIR filter algorithm to an adaptive IIR filter problem. For example, consider updating the parameters in (5.3.10) via the counterpart to (5.3.17), where $\mathbf{X}^t(k)\mathbf{V}(k) - e(k)$; that is,

$$\mathbf{W}(k+1) = \mathbf{W}(k) + \Lambda\mathbf{X}(k)e(k), \qquad (5.3.23)$$

where e is as in (5.3.13) and $\mathbf{X}$ is defined in (5.3.11). A homogeneous error system can also be formed for this candidate adaptive IIR filter algorithm. Subtracting both sides of (5.3.23) from $\mathbf{W}^\circ$ and using (5.3.16) yields the error system

$$\mathbf{V}(k+1) = \mathbf{V}(k) - \Lambda\mathbf{X}(k)\{[1 - A(q^{-1})]^{-1}[\mathbf{X}^t(k)\mathbf{V}(k)]\}. \qquad (5.3.24)$$

With the entries of Λ suitably small, the rate of time-variation $\mathbf{V}$ can be severely limited, such that the time scales of $\mathbf{X}$ and $\mathbf{V}$ can be decoupled such that

$$[1 - A(q^{-1})]^{-1}[\mathbf{X}^t(k)\mathbf{V}(k)] \approx [1 - A(q^{-1})]^{-1}[\mathbf{X}^t(k)]\mathbf{V}(k) \qquad (5.3.25)$$

for lowpass $[1 - A]^{-1}$. Recall that the pragmatic presumption of the utilization of a small step size was also exploited in Section 5.2 to promote a useful recursive approximator of the sensitivity function in the stochastic gradient. Using the approximation in (5.3.25) rewrites (5.3.24) as

$$\mathbf{V}(k+1) = \{I - \Lambda\mathbf{X}(k)[1 - A(q^{-1})]^{-1}[\mathbf{X}^t(k)]\}\mathbf{V}(k). \qquad (5.3.26)$$

As a homogeneous error system, (5.3.26) can be subjected to stability analysis similar to that described previously for the homogeneous error system in (5.3.19) associated with direct-form FIR filter adaptation using LMS. While the difference in the definitions of $\mathbf{X}$ results in different implications of various conditions, such as the meaning of the associated persistent excitation conditions [Anderson and Johnson, 1982a], the primary distinction is the presence of $[1 - A(q^{-1})]^{-1}$ in (5.3.26) that is absent in (5.3.19). However, if $[1 - A(q^{-1})]^{-1}$ were unity over all of the frequencies present in the spectra of the entries in $\mathbf{X}$, then (5.3.26) and (5.3.19) would have the same form. Thus, $[1 - A(q^{-1})]^{-1}$ need not be exactly unity for (5.3.24) to exhibit the desirable behavioral properties of (5.3.19). Indeed, if $[1 - A(q^{-1})]^{-1}$ has no phase shift out-side $(-\frac{\pi}{2}, \frac{\pi}{2})$ for any frequency component of $\mathbf{X}$, then stability/convergence can be assured. In fact, if the energy in the frequencies for which the phase of $[1 - A(q^{-1})]^{-1}$ is inside $(-\frac{\pi}{2}, \frac{\pi}{2})$ suitably dominates that in all other frequencies, stability/convergence can be proved [Anderson et al., 1986] [Bitmead and Johnson, 1987]. Other conditions on the input, such as sufficient instantaneous power of the regressor vector [Tomizuka, 1982] [Lawrence and Johnson, 1986], can be used to achieve the desired stability/convergence.

5.3.2 Error Filtering

Because foreknowledge of the spectral distribution of the regressor $\mathbf{X}$ may not be adequately proscribed prior to adaptive filter operation, we may wish to rely on satisfaction by the unknown desired denominator of the phase constraint to within $(-\frac{\pi}{2}, \frac{\pi}{2})$ across all frequencies, also known as a strictly positive real (SPR) condition on $[1 - A(q^{-1})]^{-1}$. This is generally quite impractical. Furthermore, as indicated by a simulated example in Larimore et al. [1980], without satisfaction of this SPR condition, unacceptable misbehavior can result in otherwise ideal circumstances. This prompts the concept of altering the adaptation algorithm of (5.3.23) to modify this condition to something more under the control of the designer given suitable *a priori* information. For example, if we use the filtered error

$$v(k) = e(k) + \sum_{i=1}^{n} g_i e(k - i) \tag{5.3.27}$$

in (5.3.23) in place of e, the homogeneous error system of (5.3.26) becomes

$$\mathbf{V}(k + 1) = \{I - \Lambda \mathbf{X}(k)[H(q^{-1})][\mathbf{X}^t(k)]\}\mathbf{V}(k) \tag{5.3.28}$$

where

$$H(q^{-1}) = \frac{1 + \sum_{i=1}^{n} g_i q^{-i}}{1 - \sum_{i=1}^{n} a_i q^{-i}}. \tag{5.3.29}$$

With enough, but less than exact, foreknowledge of the a_i, the g_i could be chosen (e.g., to approximate the $-a_i$) so $H(q^{-1})$ is suitably close to unity (e.g., retaining its phase within $(-\frac{\pi}{2}, \frac{\pi}{2})$) for the dominant frequencies in $\mathbf{X}$.

Thus, we have suggested a second adaptive IIR filter algorithm elaboration (i.e., fixed-error filtering) relative to the regressor and prediction error product of the update kernel used by LMS for direct-form FIR filter parameter adaptation. Previously, in Section 5.2, we extracted time-varying regressor filtering as a suit-able modification. This raises the possibilities of time-varying error filtering and fixed regressor filtering with the filters chosen in an attempt to return the under-lying error system to the robust, stable form associated with LMS for direct-form FIR filter parameter adaptation. These four possibilities are summarized in the next section.

5.4 FILTERED-ERROR AND FILTERED-REGRESSOR ALGORITHMS

The identification format in Section 5.3 revealed that the significant difference between adaptive FIR and IIR filters is the inclusion of a nonunity operator on the information vector and parameter error vector inner product generating the prediction error (refer to (5.3.16)). This difference has a substantial impact on the development of adaptive IIR filter algorithms, as indicated in Sections 5.2 and 5.3. Essentially, the information vector and prediction error product forming the update kernel in the adaptive law of adaptive FIR filters must be augmented and/or the information vector class restricted to compensate for this adaptive IIR filter prediction error operator.

More specifically, in the case where the difference between the desired signal and the adaptive filter output $d - y$ is a filtered version of the information vector $\mathbf{X}$ and the parameter error vector $\mathbf{V}$, that is, $F(q^{-1})[\mathbf{X}^t(k)\mathbf{V}(k)]$, plus an unremovable portion, we have isolated two possible algorithm forms, i.e., using regressor filtering

$$\mathbf{W}(k+1) = \mathbf{W}(k) + \Lambda\{L(q^{-1}, k)[\mathbf{X}(k)]\}\{d(k) - y(k)\} \qquad (5.4.1)$$

and using error filtering

$$\mathbf{W}(k+1) = \mathbf{W}(k) + \Lambda\{\bar{\mathbf{X}}(k)\}\{M(q^{-1}, k)[d(k) - y(k)]\}. \qquad (5.4.2)$$

We have also seen that the filter $F(q^{-1})$ in the prediction error can be composed of unknown desired signal generator parameters (i.e., a subset of $\mathbf{W}^\circ$).

In Section 5.2, using a gradient descent development of a candidate algorithm, we generated a candidate algorithm of the form of (5.4.1), where the appropriate subset of $\mathbf{W}(k)$ was used to parameterize $L(q^{-1})$ as our current estimate of $F(q^{-1})$. In other words, convergence ensued as

$$L^{-1}(q^{-1}, k)F(q^{-1}) \to 1, \quad \text{as } k \to \infty. \qquad (5.4.3)$$

In Section 5.3, by calling on nonlinear system stability theory, we supported convergent behavior when M was fixed in (5.4.2) and

$$M(q^{-1})F(q^{-1}) \approx 1. \qquad (5.4.4)$$

$M(q^{-1})F(q^{-1})$ being SPR proves sufficient. This suggested two additional possibilities, as noted at the close of Section 5.3: selecting a fixed L such that LF is ≈ 1 or using $\mathbf{W}(k)$ to appropriately parameterize a time-varying M such that $M(q^{-1}, k)F(q^{-1}) \to 1$.

Using small step sizes, appropriate in most data-rich adaptive signal-processing applications, we have arrived at the statement of four candidate algorithms for the updating of the parameters used in forming the adaptive IIR filter output

$$y(k) = \sum_{i=1}^{n} a_i(k)y(k-i) + \sum_{j=0}^{m} b_j(k)x(k-j). \qquad (5.4.5)$$

Recall that, with d formed by a similar IIR model as in (5.3.1), $F(q^{-1})$ is $[1 - A(q^{-1})]^{-1}$. To write the parameter update laws individually for each $a_i(\cdot)$ and

$b_j(\cdot)$, we select Λ as a diagonal matrix as in (5.2.17), as is commonly done. Thus, the four algorithms are as follows:

Algorithm 1:

$$a_i(k+1) = a_i(k) + \mu_i y^F(k-i)[d(k) - y(k)] \tag{5.4.6}$$

$$y^F(k) = y(k) + \sum_{i=1}^{n} a_i(k) y^F(k-i) \tag{5.4.7}$$

$$b_j(k+1) = b_j(k) + \rho_j x^F(k-j)[d(k) - y(k)] \tag{5.4.8}$$

$$x^F(k) = x(k) + \sum_{i=1}^{n} a_i(k) x^F(k-i). \tag{5.4.9}$$

Algorithm 2:

$$a_i(k+1) = a_i(k) + \mu_i y^F(k-i)[d(k) - y(k)] \tag{5.4.10}$$

$$y^F(k) = y(k) + \sum_{i=1}^{n} \alpha_i y^F(k-i) \tag{5.4.11}$$

$$b_j(k+1) = b_j(k) + \rho_j x^F(k-j)[d(k) - y(k)] \tag{5.4.12}$$

$$x^F(k) = x(k) + \sum_{i=1}^{n} \alpha_i x^F(k-i). \tag{5.4.13}$$

Algorithm 3:

$$a_i(k+1) = a_i(k) + \mu_i y(k-i)v(k) \tag{5.4.14}$$
$$b_j(k+1) = b_j(k) + \rho_j x(k-j)v(k) \tag{5.4.15}$$

$$v(k) = d(k) - y(k) - \sum_{i=1}^{n} \alpha_i[d(k-i) - y(k-i)]. \tag{5.4.16}$$

Algorithm 4:

$$a_i(k+1) = a_i(k) + \mu_i y(k-i)v(k) \tag{5.4.17}$$
$$b_j(k+1) = b_j(k) + \rho_j x(k-j)v(k) \tag{5.4.18}$$

$$v(k) = d(k) - y(k) - \sum_{i=1}^{n} a_i(k)[d(k-i) - y(k-i)]. \tag{5.4.19}$$

Algorithm 1 is the gradient-descent-based algorithm of Section 5.2 using the simplified time-varying autoregressive filtering of the information vector of Section 5.2. As noted in Section 5.2.2, assurance of local convergence of Algorithm 1 can require a stability check and projection facility on the polynomial $1 - \sum_{i=1}^{n} a_i(k+1)q^{-i}$.

Algorithm 2 is a variant of the gradient-descent-based algorithm of Section 5.2, also using a simplified form of the autoregressive filtering of the information vector, but with fixed parameters. Based on the discussion in Section 5.3.1, we predicate local convergence on conditions dependent on the desired autoregressive parameterization a_i° (i.e., the transfer function $[1 - \sum_{i=1}^n \alpha_i q^{-i}]/[1 - \sum_{i=1}^n a_i^\circ q^{-i}]$ should suitably approximate unity, which it does if $\alpha_i \approx a_i^\circ$).

Algorithm 3 is derived from the nonlinear system stability theory approach of Section 5.3 and uses a time-invariant moving-average filtering of the prediction error rather than the autoregressive information vector filtering of Algorithms 1 and 2. Local convergence should result with the same operator condition associated with Algorithm 2.

Algorithm 4 uses a time-varying moving-average filtering of the prediction error that is subject to the same stability check and projection facility as Algorithm 1 to avoid masking explosion of $d - y$.

What should be emphasized here is that these four algorithms are the logical outgrowth of the pedagogy established in this chapter. This pedagogy blends the gradient descent and average squared error minimization concepts traditionally associated with adaptive filtering, as detailed in Chapters 3 and 4, and the nonlinear system stability theory concepts exploited in recursive system identification [Ljung and Söderström, 1983], adaptive control [Goodwin and Sin, 1984], and subsequent treatises on adaptive parameter estimation systems theory [Anderson et al., 1986] [Benveniste et al., 1990] [Solo and Kong, 1995] [Mareels and Polderman, 1996].

5.5 STEIGLITZ-McBRIDE ALGORITHM

By this point we have established that the identification format of adaptive IIR filtering results in a prediction error that can be interpreted as a filtered version of the parameter error vector and regressor vector inner product. For example, see (5.3.16). Furthermore, appropriate behavior of the adaptive IIR filter parameter adjustment laws can be achieved with the addition of regressor and/or error filtering to return the error system to the robust form associated with a LMS-style update for a direct-form FIR filter. For example, refer to (5.4.6)–(5.4.19).

As we illustrate in this section, a different manipulation of the prediction error can result in a filtered version of the parameter error vector and regressor (or information) vector inner product, but with a different definition of the key information vector. Not only is this exercise pedagogically revealing, but it also leads to an algorithm that can offer [Regalia, 1995] greater robustness in reduced-order situations where the identifier model is of lower order than the system being identified.

More specifically, recall the adapted IIR model

$$y(k) = \sum_{i=1}^n a_i(k)y(k-i) + \sum_{j=0}^m b_j(k)x(k-j) \qquad (5.5.1)$$

and the presumed model generating the desired signal

$$d(k) = \sum_{i=1}^N a_i^\circ d(k-i) + \sum_{j=0}^m b_j^\circ x(k-j). \qquad (5.5.2)$$

The prediction error $e = d - y$ can be conveniently manipulated by adding zero as $\sum a_i^\circ y(k-i) - \sum a_i^\circ y(k-i)$, as was done in (5.3.13)–(5.3.16), so that

$$
e(k) = \left[\sum_{i=1}^{n} a_i^\circ d(k-i) + \sum_{j=0}^{m} b_j^\circ x(k-j) \right]
$$

$$
- \left[\sum_{i=1}^{n} a_i(k)y(k-i) + \sum_{j=0}^{m} b_j(k)x(k-j) \right]
$$

$$
+ \left[\sum_{i=1}^{n} a_i^\circ y(k-i) - \sum_{i=1}^{n} a_i^\circ y(k-i) \right]
$$

$$
= \sum_{i=1}^{n} a_i^\circ [d(k-i) - y(k-i)] + \sum_{i=1}^{n} [a_i^\circ - a_i(k)]y(k-i)
$$

$$
+ \sum_{j=0}^{m} [b_j^\circ - b_j(k)]x(k-j). \tag{5.5.3}
$$

With definition of

$$
\mathbf{X}(k) = [y(k-1) \quad \cdots \quad y(k-n) \ x(k) \quad \cdots \quad x(k-m)]^t \tag{5.5.4}
$$

and

$$
\mathbf{V}(k) = [a_1^\circ - a_1(k) \quad \cdots \quad a_n^\circ - a_n(k) \quad b_0^\circ - b_0(k) \quad \cdots \quad b_m^\circ - b_m(k)]^t, \tag{5.5.5}
$$

(5.5.3) can be rewritten as

$$
e(k) - \sum_{i=1}^{n} a_i^\circ e(k-i) = \mathbf{X}^T(k)\mathbf{V}(k) \tag{5.5.6}
$$

or

$$
e(k) = H(a_i^\circ, q^{-1})[\mathbf{X}^t(k)\mathbf{V}(k)], \tag{5.5.7}
$$

where

$$
H(a_i^\circ, q^{-1}) = \frac{1}{1 - \sum_{i=1}^{n} a_i^\circ q^{-i}}. \tag{5.5.8}
$$

As discussed in Section 5.4, two basic adaptive algorithms utilizing a prediction error of the form of (5.5.7) use either regressor filtering or error filtering.

Now return to (5.5.3) and consider adding $\sum_{i=1}^{n} a_i(k)d(k-i) - \sum_{i=1}^{n} a_i(k)d(k-i)$. This converts (5.5.3) to

$$
\begin{aligned}
e(k) &= \left[\sum_{i=1}^{n} a_i^{\circ} d(k-i) + \sum_{j=0}^{m} b_j^{\circ} x(k-j) \right] \\
&\quad - \left[\sum_{i=1}^{n} a_i(k)y(k-i) + \sum_{j=0}^{m} b_j(k)x(k-j) \right] \\
&\quad + \left[\sum_{i=1}^{n} a_i(k)d(k-i) - \sum_{i=1}^{n} a_i(k)d(k-i) \right] \\
&= \sum_{i=1}^{n} a_i(k)[d(k-i) - y(k-i)] + \sum_{i=1}^{n} [a_i^{\circ} - a_i(k)]d(k-i) \\
&\quad + \sum_{j=0}^{m} [b_j^{\circ} - b_j(k)]x(k-j).
\end{aligned}
\tag{5.5.9}
$$

With definition of

$$
\mathbf{X}(k) = [d(k-1) \quad \cdots \quad d(k-n) \; x(k) \quad \cdots \quad x(k-m)]^t
\tag{5.5.10}
$$

and

$$
\mathbf{V}(k) = [a_1 - a_1(k) \quad \cdots \quad a_n - a_n(k) \quad b_0 - b_0(k) \quad \cdots \quad b_m - b_m(k)]^t,
\tag{5.5.11}
$$

(5.5.9) can be rewritten as

$$
e(k) - \sum_{i=1}^{n} a_i(k)e(k-i) = \mathbf{X}^t(k)\mathbf{V}(k),
\tag{5.5.12}
$$

or more compactly as

$$
e(k) = H(a_i(k), q^{-1})[\mathbf{X}^t(k)\mathbf{V}(k)]
\tag{5.5.13}
$$

where

$$
H(a_i(k), q^{-1}) = \frac{1}{1 - \sum_{i=1}^{n} a_i(k)q^{-i}}.
\tag{5.5.14}
$$

Note that the $\mathbf{X}$ vector in (5.5.10) includes past values of the desired signal d (and present and past inputs u) while the $\mathbf{X}$ in (5.5.4) includes past adaptive filter outputs y. Another distinction between the prediction error of (5.5.12) and that of (5.5.6) is that the filter operating on the inner product of $\mathbf{X}$ and the parameter error vector $\mathbf{V}$ in (5.5.12) has a known parameterization (i.e., our estimates of the desired denominator coefficients) while in (5.5.6) the parameterization of H is unknown (i.e., the desired denominator coefficients that we seek to identify). This latter observation is significant for the basic algorithms of Section 5.4.

The two basic algorithm forms for updating the parameter vector

$$\mathbf{W}(k) = [a_1(k) \ \cdots \ a_n(k) \ b_0(k) \ \cdots \ b_m(k)]^t \tag{5.5.15}$$

employing regressor or error filtering to utilize a prediction error of the form of (5.5.13) as the performance assessment can be written as

$$\mathbf{W}(k+1) = \mathbf{W}(k) + \mu \mathbf{\Psi}(k) e(k) \tag{5.5.16}$$

where

$$\mathbf{\Psi}(k) = H(a_i(k), q^{-1})[\mathbf{X}(k)] = \mathbf{X}(k) + \sum_{i=1}^{n} a_i(k) \mathbf{\Psi}(k-i), \tag{5.5.17}$$

or

$$\mathbf{W}(k+1) = \mathbf{W}(k) + \mu \mathbf{X}(k) v(k) \tag{5.5.18}$$

where

$$v(k) = H^{-1}(a_i(k), q^{-1})[e(k)] = e(k) - \sum_{i=1}^{n} a_i(k) e(k-i). \tag{5.5.19}$$

The algorithm in (5.5.16)–(5.5.17) was originally formulated via a different paradigm in Steiglitz and McBride [1965]. An interpretation of (5.5.16)–(5.5.17) that is closer to that put forth in Steiglitz and McBride [1965] can be extracted from the error system diagram in Figure 5.5. The path from x to y replicates (5.5.1). The path from d to e can be seen to reduce to a unity operator, which reveals that e is indeed $d - y$. However, we now view the portion inside the dashed box in Figure 5.5 as a linear combiner as discussed in Chapter 2. The entries in $\mathbf{\Psi}$ of (5.5.17) defined as filtered versions of y and x (i.e., y^F and x^F), similar to the reduced complexity gradient approximations in (5.4.7) and (5.4.9), can be viewed as inputs to the linear combiner. Thus, the adaptive laws for adjusting the $a_i(k)$ and $b_j(k)$ driven by e would use an update term that was simply y^F or x^F times the associated prediction error e (with y^F effectively playing the role of the desired signal). This is the form of (5.5.16)–(5.5.17) (with some loose play with the fact that the operators are time-varying that can be more formally justified under our standard small step size assumption).

A comprehensive discussion of the behavior of the Steiglitz–McBride algorithm in relation to the squared output error stochastic gradient descent regressor-filtering algorithm of Section 5.2 and the stability theory based error filtering schemes of Section 5.3 appears in Regalia [1995]. Basically, when e can be made very small so y closely matches d, the information vector in (5.5.10) closely matches that in (5.5.4) and the behavior of the algorithms in (5.5.16)–(5.5.19) closely matches their counterparts in (5.4.6)–(5.4.9) and (5.4.17)–(5.4.19). However, when the parameters $a_i(k)$ and $b_j(k)$ cannot be chosen to make y closely match d, the convergence "points" of the algorithms in (5.4.6)–(5.4.9) and (5.4.17)–(5.4.19) (both of which use an information vector composed from y and x) and of the algorithms in (5.5.16)–(5.5.19) (which use an information vector composed from d and x) can be quite different.

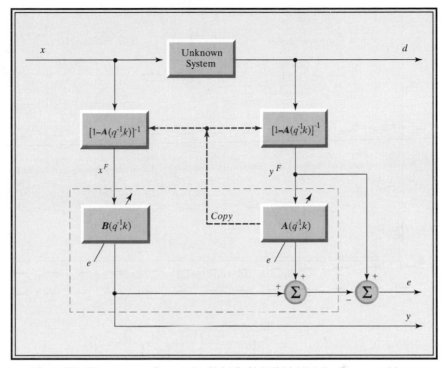

Figure 5.5   Error system diagram for (5.5.16)–(5.5.17) highlighting linear combiner extraction.

5.6 IIR WHITENER

Consider the system described by Figure 5.6. The observed signal is presumed to be a colored noise generated by passing a white noise w through an IIR filter with transfer function $[1 + C^\circ(q^{-1})]/[1 - A^\circ(q^{-1})]$. We cannot measure w; we can only measure y. Our objective is to whiten y, thereby hopefully recovering w. As illustrated in Figure 5.6, this is to be accomplished by filtering d. The particular structure of the whitening filter in Figure 5.6 is that employed by the encoder in the G.721 standard for adaptive differential pulse code modulation [Jayant and Noll, 1984] used, for example, in cordless telephone systems [Rappaport, 1996].

To see that this structure does the job, assume C and A are fixed and reduce the block diagram of the whitening filter by first reducing the feedback path from e to y as

$$y(k) = C(q^{-1})[e(k)] + A(q^{-1})[e(k) + y(k)] \tag{5.6.1}$$

or

$$[1 - A(q^{-1})][y(k)] = [C(q^{-1}) + A(q^{-1})][e(k)] \tag{5.6.2}$$

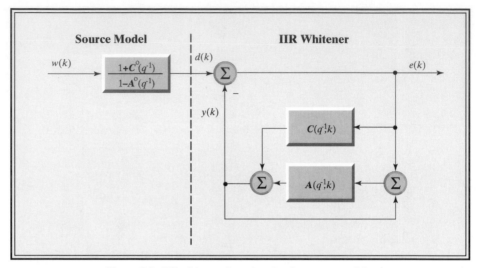

Figure 5.6   IIR whitener for colored noise source model.

or

$$y(k) = \frac{C(q^{-1}) + A(q^{-1})}{1 - A(q^{-1})}[e(k)]. \tag{5.6.3}$$

The transfer function from d to e in Figure 5.6 is the inverse of the sum of 1 and the transfer function from $e(k)$ to $y(k)$; that is,

$$e(k) = \frac{1}{1 + \left[\frac{C(q^{-1}) + A(q^{-1})}{1 - A(q^{-1})}\right]}[y(k)]$$

$$= \frac{1 - A(q^{-1})}{1 - A(q^{-1}) + C(q^{-1}) + A(q^{-1})}[y(k)] = \frac{1 - A(q^{-1})}{1 + C(q^{-1})}[y(k)]. \tag{5.6.4}$$

If A matches A° and $1 + C$ matches $1 + C^{\circ}$, the transfer function from d to e is the inverse of the transfer function generating d from w such that the transfer function from w to e is unity. Thus, e matches w and y has been whitened as desired.

With $e = d - y$ as the prediction error of interest, we follow our strategy of establishing the relationship between this observed prediction error and the parameter errors between the coefficients of A° and A and between C° and C. With the received signal

$$d(k) = \sum_{i=1}^{n} a_i^{\circ} d(k - i) + \sum_{j=1}^{m} c_j^{\circ} w(k - j) + w(k), \tag{5.6.5}$$

the prediction

$$y(k) = \sum_{i=1}^{n} a_i(k)[y(k - i) + e(k - i)] + \sum_{j=1}^{m} c_j(k)e(k - j) \tag{5.6.6}$$

that is fed back, and the relationship of d, y, and e

$$e(k) = d(k) - y(k) \implies d(k) = e(k) + y(k), \tag{5.6.7}$$

the prediction error can be written as

$$e(k) = \sum_{i=1}^{n} a_i^\circ d(k-i) + \sum_{j=1}^{m} c_j^\circ w(k-j) + w(k) - \sum_{i=1}^{n} a_i(k)d(k-i)$$

$$- \sum_{j=1}^{m} c_j(k)e(k-j). \tag{5.6.8}$$

Now we can add zero (in the form $\sum_{j=1}^{m} c_j^\circ e(k-j) - \sum_{j=1}^{m} c_j^\circ e(k-j)$) to produce

$$e(k) = \sum_{i=1}^{n} [a_i^\circ - a_i(k)]d(k-i) + \sum_{j=1}^{m} [c_j^\circ - c_j(k)]e(k-j)]$$

$$- \sum_{j=1}^{m} c_j^\circ [e(k-j) - w(k-j)] + w(k) \tag{5.6.9}$$

or

$$e(k) - w(k) + \sum_{j=1}^{m} c_j^\circ [e(k-j) - w(k-j)] = \mathbf{X}^t(k)\mathbf{V}(k) \tag{5.6.10}$$

or

$$e(k) = H(q^{-1})[\mathbf{X}^t(k)\mathbf{V}(k)] + w(k) \tag{5.6.11}$$

where

$$H(q^{-1}) = \frac{1}{1 + \sum_{j=1}^{m} c_j^\circ q^{-j}}, \tag{5.6.12}$$

$$\mathbf{X}(k) = [d(k-1) \ \cdots \ d(k-n) \ e(k-1) \ \cdots \ e(k-m)]^t, \tag{5.6.13}$$

$$\mathbf{V}(k) = [a_1^\circ - a_1(k) \ \cdots \ a_n^\circ - a_n(k) \ c_1^\circ - c_1(k) \ \cdots \ c_m^\circ - c_m(k)]^t. \tag{5.6.14}$$

The error system in (5.6.11) is a forced-error system, rather than the unforced version introduced in Section 5.3, with a relatively benign "input" (i.e., zero-mean and white) which facilitates the mechanics of "average" behavior analysis [Ljung and Söderström, 1983] [Solo and Kong, 1995].

Having cast e in the form of $F(q^{-1})[\mathbf{X}^t(k)\mathbf{V}(k)]$ as in Section 5.4, one can envision counterparts of the algorithms in (5.4.6)–(5.4.19) with the appropriate translation of time-varying filtering by the approximation of F (i.e., H in (5.6.11) and (5.6.12)) or fixed filtering such that $L^{-1}F$ or MF is suitably close to unity. The resulting algorithms turn out to be special cases of those developed in the following section for a pole-zero input-output model with colored noise in the output measurement.

The "different version of zero" of the style used in the preceding section to produce the Steiglitz–McBride algorithm (i.e., $\sum_j c_j^\circ w(k-j) - \sum_j c_j^\circ w(k-j)$) cannot be used in this IIR whitener problem because this would require using the unmeasurable w in the information vector.

5.7 ARMAX MODELING

A more general difference equation model for a desired signal generator that ac-
knowledges the presence of unmeasurable signals is the autoregressive, moving-
average model with exogenous input (termed an *ARMAX model*)

$$d(k) = \sum_{i=1}^{n} a_i^\circ d(k-i) + \sum_{j=0}^{m} b_j^\circ x(k-j) + \sum_{s=1}^{p} c_s^\circ w(k-s) + w(k), \qquad (5.7.1)$$

where d is the measurable output, x the measurable input, and w a zero-mean, unmeasurable input. The model of (5.7.1) also accommodates, with parameterization
redundancy, the Box-Jenkins model of a desired signal as the sum of an IIR filtering of the measurable x and a different IIR filtering of the unmeasurable w. For
a presentation of the suitability of this ARMAX formulation to adaptive filtering
applications, refer to Friedlander [1982].

In constructing our adapted model of (5.7.1) we cannot simply append the term
$\sum_{s=1}^{p} c_s(k)w(k-s)$ to (5.4.5) because we cannot measure w. But notice that if we
could access w and if $a_i(k) = a_i$, $b_j(k) = b_j$, and $c_s(k) = c_s$ for all k and we used d
and not y on the right of (5.4.5), then the prediction error $e = d - y$ would equal w.
This observation suggests that e might be a useful replacement for w. In other words,
we consider estimating (5.7.1) via

$$y(k) = \sum_{i=1}^{n} a_i(k)d(k-i) + \sum_{j=0}^{m} b_j(k)x(k-j) + \sum_{s=1}^{p} c_s(k)e(k-s)$$

$$= \mathbf{X}^t(k)\mathbf{W}(k), \qquad (5.7.2)$$

where

$$e(k) = d(k) - y(k), \qquad (5.7.3)$$

$$\mathbf{W}(k) = [a_1(k) \quad \cdots \quad a_n(k) \; b_0(k) \quad \cdots \quad b_m(k) \; c_1(k) \quad \cdots \quad c_p(k)]^t, \qquad (5.7.4)$$

and

$$\mathbf{X}(k) = [d(k-1) \quad \cdots \quad d(k-n) \; x(k) \quad \cdots \quad x(k-m) \; e(k-1) \quad \cdots \quad e(k-p)]^t. \qquad (5.7.5)$$

We can rewrite the prediction error equation in (5.7.3), given (5.7.1) and (5.7.2), as

$$e(k) - w(k) = \sum_{i=1}^{n} [a_i^\circ - a_i(k)]d(k-i) + \sum_{j=0}^{m} [b_j^\circ - b_j(k)]x(k-j)$$

$$+ \sum_{s=1}^{p} [c_s^\circ - c_s(k)]e(k-s) - \sum_{s=1}^{p} c_s^\circ [e(k-s) - w(k-s)] \qquad (5.7.6)$$

or

$$e(k) = [1 + C^\circ(q^{-1})]^{-1}[\mathbf{X}^t(k)\mathbf{V}(k)] + w(k). \qquad (5.7.7)$$

Compare (5.7.7) with (5.5.7)–(5.5.8). One striking difference is that the autoregression operator on the information vector and parameter estimate error vector inner product is the noise polynomial $1 + C^\circ(q^{-1})$ in the desired signal generator of (5.7.1) rather than its autoregression polynomial $1 - A^\circ(q^{-1})$. This suggests changing the information vector filtering to $[1 + C(q^{-1}, k)]^{-1}$ in the gradient descent case or relying on the fact that $[1 + C^\circ(q^{-1})]^{-1}$ satisfactorily approximates unity for a stability-theory-based scheme. These modifications are proved to yield convergent algorithms in Söderström et al. [1978] and Solo [1979], respectively. For a thorough discussion of the basis of these claims and further elaboration of the associated algorithms, see Ljung and Söderström [1983] and Solo and Kong [1995].

A second distinction between (5.7.7) and (5.3.16) is that $e \neq 0$ in (5.7.7) when $\mathbf{V} = \mathbf{0}$, as it is in (5.3.16). Thus, with a small but nonvanishing step size, $\mathbf{W}$ does not converge to a point. This behavior is described by a forced, rather than unforced, error system. Given that the underlying unforced error system is exponentially stable due to persistent excitation by the regressor, the forced error system exhibits bounded-input, bounded-output behavior.

Another important observation regarding (5.7.2) is to explicitly recognize its IIR form. Given (5.7.3), we can rewrite (5.7.2) as

$$[1 + C(q^{-1}, k)]y(k) = [C(q^{-1}, k) + A(q^{-1}, k)]d(k) + [B(q^{-1}, k)]x(k), \qquad (5.7.8)$$

where $A(q^{-1}, k)$, $B(q^{-1}, k)$, and $C(q^{-1}, k)$ are appropriately defined. Thus, we recognize that (5.7.2), as written in (5.7.8), is a two-input (d and x), single-output (y) IIR filter. This matches the input-output behavior of the system-identifier structure in Figure 5.7.

Note that if $x(k) \equiv 0$ for all k and $d(k)$ is replaced by the equivalent $y(k) + e(k)$, (5.7.8) can be written as a single-input (e), single-output (y) IIR filter

$$[1 - A(q^{-1}, k+1)]y(k) = [C(q^{-1}, k+1) + A(q^{-1}, k+1)]e(k). \qquad (5.7.9)$$

This matches the structure of the IIR whitener in Figure 5.6.

Similar to the formation of Algorithms 1–4, for (5.7.2), four algorithms are possible given the realization that, with d approximated by a similar model as in (5.7.1), $F(q^{-1})$ in Section 5.4 is $[1 + C^\circ(q^{-1})]^{-1}$ as in (5.7.7). Recall that $e(k)$ as defined in (5.7.3) is $d(k) - y(k)$.

Regressor Filtering Algorithm:

$$a_i(k+1) = a_i(k) + \mu_i d^F(k-i)e(k) \qquad (5.7.10)$$

$$b_j(k+1) = b_j(k) + \rho_j x^F(k-j)e(k) \qquad (5.7.11)$$

$$c_s(k+1) = c_s(k) + \delta_s e^F(k-s)e(k) \qquad (5.7.12)$$

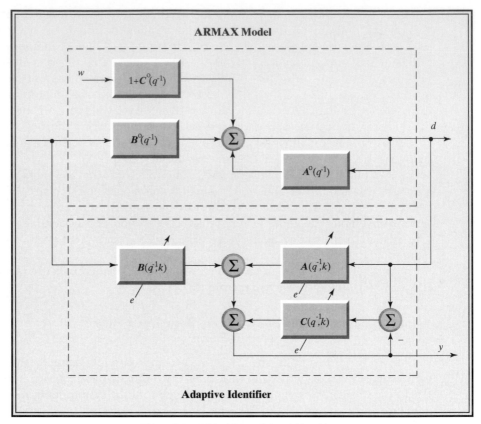

Figure 5.7   ARMAX model and identifier.

with either time-varying filtering

$$d^F(k) = d(k) - \sum_{s=1}^{p} c_s(k) d^F(k-s) \qquad (5.7.13)$$

$$x^F(k) = x(k) - \sum_{s=1}^{p} c_s(k) x^F(k-s) \qquad (5.7.14)$$

$$e^F(k) = e(k) - \sum_{s=1}^{p} c_s(k) e^F(k-s), \qquad (5.7.15)$$

or time-invariant filtering

$$d^F(k) = d(k) - \sum_{s=1}^{p} \gamma_s d^F(k-s) \qquad (5.7.16)$$

$$x^F(k) = x(k) - \sum_{s=1}^{p} \gamma_s x^F(k-s) \tag{5.7.17}$$

$$e^F(k) = e(k) - \sum_{s=1}^{p} \gamma_s e^F(k-s). \tag{5.7.18}$$

Error Filtering Algorithm:

$$a_i(k+1) = a_i(k) + \mu_i d(k-i)v(k) \tag{5.7.19}$$

$$b_j(k+1) = b_j(k) + \rho_j x(k-j)v(k) \tag{5.7.20}$$

$$c_s(k+1) = c_s(k) + \delta_s e(k-s)v(k) \tag{5.7.21}$$

with either time-invariant filtering

$$v(k) = e(k) + \sum_{s=1}^{p} \gamma_s e(k-s), \tag{5.7.22}$$

or time-varying filtering

$$v(k) = e(k) + \sum_{s=1}^{p} c_s(k)e(k-s). \tag{5.7.23}$$

Similar comments to those made for Algorithms 1–4 apply to these algorithms regarding stability checks and SPR conditions. The principal difference is that in these algorithms the stability check should be done on $[1 + C(q^{-1}, k+1)]^{-1}$ rather than $[1 - A(q^{-1}, k+1)]^{-1}$ as in Algorithms 1 and 4. Also, the operator constraint for these ARMAX identification algorithms should consider $[1 + \sum_{s=1}^{p} \gamma_s q^{-s}]/[1 + \sum_{s=1}^{p} c_s^o q^{-s}]$ rather than the transfer function $[1 - \sum_{i=1}^{n} \alpha_i q^{-1}]/[1 - \sum_{i=1}^{n} a_i^o q^{-i}]$ of concern for Algorithms 2 and 3.

5.8 SUMMARY

This chapter begins with the mission of converting our understanding (gained from the preceding chapter) of the fundamental LMS algorithm for adapting the parameters of a direct-form FIR filter to an ability to construct well-behaved algorithms for adapting the parameters of a direct-form IIR filter. A solution adding regressor filtering arose from a stochastic gradient descent view of mean squared prediction error minimization. Specialization of the adaptive IIR filter problem as an (output error) identification task proved revealing. In the direct-form FIR identification case, the basic LMS algorithm is

$$\mathbf{W}(k+1) = \mathbf{W}(k) + \mu \mathbf{X}(k)[d(k) - y(k)] \tag{5.8.1}$$

with

$$d(k) - y(k) = \mathbf{X}^t(k)\mathbf{V}(k). \tag{5.8.2}$$

where $\mathbf{V} (= \mathbf{W}^\circ - \mathbf{W})$ is the parameter error vector. In the direct-form IIR identification case

$$d(k) - y(k) = F(q^{-1})[\mathbf{X}^t(k)\mathbf{V}(k)]. \tag{5.8.3}$$

The addition of error $(d - y)$ filtering to (5.8.1) arose as a method of accommodating $F(q^{-1}) \neq 1$.

Combining the regressor filtering of (5.4.1) and the error filtering of (5.4.2) produces a filtered-regressor, filtered-error (FRFE) algorithm

$$\mathbf{W}(k + 1) = \mathbf{W}(k) + \Lambda\{L(q^{-1}, k)[\mathbf{X}(k)]\}\{M(q^{-1}, k)[d(k) - y(k)]\}. \tag{5.8.4}$$

By subtracting both sides of (5.8.4) from $\mathbf{W}^\circ$ and utilizing (5.8.3) with the small step size induced approximation in (5.3.25), we produce the homogeneous error system approximating the parameter error vector dynamics

$$\mathbf{V}(k + 1) \approx \{I - \Lambda\Phi(k)H(q^{-1}, k)[\Phi(k)]\}\mathbf{V}(k) \tag{5.8.5}$$

where

$$\Phi(k) = L(q^{-1}, k)[\mathbf{X}(k)] \tag{5.8.6}$$

and

$$H(q^{-1}, k) = \frac{M(q^{-1}, k)F(q^{-1}, k)}{L(q^{-1}, k)}. \tag{5.8.7}$$

Robust behavior relies on persistent excitation by Φ and proximity to unity by $\frac{MF}{L}$. As with the expected-moment analysis in Section 4.2.3, the setting of $\mathbf{W}$ that causes the average of the update term kernel $\{\Phi(k)H(q^{-1}, k)[\Phi(k)]\}\mathbf{V}(k)$ to be zero is an average stationary point. The formula is nonlinear in $\mathbf{W}$ for a direct-form IIR filter due to the inclusion of $\mathbf{W}$ in $\mathbf{V} = \mathbf{W}^\circ - \mathbf{W}$ and in calculating Φ from $\mathbf{X}$, which includes y produced from x through $\mathbf{W}$. In the vicinity of the stationary point $\mathbf{W}^*$, which results in $\mathbf{X}|_{\mathbf{W}=\mathbf{W}^*} = \mathbf{X}^*$, if the average of $\Phi H[\Phi]|_{(\mathbf{W}=\mathbf{W}^*, \mathbf{X}=\mathbf{X}^*)}$ plus its transpose is positive definite, local stability ensues [Sethares et al., 1989]. An $H \approx 1$ satisfies this condition.

One could ask various questions concerning extension of the underlying approach of selection of M and L to cause $MFL^{-1} \approx 1$. For example, what happens if the scalar (i.e., single-input, single-output) transfer function MFL^{-1} becomes a transfer function matrix? Such cases do occur with other alternative realizations [Williamson et al., 1991a].

A basic message of this chapter is that adaptive algorithm candidate fabrication for filters with realizations other than a direct-form FIR can be addressed through an identification setting analysis. The key is to establish the format of the connection of the regressor $\mathbf{X}$ and parameter error vector $\mathbf{V}$ to the observed prediction error $d - y$. Modifications of the adaptation algorithm, such as regressor filtering or error filtering, are contemplated for their ability to return the error system dynamics back toward the form of the direct-FIR—or linear combiner—case. This chapter illustrates this approach by consideration of a direct-form IIR filter realization. This approach can be extended, as noted in Williamson et al. [1991a,b] to other alternative realizations.

This chapter addresses the issue of altering the filter realization in Figure 5.4. The next chapter addresses the issue of altering the quality assessment component of Figure 5.4, especially to accommodate an inability to observe the desired signal.

5.9 PROBLEMS

1. Consider the following identification style scenario. The adaptive IIR filter producing

$$y(k) = a(k)y(k-1) + x(k-1) \qquad (5.9.1)$$

has only one adjustable parameter. The adaptive filter output y is meant to track the similarly composed desired signal

$$d(k) = a^\circ d(k-1) + x(k-1). \qquad (5.9.2)$$

(a) Write $e(k) = d(k) - y(k)$ as a function of $[a^\circ - a(k)]y(k-1)$ and past e.
(b) Write a filtered error adaptive algorithm for $a(k)$ in (5.9.1). Comment on conditions on $\{x\}$ and any designer-selected variables assuring convergence of $a(k)$ to a°. Confirm with simulations.
(c) Write a filtered regressor adaptive algorithm for $a(k)$ in (5.9.1). Comment on conditions on $\{x\}$ and any designer-selected variables assuring convergence of $a(k)$ to a°. Confirm with simulations.
(d) Write a Steiglitz-McBride style adaptive algorithm for $a(k)$ in (5.9.1). Comment on the conditions on $\{x\}$ and any designer-selected variables assuring convergence of $a(k)$ to a°. Confirm with simulations.
(e) Add white, zero-mean noise w to d observation so

$$e(k) = d(k) + w(k) - y(k) \qquad (5.9.3)$$

and test the three algorithms of parts (b)–(d).
(f) Increase the order of d generation to

$$d(k) = a_1^\circ d(k-1) + a_2^\circ d(k-2) + x(k-1) \qquad (5.9.4)$$

and test the three algorithms of parts (b)–(d) using first-order generation of y.

2. Consider the first-order adaptive IIR filter

$$y(k) = a(k)y(k-1) + b(k)x(k-1), \qquad (5.9.5)$$

the output of which is attempting to track the desired signal generated by

$$d(k) = a^\circ d(k-1) + b^\circ x(k-1). \qquad (5.9.6)$$

(Hint: Refer to Johnson et al. [1981].)
(a) Write a well-documented MATLAB program that simulates the first-order adaptive IIR filter of (5.9.5) and forms the filtered error of

$$v(k) = d(k) - y(k) + c[d(k-1) - y(k-1)] \qquad (5.9.7)$$

with respect to the first-order IIR system of (5.9.6). The coefficients of the adaptive filter of (5.9.5) should be updated via

$$a(k+1) = a(k) + \mu y(k-1)v(k) \qquad (5.9.8)$$

$$b(k+1) = b(k) + \rho x(k-1)v(k). \qquad (5.9.9)$$

Compose $\{x\}$ as a white, zero-mean sequence with samples drawn from a uniform distribution ranging from -0.5 to 0.5. Select appropriate step sizes μ and ρ and the error filtering coefficient c and confirm that your program results in convergence to(ward) zero of the squared prediction error $[d(k) - y(k)]^2$.

(b) With $a° = 0.75$ and $b° = 1.0$ and step sizes μ and ρ resulting in relatively smooth trajectories, draw several trajectories for $(a(\cdot), b(\cdot))$ beginning at several different equally spaced points on a circle of radius 0.025 about $(a°, b°)$.

(c) Relate the average system behavior revealed in part (b) to part c of problem 4 in Chapter 4 and use the eigenstructure of the average outer product of the regressor and appropriately filtered regressor at convergence to explain the simulated spirals.

3. The description of the prediction error for the IIR whitener in (5.6.11)–(5.6.12) identifies the numerator of the coloration filter as the denominator of the transfer function to be compensated for by regressor and/or error filtering. For a second-order IIR whitener, as in Figure 5.6,

$$C(q^{-1}, k) = c_1(k)q^{-1} + c_2(k)q^{-2} \tag{5.9.10}$$

and

$$A(q^{-1}, k) = a_1(k)q^{-1} + a_2(k)q^{-2}. \tag{5.9.11}$$

(a) For a second-order source model and whitener with $n = m = 2$ in (5.6.5)–(5.6.6) write separate formulas for the updates of all four adapted parameters and for any constituent signals, such as filtered errors, not directly measured for the counterpart to Algorithm 1 in (5.4.6)–(5.4.9). What ratio of polynomials needs to adequately approximate 1 to achieve desired (local) convergence? How can this condition be encouraged via designer-selected variables in the adaptive algorithm?

(b) Repeat part (a) for the counterpart of Algorithm 2 in (5.4.10)–(5.4.13). What ratio of polynomials needs to adequately approximate 1 to achieve desired (local) convergence? How can this condition be encouraged via designer-selected variables in the adaptive algorithm?

(c) Repeat part (a) for the counterpart of Algorithm 3 in (5.4.14)–(5.4.16). What ratio of polynomials needs to adequately approximate 1 to achieve desired (local) convergence? How can this condition be encouraged via designer-selected variables in the adaptive algorithm?

(d) Repeat part (a) for the counterpart of Algorithm 4 in (5.4.17)–(5.4.19). What ratio of polynomials needs to adequately approximate 1 to achieve desired (local) convergence? How can this condition be encouraged via designer-selected variables in the adaptive algorithm?

(e) Via simulation test the local stability of each of these adaptive second-order IIR whiteners in parts (a)–(d) for sufficiently small step sizes. Comment on the satisfaction of the associated polynomial conditions.

4. Consider the noise-cancelling problem where the desired signal d is the signal s to be recovered plus a filtered (and therefore sequentially correlated or colored) version of a white, zero-mean noise n (uncorrelated with s)

$$d(k) = s(k) + \sum_{i=0}^{m_1} f_i n(k - i). \tag{5.9.12}$$

The input x to the adaptive filter is a differently filtered version of the same noise signal

$$x(k) = n(k) + \sum_{j=1}^{m_2} g_j n(k-j) \tag{5.9.13}$$

with all roots of $z_2^m - \sum_{j=1}^{m_2} g_j z^{(m_2-j)}$ strictly inside the unit circle in the z-plane. The adapted filter uses an IIR realization to produce its output

$$y(k) = \sum_{i=0}^{\ell} b_i(k)x(k-i) + \sum_{j=1}^{p} a_j(k)y(k-j). \tag{5.9.14}$$

The prediction error to be used to drive adaptation is

$$e(k) = d(k) - y(k). \tag{5.9.15}$$

(a) Compose a two-input (s and n), single-output (e) block diagram for this system.
(b) Select ℓ, p, b_i, and a_j in terms of m_1, m_2, f_i, and g_j such that the objective $e(k) = s(k)$ is perfectly met.
(c) Using the ℓ and p from part (b) and the b_i and a_j of part (b) as b_i° and a_j°, write $e(k)$ as a function of $\sum_{i=0}^{\ell}[b_i^{\circ} - b_i(k)]x(k-i) + \sum_{j=1}^{p}[a_j^{\circ} - a_j(k)]y(k-j)$.
(d) Given the format extracted for $e(k)$, propose a suitable algorithm for updating the b_i and a_j when the f_i and g_j are extracted to wiggle a bit but basically to remain fixed in location.
(e) Test the viability of the algorithm proposed in part (d) by simulation. Plot corresponding traces of x, s, and e that illustrate (re)start transient and steady-state behaviors. (Hint: Read Section V of Larimore et al. [1980].)

5. Consider the problem of active noise control in ducts, illustrated in Figure 5.8. The idea is to measure the sound pressure waveform at the detection microphone and to drive the speaker to replicate it with a phase reversal at the error microphone. The detection microphone signal x includes (i) the sound signal s and (ii) a filtered version of the speaker output y

$$x(k) = s(k) + \sum_{i=1}^{\ell} f_i y(k-i). \tag{5.9.16}$$

The error microphone signal e is presumed to include (i) a filtered version of the sound signal at the detection microphone due to the distance (and duct dynamics) between detection and error microphones and (ii) the speaker output with no filtering due to the relative proximity of speaker and error microphone

$$e(k) = y(k) + \sum_{j=0}^{m} g_j s(k-j). \tag{5.9.17}$$

An adaptive IIR filter is used to produce the speaker output

$$y(k) = \sum_{i=1}^{\ell} a_i(k-1)y(k-i) + \sum_{j=0}^{p} b_j(k-1)x(k-j). \tag{5.9.18}$$

(Hint: For context, refer to Jiang et al. [1997], or Section 6.15 of Nelson and Elliott [1992].)
(a) Compose a single-input (s), single-output (e) block diagram for this system.

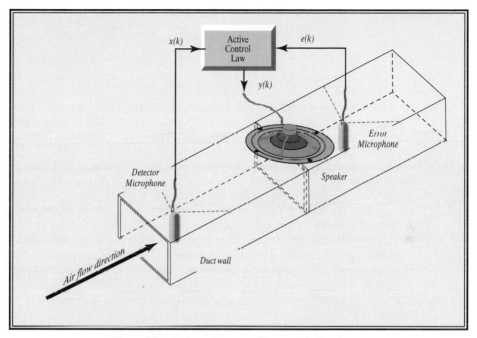

Figure 5.8   Active noise control in a ventilation duct.

(b) Select ℓ, p, b_i, and a_j in terms of n, m, f_i, and g_j such that the objective $e(k) = 0$ is perfectly met.

(c) Using the ℓ and p from part (b) and the b_i and a_j of part (b) as b_i° and a_j°, write $e(k)$ as a function of $\sum_{i=0}^{\ell}[b_i^\circ - b_i(k)]x(k-i) + \sum_{j=1}^{p}[a_j^\circ - a_j(k)]$.

(d) Given the format extracted for $e(k)$, propose a suitable algorithm for updating the b_i and a_j when the f_i and g_j are expected to wiggle a bit but basically to remain fixed in location.

(e) Test the viability of the algorithm proposed in part (d) by simulation. Plot corresponding traces of x, s, and e that illustrate (re)start transient and steady-state behaviors.

(f) In reality the path from the speaker to the error microphone has some dynamics, such that (5.9.16) becomes

$$x(k) = s(k) + \sum_{j=1}^{p} c_j s(k-j) + \sum_{i=1}^{\ell} f_i y(k-i). \qquad (5.9.19)$$

With $z^p + \sum_{j=1}^{p} c_j z^{(p-j)}$ having a phase shift between $-90°$ and $90°$ for all frequencies, propose an adaptive algorithm that would be (locally) stable to $b_j = p_j$ and $a_i = c_i - \sum_j f_j p_{i-j}$.

6. Consider the second-order (with distinct, real-valued poles), strictly causal, parallel IIR filter with input x and output y formed via

$$y(k) = v_1(k) + v_2(k) \qquad (5.9.20)$$

where

$$v_1(k) = a_1(k)v_1(k-1) + b_1(k)x(k-1) \qquad (5.9.21)$$

and

$$v_2(k) = a_2(k)v_2(k-1) + b_2(k)x(k-1). \qquad (5.9.22)$$

(a) Given the desired signal d, compose the block diagram describing the error system with inputs u and d and output $e\ (= d - y)$. This diagram should reveal the parallel structure of the model of the filter producing y from x.

(b) Using a stochastic gradient descent approach, similar to that of Section 5.2, compose an adaptive algorithm candidate for the parallel IIR model of (5.9.20)–(5.9.22)

(c) Confirm the (local) success with a simulation of the algorithm developed in part (b) that hovers about a local minimum.

(d) Because the labeling of one pole as a_1 and the other as a_2 is ambiguous (and can be reversed without effecting the output generated), the cost surface for (5.9.20)–(5.9.22) is multimodal. This means that different initializations can converge to different answers (although conceivably with the same mean-squared error performance). Illustrate this feature with simulations with different initializations and different convergence points. (Hint: Refer to Nayeri and Jenkins [1989], or Shynk [1989a].)

7. Consider the identification scenario for a bilinear IIR system generating the desired signal via

$$d(k) = a^\circ d(k-1) + b^\circ d(k-2)x(k-1) + c^\circ x(k-1) \qquad (5.9.23)$$

and the estimate of the desired signal provided via

$$y(k) = a(k)y(k-1) + b(k)y(k-2)x(k-1) + c(k)x(k-1). \qquad (5.9.24)$$

(a) For $e(k) = d(k) - y(k)$, derive an approximate stochastic gradient descent algorithm using a small step size for adapting $a(k)$, $b(k)$, and $c(k)$ to minimize $E[\frac{1}{2}e^2(k)]$. Use the same step size for updating $a(k)$, $b(k)$, and $c(k)$.

(b) For $a^\circ = 1$, $b^\circ = -0.7$, $c^\circ = 0.5$, and a zero-mean, white $\{x(k)\}$ drawn from a uniform distribution from -0.05 to 0.05, simulate the algorithm of part (a) with $a(0) = b(0) = c(0) = 0$ and approximate the range of the positive step size resulting in convergence of $a(k)$ to a°, $b(k)$ to b°, and $c(k)$ to c°.

6

Adaptive Algorithms for Restoring Signal Properties

• *Precis:* *Adaptive filtering algorithms can be developed that estimate some property of a signal and use it to guide the "training" of the filter instead of using a reference or template waveform. Such "property-restoring" algorithms can be very useful in applications in which a reference waveform is not available.*

6.1 INTRODUCTION

In Chapters 4 and 5, we developed a variety of algorithms for adapting the coefficients of a digital filter. These algorithms considered different filter structures (e.g., transversal FIR and direct-form IIR), used different algorithm construction and interpretation paradigms (e.g., summed squared error reduction and error system stability), and employed different update schemes (e.g., with and without regressor or prediction error filtering). The only aspect constant in the development of these algorithms was that of using the difference between the filter output and the desired or template signal as the prediction error, as illustrated in Figure 6.1.

The adaptive filter in Figure 6.1 contains three components. The first filters the input, the second forms the error $e(k)$, and the last adapts the filter coefficients. In the adaptive filters examined thus far, only the first and third components were allowed to change, but the simple form for the system error $e(k)$ as $d(k) - y(k)$ was maintained.

While the model assumed in Figure 6.1 allows an intuitively reasonable formulation for those algorithms, it suffers from the practical problem that a suitable reference signal $d(k)$ is often unavailable. This can be illustrated by reconsidering the troposcatter communications problem examined in Section 1.2 and shown again in the simple diagram in Figure 6.2.

A signal is sent via the "tropospheric channel" and is degraded in the process. Suppose that we consider using an adaptive filter at the receiver to correct this degradation and hence improve the quality of the received signal. The received signal, perhaps after tuning and bandpass filtering, is the input to the adaptive filter.

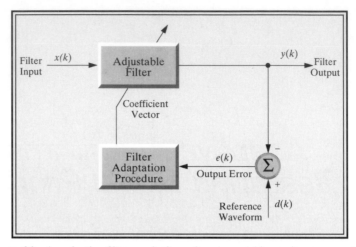

Figure 6.1   An adaptive filter employing reference matching as its assessment of performance.

The filter output is applied to the demodulator, as shown in Figure 6.2. Furthermore, as we engage the system, this equalizer is not adequately tuned to produce decisions that are correct sufficiently often. What, then, is used for the reference waveform $d(k)$? The signal we wish to have as the reference is the transmitted signal, a signal generated hundreds of miles away and in general unknown to the receiver. How then do we proceed?

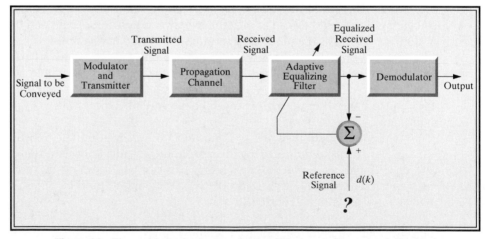

Figure 6.2   The problem of using an adaptive filter to equalize a signal dispersed by its propagation channel. How does one attain the reference waveform needed to guide the filter's adaptation?

6.2 CLASSICAL APPROACHES TO COPING WITH THE LACK OF A REFERENCE WAVEFORM

It turns out that the unavailability of the reference waveform is more the rule than the exception in the adaptive filtering field, and that many techniques have been developed to circumvent the problem. In the next section, we develop a class of algorithms that avoids a dependence on the "output error" $e(k)$ by judging the algorithm's performance in a more general way. But first, in this section, we examine some of the more classical approaches.

6.2.1 Using a Function of the Input Signal Itself as the Reference

One obvious approach is to use some function of the input signal itself as the reference waveform. An excellent, and simple, example of this is shown in Figure 6.3. This structure, often referred to as the *adaptive line enhancer* (ALE) [Widrow et al., 1975b] [Zeidler et al., 1978] [Treichler, 1979], uses the input signal itself as the reference signal and a delayed version of itself as the filter input. Using MMSE or MSSE techniques to minimize the error, the filter is adapted to become the best possible Δ-step predictor of the input signal, consistent with the constraints imposed by the filter itself (e.g., the duration of its pulse response).

This type of adaptive linear predictor is the basis for much work in the worlds of seismic processing [Robinson and Treitel, 1980] and speech compression [Jayant and Noll, 1984]. The name ALE accrues from its successful use in the extraction of

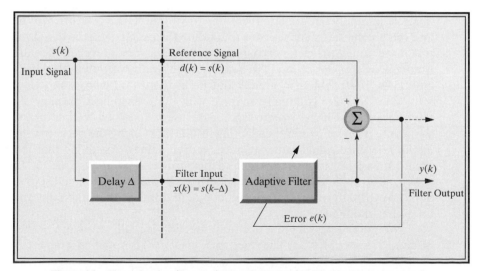

Figure 6.3   The Adaptive (Spectral) Line Enhancer (ALE). The input signal is delayed to construct the two required inputs to the adaptive filter.

spectral lines from very noisy inputs [Widrow et al., 1975b]. It has also been used to excise narrowband interference from wideband and spread-spectrum communications signals [Milstein, 1988]. A variety of filter realizations, including direct-form and lattice, FIR and IIR ones [Friedlander, 1982], and a constrained IIR one [Chang and Glover, 1993], have been studied in their use as ALEs.

The ALE is just one example of how the input signal itself or a function of it can be used to form the filter input and the reference signal. We see another example shortly. Before moving on, however, we note that the actual function to be used depends strongly on the specific application at hand and the characteristics of the input signal itself.

6.2.2 Prearrangement of a Suitable Reference Signal

An approach commonly used on point-to-point communication links is that of pre-arranging a signal to be used at both the transmitter and receiver to "train" the equalizer located at the receiving end of the link [Gersho, 1969]. When starting up the communications link, a "training signal" is transmitted for a preagreed duration. During this interval the receiver compares the equalizer's output with its own locally stored version of the prearranged signal. Differences between the two (i.e., the error signal) are used to drive the adaptive filter's coefficient adjustment algorithm. When the difference is zero, the equalizer has attained the required ability to compensate for the propagation channel's dispersion. Once the prearranged training duration is over, the transmitter begins sending the user's data and the receiver begins sending its output on to the receiving user.

While commonly used, this technique is problematic in a number of ways. Among the most important is that it works only for propagation channels that are unknown initially but are otherwise time-invariant. Once the equalizer has adapted and the transmitter switches over to sending the user's data, the equalizer's adaptation must stop. If the channel changes its characteristics, however, then the equalizer is no longer appropriate and the quality of the receiver's output declines, often precipitously. This problem is often dealt with as shown in Figure 6.4.

The equalizer is initially adapted with the prearranged training signal. Once the transmitter switches over to sending the user's "payload" rather than the training signal, the receiver continues adapting its filter, but using the decisions that it makes as the reference signal rather than the stored values. Assuming that the decisions are mostly accurate, [1] the equalizer adapts properly and tracks time variations in the propagation channel. This technique, called *decision direction* (DD) [Salz, 1973], is a part of virtually all equalized data demodulators, including all modern voiceband telephone modems.

We note in passing that decision direction is really a version of the technique discussed in Section 6.2.1. The reference signal $d(k)$ is obtained from the input signal

---

[1]Nine out of 10 is the usual rule of thumb.

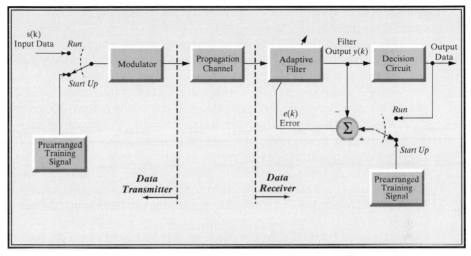

Figure 6.4   The use of decision-direction to guide an equalized data demodulator. Once running properly after start up with a prearranged training signal, the demodulator's output decisions are an accurate version of the transmitted data sequence $s(k)$ and can be used as the adaptive equalizer's reference signal.

by filtering it and applying it to a nonlinearity, the symbol decision circuit, rather than a delay as used in the ALE.

We might also note that the techniques examined in both Sections 6.2.1 and 6.2.2, while useful and practically successful, do not really meet the original objective of operating without a reference signal. In all three cases, some knowledge of the input signal and the application is used to fashion an input and/or the reference proxy, and using these, the adaptive filter operates as described in Chapter 4.

6.2.3 Using *A Priori* Statistical Knowledge about the Inputs to Avoid the Need for a Reference Signal

Both of the previous schemes used knowledge of the input signal's characteristics to craft alternative reference or filter input signals. Another approach is to use statistical knowledge about the problem at hand to modify the algorithms themselves so that they do not require the reference signal to actually be present. An excellent example of this is Griffiths' algorithm, derived in Section 4.2.6. In this case, it is assumed that the cross-correlation properties between the filter input $x(k)$ and reference $d(k)$ are known. When this is true, then the **P** vector is known and the optimal filter coefficients can be determined by any of a number of MMSE techniques. In the specific case of the Griffiths' algorithm, Widrow's LMS algorithm was modified to use the **P** vector instead of the reference signal $d(k)$. An illustration of how this might be applied occurs in the case of an antenna array [Griffiths, 1967], where the **P** vector can be computed in terms of the desired "look direction" and the statistical characteristics of the array inputs.

We should note before going on that none of the techniques we have examined here is actually practical for the FM troposcatter application shown in Figure 6.2 and described in Section 1.2. Of the three concepts discussed here, only the ones in Section 6.2.2 would appear to be appropriate. Closer examination shows that they fail as well. Because the propagation channel is time-varying in the troposcatter problem, it is not sufficient to train the receiver's equalizer only when the communications system is started up. Because the propagation channel changes considerably over even a second, the equalizer must be retrained at least that often, with the associated loss of "payload" transmission while that occurs. The decision direction technique, while useful for data transmissions over the troposcatter channel, cannot be successfully applied to analog FM transmission without the likelihood of filter divergence [Treichler, 1980]. Thus, for the particular problem examined here, the required reference signal is not available, nor can it be reasonably inferred or constructed from the signals available at the receiver.

6.3 THE PROPERTY RESTORATION CONCEPT

The property-restoration approach exploits the fact that many signals, particularly those constructed by humans for use in communications systems, have certain invariant properties that can be sensed and then used as the basis for adapting a filter. For example, many communications signals commonly used employ transmitted waveforms with constant envelopes. The use of constant-envelope signals, such as in frequency modulation (FM) and phase modulation (PM), was originally motivated by its noise immunity and its resistance to intermodulation distortion. However, this property can also be used as the basis for developing an adaptive equalizer, or antenna beamformer, which does not require explicit knowledge of the desired signal $d(k)$, which in many cases is the original transmitted waveform.

Conceptually, the idea is as follows. A signal may be designed with some invariant property (e.g., the constant envelope of an angle-modulated signal). If propagation or interference effects that degrade the receiver output also disturb this otherwise invariant property, then an algorithm can often be developed that senses this disturbance and adjusts the coefficients in such a way as to restore the should-be-invariant property. If the algorithm accomplishes this by notching the interference and/or equalizing the channel, then the signal too is corrected, not just the property, and the quality of the receiver's output is improved. It can frequently be shown that restoring the property is tantamount to correcting the signal itself. When this is true, an adaptive filtering algorithm based on property restoration can be developed and specific knowledge of a reference waveform $d(k)$ is not required.

The adaptive processor resulting from this approach has the structure shown in Figure 6.5. Two of the blocks, the filter and the coefficient adaptation, were shown in Figure 6.1. The third portion is now called *property measurement* and is used to make

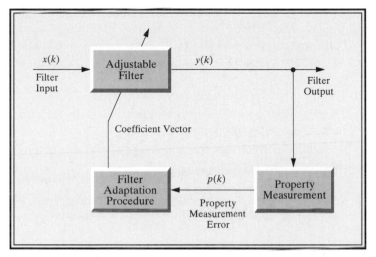

Figure 6.5   A general structure that uses property restoration to direct filter adaptation.

any measurements needed to sense the degree to which the selected signal property is attained. This property measurement block uses the filter output as its input and produces a sequence $p(k)$ which reflects the difference between the intended state of the property and its actual instantaneous value. This sequence $p(k)$ has the characteristics of an error signal and can be used to drive an adaptive algorithm that adjusts the coefficients of a filter.

Before proceeding with a specific example, we can first make two observations. The first is that this concept is quite general and subsumes a number of existing algorithm design approaches, including the prediction error techniques of Chapters 4 and 5. The second is that in practice the resulting algorithms are quite signal specific, i.e., an adaptive filter based on restoring the envelope properties of an FM signal will probably work very poorly on an AM signal. Examples of both of these points are provided later in this chapter.

6.4 THE CONSTANT-MODULUS ADAPTIVE ALGORITHM

The discussion of the previous section can be made more concrete by considering a specific example, the *constant modulus adaptive algorithm* (CMA) [Treichler and Agee, 1983]. This algorithm was developed to perform the equalization and interference reduction functions for constant-envelope signals, such as the troposcatter problem discussed in Chapter 1 and Section 6.1. If we view the transmitted constant envelope signal as a complex-valued phasor, the user's information is contained purely in the phasor angle, while the modulus, or instantaneous amplitude, is fixed at some value A. This constant modulus is the invariant property for such angle-modulated signals and is in fact corrupted by the presence of multipath propagation and/or interference.

Following the structure shown in Figure 6.5, we need to define the following in order to specify a property-restoration adaptive algorithm for such signals:

(a) The structure and parameters of the filter;

(b) The error-like signal $p(k)$ which indicates the degree of nonattainment of the constant envelope property; and

(c) An adaptive algorithm for adjusting the filter's coefficients based on some function of the error $p(k)$.

While many choices are available for each of these items, we will examine those made in Treichler and Agee [1983].

6.4.1 The Filter Structure

An N-tap transversal FIR filter was assumed as the basis of this adaptive filter. The value of N is determined by practical considerations. (Refer to Chapter 9 for an example.) An FIR filter was chosen because of its stability with any bounded parameterization. The use of a transversal structure also permits relatively straightforward construction of the filter in either hardware or firmware. Others can be used, of course, assuming that suitable adjustments are made to the adaptive coefficient updating algorithms.

6.4.2 The Error Signal

If the input and output of the filter are assumed to be complex valued, then the natural choice for the property measurement is the modulus, or instantaneous amplitude, itself. If $y(k)$ is the complex-valued filter output, then $|y(k)|$ denotes the amplitude. Because we expect the amplitude to have a value of A in the absence of signal degradations, it is quite natural to define the error signal $p(k)$ as

$$p(k) = |y(k)|^2 - A^2. \tag{6.4.1}$$

The error $p(k)$ has the desired features because it is zero when the envelope has the proper value, is nonzero otherwise, and carries sign information to indicate which direction the envelope is in error. Note, however, that other functions with the same qualifications are available, and some may in fact ultimately turn out to work better in some applications. Two examples of alternatives include

$$p_2 = |y(k)| - A \tag{6.4.2}$$

and

$$p_3 = \ln(|y(k)|/A). \tag{6.4.3}$$

6.4.3 The Adaptive Algorithm

Following the steps laid out in the previous chapters, we define the adaptive algorithm by specifying a performance function based on the error $p(k)$ and then developing a procedure that adjusts the filter's pulse response so as to minimize that performance function. Suppose that we define J, the performance function, by the expression

$$J = E\{p^2(k)\}, \tag{6.4.4}$$

where E is the statistical expectation operator. Thus J is the mean square of the error sensed in measuring the adherence to the constant envelope property.

Given this definition for J, many procedures can be developed for adapting the filter. The constant-modulus algorithm reported in Treichler and Agee [1983] employed the approximate gradient descent method presented in Section 4.2. The true gradient of J at time index k is first approximated by its instantaneous value, which can be shown to equal

$$\widehat{\nabla J} = \nabla_{\mathbf{W}}\{p^2(k)\} = 2 \cdot p(k) \cdot \nabla_{\mathbf{W}}\{p(k)\} = 4 \cdot p(k) \cdot y(k) \cdot \mathbf{X}^*(k), \tag{6.4.5}$$

where, as before, $\mathbf{X}(k)$ is the vector of the current and $N-1$ past input samples. The approximate gradient is used by updating the pulse response vector $\mathbf{W}(k)$ according to the rule

$$\mathbf{W}(k+1) = \mathbf{W}(k) - \mu \cdot \widehat{\nabla_{\mathbf{W}} J}. \tag{6.4.6}$$

Substituting (6.4.5) into (6.4.6) and suitably redefining the adaptation constant (or step size) μ, we obtain the update expression for the constant-modulus algorithm (CMA)

$$\mathbf{W}(k+1) = \mathbf{W}(k) - \mu\{|y(k)|^2 - A^2\} \cdot y(k) \cdot \mathbf{X}^*(k). \tag{6.4.7}$$

Note that this algorithm uses the input signal $x(k)$, delayed versions of it (in $\mathbf{X}(k)$), and the filter output $y(k)$, but no explicit reference signal $d(k)$. Thus the objective of "reference-free" adaptation laid out at the beginning of this chapter is satisfied by this algorithm.

The similarity between this gradient descent algorithm and others, such as LMS, can be underscored by defining the term $\epsilon(k)$ with the expression

$$\epsilon(k) = y(k)\{|y(k)|^2 - A^2\}. \tag{6.4.8}$$

With $\epsilon(k)$ written this way, the CMA recursion expression becomes

$$\mathbf{W}(k+1) = \mathbf{W}(k) - \mu\epsilon(k)\mathbf{X}^*(k). \tag{6.4.9}$$

Comparison of (6.4.9) and (4.2.7) shows that both have the same form. Only the error term itself indicates the type of performance function being minimized. In terms of the separation of (5.1.2), ϵ is $\partial J/\partial y$ (for the instantaneous version of (6.4.4) with (6.4.1)) and $\mathbf{X}^*$ is $\partial y/\partial \mathbf{W}$ (for the direct-form FIR realization).

It should be emphasized that other "constant-modulus" algorithms can be developed by making different choices for the filter structure, the error signal, the performance function, and the actual updating procedure. The particular choice of the approximate gradient technique used here was motivated originally by the need for a simple algorithm that could operate at high clock rates and for which convergence times measured in thousands of input samples was not a problem for the application at hand. When these conditions are not the case, e.g., when rapid convergence in terms of number of input samples is required, then more complicated procedures may be applied to advantage [Agee, 1986].

6.4.4 An Example Using the Gradient Descent Version of CMA

To illustrate the fact that algorithms developed using the property restoration concept can work, we now look at two examples, one very simple and the other more complicated.

First, consider an input signal given by

$$x(k) = Be^{j\omega_o kT},\tag{6.4.10}$$

a single complex-valued sinusoid of amplitude B and radian frequency ω_o. We apply it to a one-tap filter with coefficient w, producing the filter output

$$y(k) = wBe^{j\omega_o kT}.\tag{6.4.11}$$

Applying this to equation (6.4.7), we get the recursion for the update of w:

$$
\begin{aligned}
w_{k+1} &= w_k - \mu y(k)\{|y(k)|^2 - A^2\}x^*(k) \\
&= w_k - \mu w_k Be^{j\omega_o kT}\{|w_k|^2 B^2 - A^2\}Be^{-j\omega_o kT}, \\
&= w_k[1 - \mu B^2\{|w_k|^2 B^2 - A^2\}].
\end{aligned}\tag{6.4.12}
$$

For μ such that $0 < \mu < \frac{1}{B^4 w_o^2}$, CMA converges, driving w_k to w_{opt} as k grows large, where w_{opt} is given by

$$|w_{\text{opt}}| = \frac{A}{B},\tag{6.4.13}$$

making the envelope of the filter output $|y(k)| = |w_{\text{opt}}B| = A$, the desired constant.

The convergence of a one-tap filter with a simple complex-valued sinusoidal input is illustrated in Figure 6.6. A polar plot of the filter's output $y(k)$ is shown in Figure 6.6(a). The trajectory of the signal begins with an amplitude of B (assuming that $w(k)$ is initialized at unity) and spirals into the circle with radius A, the modulus value encouraged by the performance function given in (6.4.4). The angular rate of the filter output is determined by the sinusoid's radian frequency given by ω_o. Figure 6.6(b) shows the decay of the error signal $p(k)$ with time, while Figure 6.6(c) shows the progressive decline in the performance function J as the CMA algorithm adapts. Note that both $p(k)$ and J relax to zero. The rate at which they relax is determined directly by μ, the adaptation constant.

The second example is related to the first but with introduction of frequency-selective amplitude distortion. We now assume the arrangement shown in Figure 6.7.

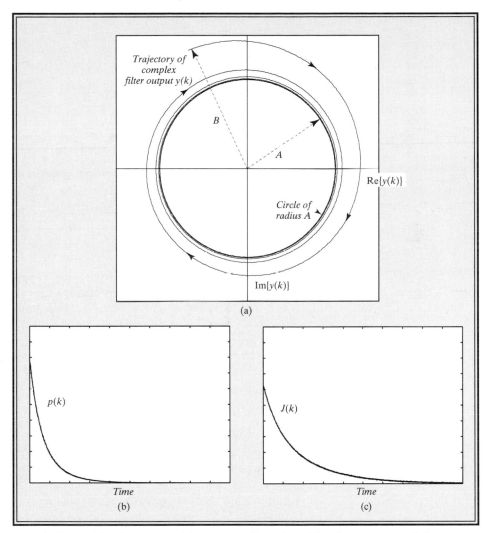

Figure 6.6 The response of a one-tap filter adapted by the constant modulus algorithm to a complex-valued sinusoid with amplitude B. (a) Polar plot of the filter output as a function of time index. (b) Plot of the error $p(k)$ as a function of time index. (c) Plot of the performance function J as a function of the time index.

The transmitted signal is a complex-valued sinusoidal carrier that has been phase-modulated by a first-order Markov process. The modulated carrier is then fed through a complex IIR filter characterized by feedback coefficients, shown in the figure as a_1 and a_2. The output of this "channel" filter, with possibly the addition of noise, forms the equalizer's input $x(k)$. We assume the use of an FIR equalizer with just enough coefficients to exactly compensate for the IIR "channel."

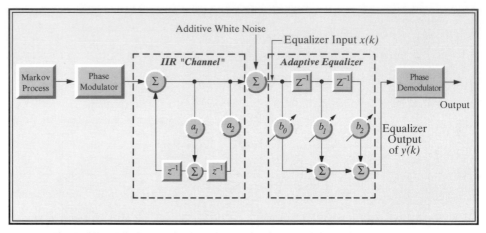

Figure 6.7 "Blind" equalization of a simple phase-modulated signal corrupted by IIR filtering.

Figure 6.8(a) shows a polar plot of the channel output during a short time interval. It is clear from this figure that the constant envelope of the transmitted carrier has been disrupted by the channel's filtering action. Figure 6.8(b) shows the equalizer output after approximately 50,000 steps of adaptation using the CMA algorithm of (6.4.7). The modulus of the signal has been restored to its initial uniform value. Figure 6.8(c) plots the performance function J as a function of time. As intended, J converges to zero, or nearly so, in the absence of additive input noise. In the presence of noise, the modulus variation cannot be completely reduced, and therefore J stabilizes at a level above zero.

The restoration of a property does not always mean that the signal itself has been properly recovered. In this case it has, however. This is shown using Figure 6.8(d), which plots the summed square of the difference between the channel parameters 1, a_1, a_2, and the equalizer parameters b_0, b_1, b_2 as a function of adaptation time. As hoped, this vector norm decreases in value to zero in the absence of noise, indicating that the equalizer has adapted to match and completely compensate for the effects of the IIR channel. In the case where the signal is received in the presence of additive white noise, the value of this error norm declines to an asymptote determined by the signal-to-noise ratio and the characteristics of the transmitted signal.

These two examples illustrate how CMA can be used to adapt simple FIR filters in the presence of simple signals and simple channels. The technique works under much more complicated circumstances as well. An extended example involving a practical FDM/FM communications signal can be found in Treichler and Agee [1983]. From these examples, it is clear that the adaptive property-restoration filter performs the desired function. Sensing the envelope variations of the received signal, the adaptation of the filter is directed toward a pulse response that desirably reduces the performance function, equalizes the channel distortion, and, most importantly, lifts the quality of the output signal to virtually its noise-limited level.

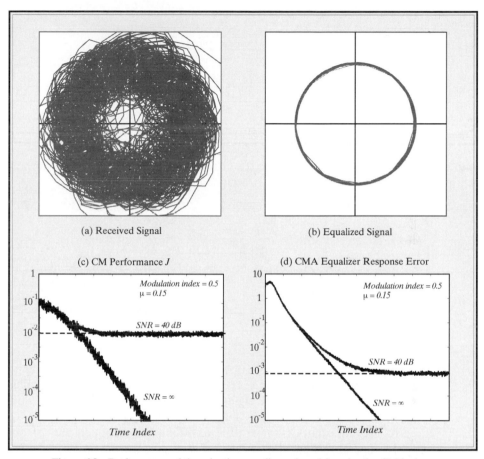

Figure 6.8   Performance of the adaptive equalizer when driven by the CMA algorithm. (a) Polar plot of the channel output. (b) Polar plot of the equalizer's output when adaptation is essentially complete. (c) Plot of the performance function J as a function of time index, both with and without additive noise at the equalizer's input. (d) Plot of the degree to which the channel is estimated by the equalizer as a function of time index, both with and without additive noise.

6.5 EXTENSION OF CMA TO DATA SIGNALS

6.5.1 "Constant Envelope" Data Signals

We just looked at "analog" FM and phase modulated signals, which, in the absence of degradation, have a constant envelope at every time index. The constant modulus algorithm (CMA) can be applied directly to data-bearing signals as well, so long as the constant envelope property on which the technique is based still prevails. In most cases this is not true, however. Data modulators built to operate efficiently through

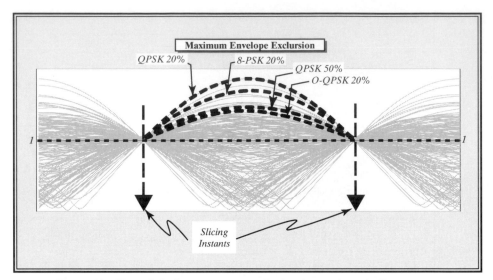

Figure 6.9 Plots of the instantaneous amplitude of several nominally constant-envelope data signals as a function of time index; (a) QPSK with 50% excess bandwidth, (b) QPSK with 20% excess bandwidth, (c) 8-PSK with 20% excess bandwidth, and (d) offset-QPSK with 20% excess bandwidth.

band-limited channels (e.g., a telephone line) usually employ pulse shaping to control the transmitted signals' power spectrum. The effect of this shaping is illustrated in Figure 6.9. Note that all of the signals' envelope values exactly equal unity at each "slicing time," that is, at integer multiples of the signal's symbol period. Between these measuring points, however, the envelope can be much greater or less than unity. In general this envelope variation is greater for the more spectrally efficient signals with smaller excess bandwidth. The variation is less when, as in the 50% QPSK case, spectral efficiency is not strived for, or, in the O-QPSK case, when the signal is specifically redesigned to maintain a constant envelope for all time, not just as the slicing instants.

The constant envelope algorithm interprets this modulus variation as a symptom of a propagation or interference problem, not as a natural part of the data signal, and its actions to correct for the perceived problem can lead to unsatisfactory performance. This problem has been solved in practice using the strategy illustrated in Figure 6.10, which draws on the *fractionally spaced equalizer* (FSE) technology commonly used in data modem design [Bingham, 1988] [Treichler et al., 1998].

Once received and converted to a complex-valued representation, the signal is sampled (or "resampled" if already digital) at a rate equal to a rational multiple of the signal's symbol (i.e., pulse) rate. (A very typical value is twice the symbol rate.) This sampled, or resampled, signal is applied to the digital filter. Its output is decimated, producing samples at exactly the symbol rate. These new samples are

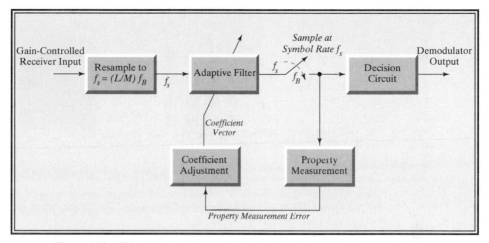

Figure 6.10   Using fractional-spaced filtering to make CMA applicable to data signals with high degrees of pulse shaping.

applied to the receiver's decision circuit in order to produce the output bit stream, and to the property measurement circuit to drive the equalizer's update algorithm.

What is achieved with this arrangement? The sampling rate at the filter's input is high enough to satisfy the Nyquist condition for the received signal, allowing the filter to equalize and remove interference without introducing aliasing. By decimating its output at the rate of one sample per symbol, the property measurement circuit can "see" the signal only at the time instants when the envelope can be expected to be constant. Provided with a signal that should attain this property when the filter is adjusted properly, CMA proceeds to operate successfully.

6.5.2 Quadrature-Amplitude Modulation (QAM) and Other Nonconstant-Envelope Signals

The receiver design shown in Figure 6.10 exploits the fact that signals with certain modulation types do have a constant envelope if that envelope measurement is made at exactly the right time. By making the measurements at these times, it is then possible to use the property restoration concept to adapt the equalizing filter properly. From this it might seem reasonable to conclude that this approach can only be used for modulations whose constellation points fall on the unit circle, such as 4- and 8-PSK. In fact this limitation turns out not to be true. The structure shown in Figure 6.10, coupled with a property restoration algorithm such as CMA, can equalize data signals that send information using both the phase and amplitude of the transmitted pulses. An important example is *quadrature-amplitude modulation* (QAM).

This observation was first made by Godard [1980], who actually came to the same scheme via an alternative viewpoint. To see this, first consider the 16-point

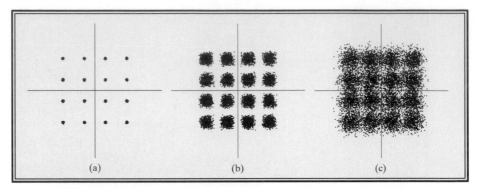

Figure 6.11   The constellation of a 16-point QAM signal, (a) as transmitted, (b) after being subjected to mild propagation dispersion, and (c) after being subjected to heavy propagation dispersion.

QAM constellation shown in Figure 6.11(a). This is typical of the signal transmitted from a digital microwave radio or a V.22*bis* 2400 b/s voiceband telephone modem. In the absence of noise and propagation-induced dispersion, the receiver can expect to see the same constellation points, and, after "time slicing" properly and removing the carrier, can recover the transmitted data by translating each received symbol into the four bits that it carries. Figure 6.11(b) shows the constellation points in the case where the propagation channel has mildly dispersed the transmitted pulses. Similarly, Figure 6.11(c) shows a heavily dispersed case. It is clear from these illustrations that the receiver's performance will be degraded when attempting to make proper decisions using the signal in Figure 6.11(b). Without equalization, a receiver encountering the signal in Figure 6.11(c) produces a random and useless output.

In confronting the "blind equalization" problem, that is, equalizing an incoming data signal without the aid of a training or reference signal, Godard suggested that a performance function be developed that sensed the *dispersion* of the constellation points, and that an approximate gradient descent algorithm be developed that would adapt an FIR equalizer by minimizing this dispersion measure. His paper postulated the use of

$$\mathbf{W}_{k+1} = \mathbf{W}_k - \mu y(k)[|y(k)|^2 - R_o]\mathbf{X}^*(k), \qquad (6.5.1)$$

where the constant R_o is selected to provide the best performance for each constellation size. He considered this algorithm to employ "dispersion direction."

A quick comparison of the "2-2" version of CMA from (6.4.7) and Godard's dispersion direction algorithm in (6.5.1) shows them to be identical when the constant R_o is chosen to equal A^2. This has two implications, one conceptual and one practical. The conceptual implication is that it is possible to arrive at the same adaptive algorithm from two very different philosophical viewpoints. Treichler and Agee [1983] developed the algorithm for truly constant-envelope signals, extended it to signals which were periodically constant-envelope, and then found that it worked as well (albeit more slowly) for those, such as QAM signals, with decidedly non-constant envelopes. Godard's work immediately addressed the QAM problem, and then observed that it applied in constant-envelope cases as well.

The practical implication is at least as important. The fact that CMA and dispersion direction are essentially identical means that one "blind" algorithm can be used in a large variety of applications, and that a large number of different modulation types can be handled by the equalizer's hardware and/or software. A survey on the design of "blind demodulators" that employ CMA/dispersion-direction can be found in Treichler et al. [1998]. An example of the use of this algorithm in the initial acquisition of a 64-QAM signal appears there.

6.5.3 Analytical Considerations in the Design of Property-Restoration Algorithms

Several basic conditions must be satisfied to make a specific property-restoration algorithm technically viable and practically useful. They include the following:

1. The signal of interest must have an invariant property that can be measured.
2. The invariant property must be sensitive to (i.e., disrupted by) the type of degradation expected to affect the signal's quality.
3. A filter with the structure selected, adaptive or otherwise, must be able to adequately solve the problem. For example, generally speaking, a filter cannot remove an uncorrelated interferer that spectrally overlaps a signal of interest.
4. The resulting adaptive algorithm must reduce the performance function with an adequate convergence rate.
5. It must be shown that restoring the invariant property of a signal is tantamount to restoring the signal itself to its original uncorrupted state.

The analysis required to examine these points has been performed in some depth for CMA operating against FM signals [Treichler and Agee, 1983] [Treichler and Larimore 1985a] [Treichler and Larimore, 1985b] and for CMA/"dispersion direction" operating against QAM signals [Godard, 1980] [Foschini, 1985] [Johnson et al., 1998] [Johnson et al., 2000]. Performance analysis has also been conducted for property restoral style algorithms other than, but similar to, CMA [Benveniste et al., 1980] [Donoho, 1981] [Bellini, 1994], including decision direction [Monson, 1977] [Macchi and Eweda, 1984] and, of course, the prediction error techniques of Chapters 4 and 5. In general the supporting analysis must be reexamined for each new algorithm and each new processing problem.

6.6 SUMMARY

This chapter considers the development of adaptive filtering algorithms that use a property of the signal of interest rather than a template of the desired signal itself to direct the adaptation. Instead of needing the desired or reference waveform itself to direct the algorithm, we use some *a priori* knowledge about the signal waveform. While a specific algorithm developed with this concept might not be as generally applicable as the algorithms of Chapters 4 and 5, they serve in applications where a reference waveform is not available, making it impossible to use the conventional approach.

The property-restoration concept hinges on the identification of an invariant property of the particular signal of interest, a property that carries no intentional information or modulation but is in fact degraded by the same propagation or interference problem that degrades the quality of the demodulated signal. If this property (e.g., the amplitude of an angle-modulated signal) can be measured and compared to its proper value, then an error signal can be formed that can be used to direct the adaptive filter. Once the error has been formed, then the remaining aspects of the adaptive filter design are the same as those considered in Chapters 4, 5, and 7: a filter structure must be decided on, a performance function or objective defined, and a procedure developed for adjusting the pulse response in such a way as to minimize the performance function or achieve the performance objective.

6.7 PROBLEMS

1. The block diagram of an adaptive line enhancer (ALE) is shown in Figure 6.3. To understand how this system got its name, we examine its response to an input consisting of a single complex-valued sinusoid plus white, zero-mean, complex-valued noise.

   (a) Suppose

   $$s(k) = Be^{j(\omega_o kT + \theta)} + An(k) \tag{6.7.1}$$

   where θ is random and uniformly distributed over $[0, 2\pi)$, $\omega_o = \frac{2\pi n}{N}$, n and N are integers, $n(k)$ is IID, zero mean with variance σ^2, and N is the length of the adaptive filter used in the ALE. Assuming that Δ, the delay, is an integer greater than or equal to one, use the mathematical machinery in Section 3.3.5 to determine
      (i) the autocorrelation function r_x,
      (ii) the cross-correlation c_{xd}, and
      (iii) the optimal weight vector $\mathbf{W}_{ms}^{\circ}$ (with the optimal weight vector written in the same general form as (3.3.75)).
   (b) Compute the transfer function of the optimal weight vector at the frequency ω_o and write its magnitude in the general form of (3.3.77).
   (c) How does the shape of the plot of transfer function magnitude from part (b) compare with that shown in Figure 3.2?
   (d) Graph the amplitude of the sinusoidal component at the filter's output as a function of its input amplitude B.
   (e) Is the tone-to-noise power at the filter's output greater than or less than its value at the ALE's input? Widrow et al. [1975b] termed the ALE a *self-tuning passband filter*. What characteristics support this name?

2. Consider the decision-directed equalizer adaptation alternative illustrated in Figure 6.4. The decision circuit creates its output as the nearest element quantization of $y(k)$. For input data $s(k)$ drawn from a binary (± 1) alphabet, this decision circuit output would be simply $\text{sgn}[y(k)]$. Thus, the decision-directed LMS (DD-LMS) algorithm would be

   $$\mathbf{W}(k + 1) = \mathbf{W}(k) + \mu \mathbf{X}(k)[\text{sgn}[y(k)] - y(k)] \tag{6.7.2}$$

   where the error in (4.2.7), which should be $s(k - \Delta) - y(k)$ during training, is replaced by $\text{sgn}[y(k)] - y(k)$. As long as $\mathbf{W}$ is chosen so $y(k)$ approximates $s(k - \Delta)$ sufficiently well so $\text{sgn}[y(k)] = s(k - \Delta)$, the behavior of DD-LMS is identical to that of trained LMS. However, once $\text{sgn}[y(k)]$ is too often not equal to $s(k - \Delta)$ for any particular fixed Δ, the behavior of DD-LMS can become totally unacceptable. The rule of thumb is that a low percentage of errors (e.g., less than 10%) can be tolerated. Your task is to test and calibrate this rule of thumb in a specific example.

   (a) Consider the channel with a mixed phase impulse response $C(z^{-1}) = (1 - az^{-1})(1 - bz^{-1})$ where $|a| > 1$ and $|b| < 1$. With $a = 1.7$ and $b = -0.8$, for an adaptive FIR filter with 20 taps and a desired overall delay for the channel and equalizer combination of $\Delta = 10$, simulate the trained LMS equalizer from a "cold" start (i.e., $\mathbf{W}(0) = \mathbf{0}$) and assess the percentage of errors at convergence. The binary (± 1) input should be zero-mean and white. If necessary, increase the length of the adapted filter tapped-delay line and/or adjust the delay Δ to reduce the occurrence of nonzero values of $s(k - \Delta) - \text{sgn}[y(k)]$ to less than 1% of the time. Document the convergent $\mathbf{W}$ and plot the impulse response of the combination of the channel $C(z^{-1})$ and the convergent equalizer. This combined impulse response should approximate $\{0, \ldots, 0, 1, 0, \ldots, 0\}$ with the unit value corresponding to the desired delay Δ.

(b) For a single-spike setting (i.e., with only one nonzero entry in a fixed $\mathbf{W}$), assess the percentage of decision errors for a zero-mean, white, binary (± 1) source. Using the equalizer length selected in part (a) that can achieve less than 1% errors, adapt the FIR equalizer parameters from a single-spike initialization using DD-LMS. Does the algorithm converge? Is its asymptotic performance capable of sustaining a low (i.e., <2%) error rate? Does success depend on the delay associated with the single initially nonzero spike? Does success depend on the magnitude of the single initially nonzero spike?

(c) Select a fixed setting of $\mathbf{W}$ that achieves an error rate of approximately 20%. Use this setting as $\mathbf{W}(0)$ and update $\mathbf{W}$ via DD-LMS. Is its asymptotic performance capable of sustaining a low (i.e., <2%) error rate? Repeat with other $\mathbf{W}(0)$ causing approximately 20% errors. Are observations the same? If asymptotic performance is typically inadequate (i.e., >2% errors) among the $\mathbf{W}(0)$ achieving a particular error rate, reinitialize $\mathbf{W}(0)$ to settings providing lower (and lower) initial error rates until subsequent adaptation via DD-LMS achieves adequate (i.e., <2% errors) performance. Comment on whether your simulated studies confirm the rule of thumb described in the footnote in Section 6.2.2 regarding the error rate at which transition from training to DD-LMS in Figure 6.4 is appropriate.

3. Consider the AR(1) channel with infinite impulse response $C(z^{-1}) = [1 + cz^{-1}]^{-1}$ driven by the binary (± 1), zero-mean, white source s and the MA(1) equalizer with finite impulse response $W(z^{-1}) = w_0 + w_1 z^{-1}$. Note that $|c| < 1$ for boundedness of the channel's output. (Hint: Refer to Ding et al. [1991].)

(a) If $w_0 = 1$ and $w_1 = c$, then $C(z^{-1})W(z^{-1}) = 1$ and perfect source recovery is possible. However, if $w_0 = 0$ as would be necessary to achieve $C(z^{-1})W(z^{-1}) \approx z^{-1}$, no value of w_1 will produce perfect recovery. Confirm these observations by simulating trained equalizer LMS adaptation, for $c = 0.6$ for the two choices (zero and unity) for the possible delay in the recovery of the sychronized training signal. Plot the trajectories in the two cases in the (w_0, w_1)-plane.

(b) For $c = 0.6$, simulate decision-directed LMS (DD-LMS) adaptation of the w_i of the equalizer from starting points in all four quadrants of the (w_0, w_1)-plane. Depending on its initialization, if convergent, the DD-LMS algorithm should converge to one of the settings associated with the local minima of MSE for the two possible delays.

(c) For $c = 0.6$, simulate constant modulus algorithm (CMA) adaptation of the w_i of the equalizer from starting points in all four quadrants of the (w_0, w_1)-plane. If convergent, does the CMA algorithm converge, as predicted by theory, to one of the settings associated with the local minima of MSE for the two possible delays or the negative of these two local minima? From a single nonzero spike initialization with $w_0 = 0$ and $w_1 \neq 0$ for various values of w_1, does CMA always converge to the vicinity of the local MSE minimum on the w_1-axis associated with the unit overall delay? From a single nonzero spike initialization with $w_1 = 0$ and $w_0 \neq 0$ for various values of w_0, does CMA always converge to the vicinity of the local MSE minimum associated with the zero overall delay?

4. Consider linear equalization with an adapted IIR equalizer

$$y(k) = b_0(k)r(k) + b_1(k)r(k-1) + b_2(k)r(k-2) + a_1(k)y(k-1) + a_2(k)y(k-2)$$

$$(6.7.3)$$

where y is the equalizer output and r is the received signal. An IIR channel is presumed to convert the binary (± 1), zero-mean, white source s into the received signal

$$r(k) = c_0 s(k) + c_1 s(k-1) + c_2 s(k-2) + d_1 r(k-1) + d_2 r(k-2). \qquad (6.7.4)$$

With the assumption that both polynomials $c_0 + c_1 z^{-1} + c_2 z^{-2}$ and $1 - d_1 z^{-1} - d_2 z^{-2}$ have all roots inside the unit circle in the z-plane, we can achieve perfect, undelayed source recovery with $b_0 = 1/c_0, b_1 = -d_1/c_0, b_2 = -d_2/c_0, a_1 = -c_1/c_0$, and $a_2 = -c_2/c_0$. Your task is to develop and test blind algorithms for this IIR equalizer that converge (locally) to this desired solution.

(a) Approximate the sensitivity function $\partial J(k)/\partial y(k)$ for the constant modulus cost

$$J(k) = \frac{1}{4}[1 - y^2(k)]^2. \qquad (6.7.5)$$

Plot $\partial J(k)/\partial y(k)$ versus $y(k)$ and note (i) the odd symmetry and (ii) zero crossings with negative slope at $|y| = 1$.

(b) Approximate the sensitivity functions $\partial y(k)/\partial a_i(k)$ and $\partial J(k)/\partial b_j(k)$ as in Section 5.2.1 for the IIR filter realization of (6.7.3) under the assumption of small step size μ in, for example,

$$a_i(k+1) = a_i(k) + \mu \cdot (\text{correction term}). \qquad (6.7.6)$$

Write out each of the updates for the five b_j and a_i.

(c) With the correction term in (6.7.6) defined for the stochastic gradient descent approach as in (5.1.1)–(5.1.2), use the results of parts (a) and (b) to compose the constant modulus IIR equalizer adaptation algorithm. Test this algorithm with a well-documented MATLAB program for initializations in the vicinity of the parameterization for perfect, undelayed source recovery. Confirm that the negative of the perfect recovery answer is also a local convergence point.

(d) Consider a variant on the constant-modulus cost function of (6.7.5) of

$$J(k) = \frac{1}{2}[1 - |y(k)|]^2. \qquad (6.7.7)$$

Repeat parts (a) and (c) for the $J(k)$ of (6.7.7). Comment on the interpretation of the resulting adaptive IIR equalizer as a decision-directed version of a trained adaptive IIR equalizer.

(e) Replace $\partial J(k)/\partial y(k)$ of part (a) with another odd function of $y(k)$ (different from that of part (a) or part (d)) that crosses $y = \pm 1$ with a negative slope. Attempt via integration to recover the associated alternative cost function that would result in the curve chosen. Repeat the simulated tests of part (c). (Hint: Refer to Bellini [1994].)

(f) Typically, utilization in nonideal circumstances reveals the differences in behavior among different candidate algorithms having the same perfect convergence point for the same idealized problem. For a modest amount of channel noise or an extra channel transfer function pole or zero, compare the performance of the three adaptive IIR blind equalizers of parts (c), (d), and (e).

5. The objective of the equalizer depicted in Figure 6.12 is to select the impulse response coefficients of F and B so the output of the decision device matches a delayed version of the original source s (i.e., $x(k) = s(k - \rho)$). The received signal r is the source s passed

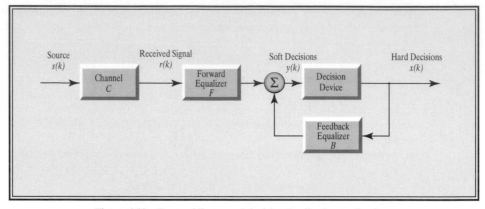

Figure 6.12   Forward linear and decision feedback equalization.

through a linear channel

$$r(k) = \sum_{j=0}^{p} c_j s(k-j). \tag{6.7.8}$$

The input to the decision device (i.e., the "soft" decision y) is composed as

$$y(k) = \sum_{i=0}^{m} f_i r(k-i) + \sum_{j=1}^{n} b_j x(k-j) \tag{6.7.9}$$

where the hard decisions x are fed back. In seeking a satisfactory setting for the f_i and b_j, it is common to assume that $y(k)$ has been set sufficiently close to $s(k-\rho)$ such that the quantization of $y(k)$ as $x(k)$ exactly matches $s(k-\rho)$ for all subsequent k.

(a) With $x(k-j)$ in (6.7.9) replaced by $s(k-\rho)$ compute the soft decision error $e(k) = s(k-\rho) - y(k)$ as a function of the convolution matrix of the channel and the impulse response vectors of the forward and feedback equalizer components.

(b) In the matrix equation established in part (a), presume that the coefficients b_j of the feedback equalizer component are selected to match the tap weights of the channel and forward equalizer combination following the cursor associated with delay ρ. Under this assumption, the coefficients f_i of the forward equalizer component can be reduced to a matrix inversion if the equalizer component lengths m and n are chosen appropriately relative to p and ρ. Write a MATLAB script that performs this design procedure for particular ρ and p and various c_i and tests its success via simulation producing plots of collapsing e.

(c) Presuming training, develop and test a well-documented MATLAB program that begins with arbitrary initial choices for the f_i and b_j and uses an LMS-based adaptive algorithm to adapt them to the desired answer. As with decision-directed adaptation discussed in Section 6.2.2, are there constraints on equalizer initialization leading to success?

(d) In the program for part (c), replace the training signal with the decision device output and test the viability of a decision-directed (and therefore blind) decision feedback equalizer (DD-DFE), in particular with regard to initialization necessities.

(e) Utilize the presumption that $x(k)$ matches $s(k - \rho)$ and develop an adaptive algorithm for updating the f_i and b_j based on stochastic gradient descent of the instantaneous constant modulus cost $J(k) = [1 - y^2(k)]^2$ for a binary (± 1), white, zero-mean source. Appropriately modify the program of part (c) to implement the constant-modulus-based DFE (or CM-DFE) and test initialization capabilities relative to those of the algorithms in parts (c) and (d). (Hint: Refer to Casas et al. [2001].)

6. Consider an adaptive FIR filter

$$y(k) = w_0(k)x(k) + w_1(k)x(k - 1) + \cdots + w_N(k)x(k - N) \qquad (6.7.10)$$

with the input a sum of sinusoids. The constant modulus algorithm (CMA) is used to adapt the w_i via

$$w_i(k + 1) = w_i(k) + \mu y(k)(1 - y^2(k))x(k - i). \qquad (6.7.11)$$

(a) With $N = 1$ and $x(k) = g\sin(\omega k)$ show that the average over a single period of the correction term $y(k)(1 - y^2(k))x(k - i)$ for $i = 0$ and 1 is zeroed by $y(k) = \frac{2}{\sqrt{3}}\sin(\omega k + \phi)$ regardless of the value of g. Confirm via simulation that this zeroing of the average update term corresponds to the small step size (average) convergent behavior of (6.7.11). Is the (average) parameterization of the convergent w_i unique? Does changing N to zero change your answers? Does changing N to 3 change your answers?

(b) With $N = 3$ and

$$x(k) = g_1\sin(\omega_1 k + \phi_1) + g_2\sin(\omega_2 k + \phi_2), \qquad (6.7.12)$$

simulate the behavior of (6.7.11). In this setting, (6.7.11) views one tone as the signal to be recovered and the other as an interferer to be rejected. Which tone is captured and which is rejected depends on the choice of the $w_i(0)$. Confirm this fact with a well-chosen set of simulations. (Hint: Refer to Treichler and Larimore [1985b] who perform such an experiment for complex sinusoids.)

7. Frequently CMA-FIR BSE is observed to converge near the MMSE design for the delay achieved by the location of the largest spike (or cursor) in the inital equalizer and channel combination. This observation has been used to validate the anticipated behavior of single-spike initializations of a CMA-FIR BSE. There are two elements in the foundation of this statement. One is that CM cost minimization is achieved by a setting in the vicinity of the MMSE solution. This assertion applies even in the presence of modest noise or other nonidealities. The second is that the cursor of single-spike initialization is retained at convergence. Each of these behavioral "facts" rests on certain assumptions about the MMSE performance achieved at the initial and desired asymptotic settings. Your task is to devise experiments that challenge both assertions on which this behavioral folklore for CMA is based in order to gain some insight into the limits of utility of the folklore.

8. Consider a multiple modulus, white, zero-mean source, such as 4-level PAM that takes on values ± 1 and ± 3. Presume an FIR channel producing the received signal r from the source s

$$r(k) = \sum_{j=0}^{p} c_j s(k - j) \qquad (6.7.13)$$

and an FIR linear baud-spaced equalizer producing the equalizer output y from the received signal r

$$y(k) = \sum_{i=0}^{m} f_i(k) r(k - i). \qquad (6.7.14)$$

With a FIR channel (with $p < \infty$) and a FIR equalizer (with $m < \infty$), there is no fixed setting for the f_i that can perfectly zero the recovery error

$$e(k) = s(k - \Delta) - y(k) \qquad (6.7.15)$$

for a finite Δ. Thus, stochastic gradient descent based algorithms with nonvanishing step sizes exhibit excess MSE above the minimum achievable with a fixed setting for the f_i. The excess MSE is proportional to the nonvanishing step size and the residual error of the desired fixed setting.

(a) Compose and test a MATLAB-based program simulating a decision-directed LMS adaptation law (DD-LMS). Confirm the linearity of the excess MSE with respect to step size variation (within the range that all choices remain suitably small).

(b) Compose and test a MATLAB-based program simulating a constant modulus based adaptation law (CMA). Confirm the linearity of the excess MSE (above the MSE associated with the CM-minimizing setting for the f_i) with respect to step sizes (within the range that all choices remain suitably small).

(c) Select a specific operating condition to document step size selection for DD-LMS and CMA that causes the total MSE to be effectively the same. For these step sizes compare the (local) convergence rate from a suboptimal initial setting for the f_i near the MMSE setting. Due to a term in the excess MSE of CMA proportional to the source (normalized) kurtosis, which increases as the PAM source takes on more levels, the DD-LMS is expected to show faster convergence. This is the argument often given to justify the use of CMA for initial capture and DD-LMS for subsequent tracking.

9. Consider a situation where the adaptive FIR model to be identified has seven parameters, e.g. the seven w_i in

$$y(k) = \sum_{i=0}^{6} w_i u(k - i). \qquad (6.7.16)$$

A training sequence is to be designed that minimizes the maximum time for reduction by LMS of the summed squared parameter error to 1% of its initial value from all possible parameterizations of the same initial summed squared parameter error on a seven-dimensional "sphere" about the correct answer. The input u during the training phase is to be binary, i.e. ± 1, periodic of period 7 with one more plus one, i.e. 4, than minus ones in each period. Two possible training sequences are

- Sequence A: $[1, \ -1, \ 1, \ -1, \ 1, \ 1, \ -1]$
- Sequence B: $[1, \ 1, \ 1, \ -1, \ -1, \ 1, \ -1]$.

So, for training sequence A

$$\{u(0), \ u(1), \ u(2), \ldots, \ u(6), \ u(7), \ u(8), \ldots\} = \{1, \ -1, \ 1, \ldots, \ -1, \ 1, \ -1, \ldots\}$$
$$(6.7.17)$$

and for training sequence B

$$\{u(0), \ u(1), \ u(2), \ldots, \ u(6), \ u(7), \ u(8), \ldots\} = \{1, \ 1, \ 1, \ldots, \ -1, \ 1, \ 1, \ldots\}:$$
$$(6.7.18)$$

(a) Perform simulated experiments of LMS behavior that reveal which of these training sequences is preferred according to the metric of minimizing the maximum time for 99% reduction from a set of all initializations with the same summed squared parameter error.

(b) Plot the magnitude spectrum of the two periodic training signals and relate your answer to part (a) to the relative flatness of these two plots.

(c) Compute the eigenvalues of the 7×7 autocorrelation matrices of the 7×1 regressors arising from the two periodic training sequences and relate your answer to part (a) to the relative condition numbers of the resulting matrices. Comment on how the autocorrelation matrix condition number is related to the topography of the mean squared error descended by LMS. Hint: The following skeleton of a sequence of Matlab commands determines the autocorrelation matrix of the periodic 7×1 regressor vector of past training symbols.

```
x=[x1 x2 x3 x4 x5 x6 x7]';
M=zeros(7,7);
shft=[0 0 0 0 0 0 1;
      1 0 0 0 0 0 0;
      0 1 0 0 0 0 0;
      0 0 1 0 0 0 0;
      0 0 0 1 0 0 0;
      0 0 0 0 1 0 0;
      0 0 0 0 0 1 0];

for ind=1:7
    M=M+x'*x;
    x= x*shft;
end

R=(1/7)*M
```

(d) Can you devise a period 7, binary (± 1) training sequence with an average of $1/7$ (or $-1/7$) that is better than either Sequence A or B in terms of minimizing the maximum decay time? Can you devise one that is worse than both sequence A and sequence B?

Hint: One of the two sequences given is a 7-symbol pseudonoise (PN) sequence, the autocorrelation sequence of which has special properties that are frequently exploited in communication system receiver training and synchronization.

7

Implementation Issues

- *Precis:* *Adaptive filters can take several forms, ranging from pure software implementation on a general-purpose computer to a variety of hardware configurations. Concerns regarding complexity, cost, bandwidth, and performance dictate the choices available to the designer.*

7.1 INTRODUCTION

To this point, we have dealt principally with the mathematical development of adaptive filtering and not really addressed the more practical aspects necessary for building working processors. In this chapter, we touch on some of the considerations required for design of useful adaptive filters, ranging from common-sense algorithmic efficiencies to the strengths and weaknesses of candidate architectures and technologies. In addition, means of assessing the performance of an implementation are discussed whereby a designer can intelligently select appropriate precision for data and weight storage.

However, as a starting point, it is useful for one to appreciate fundamental tradeoffs involved in signal processing design efforts. For example, characteristics of a signal of interest drive the sampling rate for processing fidelity; the nature of the processing further drives the computational complexity. Together they point to the technology necessary to provide sufficient computational throughput. Of course, that is not the whole story. The technology available, along with its cost and physical demands, ultimately determine the feasibility of a candidate design.

By way of illustration, Figure 7.1 depicts in vague quantitative terms the relationships of signals, computational demands, and technology. Shown is a logarithmic bandwidth axis. At the appropriate range, selected signals of interest are listed, with biomedical and control functions on the low end, radar and multichannel microwave radio at the other extreme. Then, shown below the axis are representative technologies able to sustain computational load associated with these signals.

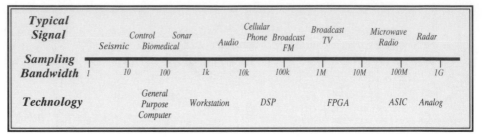

Figure 7.1   Applications and technologies.

We see that on the low end we may rely on low-cost general purpose computers, and as bandwidth and complexity increase, we are forced to resort to more exotic and specialized hardware solutions. Bear in mind that this figure is intended to simply illustrate basic relationships because absolutes are highly dependent on the state of the art in hardware technology and can be expected to change yearly.

Next, we explore further the technologies indicated in Figure 7.1. Consider the possible forms that an adaptive filter may take. First, a general-purpose computer may be programmed for off-line or "batch" processing, where digitized and recorded data of any conceivable bandwidth may be filtered in nonreal time. Typical examples of file-oriented processing software can be found in Appendix A in the form of MATLAB scripts. A pure software implementation, especially using a high-level language, has distinct advantages in that debugging, modifications, and input/output operations are inherently simple. With the current ubiquity of the desktop workstation, the cost of a low-end adaptive filter using general purpose software implementation has become relatively low, unless exotic peripherals are called upon.

The principal drawback of the software approach is that the implementation is bandwidth limited, and as such, is largely constrained to off-line applications; the flexibility of a general-purpose computer is invariably accompanied by a sacrifice in execution speed of operations critical to adaptive filtering. Even dedicated central processing units (CPUs) efficiently programmed in assembly code are normally limited in real-time use to applications having relatively low bandwidth, e.g., sampling rates serving audio-related signals. To extend real-time performance, the modern workstation can draw on a variety of add-on hardware circuit cards to provide additional specialized signal processing power.

For real-time applications where cost and size are critical factors, adaptive filters can be implemented using dedicated hardware specially designed for signal-processing functions. Since the early 1980s, the "single-chip digital signal processor" (DSP) has been refined to the point that it can well provide the computing power for most medium-bandwidth real-time applications (e.g., up to several hundred kHz). This class of device is actually a self-contained microprocessor whose instruction set and support circuitry are carefully designed for common signal-processing functions. Therefore, it is preferable to other general-purpose microprocessors for signal-processing applications in many cases. With suitable off-line development tools, this device becomes as simple to program and configure as a general-purpose CPU, but at a fraction of the cost and size, and operates at significantly higher throughput rates. The modern single-chip signal processor typically includes a number of innovative features useful for adaptive filtering applications. Specifically, these include 16-bit fixed-point or 32-bit floating point arithmetic, extended precision accumulation, cache memory, delay line shifters, and so on.

Refinements in digital technology improving the speed, cost, and size of digital circuitry have been dutifully tracking the popular "Moore's Law" prediction, steadily increasing throughput rates. Despite these advances, at least for now the single-chip DSP remains limited in terms of its real-time bandwidth. For situations requiring faster digital processing, the designer must resort to less general and more costly implementations. Field programmable gate array devices (FPGAs) now enjoy significant popularity for rates beyond the DSP, in applications where low-level programmability is still a requirement. When addressing the highest rates, often application specific integrated circuits (ASIC) may be the last resort; specialized hardwired architectures based on multiplier/accumulators and register files can service bandwidths well beyond those of the programmable processor. When necessary, use of gallium arsenide device technology (GaAs) accommodates bandwidths well in excess of hundreds of MHz. Naturally, cost, flexibility, and power are sacrificed for such high-bandwidth designs.

Finally, for bandwidths above the reaches of current digital technology, in the ranges above several hundreds of MHz, implementation calls for the use of analog components. Not only are analog systems as inherently inflexible as digital circuitry based on discrete devices, they also possess nonideal and sometimes unpredictable qualities that make them ill-suited for critical filtering applications, such as frequency dependencies, nonlinearities, instabilities, and component variations and aging. Fortunately, an adaptive structure with its performance feedback serves to correct many linear distortion, aging, and temperature effects. While the purely analog design has found use at high bandwidths in selected communication and radar applications, a hybrid arrangement with digital circuitry applied at certain critical points may greatly enhance system performance.

We return to the original thread mentioned at the beginning, one of tradeoffs between flexibility and bandwidth: As bandwidth demands increase, a design typically becomes more complex, less flexible, and more costly. This forms the basis for much of this chapter; algorithmic shortcuts are selected and discussed as means of extending bandwidth without resorting to the costs and complexities of the next level of implementation. It is important to note that the bandwidth boundaries delimiting the useful limits of technology alternatives are blurred by cost, size, and power concerns. Further, the boundaries are dynamic and expanding on a yearly basis, but will most likely always exist in some form. Special-purpose digital hardware will always serve the applications beyond the reach of the microprocessor system, just as the analog system will be the only means of processing signals with extremely high bandwidths. However, the low- to medium-bandwidth realm best addressed by the single-chip signal processor will grow as the underlying semiconductor technology and architectural efficiencies evolve.

The first part of this chapter deals with the more mundane, but important, efficiencies that a designer must be familiar with. Included are discussions of complexity and hardware impact, as well as common-sense design steps useful in both hardware and firmware. In conjunction with complexity concerns, we present some means of increasing bandwidth (i.e., clockrate) through architectures using distributed processing. Precision of time samples and filter weights has special importance when dealing with adaptive filters, and some guidelines are in order. Next, we consider specific shortcuts as they can be applied to various algorithms of Chapters 4 through 6. Also, we present arguments for reducing the rate of adaptation in the interest of efficiency. This leads to the concept of dual-mode processing (i.e., a "foreground" signal calculation and "background" adaptation processing). These concepts then serve as a basis for discussions of more block-oriented processing and associated architectures. We conclude by mentioning further alternative implementations and some of their advantages and limitations.

7.2 SIZING CONSIDERATIONS

When presented with a signal-processing requirement, the designer must first assess the value of an adaptive filtering solution. Those not familiar with the inherent limitations often consider an adaptive filter a cure-all, able to design itself and remove much of the burden from the designer. We have seen that there are definite costs, both in complexity and performance, when using an adaptive processor. Whenever possible, a fixed or programmable filter is far preferable (i.e., when enough is known *a priori* about the environment and when time variation is a secondary concern). Consequently, the designer must first objectively answer the "necessity and sufficiency" question: Will an adaptive filter satisfy the need, and is adaptation necessary? Chapter 1 provides basic insight into answering this question for typical applications.

Given that an adaptive filter is indeed called for, the next important question to be addressed concerns feasibility. Can a unit be built within size and cost constraints? The answer to this question rests largely with the bandwidth requirement coupled with the technology available. As an extreme example, equalization of voice channel modem signals (4-kHz bandwidth) was one of the earliest real-time applications of all-digital adaptive processing. But analogous equalization of radio-frequency digital signals with bandwidths above 25 MHz lagged by 20 years due to technology limitations.

Designers active in this field rely on experience to answer feasibility concerns, tempered with a grasp of today's limitations on hardware technology. Yet the novice can approach the problem using common sense and basic knowledge of the capabilities of current technology. One measure of complexity of a signal-processing circuit is the *multiplication throughput rate*. The multiply operation, a critical step in virtually all digital signal-processing functions, can be thought of as an elementary unit of complexity, and per operation it is responsible for more time, area, and heat than other simpler functions (e.g., add, compare, I/O). For the purposes of this chapter, complexity is equated with a filter's multiplication demands.

Let us illustrate by using a concrete but simplified example. Suppose we were to design a 128-tap adaptive echo canceler for use on a 4-kHz telephone voice channel. We assume an FIR architecture adapted by means of the LMS algorithm in (4.2.7). The given sampling rate for our signal is 8 kHz. The filtering operation requires 128×8 kHz $= 1.024$ megamultiplies/sec (M*/s); the update equation similarly requires 1.024 M*/s. As a first-order approximation, we may conclude that our hardware requires enough computational horsepower to perform 2M*/s; a standard single-chip signal processor would certainly suffice by a significant margin. The physical requirements for processor and support circuitry would call for modest space and low power. As an alternative, a suitable multiplier array implemented in gate array technology would provide an overkill solution in terms of multiplier throughput, and any savings in size and power would be reflected in the cost of parts and development.

Had our example involved a 100-kHz sampling rate, our multiply count would instead have been on the order of 26 M*/s. A naive, yet often adequate, extrapolation would call for about 13 times the silicon, power, and size. If the resulting scaled physical characteristics were unsuitable, a designer could draw on more exotic technologies for faster multipliers to reduce size or to lower power, but usually not both. Needless to say, the concrete numbers in this paragraph reflect current technology at time of publication. Higher multiply rates, higher density, and lower power are evolving yearly, and an effective designer must dutifully track industry trends.

For a first cut at sizing, use of the multiplier throughput factor in this manner is often adequate. However, if a more accurate answer were needed, there are additional subtleties that must be considered. First, high sampling rates, such as the 100-kHz case above, may call for some rudimentary type of distributed processing; the net multiply throughput may be spread among several processors or multipliers. As might be suspected, the complexities of distributing data and orchestrating their remultiplexing can contribute to a significant amount of circuitry. In such cases, rather than linear scaling of complexity and circuitry with bandwidth, it can be argued that a quadratic factor appears at bandwidths where distributed processing enters. That is, at a 1-MHz sampling rate, a brute-force scaling of the architecture outlined above might very well represent a formidable physical package. The bandwidth at which multiplexing effects become significant is naturally dependent on architecture.

Interestingly, an analogous effect can be seen for bandwidth reductions as well. Given a lower clock rate, circuit complexity is reduced according to our earlier definition. However, hardware savings can be realized only when a single processor or multiplier can take on the duties of other circuit elements. Returning to the example of a 128-tap echo canceller, were multiple channels involved, each sampled at 8 kHz, an approach using a single-device FPGA a 10–20 M*/s rate could service on the order of eight voice channels and offer a competitive solution to a multiple, independent single-chip signal processor implementation. However, this requires multiplexing and control hardware to "funnel" data into the high-rate device from several sources and to commutate its output port among subsequent parallel stages, implying an effective increase in complexity and development cost. When multiplexing a processor, this complexity similarly translates into more involved microcode. Such a complexity increase resulting from multiplexing is tolerable when cost or size savings through elimination of large or expensive components offsets the impact on design.

The qualitative effect of bandwidth on complexity is shown in Figure 7.2 for a hypothetical digital signal-processing architecture. Reiterating, a region exists for which frequency scaling is essentially linear. Adapting this same architecture to extremes of bandwidth by means of distributed or consolidated processing adversely affects complexity. These end effects often serve as sufficient motivation for a designer to consider alternative architectures and signal distribution that better match the particular bandwidth requirement.

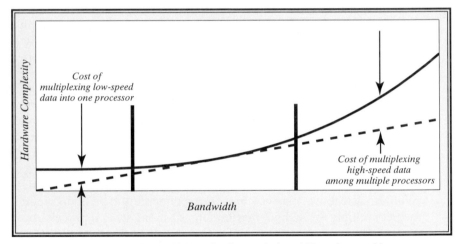

Figure 7.2   Effect of bandwidth on circuit complexity within a given architecture.

A second subtlety of our first-order complexity assessment involves the type of multiplier used in the function. This is of particular importance for adaptive processing, where there are two distinct contexts for multiply operations. Recall that an adaptive FIR filter involves (i) an output calculation and (ii) a weight update. In the first, N multiplies are done, and the results accumulated, forming a convolutional sum. This operation can be made particularly concise in hardware and has led to the signal processor building block, the multiplier/accumulator (MAC), which includes a pipelined multiplier and on-chip integral accumulator. For convolution operations, such a multiplier can be run at nearly a 100% duty cycle. In the latter case, for each updating multiply operation (e.g., error sample times a delayed input sample), there is again an add operation, but also a memory read (old weight) and a memory write (new updated weight). Consequently, the input/output (I/O) of the multiplier can slow the throughput by a significant fraction. For our original example, while a single-chip signal processor could easily sustain a high rate for convolutional operations, the weight update operation and its associated memory I/O may represent a sizable and inefficient burden on the resource, when adaptation is performed at the sampling rate. This fact alone serves as sufficient motivation to find means of reducing adaptive filter complexity, specifically of the update computation.

Clearly, this discussion has provided only general statements regarding complexity estimates and the assessment of feasibility. We only wish to indicate here that a designer should be aware of certain facets of adaptive filter "lore" and consider seeking an implementation to fit the application's performance and speed requirements. Often we find that sacrifices of theoretical rigor are necessary to accommodate real-time operation.

7.3 REAL-TIME OPERATION

Before investigating such specific shortcuts, it is instructive to review the necessary steps involved in a typical digital adaptive filter implementation. The list of steps to be completed for each sample taken has special significance in real-time operation, where the loop of operations must be completed in one sampling interval. While our procedure breakdown is based on the LMS algorithm of (4.2.7), it is easily generalized to any adaptation approach. For the analog alternative, the enumerated items correspond to continuous-time calculations and are no longer discrete events.

1. *Get input sample.* Read the analog-to-digital converter (ADC) port to bring in the next input sample. An interrupt of a time source or the digitizer itself has brought us to this point. If an external "desired" waveform or training signal is required by the algorithm, it will also be measured at this point; in the case of a stored replica training signal, the sample is accessed from memory.
2. *Inject sample into delay line.* This newest sample must be saved for future use in the convolution and update calculations. Storage may be a hardware shift register or a queued random access memory (RAM).
3. *Compute output.* The convolutional sum of N taps and N input samples is performed using a series of multiply/accumulate operations. Depending on the specific implementation, the accumulator may be implemented using up to full double-word precision.
4. *Output result.* The output as accumulated is sent out to the appropriate port. Under normal circumstances, rounding or truncation of the accumulator assures that only the most significant part of the convolutional sum is transferred (e.g., 8 to 16 bits).
5. *Compute error.* A subtraction involving desired and computed output is performed. Normally, a means of monitoring error performance is desirable, e.g., a smoothed error "power" provides a quantitative history of adaptive performance.

6. *Compute update.* For each weight, an update term is computed from the product of error (from step (5)) and appropriately delayed input (step (2)). According to (4.2.7), this operation must be repeated for each weight, and as mentioned, this operation becomes the dominant burden in the processing loop. It is here that algorithmic sacrifices can make the difference between loop completion and processor overload. Among other things, we note that the precision of this product can be as coarse as a single sign bit, requiring no multiplication at all.

7. *Wait state.* On completion, the processor can enter an idle state, awaiting the next sampling instant. It is here also that lower-priority "background" processing can be carried out. For example, performance measures (filter frequency response, error power estimate, etc.) can be computed and formatted for display as time permits.

For batch or off-line applications, the timing of this basic loop simply translates into the net execution time. Yet in real-time applications, the designer must carefully tabulate the execution time for each step because the maximum sampling rate becomes the inverse of the basic loop interval. Note that in practical cases this neglects a necessary margin to accommodate, for example, system functions, operator interfacing, and other interrupts. The remainder of this chapter focuses on the variety of means available that contribute to a reduction of the net computation time.

7.4 IMPLEMENTATION EFFICIENCIES

The suitability of a hardware implementation is often determined by clever architectural efficiencies. These shortcuts are admittedly not obvious, but nonetheless may be critical to minimize hardware necessary to sustain a required sampling rate. In this section, we highlight several issues to consider when defining a viable design, concerning the nature of the filter response, the signal structure, and the update calculation.

7.4.1 Data Storage

Data samples must be retained for use in the weight update as well as the output convolution sum. For digital implementation this can be done by means of a hardware shift register or delay line; analog filters may instead use broadband, passive delay elements (i.e., L-C sections) surface acoustic wave (SAW) devices, or charge-coupled device (CCD) delay lines. For the remainder of this discussion, we concentrate on digital architectures. As a sample enters the processor, the delay line is clocked, physically advancing past samples. It should not be surprising that while this form of storage arises naturally from the filtering block diagrams, it has severe limitations for long filters. Propagation delays can skew data arrivals at nodes of the delay line. More importantly, component count can become unwieldy.

An alternative approach that can be attractive from both efficiency and timing viewpoints is a queued random access memory (RAM). Samples arriving at the filter are written into a RAM, where an address register keeps track of the next available memory location. Data samples need not shift down the delay line, but rather simply overwrite values that are no longer needed. Of course, advancing the pointer register requires "wrap-around" logic, forcing the register to point back to the beginning of the memory when the memory size is exceeded. The single-chip processor is often configured in such a way that this delay line bookkeeping is handled by special instructions. Each memory location corresponds to a node of the delay line, with the pointer register indicating the most recent arrival. As memory can be had in extremely efficient packaging, discrete delay line hardware can be minimal.

When using this storage scheme, the maximum filter length is limited by the memory size, usually a power of two (e.g., 2^M). The M-bit address register is simply allowed to increment with no regard for overflow conditions. A separate read-address register is maintained for output of data in correct sequence for convolution and update operations. Care must be exercised for the synchronization of write and read operations, and access time must be consistent with the loop timing requirements. That is to say, an N-tap filter must complete $2N$ delay line read operations for every sampling interval, N for the convolution and N for the update. Rates exceeding memory speed must be achieved by algorithmic shortcuts, as well as improved or distributed hardware.

Analogous storage efficiencies can be achieved in software implementations. Most novice programmers choose to emulate the shift register operation. That is, incoming data samples are stored into an array, and as new samples enter, the entire array is shifted one element at a time. Needless to say, this can cause a considerable drain on the execution time, no matter how powerful the CPU. Therefore, for longer filters, say, more than 20 taps, it is usually more efficient to use a queue structure of the array and a pointer variable indicating the top of the queue. In a MATLAB implementation, where large blocks of data samples may be available, such data shuffling may be minimized by simply referencing subvectors of the block, as illustrated in Appendix A.

7.4.2 Symmetric Filtering

Situations arise where it is very desirable to maintain symmetry of an FIR filter, which may provide a means of improving throughput. Filter symmetry implies that the impulse response reflects about the center tap,[1] so that for an N-tap filter, $h(0) = h(N - 1), h(1) = h(N - 2)$, and so on.[2] The possibility of controlled symmetry in the impulse response is one of several attractive features of the FIR filter structure. A filter with time domain symmetry has a "linear phase response" in the frequency

---

[1] In the case of a complex-valued impulse response, symmetry is defined in Hermitian terms, i.e., $h(\ell) = h^*(N - 1 - \ell)$.

[2] When N is odd, the center tap stands alone.

domain; i.e., a sinusoidal component experiences a phase shift proportional to its frequency. In more practical terms, everything passing through the filter is delayed the same amount in time, helping to preserve pulse integrity.

Where might such a property be of interest? Signals sensitive to phase distortion, that is, a nonlinear phase response, often must be processed with due attention to maintaining phase relationships. As a common example, quality of visual images are degraded by smearing caused by phase distortion; in contrast, the relative insensitivity of the human ear to phase distortion means that audio signals often can undergo serious but largely imperceptible phase disturbances. In the area of digital communications, nonlinear phase distortion can be responsible for serious pulse deformation that degrades reliable transmission at high data rates.

At any rate, applications arise where it may be advantageous to maintain the linearity of a filter's phase response. This allows rejecting or shaping energy bands of the spectrum while maintaining the basic pulse integrity with a constant filter group delay. For this reason, design of nonadaptive symmetric, linear phase filters has received a good deal of attention and can be found in most filter design software packages such as MATLAB.

In the case of a real-valued impulse response this symmetry can be exploited to reduce computational complexity, defined earlier in terms of multiplication rate. That is to say, such a filter requires only half the multiply operations of the general filter per output sample. To take advantage of this structure, we simply "fold" the delay line as shown in Figure 7.3 and add values appearing at corresponding nodes prior to the convolutional accumulation. Values $x(k)$ and $x(k - N + 1)$ both multiply $h(0) = h(N - 1)$ in the calculation of the output sample; adding them first and then multiplying by $h(0)$ eliminates one multiply. Symbolically, assuming N is an even

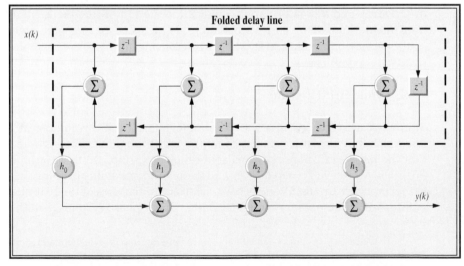

Figure 7.3   Implementation of an 8-tap symmetric filter with a folded delay line.

number,

$$y(k) = \sum_{\ell=0}^{N/2-1} h(\ell)[x(k-\ell) + x(k-N+\ell+1)]. \qquad (7.4.1)$$

Approached in this manner, the storage requirement for filter coefficients is likewise halved. However, also note that introducing an add operation into the architecture prior to the multiply/accumulation may actually not reduce the complexity in a processor intended for general impulse responses.

In the more general case of a complex-valued symmetric (Hermitian) impulse response, the "folding" operation is a bit more involved. Prior to addition, the folded input sample must be rotated by the phase differential between corresponding tap values. In this case, the additional degree of complexity may offset any gain realized by folding. The notable exception occurs when the phase differential is $180°$, giving a sign change between $h(\ell)$ and $h(N-1-\ell)$ so that $h(N-1-\ell) = -h(\ell)$ for each tap position. Such antisymmetry assures phase linearity across the high-frequency passband portion. In this case, the folding operation now involves a simple subtraction prior to multiplying.

The computational benefits of symmetry extend to the adaptation segment as well, by enforcing the symmetry constraint within the weight update operation. Symmetric adaptation of filter coefficients is done to maintain linearity of phase when necessary. For example, a pulsed signal in need of isolation from independent, additive interference might require an adaptive filter to track any time variations in the environment. To prevent arbitrary phase shaping by the filter, its impulse response (or its taps) must be constrained to be symmetric. Constrained adaptation performed on only half the weights reduces the complexity by almost half.

At first glance, it might seem that we must simply perform the update of (4.2.7) on the first half of the weight vector (i.e., using samples $x(k)$ through $x(k-N/2)$). However, this ignores the contribution of the "folded" samples on the output. Rather, noting the form of the output calculation for the symmetric filter above, the derivative of $e(k)$ with respect to w_ℓ is

$$\frac{\partial e(k)}{\partial w_\ell} = -[x(k-\ell) + x(k-N+1+\ell)]. \qquad (7.4.2)$$

Consequently, (4.2.7) is modified for adapting the length $N/2$ weight vector

$$\mathbf{W}(k+1) = \mathbf{W}(k) + \mu e(k)[x(k-\ell) + x(k-N+1+\ell)], \qquad (7.4.3)$$

requiring $N/2$ multiplies and N add operations. Again, this can be generalized to the Hermitian complex-valued filter as well, but the necessary phase alignment of folded samples tends to reduce any computational benefit to adaptation that special handling might offer.

7.4.3 Complex Filtering and Narrowband Signals

Under certain conditions, a signal may be represented in complex form, i.e., with both real and imaginary components, which may lead to architectural benefits for digital processing. The concept of a "complex-valued signal" often is treated in traditional texts as a mathematical abstraction and a generalization of linear processing formulation. In keeping with the tone of this chapter, we address the more practical aspects of this representation in the context of architectural shortcuts. For purposes of this discussion, we use j to denote the imaginary dimension.

Relating a real-valued physical phenomenon to a complex representation can be quite a leap. However, for the moment simply view the complex form as a notational means of accommodating two distinct versions of a real signal. Complex notation assigns one version to the real component, and the second to the imaginary component. There is, of course, more to it than a simple matter of notational convenience.

What does it mean for a signal to be "complex" in this sense? Recall that in the frequency domain, a real-valued signal possesses a Hermitian symmetry about 0 Hz (i.e., symmetric magnitude and antisymmetric phase). Deviation from this frequency-domain constraint can only result from a complex function in the time domain. So, what we are addressing is a time function that may lack symmetry in the frequency domain.

That observation is key to linking real phenomona to a complex representation. For example, suppose that we were to "frequency translate" a real-valued time function $x(t)$, i.e. displace its Fourier transform $X(f)$ to the left by an amount f_o, giving $X(f + f_o)$. Intuitively, translation preserves spectral distribution, and because the operation is reversible, information is also preserved. From basic Fourier principles, this equates to a multiplication in the time-domain,

$$X(f + f_o) \leftrightarrow x(t)e^{-j2\pi f_o t}. \tag{7.4.4}$$

The translating time function is a complex trigonometric, expressible as

$$e^{-j2\pi f_o t} = \cos(2\pi f_o t) - j\sin(2\pi f_o t). \tag{7.4.5}$$

So in a sense, a complex time function might simply be a real-valued one that has undergone a frequency shift to offset its symmetric spectrum with respect to 0 Hz.

What does this mean in the physical sense? This concept is perhaps best illustrated graphically. A narrowband (real) signal has the symmetric spectrum seen in Figure 7.4(a) with energy concentrated about f_c and $-f_c$. Multiplying by $\cos(2\pi f_c t)$ results in the spectrum shown in Figure 7.4(b), with a composite overlap at 0 Hz, and double frequency images at $\pm 2 f_c$. In Figure 7.4(c) is seen the corresponding result after multiplying by $-j\sin(2\pi f_c t)$, a partial cancellation composite at 0 Hz accompanied by double frequency components. Adding the two (b) and (c) results in the spectrum of Figure 7.4(d), the original spectrum shifted by $-f_c$ as predicted by Fourier theory.

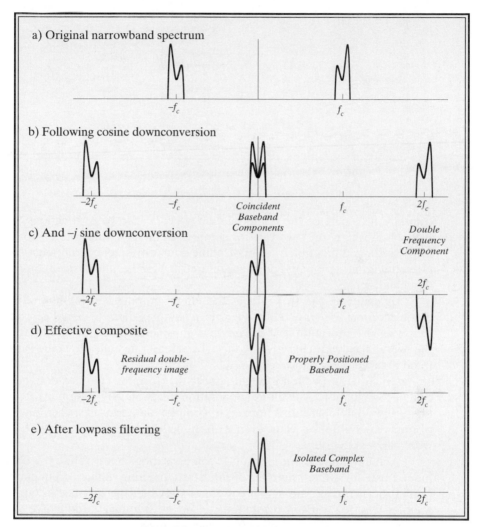

Figure 7.4   Complex frequency translation.

Now suppose we apply a lowpass filter to the translated signal shown in Figure 7.4(d). The result is shown in Figure 7.4(e), the complex-valued signal centered around 0 Hz with a very concentrated spectrum, i.e., bandwidth considerably less than its original form positioned at f_c. This means that in complex form, this particular example can be sampled at a rate dictated by the width of its narrowband spectrum, not by its center frequency in its original real-valued form.

A prime application of this concept can be seen in down conversion appearing in single sideband (SSB) communications receivers [Rohde and Bucher, 1988]. A narrowband signal carries the desired information, and a receiver must isolate and

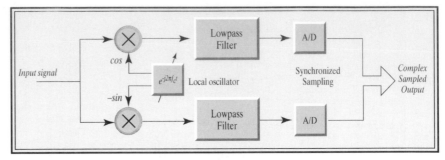

Figure 7.5   Conventional communications receiver using complex sampling.

translate it as part of the demodulation process. The basic functions are seen in Figure 7.5, where the "two-rail" or complex frequency translation is followed by a lowpass filter; its function is rejection of the double-frequency component, so that the net result is the asymmetric portion centered at 0 Hz, i.e., the desired complex-valued baseband signal.

By sampling the two rails at the filters' outputs and maintaining time synchronization of the two A/D converters, a complex discrete signal is produced that preserves the information of the original. In isolating one sideband in this manner, the overall bandwidth has been reduced by at least one half, allowing a sampling rate to be reduced accordingly.

On closer inspection it might appear that forming complex data has a hidden cost in computation. Any filtering operation following conversion involves complex taps or multiply operations applied to complex data samples, each one composed of four real multiplies. Thus, even with the halved sampling rate, net computation would appear to double!

Actually, there is another subtle compensating factor. While this conclusion is indeed true for a fixed number of filter taps, meeting a given frequency response at half the sampling rate actually requires only half the number of taps. Stated in another way, for a given resolution Δf in the frequency domain (e.g. transition band), determined by (sampling frequency/number of taps), use of complex processing at half-speed requires only half the number of taps. The net multiply rate is then

$$B \text{ samp/sec} \times N/2 \text{ taps } \times 4 * /\text{tap } = 2BN * /\text{sec.} \qquad (7.4.6)$$

For a real filter operating at twice the sampling frequency,

$$2B \text{ samp/sec} \times N \text{ taps } \times 1 * /\text{tap } = 2BN * /\text{sec.} \qquad (7.4.7)$$

Therefore, after all is accounted for, complex processing requires exactly the same multiplier throughput as equivalent real processing. (Note, however, that the actual operations for complex conversion may account for a fair burden as well.)

Given that there appears no reduction in net computation rate, of what value is the complex representation? The key is to recognize that we have in effect distributed any subsequent filtering computation between two parallel paths, the real and imaginary rails of the signal path. From an implementational point of view, we now need duplicate processes, but each requiring multipliers that run at half the original rate.

Extrapolation of this discussion to adaptive filtering in the complex domain is fairly straightforward. The statement of a complex form of LMS was given in (4.2.39). From the implementational perspective, the input and weight vectors as defined earlier now become complex-valued, and the scalar output and its error sequence are likewise complex-valued. However, there is a subtle difference in the actual adaptation expression, (4.2.39), that can be easily overlooked. Rather than a squared error cost function, we base optimization on a magnitude-squared error, that is, $e(k)e^*(k) = e_R^2(k) + e_I^2(k)$. This necessitates developing a separate gradient expression with respect to the real component of the weight vector, and a second with respect to the imaginary component:

$$\nabla_{\mathbf{W}_R} J = -2e_R(k)\mathbf{X}_R(k) - 2e_I(t)\mathbf{X}_I(k)$$
$$\nabla_{\mathbf{W}_I} J = 2e_R(k)\mathbf{X}_I(k) - 2e_I(t)\mathbf{X}_R(k).$$

Combining the individual components,

$$\nabla_{\mathbf{W}} J = \nabla_{\mathbf{W}_R} J + j\nabla_{\mathbf{W}_I} J$$
$$= -2(e_R(k)\mathbf{X}_R(k) + e_I(t)\mathbf{X}_I(k))$$
$$\quad -2j(e_I(k)\mathbf{X}_R(k) - e_R(t)\mathbf{X}_I(k))$$
$$= -2e(k)\mathbf{X}^*(k). \tag{7.4.8}$$

Details are available in Widrow et al. [1975a]. Recombining the update vectors into complex form leads to the complex LMS algorithm, as in (4.2.39); that is,

$$\mathbf{W}(k+1) = \mathbf{W}(k) + \mu e(k)\mathbf{X}^*(k). \tag{7.4.9}$$

Note the presence of the conjugation on the complex input vector. Omission of the conjugate is equivalent to a minus sign on the step size of the imaginary part of the weight vector and leads to a somewhat peculiar divergent mode.[3]

In this section, the subtle efficiencies of complex signal representation and complex filtering have been presented. The associated adaptive algorithm results from a derivation paralleling the conventional real arithmetic version, with essentially the same computational burden distributed between the real and imaginary signal paths.

---

[3] *Syntax Alert*: In MATLAB, the symbols a' produce the complex conjugate transpose of a, while $a.'$ delivers a transpose without conjugation.

7.4.4 Algorithmic Shortcuts

When operating at high sampling rates, it is often necessary to reduce the complexity of calculations to allow completion of the steps enumerated at the beginning of Section 7.3. This could mean skipping operations outright when the timing of the processing loop requires it, or perhaps reducing precision to simplify data manipulations. In this section, we discuss the general effects of these alternatives and their impact on implementation.

Partitioned architectures.   Elimination of operations is a natural consequence of insufficient time for completion of all steps enumerated in Section 7.3. Omission of operations may not be as serious as we might first imagine. For adaptive filtering applications, we can classify operations into two distinct categories: those associated with output calculation (the signal flowpath) and those associated with weight update (the performance feedback path). Calculation of the output clearly is of highest priority; that is, we must produce an accurate response value by the end of each sampling instant. The rule is: If the output cannot be calculated at the sampling rate, abandon the current implementation. For a digital design, this means one must either provide more computing power or reduce the filter length. In cases where neither is a satisfactory solution, an analog implementation may provide an alternative with the associated cost to performance, as discussed in Section 7.7.

Fortunately, such a grave verdict is not necessary for the second class of operation, the updating of the filter weights. Clearly, adjustment of a weight is of lesser priority. If an update is lost every now and then, the principal cost is a slower convergence rate. Specifically, if theory predicts L samples for convergence of the weights of an N-tap filter, to a first order there must be NL individual weight update calculations completed. If only one weight of the N can be updated per sample, we might expect a convergence time of NL samples, an increase by a factor of N to on the order of $N^2 L$ samples. We can view the update operation as a "background" computation, sandwiched in between the "foreground" output calculations. Thus, each weight is updated in turn, as many per sampling instant as possible.

Of course, asynchronous computation can be awkward for a small processor, so it is usually advantageous to structure the firmware/software to update given weights at specific times. For example, we might update one weight per sampling instant, once the output convolution has been completed; we leave enough idle time to assure completion of this task. At the next sampling instant, the next weight would be updated, and so on. In effect, the limited computing power of the single processor is being distributed among the N taps of the filter. This could be extended, time permitting, to update groups of two or more during each sampling instant, with a suitable increase in complexity. In higher-speed cases where the entire update cannot be completed during the "background" fraction of the sampling loop, the update operations can be split; i.e., the error-data multiply can be completed during one sampling period, and the add during the next. This again slows response time by roughly another factor of 2.

In such cases, the original adaptation algorithm has effectively overloaded the processing hardware, unfavorably impacting filter evolution rate. Under certain circumstances where tracking ability of the filter is important, it may be necessary to seek an alternative to update skipping. Clearly, this requires introduction of additional hardware. What are the best ways to structure the adaptive filter to use a second processor? Recall that the output convolution and the weight updating involve roughly the same complexity, i.e., the same number of multiplies, but more data manipulations in the addition operations. One division of labor might be to dedicate one processor to the output calculation, and a second to the update calculation. The former computes output and error terms and passes the error to the update processor. The second processor reads out the delay line data and performs the product and updating for each weight. In this way, the updating is completed in parallel with the calculation of the next output. The two processors share the same data and weight memory, as shown in Figure 7.6, so access must be synchronized. Global memory access associated with single-chip signal processors makes such I/O operations simple. This structure allows adaptation in accordance with the original algorithm, with one subtle difference. The update of weights lags by one sample; i.e., output at time k is computed using weights not yet incorporating the output performance at time $k - 1$. As we have come to expect when small adaptation step size is involved, such a small time lag is insignificant when compared to the overall time constants of the filter and makes little practical difference to filter evolution.

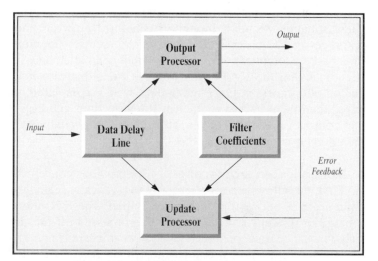

Figure 7.6   Distributed processing architecture.

Sharing memory resources provides certain practical limitations on this dual processor structure; after all, we have effectively doubled the number of memory accesses. By further divorcing output and update processors, this concept can be extended to even faster sampling rates. Suppose that each processor were provided

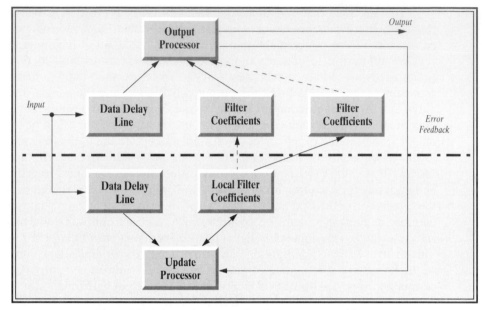

Figure 7.7   Divorced output and update processor architecture.

its own data and coefficient memory, as shown in Figure 7.7. Note that the output processor draws its coefficients from one of two RAM sections; the second serves as the destination of updated weights. As before, the error sample would be passed from processor 1 to processor 2. Then, each processor operates in parallel without memory access complications. As an update is completed, not only is the new weight written back into the RAM from where it came, but also into the inactive RAM of the output processor. Once the update cycle is completed, the output processor "swaps" the role of its two coefficient RAM sections and uses the new weights for its next output calculation. Again, global memory available to both processors can make interchip communication trivial.

Block-oriented architectures.   The previous concept has several ramifications. First, this allows a convenient way to physically segment the hardware, since communications between processors is limited. The FIR filter itself can reside on one board or package (such units can be purchased off-the-shelf), and the weight calculation can be done on a second. New weights are transferred *en bloc*.

Second, as mentioned before, there is no reason that updated weights need be transferred every sampling period. The output processor can very well use fixed weights for an interval and later accept a new set of improved weights. This leads us to the concept of *block adaptation*. Recall that when the speed of update processing was a concern, adaptations were simply skipped, lengthening the convergence rate. With block adaptation, the problem is more one of interboard communication. To minimize the transfer of updated weights between processors, we can keep updating the weights locally, but not pass them on to the filter processor. In effect, subsequent updates are accumulated before an adjustment is seen by the output processor. In terms of the gradient approximation discussion of Section 4.2.2, accumulation of update terms effectively improves the accuracy of the estimate of the error gradient. Consequently, the net update has a lower variance and represents a more accurate adjustment. The rate of convergence is not affected to first order.

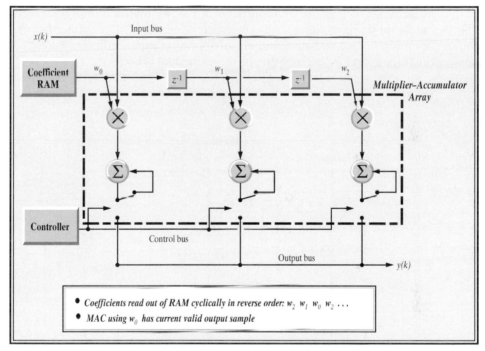

Figure 7.8   Reverse form FIR filter.

Use of block adaptation is especially well-suited to the reverse form of the FIR digital filter, shown in Figure 7.8. Using this dual architecture allows a convenient means of applying multiple processors to the output convolution, and is thereby useful at very high sampling rates. Instead of a delay line holding data samples, this form has filter weights advancing through a delay line in time-reversed order. As a result, each input data sample can be discarded as a new one becomes available. For each node in the N-tap filter there is an independent accumulator that provides a completed convolutional sum once every N input samples. Following initialization, its content builds up over time as

$$
\begin{aligned}
\text{At time } k: \quad & w_{N-1}x(k) \\
\text{At time } k+1: \quad & w_{N-2}x(k+1) + w_{N-1}x(k) \\
\text{At time } k+2: \quad & w_{N-3}x(k+2) + w_{N-2}x(k+1) + w_{N-1}x(k) \\
\text{At time } k+N-1: \quad & w_0 x(k+N-1) + \cdots + w_{N-1}x(k)
\end{aligned}
$$

(7.4.10)

so that at this last point in time it contains a completed output convolution $\mathbf{X}(k)^T\mathbf{W}$. Staggering the filter coefficients with the delay line will phase the accumulator array such that sequentially sampling (i.e., multiplexing) the N nodes provides the output at the full rate. Following its polling for output, the node's accumulator is reset to zero for the next cycle.

In this architecture, the N weights multiply the input sample, N multiplies as before, but it is the accumulation of results that is entirely different. From a hardware point of view this is a convenient means of decoupling the operations of N multiplier/accumulators and of distributing computation. The throughput rate of the filter is then essentially that of the individual processor.

The same basic architecture also serves the update operation, as shown in Figure 7.9. Thus, a circuit with modified I/O and control firmware acts as both

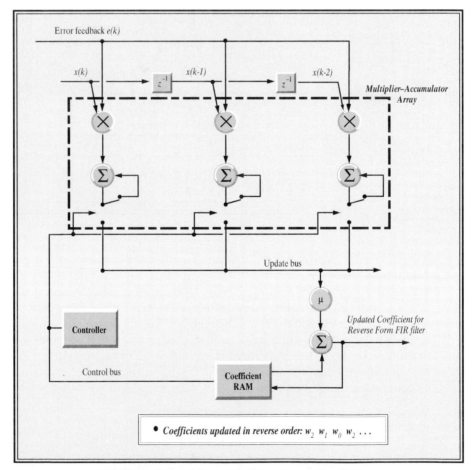

Figure 7.9   Reverse form architecture for weight updating.

output processor and update processor, suitable for very high sampling rates. In the update mode, the error signal fed back from the output processor enters to multiply data samples advancing along a delay line. The resulting error-data products are accumulated at each node; each accumulator then contains the respective weight update prior to step size scaling. Step size is incorporated either by scaling of multiplier inputs or scaling outputs from the accumulators. During each sampling period, one weight is read out and passed to the output processor, where it enters the weight delay line. Note that this architecture relies on block adaptation on a weight-by-weight basis; once an updated weight is sent to the output processor, it does not change for N samples. During this interval, N updates are accumulated.

Reduced precision structures.   The two preceding architectural concepts represent a sampling of ways that an adaptive filter may be configured for speed or size efficiency. Note that as general rule, efficiency costs not only filter bandwidth, but convergence rate as well. What else may a designer try in order to reduce computation time and/or hardware? Often, gains can be made by resorting to lower-precision data and coefficients, with the obvious cost to output distortion and quantization noise level. Not only does coefficient and data storage require fewer memory chips, but a reduction in multiplier width can result in faster throughput per unit of board area. Depending on the I/O bus of a processor, wider data samples may require multiple accesses; for example, I/O is often limited to transfers of one byte at a time.

A discussion of performance and precision issues is found in Section 7.6. Here we are concerned specifically with the effect of precision on update computation. While modest gains may be possible by use of a lower-precision product of error and data, significant simplification results from use of single-bit update operations, i.e., reduction of precision to the sign bit only. Chapter 4 enumerated the algorithms using "signum-based" adaptation in (4.2.55)–(4.2.57), where the update might involve the terms

$$\text{sgn}(x(k-j))e(k), \tag{7.4.11}$$

$$\text{sgn}(e(k))x(k-j), \tag{7.4.12}$$

or

$$\text{sgn}(e(k)x(k-j)). \tag{7.4.13}$$

In all cases, there is no multiply as such; in the first two forms, the update reduces to an add/subtract. The last form is particularly convenient; the update is simply an increment or decrement operation. Architectures for these algorithms are shown in Figure 7.10. Note that multipliers and multiplier/accumulators have been replaced by signed adders, or in the last case, combinatorial logic driving an up/down counter. Such algorithms may be of particular value for very high sampling rates, where use of a full multiply might involve considerable expense.

Not surprisingly, convergence behavior of these forms is degraded by the lower precision. As noted in Section 4.2.7, taking the sign of the data alters the update

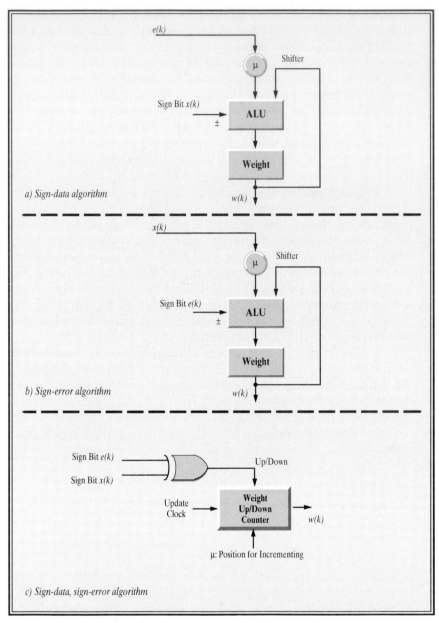

Figure 7.10   Signum-type algorithm update hardware.

direction, thereby threatening the capability for convergence without further restrictions on the acceptable input data. Convergence rate is also impacted. Note that only for the first does the "size" of the error enter into the update, thereby providing finer adjustment as convergence is approached; this retains the flavor of a quadratic cost function with its exponential weight evolution. In contrast, the update associated with the last two algorithms is of constant "size"; near convergence, it is the sign of the error sample that keeps the weight jittering around its steady-state value. This behavior can be likened to that seen with a "linear" cost function, e.g., an absolute value function, where slope magnitude (convergence rate) is constant. Using this intuitive characterization, we might expect that acceptable behavior at convergence (low-weight jitter) would require reduced step size and an overall loss in convergence rate. Therefore, while "signum-based" adaptation is convenient and efficient in its hardware requirements, it may be of limited use in highly dynamic environments.

7.4.5 Cyclostationary Filtering

Most of the discussion to this point has dealt with signals having a stationary character. Mathematically, this means that the statistics of the signal are constant over time. Of particular interest for the adaptive filtering problem are signal power and time correlation, i.e., the second-order statistics. One of the major attractions of adaptive filters is their ability to track variations in the signal. We usually assume that such variations occur slowly when compared to convergence modes of the filter, defining the so-called quasi-stationary signal. Such a characterization is suitable for numerous applications involving random continuous waveforms, as found in communication problems.

   There is a large class of problems involving signals that are not strictly stationary, but possess statistics that vary in a periodic or cyclic manner. During a "cycle," the statistics may vary widely, but the variations are the same from cycle to cycle. Sparing any further mathematical qualifications, such signals are referred to as *cyclostationary*. The standard example concerns a periodic pulsed waveform in stationary noise, as depicted in Figure 7.11; measured biological phenomena such as noisy voiced

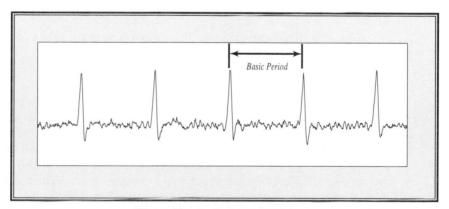

Basic Period

Figure 7.11   Cyclostationary process.

speech are often sources of such data. The wave has a basic period, and at any given instant its variance is constant, so that the mean traces out the underlying pulse shape.

When the rate of statistical variation is slow compared to the adaptive filter convergence rate, the signal can be treated as a quasi-stationary process. In such cases, the filter can track the optimum setting that traces out a periodic trajectory. However, when the signal changes at a rate comparable to the filter time constant, we can no longer expect the normal adaptive algorithm to track accurately the optimal filter settings. In such cases, the filter resorts to some "average" response that typically degrades the quality of the signal.

Fortunately, such problems can be countered by means of *cyclostationary adaptive filtering* [Ferrara, 1981]; we offer an intuitive treatment in this section. For the moment, assume that the statistics cycle over a well-defined period. Consider the pulsed signal shown in Figure 7.11. If the filter's task is to isolate the signal and reduce the noise, then it is clear that the "optimum" filter involves some spectral shaping during the "on" time and a zero response during the "off" time. In other words, at a given instant the optimum filter setting is determined by the input statistics at that instant. This implies that in steady state, the filter taps should cycle among a set of weight vectors, each one optimum for a relative position within the period of the statistics. Therefore for a cycle of M samples, there are M vectors of N filter taps each necessary to provide optimal signal recovery. For a given relative position within the period, the best output is computed by using one set of weights, and subsequent outputs by using other sets of weights.

Each such weight vector can be adapted independently, using a cyclic update. That is, each vector is adapted once per cycle following computation of its output. The converged result is dependent only on the statistics of the input at that instant, an invariant. Thus, each of the M filter responses converges to a unique vector. Mathematically, we define a doubly indexed weight vector, with the time index referencing the cycle's starting edge, and a subscript to denote the filter position within the cycle:

$$\mathbf{W}_\ell(kM), \qquad 0 \le \ell \le M - 1. \qquad (7.4.14)$$

Note that the effective composite time index involves the number of cycles k plus an offset ℓ within the cycle. As each vector is adapted only once per cycle, we might correctly assume that convergence time is roughly proportional to the length of the cycle time M.

The implementation of a cyclostationary adaptive filter requires only slight modification of the conventional structure. As before, the output is computed every sample, but must involve a different set of weights. These weights are normally stored in small addressable segments of a single RAM, where firmware enables access of the correct segment at the appropriate time. Following calculation of the output error, the update operation reads the correct weight, makes the weight adjustment, and writes back into the same segment of RAM. For the next sampling instant, firmware increments access to the next weight RAM segment.

Use of cyclostationary filters can greatly enhance performance for applications involving periodic signal or noise waveforms. The basic implementational cost is minimal, but does require measurement and tracking of cycle synchronization information.

7.4.6 Algorithmic Leaking

There are certain conditions under which adaptive strategies may prove unsatisfactory, despite the reasonable nature of the environment. Divergence or stalling of weights for stochastic descent adaptation can often be avoided by means of a "leaking" mechanism used during the update calculation. The benefits of adding a noise to the input of an adaptive filter has been alluded to in Section 4.2.7; the equivalent effect can be achieved indirectly by an algorithmic adjustment, avoiding unnecessary corruption of the input environment. Specifically, rather than simply adding the update term $e(k)\mathbf{X}(k)$ to the previous weight vector, we first reduce the old weights by a small amount. This action effectively simulates a small "leak" in the integration operation, borrowing from terminology associated with analog operational amplifiers. The resulting expression is as in (4.2.58), that is,

$$\mathbf{W}(k+1) = (1 - \mu\gamma)\mathbf{W}(k) + \mu e(k)\mathbf{X}(k), \qquad (7.4.15)$$

where γ is small and positive such that $(1 - \mu\gamma)$ is very close to unity. This has the same effect as adding a white noise with power γ to the input (or penalizing larger $\mathbf{W}'\mathbf{W}$ as in (4.6.32)). Biases away from the optimal filter solution result from nonzero γ, yet can be minimized by specifying $\gamma \ll 1$.

Use of this technique can be beneficial in a number of situations. Conditions where conventional iteration may be inadequate include the following:

1. *Insufficient spectral excitation.* When the input spectrum exhibits a wide range of energy densities, the convergence time constants are correspondingly disparate. In particular, when there are regions for which energy is nearly negligible, adaptive algorithms may respond in odd ways. Absence of energy at a given frequency in the input, and consequently in the output, implies that the filter has no feedback mechanism by which to sense its response at that frequency. Its growth at that frequency may continue unchecked and result in weight divergence. Such divergence is associated with the inversion of the ill-conditioned input correlation matrix.

2. *Finite precision effects.* A related effect concerns the quantization of the algorithm computations. The resulting quantization effects may serve as a low-level noise that appears at the output, with no corresponding stimulus at the input. Depending on the specific algorithm, the weights may react in an undesirable fashion.

3. *Stalling or biasing.* Weight recursions of Chapters 4 through 6 serve to "integrate" or sum all update contributions, which are derived by means of a performance feedback path. Disturbance of this path (noise, finite precision calculation and storage, transmission errors) may introduce a bias or "glitch" to the weight vector components. Recovery is dependent on the modes of the system, often involving the eigenstructure of the input, and in some cases may come at an insufficient rate. In some adaptive configurations, which may lack a true feedback path, recovery does not occur at all. A simple leak factor assures that such errors decay at an adequate rate, as discussed in Section 4.2.7.

7.5 FREQUENCY DOMAIN IMPLEMENTATIONS

To this point, all discussion has been limited to the implementation of adaptive filters using time domain techniques. There is a certain consistency and simplicity of the operations that is comforting: a sample enters a delay line, all delay line contents are multiplied in turn by appropriate impulse response or tap values, and the contributing products are accumulated to form the output sample. As we have pointed out along the way, filter performance improves with the number of taps, at a cost in complexity that increases approximately linearly with filter length. However, as we have seen for a given bandwidth, long filters may well lead to impractical hardware sizing. It turns out that significant processing efficiencies can be realized by using block-oriented frequency domain operations. The computational efficiency of the *fast Fourier transform algorithm* (FFT) reduces the overall complexity of the convolutional sum as well as the adaptation cycle. These ideas were first formalized in Dentino et al. [1978] and Ferrara [1980]. This concept can be extended to a variety of transform domain implementations [Shynk, 1992] and also can allow the imposition of transform domain constraints on the adapted parameters [Rafaely and Elliott, 2000]. In this section, we present an intuitive approach to the development of frequency domain implementation and adaptation.

7.5.1 Fast Output Convolution: A Complexity Analysis

We first review the efficiencies of performing linear filtering using the FFT, in keeping with the tone of this chapter, by addressing architectural implications. Recall that we found the bulk of computation is associated with the calculation of filter output. That is, adaptation of weights need be done only as time permits, and stretching out update operations need only affect net convergence rate. For an N-tap filter, the convolution itself involves N multiplies and $N - 1$ adds. (This assumes real data and weights; complex operations implies a fourfold increase in multiplies and doubling of adds.) Therefore, processing N contiguous input samples and generating the N corresponding output samples involves net computation of N^2 multiplies.

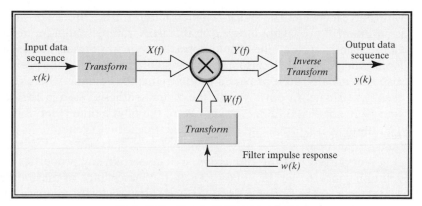

Figure 7.12   Concept of fast convolution.

In applications involving fixed filtering, significant reduction in hardware can be achieved by using a block-oriented architecture instead of more simple and concise single-sample processing. The costs of block processing, i.e., the addition of memory buffers and more involved control functions, are more than outweighed by the reduction of multiply and accumulate operations. The basic "fast convolution" implementation of a digital filter is shown in Figure 7.12. Owing to its impact on signal processing, details of fast convolution in Fourier analysis are usually prominent in many texts on digital signal processing; for that reason, background discussion here is purposely kept brief. (See, for example, Burrus and Parks, 1985.)

Here the convolution sum is replaced by a product in the frequency domain, exploiting the property

$$\mathcal{F}[y(k)] = Y(f) = X(f)W(f). \tag{7.5.1}$$

From the implementational perspective, the samples still enter and leave in time sequence form. Incoming samples are written into half of a "double buffer" memory; when a block of new N samples is filled, an FFT processor operates on the block to generate complex frequency samples. During this computation in a real-time environment, incoming samples are directed into the second half of the buffer. The filter response is likewise specified in the frequency domain and is applied as a point-for-point complex product with the input spectrum. The block of complex results are then inverse-transformed by another FFT processor and written into an output buffer. At appropriate sample times, each real value is read from the buffer as an output sample. Many of the architectural features of single-chip signal processors are motivated by the operations associated with the fast Fourier transform. Consequently, very concise transform implementations can be realized with dedicated chips.

It is important to realize that despite its internal differences, this function is identical to the time domain implementation from an input/output point of view, with one exception. The block-oriented nature of the processor means that there is an inherent propagation delay of at least N samples from input to output port. Consequently, such a filter would normally be inappropriate for use in a feedback loop, as might appear in certain control system functions. On the positive side, a filter response itself is often provided in the frequency domain, where its specifications usually originate. In other words, the "filter synthesis" step in the design of a fast convolutional digital filter is trivial. Were the filter's time response designated, we would simply perform a one-time, off-line transform to generate its complex-valued transfer function.

For purposes of this discussion, we cite certain key properties of the fast convolution concept. We then elaborate on the importance of these properties in the context of adaptive filtering. First, as a basis for complexity comparison, we note that the number of real multiplication operations involved in an N-point radix-2 complex FFT is $2N \log_2(N)$. (This includes "degenerate multiplies" by $+1$ in one stage.) Second, it is important to note that the FFT of an N-point block of real samples can be achieved by a complex $N/2$-point FFT, plus $2N$ additional multiplies. Finally, we must be aware of the peculiarities of "circular convolution" associated with the periodic nature of the discrete Fourier transform. Avoiding the distortion effects can be assured by proper blocking of input data. Leaving details to fundamental texts in signal processing, we note that the product of N-point transforms results in a time sequence that exhibits circular end-effects distorting the true convolutional values. Suppressing this effect calls for arranging time samples into blocks of $2N$ points (i.e., both time data and filter impulse response). Inverting the product of transforms for the $2N$-length block yields only N true samples of the output convolution. The remaining N output values are discarded in this, the so-called "overlap and save" convolutional method.

Notationally, this might be expressed as

$$W(f) = \mathcal{F}_{2N}[w_0 \ w_1 \ \cdots w_{N-1} \ 0 \cdots \ 0]$$
$$X(f) = \mathcal{F}_{2N}[x((k-1)N) \ x((k-1)N+1) \ \cdots \ x((k-1)N+2N-1)] \quad (7.5.2)$$
$$Y(f) = \mathcal{F}_{2N}[N \text{ discarded values} \vdots \ y(kN) \ y(kN+1) \cdots \ y((k-1)N+2N-1)].$$

In the "overlap and save" fast convolution technique, half of this $2N$ record of input samples must be retained for use in the next block transform.

Consider the net complexity of the fast convolutional filter. For an N-point impulse response, the real input data is blocked into $2N$ samples and transformed. The product with the filter frequency response is performed, and the output sequence is recovered by a $2N$-point inverse FFT; the proper N output time samples are retained. As a basis for comparison, this requires a net $[4N \log_2(N) + 12N]$ multiplies, assuming spectral symmetry is exploited to the full extent. The time domain computation of the same N output samples corresponding to a block of N input samples is N^2.

Based solely on the number of multiplies, a complexity ratio for radix-2 block sizes can be tabulated:

N	Complexity Ratio (FFT/Time Domain)
32	1
64	0.56
128	0.31
256	0.17
512	0.09
1024	0.05

Thus, for fixed FIR filtering, we see a dramatic reduction of complexity for large filters. Note that this table disregards the one-time transform associated with the filter transfer function.

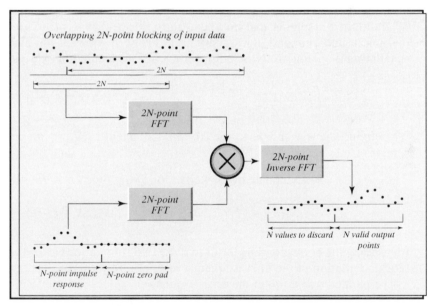

Figure 7.13   FIR filtering using fast convolution.

Therefore, for sampling rates where the output computation becomes a significant bottleneck, replacement of the FIR time domain filter by a frequency domain implementation may be warranted, as shown in Figure 7.13. Note that this exploits the division of labor mentioned in the previous section and allows the slower, less critical update computation to remain in the time domain. This requires that the update processor have access to the input data with sufficient memory to account for the bulk delay in the output calculation. Updated weights are again accumulated by the update processor and passed to the output processor. Each time weights are adjusted, a new frequency response is required, involving another $2N$-point transform.

7.5.2 Fast Update Calculation

While this approach to reducing output computational load has merit in some situations, it turns out that frequency domain techniques can be further exploited, allowing virtually all operations to be done at a reduced total computational burden. In other words, in situations where the rate of adaptation is critical and loss of update steps is unacceptable, frequency domain implementation of the update processor results in further savings for large filters. Of course, update calculations made in the frequency domain are a form of block adaptation, where N filter taps are adjusted once every N samples.

Consider the computation in the update process. For each filter update operation, there are N real multiplies required, that is, the error times the N input samples in the filter delay line. Thus, for a block of N samples, the update process involves N^2 multiplies, assuming that no updates are skipped; this is true for both sample-by-sample updating and block adaptation. Properly viewed, the block adaptation calculation is analogous to the output convolution calculation expression,

$$\text{Output at time } kN + i: \quad y(kN + i) = \sum_{\ell=0}^{N-1} w_\ell x(kN + i - \ell).$$

By defining the net update to the ith tap coefficient as ∇_i, it can be expressed in similar terms:

$$\text{Block update of } i\text{th weight following time } kN + N - 1:$$

$$\nabla_i(kN + N - 1) = \sum_{\ell=0}^{N-1} e(kN + \ell)x^*(kN + i - \ell).$$

Identifying the corresponding terms in these two summations leads to an FFT-based block adaptation of the filter frequency response. In terms of (7.5.2), we can define a zero-padded transform of the error sequence,

$$E(f) = \mathcal{F}_{2N}[e(kN)\, e(kN+1)\cdots e(kN+N-1)\, 0\cdots 0],$$

a transform of the time-reversed, conjugated data sequence,

$$\tilde{X}(f) = \mathcal{F}_{2N}[x^*((kN+N-1)\, x^*(kN+N-2)\cdots x^*((k-1)N)]$$

$$(7.5.3)$$

and the resultant convolution,

$$\nabla(f) = \mathcal{F}_{2n}[N \text{ discarded values} \vdots \nabla_0\, \nabla_1\cdots \nabla_{N-1}].$$

Furthermore, the Fourier transform conjugation/time-reversal property whereby $\mathcal{F}[x^*(-t)] = \mathcal{F}[x(t)]^*$ [Burrus and Parks, 1985] enables us to note that

$$\tilde{X}(f) = X^*(f)$$

so that

$$\nabla(f) = E(f)X^*(f).$$

This allows use of the input data transform already available, and requires only transformation of the error sequence. Thus, the vector to adapt the filter weight values is simply the last N points of the inverse transform:

$$\nabla(kN + N - 1) = \mathcal{F}_{2N}^{-1}[E(f)X^*(f)]. \tag{7.5.4}$$

This N-point vector can then be scaled by the constant μ and accumulated into the weight vector as before.

However, rather than updating the weights in the time domain, it is advantageous to apply adjustment in the frequency domain directly. (Clearly, in an implementation using the frequency domain output calculation, the weights themselves may need never revert to the time domain.) The gradient can be transformed using a zero-padded $2N$-point FFT and then accumulated according to

$$W(f, k + 1) = W(f, k) + \mu\mathcal{F}_{2N}[\nabla_0\nabla_1 \cdots \nabla_{N-1} \, 0 \cdots 0]. \tag{7.5.5}$$

This expression is nothing more than a spectral domain version of (4.2.7).

Using this overall frequency domain implementation, concrete savings in complexity and hardware can be realized. Referring to Figure 7.14, we see that five $2N$-point real FFTs are required, as well as two N-point complex vector multiplications. Net computational complexity for the frequency domain version of the adaptive filter is

$$5 \times [2N \log_2 N + 4N] + 2 \times 4N = 10N \log_2 N + 28N \tag{7.5.6}$$

real multiplies per N-point block. The equivalent complexity of the time domain filter involves simply $2N^2$ real multiplies, leading to a complexity ratio of $(5 \log_2 N + 14)/N$. Tabulated for radix-2 block sizes, this expression provides an indication of the dramatic savings that can be realized over traditional time-domain methods:

N	Complexity Ratio (FFT/Time Domain)
32	1.2
64	0.69
128	0.38
256	0.21
512	0.12
1024	0.063

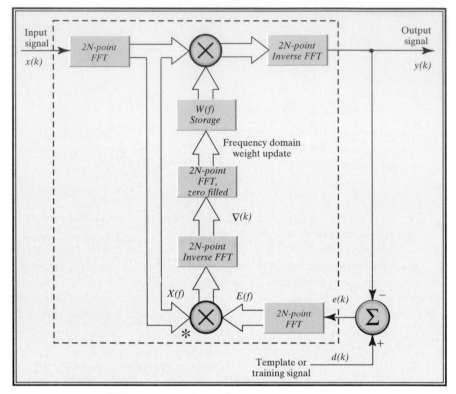

Figure 7.14   Frequency domain implementation of adaptive filter.

Note that there is a slight loss over the previous table, due to the fifth transform linking the update and output calculations. While there are subtle costs associated with frequency domain implementations not quantified by this measure (e.g., lack of flexibility, time delays, memory requirements), it is clear that filters using in excess of 100 taps may often require simpler hardware using the architecture of Figure 7.14. As a variety of hardware is available that can implement the FFT over a wide range of real-time bandwidths, such an architecture may provide benefits that far outweigh its limitations.

It is important to note that implementation of Figure 7.14 is quite general; it represents the equivalent of (4.2.7), which is itself a general recursive expression. In Chapter 6 it is stated that suitable redefinition of the performance cost function could result in other adaptive algorithms having this general form. Calculation of an alternative performance "error" quantity $e(k)$ can still be easily incorporated in this more efficient implementation. That is, the summing junction in Figure 7.14 where the error $e(k)$ is computed can be replaced by a far more general operation.

7.5.3 Channelized Adaptation

In Chapter 4, it was mentioned that the frequency response of a gradient-based adaptive filter evolves fastest in bands of highest energy concentration. Having just derived frequency domain relationships for the update expression, we can see this phenomenon directly. That is, frequency bands where input energy correlates with error receive the largest perturbations. For example, were a strong undesired narrow-band component present in the input spectrum, the filter's response in the appropriate frequency band would be rapidly reduced until the error energy were nulled at that frequency, i.e., $E(f_0)X(f_0) = 0$. Conversely, a low level of broadband noise at the input would be reduced by decay of the filter frequency response in the noise-only band, but at a relatively slow rate. The disparity of time constants, related inversely to the eigenvalues of the autocorrelation matrix, governs the convergence of adaptive filter parameters and often limits the level of performance that can be achieved. In other words, initial convergence rate and misadjustment effects are dominated by fast time constants, while overall rate of convergence is dictated by the slow time constants. For the most part, the effect of disparate time constants can only be reduced by techniques accelerating convergence by varying the adaptive step size over time.

However, once we resort to the frequency domain implementation, there is an obvious means of improving convergence behavior. The input spectrum has now been "channelized" or decomposed in the sense discussed in Section 3.4.6. Under adaptation, each band has its own convergence rate, decoupled from its neighbors. So, each band can possess its own adaptive step size, dependent on its relative input energy level. By incorporating any *a priori* information about the energy distribution of the input and desired signal, the convergence modes of the adaptive filter can be compressed to a more reasonable range, thereby improving convergence properties.

Mathematically, it is the transformation to the frequency domain that tends to decouple the adaptation modes. Recall that in the time domain, convergence dynamics are governed by the input correlation matrix. As detailed in Section 3.4.6, a set of orthogonal eigenvectors can be defined that spans the space of all input data vectors. A similarity transformation using this basis results in a matrix with the correlation eigenvalues on the diagonal. Adaptation of each channel or frequency band is governed by its eigenvalue alone. Filtering and adaptation is carried out in this transformed space, and the output is recovered by retransforming the result back to the composite space.

The FFT is merely one means of "orthogonalizing" the input data. It is far preferable to linear algebraic alternatives, which involve not only eigenanalysis of the input correlation matrix, but accurate measurement of the correlation samples making up the matrix as well. It is interesting to note that as the filter length gets large, the Fourier transformation asymptotically approaches a true eigenanalysis of the input correlation matrix [Gray, 1972]. Nevertheless, when input statistics are known *a priori*, there are adaptive algorithms which approximately orthogonalize the data during the adaptation update. Section 4.3 dealt with a recursive least squares technique using an orthogonalized update calculation.

However, it must be recognized that while the discrete Fourier transform produces a convenient and intuitive dissection of the input signal space (i.e., into frequency bins of the FFT), transformation of any finite record or block of data results in energy leakage between bins. As a simple example, a sinusoid input results in energy appearing in all bins of the FFT rather than the single bin containing its frequency. (Leakage does not occur only when the sinusoid frequency falls exactly at the center of a bin.) Such leakage represents a small coupling of the dynamics of the adaptive filter in the frequency domain. In certain cases, this small coupling can have a significant impact on convergence modes. For example, consider the same sinusoid component serving as an undesired element of a broadband input. Were we using the frequency domain implementation as described earlier, we might be tempted to assign a small step size to the bin containing the tone and larger step sizes to the rest of the frequency bins. However, leakage from the interfering sinusoid component into adjacent bins may dominate the broadband signal component; this extra energy may induce significant variance of the weight governing this neighboring bin, i.e., performance degradation. In other words, while the frequency domain implementation does provide an efficient architecture, weight behavior is not perfectly decoupled.

For many applications this residual coupling is of minor concern. However, in cases where leakage effects result in a performance degradation, e.g., an array of densely-spaced strong sinusoids corrupting a broadband signal, it is often necessary to provide further bin isolation. As was illustrated in Section 3.4.6 we wish to isolate bands of the input spectrum, passing all energy within the band with no frequency dependence. One simple means of performing this ideal orthogonalization is to use a "comb" of N bandpass filters spanning the input bandwidth. For each band, the magnitude and phase (relative to the filter's center frequency) is determined, weighted by a complex "tap," and used to "remodulate" a corresponding output band of energy. The sum of all such output bands generates the composite time domain output.

7.5.4 Designed Channelization

It can be seen that the FFT is simply an efficient means of doing the bandpass filtering and reconstruction. However, the equivalent "frequency response" of the FFT is not flat across the bin and does not provide a great deal of band isolation. The response for the unwindowed FFT is seen in Figure 7.15, i.e., closely approximated by the familiar $(\sin x/x)$ function: windowing the data provides some improvement, but may still be inadequate. Fortunately, a means does exist to improve the effective filter response while still exploiting the efficiencies of the FFT. This technique has been popularized by use in the generation and demodulation of frequency division multiplexed basebands, i.e., independent channels stacked in frequency. In the telephone

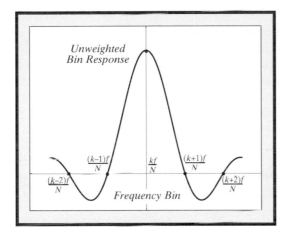

Figure 7.15 Approximate spectral response for a bin of an unwindowed DFT: $(\sin x/x)$ function.

industry, conversion between time and frequency-division-multiplexed formats has become known as "transmultiplexing" and has become an important application of digital signal processing. The details of transmultiplexer theory can be found in numerous publications (e.g., Freeny [1980], Narasimha and Peterson [1979], Yam and Redman [1983]).

Suppose that our input were sampled at f_s, and as before we wish to apply an adaptive filter of N weights. To perform the fast convolution, we must block the samples into $2N$ points and transform; the N filter weights are zero-padded to $2N$ values and likewise transformed. Subsequent transformations involve input data blocks overlapping the previous block by N samples. The net bin resolution of this filtering operation is $f_s/2N$. But suppose that the channelizing or bin shaping of the input provided by the $2N$-point FFT were inadequate, and that we insist on lower levels of interbin leakage, while preserving the basic resolution afforded by $2N$ points. To improve the isolation we might work backwards, specifying the bin shape in the frequency domain, and then inverse transforming to determine the weighting sequence necessary to apply to the input prior to the FFT, that is, a frequency-sampling design of the window. Specifying the shape of the bin response with fine-grain resolution results in a weighting sequence that exceeds $2N$ values, instead spanning $L = 2NQ$ samples, where Q is the integer number of specified frequency samples per $f_s/2N$ interval. Thus, our desire for better channelization has translated directly into a higher resolution spectral analysis, that is, an L-point transform of the input data applied to an L-point frequency response. Again, subsequent transforms must overlap the previous data block by N values. When inverse transformed, N points of the output are valid, as before in the "overlap and save" method of fast convolution.

Therefore, with this initial explanation, the processing burden has gone up with the need for a longer FFT. However, recall that the intent was to channelize the input into only $2N$ bins spaced at $f_s/2N$, not L higher resolution bins spaced at $f_s/2NQ$. The longer transform provides an excess of information, an unnecessary $Q - 1$ bin measurements or channels between each desired channel; this information can simply be discarded. With this in mind, the operations involved in the L-point FFT can be examined and "pruned" to eliminate the unnecessary calculations. It turns out that the longer FFT reduces to the $2N$-point FFT, preceded by the appropriate weighting of L input points, overlapped or "folded" into a single $2N$-point block. The resulting transform provides a channelized version of the input with bin measurements properly decoupled, occurring at a rate of $f_s/2N$.

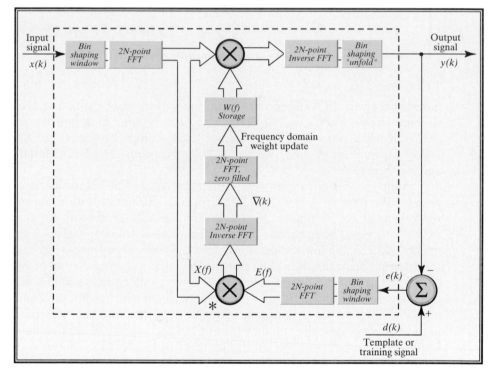

Figure 7.16   Frequency domain adaptive filter using an FFT-based filter bank.

Once properly channelized, the adaptive filtering operation proceeds as shown in Figure 7.16. An analogous inversion operation recovers the output time domain data from the adaptively weighted, channelized representation. Q sequential time samples emerging from the $2N$-point inverse FFT are interpolated for commutation into an output data stream at the original sampling rate. The interpolation filters applied to each leg of the FFT output must have a "polyphase" relationship. That is, they have identical all-pass characteristics and a flat delay response at exact multiples of $1/f_s$. (For example, the filter for bin 0 data has no delay, and for bin i data has delay i/f_s, etc.) The filter is often derived by decimating the

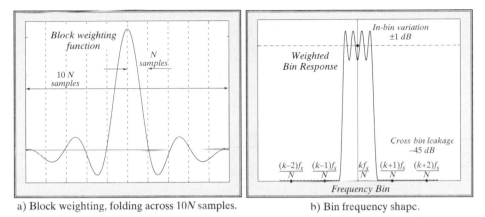

a) Block weighting, folding across 10N samples.   b) Bin frequency shape.

Figure 7.17   Typical shaping function for the FFT-based filter bank and its corresponding impulse response.

weighting impulse response used to condition data for the input FFT, as shown in Figure 7.17.

From a computational perspective, incorporation of data conditioning with each FFT results in an additional QN real multiplies per block of N points. The value of Q is determined by the quality of bin isolation required, i.e., preconditioning filter length, and may range from 3 for an isolation adequate for adaptive filtering applications to 22 for critical telephone transmultiplexer applications. Clearly, this data conditioning can be costly not only in terms of computational complexity, but in terms of memory requirements as well. Nevertheless, it is a powerful means of enhancing resolution of an adaptive filter without increasing its number of adaptive parameters.

A fitting closing comment to this section would note that orthogonalization of the input may have great benefit to convergence properties. We have seen the spectral decoupling using block processing with the FFT, perhaps enhanced by transmultiplexer weighting, allows the disparity in convergence modes to be resolved. That is, each time constant can be controlled by assigning an individual step size. Mathematical alternatives exist, of course, but are not always practical for the general case.

7.5.5 Modal Decoupling Architecture

One very important means of decoupling adaptive modes does lend itself to practice. This concerns an alternative implementation, the so-called lattice or ladder form for the filter, shown in Figure 7.18. This configuration was shown in Gray and Markel [1973] to possess certain favorable numerical properties in terms of coefficient sensitivity. Furthermore, in the context of modeling voice generation, or in autoregressive processes in general, the coefficients may equate to parameters describing energy reflection, and therefore have physical significance.

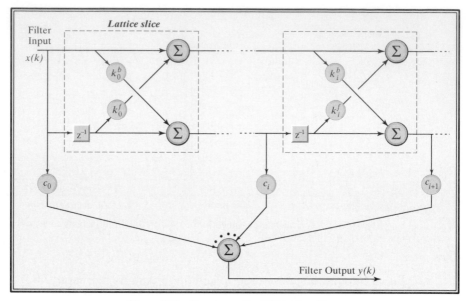

Figure 7.18   Structure of an FIR lattice filter.

Adaptive forms using the lattice filter evolved from a recursive least squares solution. In this form, the filter produces the exact least squares solution at each time instant, as described in Chapter 4. To simplify the update calculation, the step size can be made constant as in LMS-type algorithms. By virtue of its architecture involving a cascade of identical sections, the adjustment of each coefficient depends on the output of its section alone; there is no feedback mechanism relating performance of later sections to earlier sections. In a sense, each section acts as a one-tap filter removing the dominant correlation term and orthogonalizing the input one dimension at a time. Its convergence rate is not dictated by disparity of input correlation modes. Of course, a section cannot converge until those preceding it have converged. Yet such an architecture has demonstrated favorable convergence behavior compared to equivalent FIR-LMS adaptive filters. Satorius and Alexander [1979] discuss a comparison in the adaptive equalization context.

It is worth noting also that this configuration has great appeal for sliced architectures, where a filter can be lengthened by simply adding another section. This is in contrast to FIR implementations, where additional weights have an impact on both delay line and adder tree.

7.6 PRECISION EFFECTS

Arithmetic precision has a profound impact on implementation complexity. For a given processor and memory configuration, increasing precision of data or filter coefficients can often only be accomplished by multiple memory accesses and storage of intermediate partial products. Therefore, an understanding of precision effects as they impact adaptive filter performance is necessary to a designer for selection of appropriate processor and components. Again, the general topic of precision is normally treated in digital signal processing texts addressing hardware considerations [Rabiner and Gold, 1975]. However, fundamentals are included here to motivate special considerations due adaptive filtering applications.

The first fundamental design choice centers around the use of fixed or floating point arithmetic and storage. An increasing number of processors offer the luxury of floating point manipulation, thereby relieving the designer of headaches associated with fixed point operations, such as scaling and quantization performance. The advantages of floating point computation are many, enabling the designer to all but ignore limitations on sample range and overflow. Often the implementation phase of a hardware design reduces to transporting simulation software to a real-time platform. All that remains is the interfacing of a floating point design to the analog world, requiring an appreciation of fixed point representation and scaling.

While the convenience of floating point implementation may indeed be appropriate, as in the case of prototyping and concept demonstration, or in detectors requiring very large number ranges, it is important that the designer keep in mind the tangible costs in terms of processor, memory, and I/O. Often substantial reduction in recurring product costs can be realized with fixed point components. And of course, when dealing with high bandwidth applications, the choice may not exist at all; devices supporting fixed point arithmetic may be the only alternative available. To make an informed choice, it is important that a designer be aware of the tradeoffs involved in the fundamental architectural decision: ease of implementation versus cost/size/bandwidth. To this end, this section addresses the limitations of the fixed point implementation, in terms of scaling and arithmetic roundoff.

7.6.1 Scaling

By definition, fixed point implementation is constrained to store all signal samples and filter coefficients in integer form, usually in two's complement representation. The number of bits of storage n limits the range of integers available, from -2^{n-1} through $2^{n-1} - 1$, defining the *dynamic range* for the n-bit representation as $20 \log 2^{n-1} = 6n - 6$ dB. That is, for each additional bit the stored values can accommodate 6 dB more in signal power level. The cost of acquiring and maintaining that additional bit motivates a well-defined scaling strategy from input through output.

Scaling of data and coefficients to best fit within the available dynamic range requires some care. Prior to analog-to-digital conversion there is usually some form of gain adjustment, making certain that the input signal best utilizes the available range of values. Similarly, once digitized, a signal passing through sequential stages of processing may require adjustment in its level to keep the sample values within the allowable range.

A signal with level too high has values that exceed the maximum range, the *clipping level*. Clipping a waveform at any point introduces a serious nonlinear distortion, which can be viewed as a bursty signal-dependent noise component that destroys the fidelity of the original signal during its peak intervals. Once introduced, the nonlinear nature of this noise means that under many circumstances there is little hope of restoring fidelity.

On the other hand, a signal with level too low in the available dynamic range suffers from degradations due to quantization. Quantizing signal samples to integer values introduces an error component in the form of *quantization noise*, often modeled as a uniform white process with a fixed power level of 1/12, i.e., 11 dB below the level of a sample's least significant bit [Widrow, 1961].

For purposes of this discussion we introduce the concept of *loading crest factor* or CF, a measure of the signal power relative to the clipping level, expressed in positive terms. More precisely,

$$\textit{Crest factor, } CF = 10\log\frac{(2^{n-1})^2}{(\text{Signal power})}, \tag{7.6.1}$$

that is, the difference in dB between the upper limit (clipping level) and the total signal power. In colloquial terms crest factor is a measure of "headroom" available to accommodate signal excursions above their average power.

Proper scaling becomes a matter of adjusting the signal level, or its CF, to balance the effects of clipping with those of quantization. This relationship is highly dependent on the nature of the signal and its distribution. Consider Figure 7.19 showing the distribution of sample magnitude for four common signals: an ideal Gaussian, an ideal sinusoid, an actual speech record, and an actual modem waveform record. All have been scaled to the same average power level on an 8-bit range. We see that all but the sinusoid exhibit a monotonically decreasing behavior with a tail that approaches zero at the clipping point of 128. The sinusoid, limited to a peak value of $\sqrt{2}$ times its RMS level of 32, has a sample range confined to ±45. Since the waveform flattens out at its peak, the distribution has a singular point at that value. For this simple case, a CF of 3 dB minimizes quantization effects with no loss to clipping. This type of behavior carries over to many narrowband situations; for practical reasons, one usually allows a margin of safety of a couple of dB to accommodate amplitude variations and noise components.

The other three cases are not as easily analyzed. It is important to note the relationship of the two real signals to the ideal Gaussian distribution. Since an optimal scaling can be derived numerically for the Gaussian distribution, it serves as a baseline for evaluating other signals whose general behavior is similar. In this instance, speech by its nature is concentrated at lower values, with brief excursions during transients associated with "voiced" and "stopped consonant" sounds [Jayant and Noll, 1984]. This generates a longer-reaching tail than that of the Gaussian signal, one that must be accommodated when specifying a scaling approach. However, owing to its defined pulse amplitude structure, the modem waveform is more concentrated than the Gaussian case, and has a shorter reaching tail.

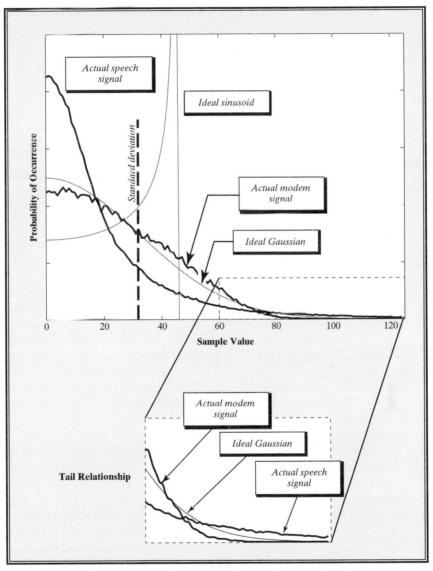

Figure 7.19   Probability of sample value for various signals.

One intuitive approach to scaling is to adjust the gain so that the average effect of the clipping noise contribution roughly equals that of the quantization noise.[4] In terms of Figure 7.19, this means that the power in the upper tail area should roughly equal that of the quantization noise. In the case of a Gaussian distribution

---

[4]This ignores subjective penalties that might be assigned to more serious clipping distortion.

this relationship can be evaluated numerically for various numbers of bits, giving rise to the following table of optimal CF:

Number of bits	CF (dB)
8	11.9
9	12.5
10	13.1
11	13.6
12	14.0
14	15
16	16
n	$\sim n/2 + 8$

For example, when representing a Gaussian signal in 14 bits, the optimal power level is about 15 dB below the maximum clipping level of 8192, so that the RMS level is about 18% or 1457. At that point the contribution of clipped distortion equals the quantization noise power, about $6 \times (n-1) + 11 = 89$ dB below clipping.[5]

While this table is useful for true Gaussian cases, on the surface it would appear to offer little help when dealing with real non-Gaussian signals, such as those depicted in Figure 7.19. However, an understanding of the distribution's tail indicates an appropriate adjustment to the tabulated CF. For example, speech with its longer tail should require a larger CF, whereas the more compact modem waveform should accommodate a smaller CF. To quantitatively underscore this, consider Figure 7.20, which shows for all four of the signals the numerical representation of clipping noise versus CF. Superimposed on this graph is the quantization noise power for sample widths of 8 through 16 bits, shown as horizontal dashed lines. The points in the table above are highlighted along the Gaussian curve.

As expected, the modem signal requires a CF smaller than the Gaussian process, approaching 10 dB, reflecting its relative compactness.[6] However, the clipping noise for the speech waveform parallels that of the Gaussian signal, calling for an additional 5 dB in CF; this particular example stops at about 18 dB, reflecting the sparsity of outliers for the window of observation. Depending on objectives for the level of speech fidelity, a designer may choose to limit the increase in CF to 2–3 dB.

Characterization of the Gaussian case has value beyond its role as a baseline of comparison. While individual sources may have waveform distributions that deviate from the Gaussian case, for most practical situations superposition of several such signals takes on a Gaussian flavor in accordance with the Central Limit Theorem. In cases where six or more independent speech, modem, and even tone signals of roughly the same power level are added, the result can often be treated as a Gaussian process,

---

[5]It is interesting to note that the clipping and quantization components do not actually add, because quantization noise only exists for samples that are not clipped and *vice versa*.

[6]This particular modem sample involves a 16-level modulation format. As the complexity of the signal's format increases, its distribution in turn expands and drives up the necessary CF.

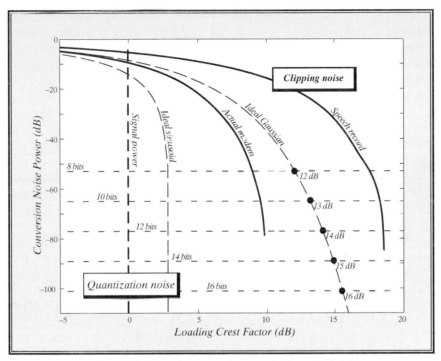

Figure 7.20   Crest factor requirements for four signal classes.

with a CF chosen accordingly. A common example is seen in frequency division multiplexing, where spectrally non-overlapping independent signals are combined as part of a transmission system.

7.6.2 Performance Issues

As detailed in the previous section, signal quality is limited by the dynamic range of its representation, and in the case of fixed point storage, the *noise floor* is determined by the combination of quantization and clipping effects. This basic noise floor can be further degraded by the introduction of round-off error in subsequent fixed precision arithmetic operations. The net effect can be minimized by proper use of floating point arithmetic; however, even then, round-off effects may accumulate in ways that force the designer to consider alternative structural arrangements in the interest of system performance. In this section we address the mechanisms and their contributions to signal quality.

To begin, it is instructive to digress on the topic of performance measurement. A common figure of merit when dealing with noise effects is the signal-to-noise ratio (SNR), i.e., the ratio of signal power to noise power expressed in dB. This is a measure that makes most sense when dealing with additive and independent noise.

However, the discussion here deals with noise that is highly dependent on the signal component; specifically, in the absence of signal there is neither quantization, clipping, or arithmetic noise present. Furthermore, in a digital representation, the noise's dependence on signal may also imply some level of frequency shaping. When dealing with non-white noise the reduction to its net power may be inappropriate or misleading.

For example, consider a sinusoid digitized with n-bit resolution, whose amplitude spans the entire $2^{n-1} - 1$ range. Its representation includes the usual level of quantization noise, 1/12. This textbook example then has an overall SNR of about $6n + 1.8$ dB. But how meaningful is this quantity? After all, the noise is spread across the whole band, but the sinusoid is concentrated at only one frequency. In many narrowband cases like this, SNR is of little value to characterize signal fidelity. Furthermore, if noise has spectral shaping, its composite power may be a misleading figure of merit.

For this reason it is useful to approach the idea of performance from a different direction. We draw on a technique originally developed for assessing nonlinear effects in analog circuitry. Degradation associated with effects such as amplifier saturation, detection devices, bias dependencies, magnetic hysteresis losses, as well as additive noise, result in an underlying floor whose signal dependence and frequency distribution is highly complex. Relationships between signal and individual noise contributors are difficult to characterize. But from a system point of view, unraveling such dependencies is unnecessary; it is sufficient to have a "bottom line" figure of merit for the nominal operating conditions. One approach to quantifying the net system performance is to measure the level of the noise floor for nominal signal excitation, i.e., power level and bandwidth occupancy. By convention, a specific test signal is used, a Gaussian noise-like signal with a flat spectrum that covers the specific band of interest at the nominal power level, so-called *noise loading*.

Given a signal that fills the band, the associated noise floor will be obscured and not directly measurable. To allow a glimpse of the noise floor, the signal is deliberately notched very deeply so that the noise level within the band is visible. The notch is kept relatively narrow to minimize its impact on the signal-dependent components of the noise floor. The measurement of net notch depth is termed the *noise power ratio* or NPR, and is used as a system figure of merit, providing a measure of end-to-end signal quality in light of complex degradation effects.

While originally developed to address nonlinear analog effects, the NPR approach is well-suited to characterize noise effects in digital circuits. For example, Figure 7.21(a) shows the spectrum of a digital test signal spanning about 36% of the sampling bandwidth, starting slightly above 0 Hz. Note the notch near the bottom edge. The signal's level has been set to 16 dB below the maximum, i.e., the optimal CF for a Gaussian signal represented by 16 bits. Then, to simulate fixed point behavior, the samples have been rounded to 16-bit precision. The resulting spectrum is shown in Figure 7.21(b). Note that the signal bandwidth itself is still well-defined at the same power level, but the out-of-band portion now exhibits a noisy floor associated

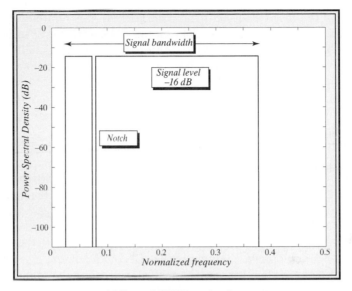

(a) Example NPR test signal.

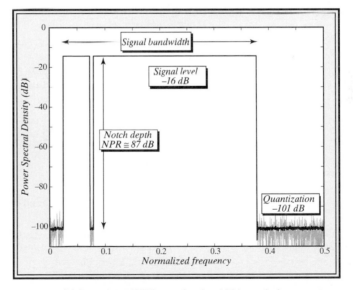

(b) Spectrum of NPR test signal at 16-bit resolution.

Figure 7.21   Typical NPR test signal.

with quantization. The noisy plot in grey corresponds to a single test; by averaging over a long interval, the noise spectrum becomes the well-defined dark line at the -101 dB level. The net NPR can be determined from the noise level in the notch, about $101 - 14.5 \simeq 86.5$ dB.

In the case of perfectly flat noise, the NPR is related to the SNR by a bandwidth normalization factor. That is, the SNR for this example is approximately $(-16 - (-101)) = 85$ dB. A fraction of that noise is actually out of band, and is irrelevant. Because the signal covers only about 0.35 of the 0.5 Hz range, the out-of-band portion of the noise accounts for $10 \log (.5/.35) \simeq 1.55$ dB of rejected noise power, which is exactly the difference between NPR and SNR. Of course, the relationship breaks down when the noise power has any shaping related to filtering or aliasing effects.

It is interesting to note that traditional NPR test equipment has often been costly to produce and maintain. Calibration of filters to maintain notches sufficiently narrow and deep requires precise analog adjustment. By contrast, digital test signals are truly trivial to generate. For this reason, modern test configurations may actually source the signal in digital form, stored in RAM and played back through a digital-to-analog converter, to provide a test signal for analog systems.

One common way to synthesize a noise-loading flat signal is to start in the frequency domain. We simply specify the frequency content as uniform in magnitude, and zero out the bands not of interest, along with the notch interval. Then, a simple inverse FFT provides the suitable time sequence. To assure randomness we specify the phase of each "bin" as a uniformly random value from $[0, 2\pi)$. In MATLAB the steps to generate a test record might look like this:

```
nsize=4096;                    %Time duration of test signal
nbits=16;                      %16 bit representation
CF=16;                         %Optimal crest factor for 16 bits

nscale=2^(nbits-1);            %Scale factor for 16-bit integers
amp=10^(-CF/20)*nscale;        %Amplitude

%===================================
phi=2*pi*rand(nsize,1);        %Random phase array
X=exp(-i*phi);                 %Set up randomly phased values of one

X(1:100)=0;                    %Below the band of interest
X(nsize/2-500:nsize)=0;        %Above the band
X(300:325)=0;                  %Notch frequencies

x=ifft(X);                     %Invert the spectrum
x=real(x);                     %Toss the imaginary part
%===================================

xpow=x'*x/nsize;               %Find the power
x=amp*x/sqrt(xpow);            %Scale to proper level
x=round(x);                    %Fixed point integer values
```

Note that the actual signal definition occurs between the barred lines; this is followed by scaling and fixed-point formatting. The resulting waveform is a noise-loading test signal of 4096 samples. Because it has been generated in the frequency domain, its sequence has endpoint continuity and can be repeated continuously.[7]

Note that we have not explicitly addressed the Gaussian nature of the test signal in the above generation process. In this method we are using the power of the FFT algorithm to add a large number of stationary independent, randomly phased sinusoids of equal power level. By the Central Limit Theorem, this result approaches a Gaussian distribution with probability one.

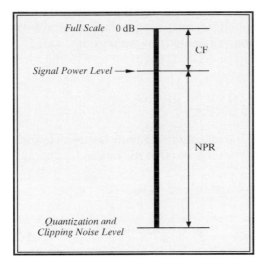

Figure 7.22   Input level diagram.

As a concluding note, tracking NPR through several processing stages is made easier by adopting a schematic shorthand. Figure 7.22 depicts the relevant information on a single vertical bar; it spans the full scale or clipping level at the top, to the noise floor associated with the least significant bit on the bottom. The signal power level is shown at its CF below the clipping level. The distance separating the signal power level and the noise floor, adjusted by the spectral bandwidth occupancy ratio, becomes the NPR. This form of notation provides a concise way to analyze a design, its scaling and performance, stage by stage, and finds use in the next section.

7.6.3 Arithmetic Effects in Fixed Designs

Given the means to quantify implementation performance, we can now evaluate the impact of various processing functions. Let us first consider the output calculation,

---

[7]Any discontinuity in the pattern will result in a glitch that artificially fills in the notch, thereby degrading the apparent NPR.

assuming an FIR filter with N finite precision coefficients operating on finite precision data samples. As noted earlier, FIR convolution is best implemented using a multiply/accumulate device, with each product summed into an internal accumulator. The reason for this is simple: The product of an n-bit data sample and an m-bit filter coefficient is an $(n+m)$-bit result. The use of an internal accumulator means the entire product can be retained and summed without prematurely truncating its precision and without resorting to extended-width off-chip I/O and storage. Most common DSP architectures accommodate multiplication of 16-bit data and 16-bit filter coefficients, accumulating the product terms with precision ranging from 24 to 32 bits. Only after the N terms of the convolution sum are completed, is the extended precision result rounded back to 16 bits for output to subsequent stages.

Accumulation of fixed point intermediate product terms in a convolution sum also results in an accumulation of quantization noise terms, so that the noise floor increases with filter length N. The desired output for an FIR filter is expressible as

$$y(k) = \sum_{\ell=0}^{N-1} w(\ell)x(k-\ell). \tag{7.6.2}$$

A simple model assumes that each element of the sum is subject to some quantization error, denoted as $\delta w(i)$ and $\delta x(k-i)$, and that the output is actually

$$y(k) + \delta y(k) = \sum_{\ell=0}^{N-1} [w(\ell) + \delta w(\ell)][x(k-\ell) + \delta x(k-\ell)]$$

$$\approx \sum_{\ell=0}^{N-1} w(\ell)x(k-\ell) + \sum_{\ell=0}^{N-1} \delta x(k-\ell)w(\ell) + \sum_{\ell=0}^{N-1} \delta w(\ell)x(k-\ell),$$

$$\tag{7.6.3}$$

neglecting the second-order error product.[8] The net error of the output summation is expressible as

$$\delta y(k) \approx \sum_{\ell=0}^{N-1} \delta x(k-\ell)w(\ell) + \sum_{\ell=0}^{N-1} \delta w(\ell)x(k-\ell). \tag{7.6.4}$$

To this point, we have assumed that precision of the output sum is maintained by means of an extended-length accumulator.

Actual calculation of the resulting signal level, noise floor, and NPR depend on specific filter characteristics. We can only make certain general statements that can be useful to a designer in assessment of an implementation. Signal power (i.e., the strength of the first term) is determined by the input signal power (i.e., $-CF$ with respect to the dipping level) and by the effective filter passband gain. Adjustment of the output crest factor, that is, output power level, is accomplished through scaling

---

[8]Note that for the fixed-coefficient filters, appropriate optimization can be used to limit these error terms. However, under coefficient adaptation, modeling of their contribution in the manner of (7.6.3) is useful to characterize performance losses.

via the filter's gain setting. The level of the output noise floor may depend on the number of calculations and their precision as detailed in the following.

The first error term in (7.6.4) is simply the input quantization noise samples, shaped and scaled by the specified filter response. Its level relative to the signal power is nominally the same as that at the input, with perhaps minor improvements afforded by the filter selectivity.

The second term in (7.6.4) depends on the number of coefficients N and their accuracy. We can think of each tap as having an associated noise generator, each with the same power, that of the half-bit quantization noise [Rabiner and Gold, 1975]. Assuming that coefficient error is uniformly distributed, the composite strength seen at the output is

$$NP_s E\{\delta w^2\} = (N/12)P_s \qquad (7.6.5)$$

where N is the number of filter coefficients in the convolution sum, and P_s is the signal power at the filter input. Because the signal level is $-CF$, (7.6.5) becomes $10\log(N) - CF - 11$ dB.

To illustrate the effects in terms of the NPR, consider Figure 7.23. A lowpass FIR filter with 151 taps has been designed with cutoff at 0.22 and equiripple suppression. Shown in Figure 7.23(a) is the magnitude response; the original design was optimized in floating point to provide a suppression band of nearly -120 dB of rejection. Shown in the figure is the response of the 16-bit fixed point approximation. Note the sensitivity of the stopband to the coefficient precision has eroded the out-of-band suppression from nearly -120 dB to almost -70 dB.[9] Applying that filter to the 16-bit NPR signal of Figure 7.21, we see that the resulting signal has the spectrum shown in Figure 7.23(b).

Figure 7.24 shows a typical level schematic associated with an FIR filter output calculation using 16-bit coefficients and data. On the left, 7.24(a) shows the input level diagram with the crest factor of 16 dB and the ideal noise floor at $-6 \times 15 - 11$ dB $= -101$ dB. The net NPR at the input is then -16 dB $+ 101$ dB $= 85$ dB. Figures 7.24(b) and 7.24(c) show the corresponding output level diagrams for a short filter (small N) and a long filter (large N), respectively. In both cases, the signal power appears at a level that has been reduced by 8 dB, reflecting rejection or downscaling by the filter response for this example. For this hypothetical case, the output crest factor has been improved to 24 dB, most likely an excessive value, a condition that can be compensated by a bulk shift in the accumulation. (In certain cases, such increases may be necessary. For example, the filter may isolate an individual component that requires a high crest factor when viewed by itself.)

When the convolutional sum is calculated using a multiplier with an internal 32-bit accumulator, the internal quantization floor is far below the level of the input quantization noise, shown in Figures 7.24(b) and 7.24(c) at -197 dB. When transferred out of the accumulator, the result is rounded to 16 bits, and the inherent quantization

---

[9]This band shape degradation can be partially mitigated by including fixed point representation within the numerical design procedure.

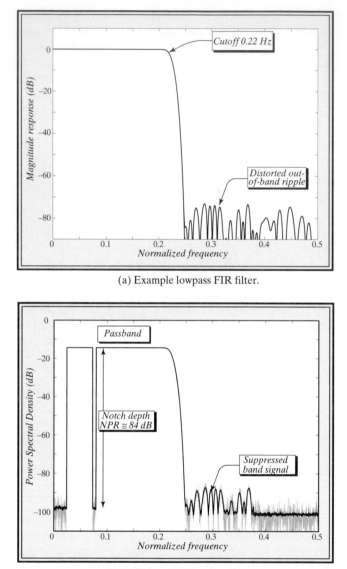

(a) Example lowpass FIR filter.

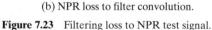

(b) NPR loss to filter convolution.

Figure 7.23   Filtering loss to NPR test signal.

floor is returned to the −101-dB level. At first glance it might seem that discarding the lower 16 bits has increased output noise level by 96 dB and thereby degraded the output NPR a similar amount. However, the self-generated noise terms associated with the convolutional sum (7.6.3) actually set the dominant noise floor far above this inherent double-precision quantization noise floor, so that very little if anything is lost by the rounding operation.

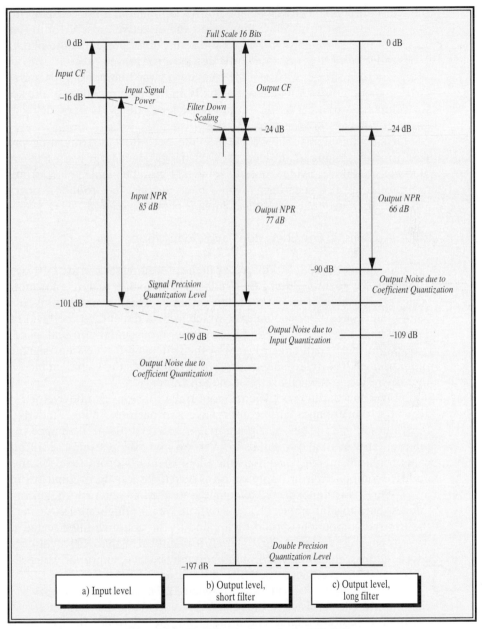

Figure 7.24   Signal level schematics for FIR filter.

The first of these two noise terms that appear in the convolutional sum of (7.6.3) i.e., the filtered input noise, is shown at a reduced level at the output, and again reflects some degree of band isolation by the filter. Recall that the second noise term is dependent on the number of taps in the filter. In Figure 7.24(b), the short filter case, this noise term is shown at a level below its companion noise component; rounding of the accumulator to 16 bits then raises the effective noise level to the -101-dB level, in this case roughly 8 dB above the actual noise present in the signal. The NPR is degraded to 77 dB due to the 8-dB loss in signal power.

Figure 7.24(c), involving a filter having a large number of taps, shows the level of this second noise term at about -90 dB. In this case rounding of the accumulator to 16 bits has no effect on the output noise level; the NPR of 66 dB is determined strictly by the level of this second term.

Using this approach, we can see the net effect of truncating prematurely, i.e., prior to accumulation. Had each partial product term been truncated to single precision, the individual noise level would have been unchanged from the input; accumulation of N such terms would have meant a net roundoff degradation of $10 \log N$ dB worse than proper accumulation and truncation.

7.6.4 Arithmetic Considerations and Adaptation

For fixed filters, the concepts discussed in the preceding section are fairly well defined. However, for adaptive filters, the feedback path makes scaling a far more complex issue. The location of the filter output within its dynamic range is given by the yet-to-be-determined filter coefficients, which in turn depend on the level of the error feedback. In a sense, for the LMS algorithm in particular, the scaling of the entire process (output and filter gain) is set by the scaling of the "desired" signal. Reducing the power of $d(k)$ (increasing its crest factor) reduces the gain demand on the filter, thereby reducing the actual size of the tap values.

Overflow of filter coefficients is naturally something to be avoided, and it usually pays to maintain a fairly conservative approach to scaling. Actually, saturated tap values clipped at the maximum magnitude degrade performance in a graceful manner. However, allowing taps to overflow and "wrap around" invariably proves catastrophic. In many applications, the adaptive filter's job is to excise some offending additive component from its input, and as such it reduces the original incoming power level. Were it further expected to compensate the loss and restore the component of interest back to a favorable CF at the output, weights might well saturate. Therefore, the desired component should be applied to the adaptive filter scaled down from its optimal crest factor. At first glance, it might seem that NPR will necessarily be degraded by such an approach. While this may be true, improperly increased scaling can do nothing to enhance the NPR of the component of interest.

When updating weights according to (4.2.7), it is again necessary to make provision for ample precision in the accumulation. That is, the product $x(k)e(k)$ defines a double precision number, and downscaling by μ extends the dynamic range further. This result must then be added to the original stored weight value to form the updated value. We are faced by the same fundamental problem as in the convolution calculation. Insufficient precision provided in the weight register will be responsible for a performance degradation. Only in this case, it is not evident as an increased noise floor, but rather as a coefficient bias or stalling of convergence. Stalling of weights short of the optimal setting is then responsible for excess error.

Recall that, at startup, weights are normally far away from their optimal settings, thus generating a sizable error. For a given weight precision and step size μ the update term decreases and eventually achieves a near-zero mean. This does not mean that the weight has the optimal setting, but rather that it varies around the proper value. When weights jitter due to such ongoing adjustment, they degrade performance or error power by misadjustment noise, proportional to μ. Theory tells us to reduce step size μ to the point where a suitable trade-off of misadjustment noise and fast response time is reached [Widrow et al., 1976].

However, there is another factor entering into selection of step size. At some point the update term will "slide off" the bottom of the allotted dynamic range of the accumulator used for weight updating. In effect, $e(k)x(k)$ is truncated to zero and the weight stalls at a location dependent on its initial value. In reality, because $x(k)e(k)$ is a random quantity, stalling occurs gradually; fewer and fewer values exceed the quantization level and continue to prod the weight. As the weights improve and the error term decreases further, eventually the weight will stop changing almost completely.

A suboptimal weight setting may or may not result in a significant performance degradation. This largely depends on the processing configuration and bandwidths of signal components. Before considering an example, a discussion of reasonable design steps is in order.

Clearly, to minimize bias effects due to stalling, we simply need to make the weight accumulator longer, i.e., tolerant to small update contributions. Practicality, however, requires that a reasonably short length be maintained to simplify hardware. Extended precision accumulation often requires multiple memory accesses and objectionably wide adders. It should be noted that block adaptation with its update accumulation accomplishes a degree of extended precision, thereby reducing the stalling effects. Thus, a designer must examine the application carefully and weigh the performance sensitivity to weight bias error against the misadjustment error seen with larger step size μ. This is made clearer by an example that follows.

For these reasons the weight storage precision may well exceed that of the input data. In such cases, the output convolution may use only the upper portion of the weight. Therefore, only when the accumulation of small update terms carries a change into this upper part will the output calculation use a new weight.

A simple example serves to illustrate most effects governing choice of step size. We consider the sinusoid cancellation problem, where effects are pronounced and easily characterized. In the context of noise canceling described in Section 1.1, suppose the *primary* input $d(k)$ contains a dominant sinusoidal $A \cos(\omega_0 k)$ and the *reference* input to the filter $x(k)$ contains the same tone at a different amplitude, $a \cos(\omega_0 k)$. Primary crest factor is set to 9 dB, that is, A equals one-half of full scale. A single weight w is adapted to minimize the error power

$$e(k) = (A - w(k)a) \cos(\omega_0 k)$$

so that the update is

$$w(k+1) = w(k) + \mu e(k)a\cos(\omega_0 k) \tag{7.6.6}$$

$$\approx w(k) + \mu[A - w(k)a]a/2$$

neglecting the double frequency product. In time, and with infinite precision, the weight converges to A/a and provides perfect cancellation.

However, suppose that this were implemented in fixed-point arithmetic with n bits. At some point, the update term $\mu e(k)x(k)$ crosses the quantization level, i.e.,

$$\mu(A - wa)\frac{a}{2} \approx 2^{-n+1}, \tag{7.6.7}$$

at which point

$$w \approx \frac{A}{a} - \frac{2^{-n+2}}{a^2\mu} \approx \frac{A}{a} - \delta, \tag{7.6.8}$$

where the weight error $\delta = (4/a^2\mu)2^{-n}$. The resulting error, that is, the amplitude of the residual sinusoid, is

$$a\delta = \frac{4 \cdot 2^{-n}}{a\mu}. \tag{7.6.9}$$

Cancellation, quantified as $20\log$ (amplitude before/amplitude after), is then

$$20\log\frac{A}{4 \cdot 2^{-n}/a\mu} = 20\log 2^{n-2} + 20\log Aa\mu$$

$$= 6n - 12 + 20\log Aa\mu \text{ dB}. \tag{7.6.10}$$

For 10-bit weights with $\mu = 2^{-4}$ and $A = a = 0.5$, this provides only 12 dB of cancellation, or 75 percent. Increasing μ to 2^{-3} improves the suppression by another 6 dB.

For this example the opposite effects of larger μ can also be shown in closed form. Suppose that underlying the primary input with its dominant tone is a noiselike process of interest with power σ_2^2. This randomness is present in the error, and consequently serves to jitter the weight. This case has been examined in detail in Glover [1977] and Treichler [1979]. In infinite precision, the weight converges to a random variable with mean A/a and variance $\mu\sigma_s^2$; the amplitude of the residual sinusoidal component is likewise random with variance $a^2\mu\sigma_s^2$. This leads to a clear trade-off: Large step size generates an undesirable error due to weight jitter; and small step size is responsible for error due to weight stalling. In this simplified case, the effects can be quantified, but in general (longer filters and correlated signals) the exact expressions cannot be found in closed form. However, the relationships, and thus the compromise, concerning μ still hold, and an experienced designer can form fairly reliable choices for μ and n, dependent on application details. For example, depending on the strength of the error waveform expected at convergence, the length of the weight accumulator can be specified. In applications where larger errors may be acceptable it may need no more than the filter input precision; in other critical cases where residual error may be very small, weight storage may require in excess of twice the data precision. Likewise, choice of step size should be such that the update term at convergence drops no closer than 2–3 bits to the accumulator's quantization level.

We conclude our example by demonstrating certain design choices that result. Certain key remaining parameters need to be specified. Presume the primary input has a signal-to-interference ratio (SIR) of -14 dB with a CF of 9 dB ($\sigma_s^2 = 0.005$ and $A = 0.5$); we wish to eliminate essentially all of the tonal interferer so that we know the acceptable error power is $\sim\sigma_s^2$. A CF of 9 dB at the filter input means that the input level a is 0.5. In this example, cancellation must be done quite accurately for significant suppression to be achieved, so we might expect that a high precision accumulator will be required. If the input were provided with 12 bits of precision (66-dB dynamic range), cancellation will be limited to 57 dB (the original input level of -9 dB reduced to the quantization level) given infinite precision updating. Were $\mu = 2^{-8}$ (i.e., an 8-bit shift), the misadjustment error would limit cancellation to only 47 dB; decreasing to $\mu = 2^{-10}$ allows 53 dB. However, this level can only be reached if the accumulator has adequate precision. In this case $n > 22.8$ bits, nearly twice the input data precision. For convenience in operations, this would be rounded to 24 bits, or double precision. Thus, weights would be maintained through the update process in double precision, but only the most significant half would enter into the output calculation.

This example is not meant to imply that extra weight precision is always required. However, it does show that instances exist for which an adaptive filter will be severely constrained by truncation of weight precision. For a further discussion on precision effects, see, for example, Caraiscos and Liu [1984].

7.7 ANALOG ALTERNATIVES

Recall that for purposes of discussion in this chapter a measure of complexity was defined in terms of net multiplication rate, only because the size and power of digital circuitry is dominated by multipliers, augmented by memory control and multiplexing hardware. There are situations where this complexity measure maps to a device that is undesirable: (i) cases where performance requirements do not require the accuracy and flexibility of digital hardware, and (ii) cases where bandwidth does not lend itself to acceptable forms of digital hardware. In such applications a designer may wish to consider analog or hybrid implementations.

The principal attraction of digital hardware is its accuracy; that is, it operates repeatably just as theory predicts. Analog devices are notorious for nonideal effects, e.g., trim adjustments, ripple, reflected energy, and frequency rolloff, which make them less than desirable for applications requiring accurate placement of resonances and notches. Thermal effects and aging further serve to complicate critical designs. However, in an adaptive mode, where there is an effective feedback closure around the filter, nonideal effects tend to be compensated, although leakage of analog weight storage is an unavoidable phenomenon. In a sense, an adaptive configuration optimizes performance of its components even when subjected to such handicaps. Assuming that reasonable care is taken in design to minimize the severity, a perfectly workable analog or hybrid system may be realizable with considerably lower power, size, and/or cost.

The basic analog building blocks include some form of signed product, e.g., a four-quadrant attenuator or mixer, summing amplifiers, and some form of "delay." This last element is loosely defined to be any component that provides "linear independence" of its input and output, i.e., some dynamic and hopefully linear time response. The resulting set of linearly independent versions of the input process then defines some subspace of the desired waveform.

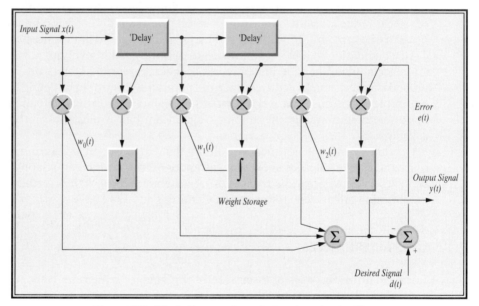

Figure 7.25   Block diagram of a typical analog adaptive filter.

Figure 7.25 shows a typical analog adaptive filter. Note that the "delay line" of the FIR structure may involve anything resembling a delay element with a suitably wide bandwidth. The weighting operation in the convolution is performed by analog mixers, whose outputs are summed. The error waveform then feeds back into other mixer components, and each is integrated to generate a voltage corresponding to a weight.

Recall that in any adaptive implementation the principal source of complexity is the output convolution; the update process can be performed at a pace permitted by the hardware. The analog implementation can be tailored to take advantage of this fact. Instead of totally analog circuitry, the output calculation can be controlled by digital feedback. That is, the output (or error waveform) can be digitized, as can the delay line nodes, and the weights maintained and updated using the digital techniques discussed earlier; digital-to-analog converters provide the weighting voltage to the tap mixers. Block adaptation and/or sign-bit adaptation can make such adjustments suitably simple so that their hardware contribution can be minimal. The advantage is that the accuracy afforded by even this fraction of digital hardware improves convergent behavior.

Such techniques have their place for low-complexity, low-bandwidth applications, as in the hum cancellation problem. However, even while development of digital hardware and associated software may be more costly, the recurring cost of production is most likely considerably less due to simplified testing. Consequently, a designer must also weigh volume of production.

For the other extreme, there may be no other practical alternative. For equalization or cancellation of wideband signals, for example, digital radio signals in excess of 100-MHz bandwidth, a totally digital implementation might well require excessive equipment, i.e., high power and volume, whereas an analog system could require much less. Such systems have found use in microwave systems for equalization, sidelobe cancellation, and beam steering.

7.8 IIR CONSIDERATIONS

The attentive reader will note that this chapter has discussed only implementations involving the FIR filter structure. For the most part, this reflects the fact that the overwhelming majority of current applications involve an FIR implementation, whereby the present competitive constraints on performance and complexity are best met. As discussed in earlier chapters, the FIR structure has the definite advantage of guaranteed bounded-input, bounded-output stability. Yet there are selected instances where an adaptive IIR filter appears to offer significant theoretical advantages. However, a designer must be aware of certain subtle practical costs associated with the IIR filter.

For example, suppose that the optimal processing filter in a given application were to achieve a narrowband resonance or passband; in such a case, an FIR implementation might require an extremely large number of taps to emulate a long impulse-response duration. (Refer to Section 5.1.1.) Such a structure not only would require a good deal of hardware for storage and calculation, but would no doubt be sluggish in its behavior. However, an IIR structure with the proper number of poles might require only a few adaptive parameters, and in a sense greatly reduce the basic complexity.

Overlooking the complications associated with adapting parameters that define pole locations (detailed in Chapter 5), there are other problems inherent in the feedback structure. First, accuracy of tap values becomes far more critical in cases where feedback is involved. In situations where a sharp resonance is of interest, the corresponding pole position will be near the unit circle. As tap values dither around their optimal values, this pole will tend to wobble in radius and may

actually enter the region of instability. Proper algorithm behavior will prompt recovery from this momentary foray, but perhaps only after the associated transient is
evident at the output. The basic sensitivity of pole positions to tap values becomes
more pronounced for higher-order denominators and for poles near unity radius.
From a hardware point of view, this would mean not only that storage of feedback
taps require extra precision, but also that the output calculation would need to be
done with a wider multiplier/accumulator. Thus, a single-chip signal processor using
finite precision arithmetic might well be limited to low-order adaptive IIR implementations.

Secondly, the IIR structure tends to aggravate the self-generated computation
noise associated with multiplier roundoff. When poles approach the unit circle, the
effective noise seen at the filter's output exhibits spectral emphasis near the resonance
[Rabiner and Gold, 1975]. Such noise properties tend to counterbalance much of the
gain in hardware by costs in performance.

One interesting use of adaptive IIR filters occurs in conjunction with an FFT-
based filter bank. Bershad and Feintuch [1980] used one-pole LMS-adapted IIR
adaptive predictors at the outputs of the filter bank to improve the degrees of spectral
resolution attainable. This technique was refined [Shynk and Gooch, 1985] considerably by using an accelerated algorithm to adapt the coefficients of second-order IIR
filters.

7.9 SUMMARY

In this chapter we have presented certain practical aspects of adaptive filtering.
Probably the most important points of this chapter can be summarized as shown
in Table 7.1. This provides the designer with an overview of the implementation
possibilities and their attributes. Each of the five implementations is compared in
terms of speed, performance, and cost of development, production, and modification. We see that software approaches (the general purpose CPU and the single-chip
signal processor) have favorable performance and cost attributes and currently service low- to medium-bandwidth applications. For wider-bandwidth signals, discrete
special-purpose digital designs can perform equally well, but at significantly higher
cost figures. Higher speed and lower production cost can often be realized using
custom integrated digital designs, but with extremely high development and modification costs. At the high extreme, we find the analog approach a relatively higher
cost and lower performance means of implementation.

As digital technology improves in cost and speed in the next several years,
inevitably the absolute definitions of bandwidth capability will expand. Nevertheless,
the use of the general-purpose CPU, by virtue of architectural flexibility, will likely
yield in most high-rate applications to the more specialized, low-cost single-chip
signal processor alternative for volume applications. Many of the applications now
serviced by discrete special-purpose digital hardware will likewise be taken over
by the signal-processing chip, due to cost and reprogrammability advantages. On

TABLE 7.1   COMPARISON OF THE ATTRIBUTES OF VARIOUS ADAPTIVE
FILTER IMPLEMENTATIONS

Implementation	Real-time bandwidth per device	Incremental cost	Initial development cost	Cost of modification	Preservation of signal quality
Programmable signal-processing chip	≤ 500 kHz	Low	Medium	Moderately low	Good
Discrete MSI/LSI/VLSI components	≤ 50 MHz	Medium	High	High	Good
Custom VLSI devices	≤ 100 MHz	Very low	Very high	Very high	Good
Analog components	≤ 1000 MHz	High	High	High	Poor to moderate
Computer software	≤ 20 kHz	Medium	Low	Low	Good

the other hand, the more costly digital designs with their improved speed will also
gain ground on applications now reserved for analog systems. The ever-increasing
demands on bandwidth in communication and radar systems will most likely provide
the only applications requiring analog processing.

8

Design Example:
Hum Removal for an
Electrocardiagram Monitor

- *Precis: Hum removal is one example of the broad-ranging applications of adaptive filtering for noise/interference cancellation.*

8.1 INTRODUCTION

Recall that Chapter 1 presented four sample applications for which adaptive processing has proved useful. Each case involved a phenomenon that was unknown and slowly time varying, and required a self-tuning filter to adjust to such changes. This chapter is the first of four that revisit each of those applications and elaborate on considerations that enter into a practical design. While we do not attempt to weigh all of the alternatives in each implementation, the examples do serve to illustrate the evaluation of a design and the ultimate complexity required for favorable performance. The examples have been chosen intentionally as a set that spans the range of signal bandwidth and circuit complexity.

8.2 REVIEW OF THE PROBLEM

In Section 1.1 we introduced the general concept of adaptive cancellation of tonal interference. Here we concentrate on the details associated with biomedical instrumentation and outline a specific functional design. In light of the computational requirements of the hum canceller, an assessment of the necessary hardware is given. Measurement of biological activity by means of monitoring electrical discharge, as typified by the monitoring of heart patients, parallels the communications problem: A transmitter (the electrical discharge) radiates energy through a propagation path (the body's tissue) to a receiving antenna (an electrode) positioned to maximize energy reception. Because the electrical discharge involves very small potentials, the received energy is very weak and requires care to prevent degradation of the signal content by added noises or filtering. Probably the strongest source of interference is 50/60-Hz pickup and its harmonics emanating from nearby electrical equipment such as lighting and instrument power supplies. The conventional means for dealing with such strong, spectrally concentrated interference is a fixed, low-pass filter, which sacrifices waveform detail associated with spectral components above 50 Hz. Use of a notch filter suppressing the energy in the appropriate narrow spectral band represents an improvement; however, it still distorts the signal component of interest.

Chapter 1 described a means of removing the additive interference, not by filtering in the signal path, but by coherently subtracting a replica of the interference waveform. This noise-cancellation approach to the problem requires a very accurate match of the replica to the actual interference to achieve adequate suppression. For 30 dB of suppression, for example, the match in amplitude must be better than 3%, with a phase match of better than 2°. To account for variations in frequency and amplitude of the stray interference, an adaptive filter can be used to adjust the phase and amplitude of the replica to maximize cancellation. The concept is shown in Figure 8.1.

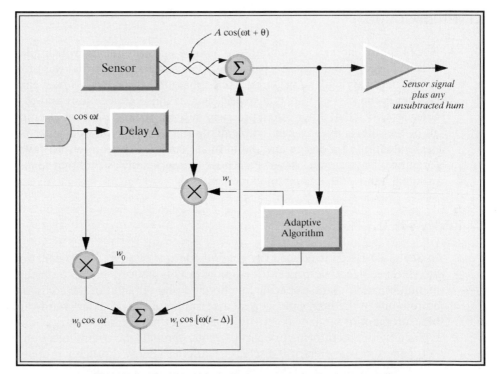

Figure 8.1   Simplified block diagram of an adaptive hum canceller.

8.3 DESIGN APPROACH

Consider the development of a circuit for use with off-the-shelf medical instrumentation. It must provide significant rejection of the offending 50/60 Hz (nominally) component, say in excess of 30 dB, and provide the enhanced output in real time. The goal is to degrade the real biomedical signal as little as possible. The processed signal is normally displayed using cathode-ray tube (CRT) deflection, so it must be available in analog form, although it would be attractive to have the signal available in digital form as well for further computer monitoring and analysis. There are two operational and economic concerns. First, the setup of the equipment must be as simple as possible, with no adjustment unfamiliar to a competent medical technician. Adequate internal self-testing is necessary to assure the user of proper operation. Second, as such signal enhancement might initially be viewed as a luxury, manufacturing costs should be kept as low as possible. These concerns are very important when developing instrumentation for a nonengineering field; potential for sales may exist, but only if the design is kept attractively simple.

Fortunately, this problem lends itself to a simple solution. First, its bandwidth is low, so that we have a wide range of devices over which we can minimize costs and complexity. Arguments can be made that information of interest for the ECG waveform extends no higher than 100 Hz. This implies that a sampling rate of 512 Hz would be more than adequate—high enough to satisfy the Nyquist condition for the signal of interest and the interference, yet low enough to keep the processor complexity down. We observe that the offending interference is made up of a dominant 50/60-Hz component, a second harmonic (from rectifiers in power supplies), a third harmonic (from nonlinearities in motors and transformers), and perhaps some low-energy higher harmonics. As implied by discussion in Chapter 3, the cancelling filter requires two degrees of freedom for each sinusoidal component, which can be thought of as one for amplitude setting and one for phase alignment. Thus, at least six to eight active weights are required. The reference to be applied to the filter input is easily obtained. The power supply of the adaptive filter itself can be tapped to provide a 50/60-Hz source that operates at exactly the same frequency as radiated by nearby equipment. Simple harmonic-generating distortion (e.g., with a diode) can provide all of the spectral lines of interest to the filter. The waveform of interest is always present and its amplitude and frequency vary slowly, so speed of adaptation is not a concern. Rapidly converging algorithms are unnecessary, and the simplicity of the LMS implementation is another place where significant cost saving can result.

To first order, the net complexity of this hum-reducing device can be determined by the number of multiplications needed per second. Eight weights, each operating at the sampling rate of 512 Hz, and each updated at the same rate, require less than 9000 multiplications per second. This low rate permits the hum canceller to be easily implemented in either of two ways—in a "low-end" digital signal microprocessor, or in high-level language (e.g., C) on a computer's floating point processor as a part of other analytical and display functions.

As discussed in Chapter 7, it is necessary to specify the scaling of the two analog-to-digital converter (ADC) inputs. Both are dominated by sinusoids, so it is safe to use a relatively low crest factor (CF) as defined in (7.6.1), e.g., 6 dB. The primary input, with its pulse-like signal, would require a larger crest factor were the 50/60-Hz component not dominant. Were the ADC to provide an 8-bit sample, with dynamic range of $6(n - 1) = 42$ dB, suppression could theoretically be as high as $42 - \text{CF} = 36$ dB. Accumulation should be done with at least 12 bits so that roundoff noise in an 8-term convolution would not degrade performance significantly. The effect of weight storage precision is the next concern. Typically, the precision of the weights is chosen to at least equal that of the input sample data, 8 bits in this case. In practice, better performance is attained if more precision is used. If 16-bit weights are employed, then μ could be set at a 6-bit shift (e.g., 2^{-6}), and the degradation due to weight stalling would still allow in excess of 36 dB of tone suppression. Under normal circumstances, this relatively large step size would tend to generate an unacceptable amount of weight jitter and residual tone interference.

Fortunately, this particular application permits a trick to be used to mitigate this problem. The signal of interest is a low duty cycle pulse waveform. Once the interference has been reduced by 10 to 20 dB and the pulses of interest are apparent, our processor can sense the pulses and then disable adaptation during the interval containing each pulse. This is termed *gating* the adaptation process. By adapting the filter when only the interference is present, there is very little weight jitter introduced by the signal of interest. Thus, even with the big step size needed to prevent weight stalling, there is little degradation of the signal of interest. Aside from the front end analog circuitry, the hardware requirements include two 8-bit A/D converters, a processor, and a D/A converter if an analog version of the signal of interest is needed by downstream equipment. Some form of analog automatic gain control (AGC) and low-pass anti-aliasing filters are needed to condition the A/D inputs. Figure 8.2 shows the behavior of a fixed-point simulation of this proposed hum canceller. Note that the "heartbeat" spike is nearly totally masked initially, and within 2 seconds becomes

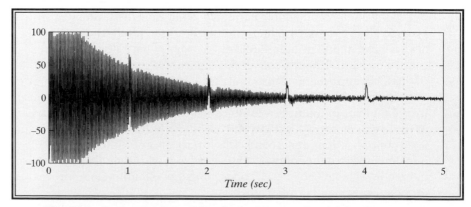

Figure 8.2 Output waveform of the adaptive hum canceller showing the error transient and the periodic signal of interest.

essentially hum-free. The residual noise is due principally to additive measurement noise at a level near that expected for 8-bit input quantization. Note that better fidelity of the underlying signal of interest might well require higher-precision input sampling.

8.4 THE ADAPTIVE NOISE CANCELLER (ANC)

The hum remover just described uses an adaptive filter to produce an estimate of an interfering signal and then subtract it away from the corrupted signal of interest. This concept has proved to be very useful in a variety of applications and has been generalized as shown in Figure 8.3. It is termed the *Adaptive Noise Canceller* (ANC) [Widrow et al., 1975b]. It has two inputs and a single output. The *primary input* $p(k)$ contains the signal of interest plus one or more interfering signals. The second input, termed the *reference input* $x(k)$, is applied to the input of the adaptive filter. This reference input should be as rich as possible in the signals interfering with the signal of interest and should contain as little of the signal of interest as possible. The objective in adapting the coefficients of the filter is to produce a filter output $y(k)$ that matches, to the greatest extent possible, the exact waveshape of the interference signals appearing in the primary input. The filter output is subtracted from the primary input to produce the system output $e(k)$. If the filter can be adjusted to achieve a perfect match between filter output $y(k)$ and the interference present in the primary signal $p(k)$, then $e(k)$, the system output, contains only the signal of interest. To the extent that the filter cannot be so adjusted, then a certain amount of the interference remains.

Note that the ANC uses the system output $e(k)$ as the error signal to drive the filter's adaptation. The rationale for this can be seen from the above discussion. When the filter's coefficients are optimally adjusted, the presence of the interference in the error is minimized. By using an adaptive algorithm that minimizes the presence of

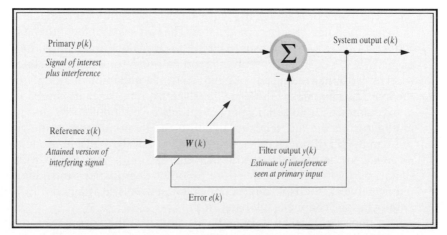

Figure 8.3 Block diagram of the adaptive noise canceller [Widrow, 1975].

the interference, the best coefficients can be found. A reexamination of Figure 8.1 shows that it is in fact an ANC. The primary signal is that provided by the medical instrumentation containing both the ECG signal of interest and the 50/60-Hz interfering signal component received from the room's power system. The reference input $x(k)$ is obtained from the power mains themselves, thus being rich in the interference signal and containing very little of the medical signal of interest. The difference signal $e(k)$ is both the system output and the error signal used to drive the filter's adaptive algorithm. As mentioned earlier, the ANC is widely used in practice. While the full range of design possibilities are available in terms of filter structure, performance functions, and adaptive algorithms, the most common designs use FIR filters, least-squares performance criteria, and the LMS approximate-gradient-descent adaptive algorithm of (4.2.7). In light of this, the theory developed in Chapter 4 can be used to analyze both the transient and convergent behavior of most ANC implementations. To demonstrate its flexibility and utility, we consider in the next section another common application of the ANC.

8.5 USING THE ADAPTIVE NOISE CANCELLER TO CANCEL ECHO IN TWO-WIRE TELEPHONE MODEMS

The rapidly falling cost of semiconductors and computation made possible the personal computer and with it the ability to have computers at both home and work. This led directly to the strong desire to connect these computers to each other using the dial-up telephone network [Treichler et al., 1999]. Early dial-up modems were limited to speeds of up to 2400 b/s and operated by splitting the roughly 3000 Hz of telephone channel bandwidth into two nonoverlapping portions, one used for each direction of transmission. As demand grew for faster transmission rates, however, it became clear that it would be desirable to increase the symbol rates and for both directions of transmission to be able to use the full bandwidth of the telephone channel simultaneously.

This concept is shown in Figure 8.4. At each end of the telephone connection there is a modulator and a demodulator. The two are coupled into the two-wire "subscriber loop" at each end using a circuit historically termed a *hybrid*. The objective of the hybrid's design is to send the modulator's output down the line to the distant receiver without sending any of it into its own companion demodulator. Conversely, the hybrid should direct the signal received from the distant modulator onto its own demodulator without sending any of it to its own modulator. Thus, in principle, the modulator on the left sends its signal to the demodulator on the right, using the full bandwidth of the channel, while simultaneously the right modulator is sending its signal to the demodulator on the left. Assuming that the hybrids separate the signals perfectly, and that there are no other degradations introduced by the telephone network, then full-duplex transmission would be attained with both directions employing the channel's full bandwidth.

Life is rarely so kind. In fact, virtually all of the assumptions made above are not true. Some portion of the signal transmitted from each end flows right through

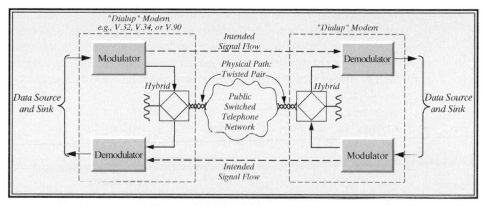

Figure 8.4   The block diagram of two dial-up modems operating simultaneously over the shared medium of a two-wire telephone connection.

its own hybrid and into its companion demodulator, creating very significant interference. Moreover, as the transmitted signal travels through the telephone system, it is reflected back at various points. These reflections are often termed *echoes* because that is their apparent effect on voice signals. Figure 8.5(a) shows various causes of these reflections from the perspective of the modulator on the left side of Figure 8.4. Thus, in addition to the relatively weak signal sent from the modulator on the right

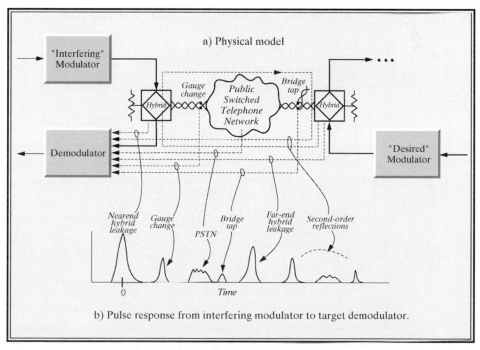

Figure 8.5   Undesired signal paths from the left modulator to its own demodulator.

side (which is the signal we desire, of course), the left-most demodulator receives the signal from its own modulator directly through the hybrid, and reflected back from wire gauge changes, bridging subscriber loops, multiplexing equipment, digital switching equipment, and the hybrid on the right side. If the echo levels are high enough, it is possible for the interfering signal to actually loop around the telephone network twice.

We now examine another view of this situation. Assuming that the telephone connection is linear and time invariant (which is adequately true), it is possible

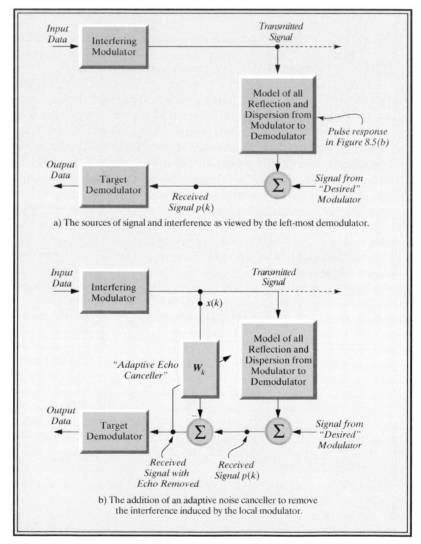

a) The sources of signal and interference as viewed by the left-most demodulator.

b) The addition of an adaptive noise canceller to remove the interference induced by the local modulator.

Figure 8.6   Reduction of the modem echo cancellation problem into a simple model.

to represent the path from the left-most modulator to the left-most demodulator by a pulse response function. A typical example is shown in Figure 8.5(b). The strong response at zero delay is the undesired signal passing directly through the left-most hybrid. All of the other terms arrive with some delay, the degree of which depends on how far down the telephone line that the associated "echo" occurred.

A practical solution to this problem can be found by starting with the model in Figure 8.6(a). From the perspective of the left-most demodulator, its input consists of two terms, its desired input, the signal from the distant modulator, and interference, all accruing from its companion modulator, but filtered through the telephone network with the effective pulse response shown in Figure 8.5(b). The solution comes by applying the concept of adaptive noise cancellation. An excellent reference for the interfering signal, the modulator itself, is available in the left-most modem. This observation leads to the echo canceller structure shown in Figure 8.6(b). An adaptive filter is added to the modem [Bingham, 1988]. Its input is the interfering signal, the modulator's output. The filter's output is subtracted from the incoming signal. The difference between the received signal is sent on to the demodulator, and is used to adapt the echo-cancelling filter. Once the adaptive filter's coefficients have adapted to match the dispersion and echo characteristics of the telephone channel, as viewed at the demodulator, then the effects of the hybrid and echo are removed, and the demodulator can operate near its theoretically maximum level on the signal coming from the right-most modulator.

This type of echo cancellation was crucial in the improvement of dial-up modems in the 1980s and 1990s. Modems conforming the International Telecommunications Union's V.32, V.34, and V.90 standards all use this approach. It is also an important part of ISDN and Digital Subscriber Loop (DSL) equipment as well [Starr et al., 1999].

8.6 HANDLING INTERFERENCE FROM MULTIPLE SOURCES

An attractive practical aspect of the adaptive noise cancelling concept is that it can be applied in situations where there are multiple sources of interference (as indicated in Appendix C of Widrow et al. [1975b]). This can be best illustrated with an example. Figure 8.7 illustrates a common problem in the use of ship-borne sonar. The sonar's transmitting and receiving transducer is mounted to the ship's hull. Even with careful design and construction, it is common for mechanical vibration from the ship's rotating machinery (e.g., pumps and turbines) to be mechanically transmitted through the ship's hull and into the receiving transducers. This mechanically induced and mechanically transmitted noise enters the transducer and interferes with the reception of active and passive sonar signals.

A simple model of this problem is shown in Figure 8.8. The sonar receiver sees a combination of many signals—the desired one and one from each of the interfering pieces of machinery. Notice that path from each of the pieces of machinery to the

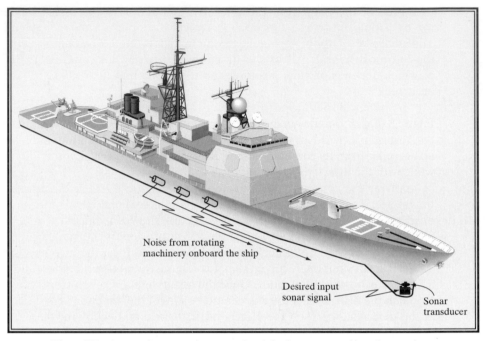

Figure 8.7   Attempting to receive sonar signals in the presence of interference from shipboard machinery.

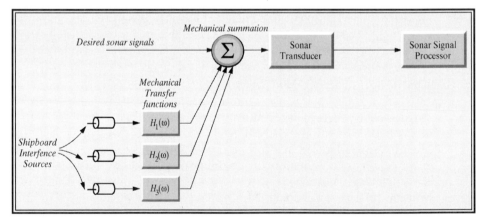

Figure 8.8   A model describing the signals arriving at the sonar's receiving transducer.

sonar transducer is different, and therefore each has its own transfer function from source to the transducer.

One solution to the problem is to attempt to filter out all of the machinery-induced interference apparent at the electrical output of the sonar transducer.

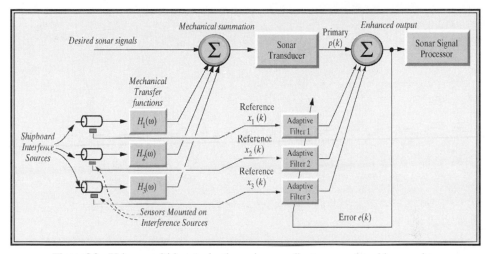

Figure 8.9   Using a multi-input adaptive noise canceller to remove machinery noise from a sonar signal.

Another is to attempt to "quiet" the mechanical equipment as much as possible. Yet another approach is to employ the adaptive noise cancellation concept, but in this case, using a separate filter for every identifiable mechanical interference source. This solution is shown in Figure 8.9, which matches Figure 32 in Widrow et al. [1975b]. A reference signal is obtained from each piece of machinery contributing interference to the sonar. A practical method of doing it is the attachment of an accelerometer to the machinery casing itself. Each of these sensor signals is then applied to an adaptive filter. These filter outputs are subtracted from the sonar transducer signal to reduce the interference to its lowest possible value. To the limit that each of the adaptive filters can match exactly the transfer function characteristics carrying their interference source to the transducer, the transducer output can be "cleaned up" completely.

Notice that there is only one error signal $e(k)$ in this arrangement and that it is fed back to all of the adaptive filters to guide their adaptation. A simple extension of the analytical techniques used in Chapters 3 and 4 can be used to describe the behavior of the "multisensor" arrangements. Most of the intuition gained from the single-input case can be applied directly, as can the adaptive algorithms, such as LMS, developed from that intuition due to the underlying linear combiner format.

9

Design Example:
Multipath Correction for
Troposcatter Signals

• *Precis: An important application of adaptive filters is the correction or "equalization"
of communications signals that have been distorted by their propagation through a transmission medium. This chapter examines one such practical example, then extends the
solution to several others.*

9.1 THE PROBLEM

Section 1.2 introduced the problem of correcting or equalizing radio signals dispersed
by propagating through the "tropospheric channel." In this section, the tropospheric
communication problem is described in more detail. An approach to solving the
problem is discussed in the next section, along with a description of the engineering
steps needed to specify the resulting adaptive filter.

The basic troposcatter communications link was depicted in the abstract in
Figure 1.4, exploiting scattering in the earth's atmosphere to achieve over-the-horizon
point-to-point connections. A powerful transmitter sends a UHF or microwave signal
in the direction of the receiving site. The large antennas necessary are illustrated by
Figure 9.1—in this case for defense communications across remote parts of North
America. Even though the transmitter and receiver are obscured from each other
by the curvature of the earth or its terrain, enough energy is refracted by turbulence
in the troposphere toward the receiver to be able to demodulate the signal most of
the time. Because troposcatter links use powerful transmitters, large antennas, and
sensitive receivers, they can be quite expensive to build and operate. This is offset,
however, by the fact that each "hop" can cover 300 to 800 km, making the cost per
circuit mile competitive with communications satellites and undersea cables.

The principal shortcoming of tropo systems is circuit reliability, i.e., how much a
given circuit is available to the overall telecommunications system. The objective for
a typical end-to-end circuit is a maximum average outage rate of 0.01% or less, making the requirement for each hop of a circuit more stringent yet. In troposcatter systems, outages stem mainly from the deleterious effects of multipath propagation. As

Figure 9.1 Sixty-foot UHF troposcatter antennas, Far North Communications Systems, Labrador. (Property of AT&T Archives. Reprinted with permission of AT&T.)

explained in Chapter 1, the multipath propagation effectively filters the transmitted signal in a way that can cause severe distortion at the receiver. This distortion, when it occurs, can make all circuits carried on the affected tropo unusable. This multipath distortion problem becomes worse as the bandwidth (and hence circuit-carrying capacity) is increased. Thus, the communications link designer must trade-off between capacity (hence revenue) and circuit reliability.

Link designers have traditionally used several approaches to improve link reliability to an adequate level. Straightforward approaches include increasing transmitter power, increasing receiver sensitivity, and increasing the sizes of the antennas at both sites. These methods serve only to increase the "link margin," the amount of signal strength that can be diluted by multipath-induced signal cancellation before the output quality falls to an intolerable level. They do not deal with so-called frequency-selective multipath, which leads to output distortion even when adequate power is seen at the receiver.

Both selective and nonselective multipath can be treated with "diversity reception." A diagram of so-called four-way diversity is shown in Figure 9.2. Two transmitters are used, sending the same signal but at different frequencies. Four receivers are used at the receiving site, two with each of two antennas. Both transmitted signals are received at each of the two receiving antennas. The result is the reception of four versions of the transmitted signal. If the transmitting frequencies are sufficiently different and the receiving antennas far enough apart, the multipath fading behavior of each of the four propagation channels is essentially statistically independent. Therefore, the probability of all four signals having poor quality at the same instant is much less than any individual one. Capitalizing on this fact, a switch is used to connect the best of the four signals to the system output, thus producing the best end-to-end quality.

Diversity reception has proved a very powerful technique for improving the quality of troposcatter links, but this improvement comes at substantial cost. In particular, two transmitters are required instead of one, four receivers instead of one, and the number of large antennas is doubled. The large financial outlay for this

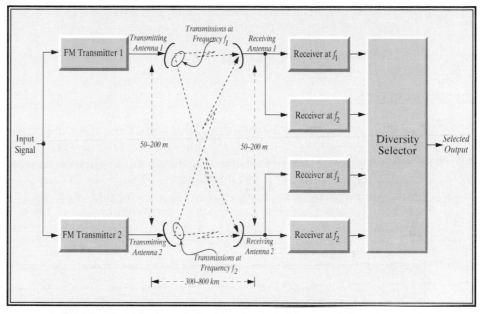

Figure 9.2   Block diagram of a four-way (space and frequency) diversity transmission system.

diversity equipment motivates the investigation of cheaper techniques that might attain the same performance level. In particular, we examine here the design of an adaptive filter which provides relief from frequency-selective multipath, leaving the "flat-fading," i.e., nonselective multipath as the only cause of channel outage. Correction of frequency-selective fading can also allow extension of the bandwidth and hence channel capacity of the link, further lowering the cost per circuit.

For the purposes of this design example, we expect the multipath correction filter to operate in the following environment:

(a) The transmitted signal is frequency-modulated using an analog frequency-division multiplex (FDM) signal. The tropo system can be upgraded at any time to carry time-division multiplex (TDM) signals on a constant-envelope bauded-modulation type, such as phase shift keying.

(b) The bandwidth of the modulated signal may be as wide as 4 MHz, but perhaps as narrow as 1 MHz.

(c) The multipath propagation channel introduces a time spread of typically 0.5 μsec and at most 2 μsec. The Doppler spread is typically a few Hz and no more than 20 Hz.

(d) The characteristics of the modulating signal are completely unknown to the receiver and may change at any time. (No special signal is added to the "payload" for the express purpose of training the adaptive filter.)

(e) The tropo system may already be equipped with two- or four-way diversity reception.

Given these conditions, we are ready to design the appropriate adaptive filter.

9.2 DESIGN STEPS

A prudent system design uses both adaptive equalization and diversity reception, since each accomplishes something the other cannot. Diversity reception neatly accommodates the problem of flat fading, i.e., the condition when the signal at the input of one of the receivers is cancelled by antiphased paths. In this case, the diversity receiver simply picks the stronger signal and thereby maximizes output quality. In the case of frequency-selective fading, however, only equalization of the propagation-induced filtering restores quality. For this reason, we begin with the system design

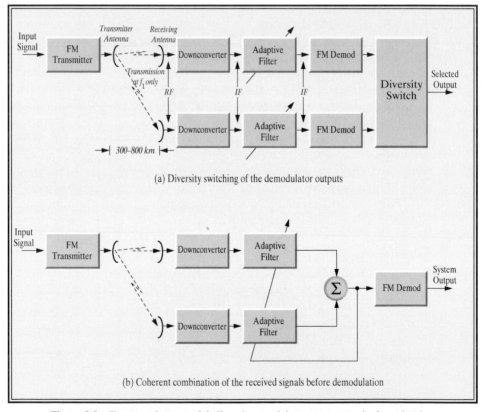

(a) Diversity switching of the demodulator outputs

(b) Coherent combination of the received signals before demodulation

Figure 9.3   Two-way (space only) diversity receiving systems employing adaptive multipath correction in each path.

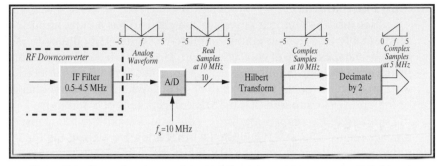

Figure 9.4 Processing steps and associated spectra used to generate digital input for the adaptive filter.

shown in Figure 9.3(a). One transmitter, two receivers, and two receiving antennas are used. The receivers downconvert the input signals to a convenient intermediate frequency (IF). The correction filtering is applied at this point, and the resulting filter outputs are demodulated. A diversity switch then picks the best output. The correction filtering must be applied before the demodulator because frequency modulation is a nonlinear process. That is, any filtering introduced by the channel after the transmitting modulator must be removed before the nonlinear receiver. The diversity switching is usually done after the demodulators for convenience, but also because it is usually necessary to demodulate both signals to decide which one of the two signals is the better.

Given the specifications listed, the following conclusions and observations can be made:

(a) Digital Implementation

Digital implementations are usually chosen for adaptive filters if the bandwidth to be processed is not so high as to make the filter's construction prohibitively expensive. The principal reason for the inclination toward a digital implementation is that the filter and adaptive algorithm can be implemented with fewer errors and hence better performance.

Given a maximum bandwidth of 4 MHz, the input IF signal must be sampled at a rate of at least 5 MHz complex or 10 MHz real. For this example, we will use the structure shown in Figure 9.4. The IF signal is centered at 2.5 MHz and digitized with 10-bit accuracy at a rate of 10 MHz. A digital Hilbert transformer [Gold and Rader, 1969] converts the real samples into quadrature pairs, i.e., complex samples, at a 5 MHz rate. These samples form the input to the correction filter itself.

The digital implementation is not inexpensive. However, it performs substantially better than known analog implementations. Its cost is amortized over many circuits, and it is substantially cheaper than the transmitters and antennas it is meant to replace.

(b) Filter Structure

Because the multipath propagation channel has a finite impulse response, it is theoretically true that an infinite-impulse-response (IIR) filter offers the computationally cheapest form of correction filter. However the multipath channel cannot be guaranteed to have "minimum phase," i.e., that all the zeros of its transfer function would be inside the unit circle in the z-plane. When the channel has a zero outside of the unit circle, suppose that the IIR correction filter could move a pole outside of the unit circle to compensate for it. This would make the filter unstable and chaos quickly reigns. This effect and the fact that adaptive algorithms for IIR filters have not yet reached maturity make FIR filters the proper choice.

Given the choice of an FIR filter, we must now determine how many taps to use. The multipath channel itself can be modeled with 10 taps because 10 taps at a 5 MHz sampling rate covers the maximum channel spread of 2 μsec. The correction filter, however, must be longer. Engineering experience has shown that the correction filter needs to be three to five times the length of the multipath spread to be effective [Treichler et al., 1996]. This can be rationalized by observing that the FIR correction filter is in some sense approximating the response of the theoretically optimal IIR filter. An IIR filter with 10 taps would normally have an impulse response much longer than 10 time samples. Based on this analysis, we choose a 30-tap FIR filter as the basis for the adaptive correction filter. This filter is 12 times longer than the 0.5 μsec expected multipath delay and three times the maximum delay.

While many forms of FIR structure are available, including lattice, transmultiplexer, and fast convolution approaches, we will assume here the use of a conventional tapped-delay-line filter employing multiplier/accumulators, such as those discussed in Section 7.4. This type of filter is straightforward to design and test compared to the others and does not incur large penalties in size or performance.

(c) Choice of Adaptive Algorithm

For the problem of tropo multipath correction, the types of algorithms used are very restricted. Because the input to the FM or QPSK modulator is assumed to be unknown, and because no training or pilot signals are added at the transmitter, no desired signal $d(k)$ is available. This in turn implies that none of the algorithms discussed in Chapters 4 and 5 can be employed directly. A possible exception occurs in the case of digital or bauded signals in which decision direction (see Section 6.2.2) can be used, but because this equalizer must work for both analog and digital modulation types, the sole use of decision direction does not meet the requirements stated earlier.

The problem can be solved by observing that all of the modulation types of interest are of the constant envelope variety. This is not unusual in radio systems since constant-envelope signals have good resistance to the nonlinearity of powerful transmitters and have the optimum peak-to-average power ratio. The fact that the tropo systems use FM and PSK with constant envelopes means that property-restoral algorithms of the type explored in Chapter 6 can be employed. In particular, the constant-modulus algorithm (CMA) is an obvious choice for this problem.

(d) Adaptation Rate

The adaptive filter must change its coefficients fast enough to "track" the changing impulse response of the multipath propagation channel closely enough to achieve the desired high degree of multipath correction.

The degree of time variation in a propagation channel is indicated by the channel's Doppler spread. While Doppler spread has a well-defined technical meaning [Bello, 1963], as a practical matter it specifies the interval between significantly different realizations of the channel impulse response. In particular, a Doppler spread of 20 Hz indicates that a comparison between impulse responses taken 50 msec apart would show significant differences. Practical experience has shown that tracking this time variation means developing adaptive solutions at least 10 times faster than the maximum Doppler spread. In this case, the adaptive algorithm driving the correction filter must be capable of essentially converging to new solutions in 5 msec.

Some theoretical work and extensive computer simulation [Treichler and Agee, 1983] have shown that at this sampling rate, the gradient descent version of CMA will converge reliably within 500 μsec for a wide variety of multipath channels using either FM or phase shift keying. Thus, even the simplest type of adaptation algorithm converges more than fast enough to meet the 5 msec requirement.

At this point, given the filter's excessive agility, the designer has at least two choices: (1) she can adapt the filter using only one-tenth the input data, leading to a reduction of 90% in the processing load needed to compute the filter coefficients, or (2) she can use all the data, allowing for either anomalously high Doppler spreads or, using a lower adaptation coefficient, providing smoother adaptation and lower misadjustment. Adapting only one-tenth the time also reduces the finite word length requirements by 3 bits.

For the purpose of this design example, we assume that the coefficients are computed anew every 5 msec, allowing the coefficient update processor to be scaled down proportionately.

(e) Word Length Determination

The sampled data entering the adaptive filter is assumed to be quantized to 10-bit accuracy. To provide for adequate dynamic range in the frequency response, the filter impulse response should be quantized no more coarsely than 12 bits. Assuming the use of 30 complex taps in the filter impulse response, each sample of the filter output would require 28 bits, even though only 10 or 11 are needed to describe the output waveform with sufficient quality.

The word lengths required to compute the error signal and adaptive updates depend strongly on the particular performance function chosen. Even within the limited class of gradient descent constant-modulus algorithms, several are available. We choose here a block-averaged version of "1 − 1 CMA," given by the performance function

$$J = \sum_{k=1}^{M} ||y(k)| - 1|. \tag{9.2.1}$$

Both the signal modulus and its magnitude deviation are raised only to the first power. The impact of this is that if $y(k)$ is adequately represented with N bits, then so are the elements of the instantaneous gradient estimate. This contrasts with the $2-2$ version of CMA, discussed in Section 6.4, which requires $4N$ bits since the signal is squared twice.

The estimated gradient of J in (9.2.1) with respect to the adapted filter weights $\mathbf{W}$ in $y = \mathbf{W}^t\mathbf{X}$ is given by

$$\frac{\partial J}{\partial \mathbf{W}(k)} = \sum_{k=1}^{M} \mathbf{X}^*(k)\{\operatorname{sgn}(|y(k)| - 1)|\} \lim\{y(k)\}, \qquad (9.2.2)$$

where $\lim\{\cdot\}$ denotes the unit length phasor in the direction of the argument. Because the last two terms in the product have unit length, each term of the gradient vector can be seen to specify $N + \log_2 M$ bits, where N is the input quantization and M is the size of the block and therefore the number of terms in the sum. An averaging interval of 500 μsec and a sampling interval of 0.2 μsec imply that M is about 2500. If the input is quantized to 10 bits, then each term of the estimated gradient requires 21 bits to preserve full accuracy. If the adaptation constant μ is chosen to be in the range of 0.01 to 0.001 (usually in values equaling binary shifts), then the scaled gradient may require up to 30 bits to represent each term.

By working through the requirements, we developed the following technical approach to the design of the adaptive correction filter. The input signal is down-converted to a center frequency of 2.5 MHz, sampled at 10 MHz with 10-bit accuracy, and converted to a 5-megasamples/sec complex format. The filter itself is a tapped-delay-line FIR structure with 30 complex-valued taps. The $1-1$ constant-modulus algorithm is used to update the coefficients, but the channel variation is slow enough to allow a 90% reduction in the processing required by the adaptation hardware. The filter input would be presented in 10-bit samples, and the output computed to 28 bits, but the actual output would be the most significant 12 bits. The coefficients must be updated with about 30 bits of accuracy but can be rounded and used with only the top 12 bits of accuracy in the filter output computation.

Even with the approach specified to this degree, there are still many implementation techniques open to the system designer. An important consideration at this point is the rapid improvement in semiconductor technology. No simple guidance can be given that will prevail for more than a few years. As an example, consider the two adaptive digital filters shown in Figure 9.5. The circuit board shown in Figure 9.5(a) represented the state of the art in 1984 (when this problem was originally addressed). It is capable of performing roughly 130 million multiply-and-add operations per second. It was used as a part of an adaptive filter used to equalize multipath- and interference-corrupted "wideband" radio signals. The Application-Specific Integrated Circuit (ASIC) shown in Figure 9.5(b), built not even eight years later, executes roughly 1.6 billion multiply/adds per second and can accept signals with bandwidths in excess of 50 MHz. Clearly the design engineer must frequently check the current state of semiconductor technology to ensure that the selected approach is still appropriate.

a) *Circa 1984*: A 10-tap FIR digital filtering circuit card used to process complex-valued data samples at a 6-MHz rate.

b) *Circa 1994*: A 32-tap digital filter ASIC used to process complex-valued samples at 50 Msps.
Courtesy Applied Signal Technology, Inc

Figure 9.5   Digital filter implementation a decade apart.

The final system consideration involves the form of the filter output. The filter's natural output is in the form of complex-valued digital samples at a rate of 5 MHz. This signal must be processed in some fashion to make it compatible with the demodulator which follows it, whether for FM or PSK. Any of three approaches might be used:

(a) Convert the complex-valued samples into a 10 megasample/sec real-valued format and apply those to a D/A converter. The resulting analog signal is then applied to a conventional analog demodulator.

(b) Instead of employing a complex-valued adaptive filter, use a version with real-valued coefficients. The real-valued samples derived at 10 megasamples/sec from the input A/D are applied directly to the filter and the output is sent directly to the D/A. A version of the constant-modulus algorithm has been developed [Treichler and Larimore, 1985a] that allows adaptation of the real coefficients. The amount of filter computation is the same with the real filter, but the Hilbert transformer and output complex-to-real conversion are no longer necessary.

(c) Perform the demodulation in the digital domain as well. The complex filter output is a natural input to such a demodulator, and techniques have been developed which allow quality demodulation at the bandwidths required here [Treichler, 1980].

The overall system block diagram of the multipath correction filter outlined above is shown in Figure 9.6. Adaptive filters of this type have actually been built [Larimore and Goodman, 1985], and the degree of multipath correction and output signal quality match very well with the values predicted by the computer simulations presented in Treichler and Agee [1983].

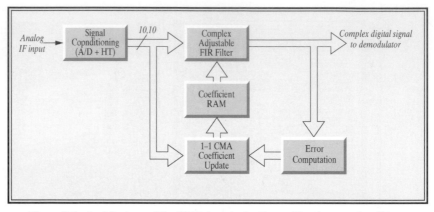

Figure 9.6   Architecture of the CMA-based adaptive multipath correction filter.

9.3 INCORPORATION OF DIVERSITY COMBINATION

Part of the system concept for the tropo receiving processor was the use of diversity combination, i.e., receiving and processing two independent versions of the transmitted signal and then choosing the better of the two, as shown in Figure 9.3(a). This is usually accomplished by measuring the signal quality at the output of the two demodulators and then choosing the better of the two. So-called predetection combination is shown in Figure 9.3(b). In this case, the two IF signals are properly phased and then added coherently. Historically this technique was infrequently used because of the difficulty in implementing it with analog technology. Even so, at the cost of slightly increased complexity, this technique can improve signal quality over that attained by switching alone because the sum of the signal powers is usually more than either received signal separately.

The adaptive filter designed in the previous section can actually be extended to offer diversity combination as well. Consider the block diagram shown in Figure 9.7. The IF signals from the space-diversity receivers are both sampled and converted to a complex format. They are then applied to their own filters and the outputs added. The added signal forms both the input to the demodulator (by any of the three means discussed above) and the "output" to be used by the constant-modulus algorithm. The details are presented in Treichler and Larimore [1985a] and in a variety of more modern literature on "blind signal separation" [Cardoso, 1998]. In essence, CMA is used to adapt both filters simultaneously, introducing the spectral shaping, the gain, and the phase shifting required to coherently combine the two signals. The algorithm is no more complicated than before, a second demodulator is not needed, and no measurements of signal quality are required. The CMA adjusts both filters to make the sum signal as close to a constant-envelope signal as possible. In effect, this structure performs both the diversity combination needed to deal with non-frequency-selective multipath flat-fading and the spectral shaping needed to

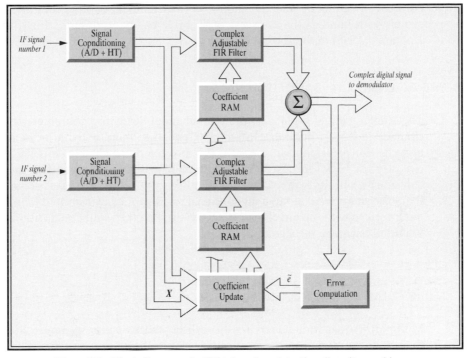

Figure 9.7   Block diagram of a CMA-based predetection diversity combiner.

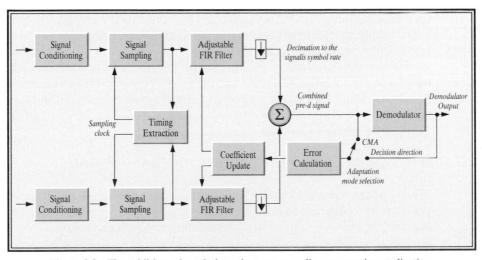

Figure 9.8   The addition of symbol-synchronous sampling to permit equalization and coherent combination of QPSK and QAM signals.

correct for frequency-selective fading. A two-channel adaptive combiner for digital signals with bandwidths in excess of 40 MHz has been described in Treichler and Bohanon [1998] in the format of Figure 9.8.

9.4 THE EXTENSION TO BAUDED SIGNALS

The single-channel equalizer, the dual-channel switching combiner, and the two-channel additive combiner can all be extended to handle digital or bauded signals as well. The principal adjustment needed to handle such signals is the addition of circuitry (or logic) to ensure that the incoming signal (or signals) is sampled synchronously with its symbol rate. As discussed in Chapter 6, this is required so that the pulse shaping added to a digital signal to control its transmitted bandwidth does not interfere with the envelope properties used by the blind equalization algorithms to initially acquire the signal.

9.5 ADAPTIVE CHANNEL EQUALIZATION FOR TERRESTRIAL DIGITAL MICROWAVE RADIOS

Multipath propagation effects like those discussed in Sections 1.2 and 9.1 also degrade the quality of digital microwave radio relay transmission systems used to convey high-capacity telephone signals. These signals tend to use complicated modulation types, such as 16-level (and higher) quadrature amplitude modulation (QAM), and occupy bandwidths of 20 to 50 MHz. Because of these high bandwidths, fully digital implementation of the adaptive filter was once economically infeasible. Equalizers for "digital radios" built during the 1980s and early 1990s typically employed an adjustable analog filter with some form of digital quality assessment and adaptation control. The rapid improvement in the speed-to-cost ratio in semiconductors, such as that illustrated in Figure 9.5, has made fully digital implementation feasible in the late 1990s. Treichler et al. [1998] survey the state of the art in the design of blind equalized demodulators for a variety of signals, including digital microwave radio modems.

9.6 ADAPTIVE CHANNEL EQUALIZATION FOR VOICEBAND MODEMS

While this chapter has focused so far on radio transmission systems, it should be clear that the concepts apply to other types of communications systems as well. One of the most important examples of this are the modems designed for use over the dial-up telephone network. In fact, the analytical problem to be solved is almost exactly the same as that just addressed for bauded signal transmission over radio systems. A telephone modem sends its information encoded on pulses that are transmitted over the telephone line. The telephone line, and all of the equipment through which the

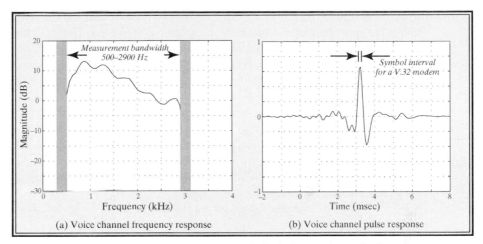

Figure 9.9   The pulse response of a typical telephone voice grade channel.

signal must pass along the way, smears and distorts the transmitted pulses, making it impossible for the receiver to distinguish one pulse from the next. To illustrate this, consider the telephone channel pulse response shown in Figure 9.9. The delay spread of the channel response, the time over which each transmitted pulse is smeared, is much longer than the inter-pulse interval, a condition that must be equalized or corrected before the encoded data can be accurately extracted at the receiver.

The block diagram of the equalized receiver for a telephone modem is essentially the same as laid out earlier, with a few important exceptions:

(a) Telephone channels have much lower bandwidths than the tropo or microwave radio signals discussed earlier. Therefore much less computation is needed. As a result, most are implemented with programmable DSP microprocessors instead of dedicated hardware.

(b) Most telephone modems operate in a point-to-point mode, permitting the use of training when the communications channel is initialized. The need for blind equalization for telephone modems is limited to test equipment and some special cases such as point-to-multipoint applications.

(c) The propagation channel over which the modems converse is typically completely unknown when the modems first connect, but thereafter the channel varies very little. This differs from the radio transmission case where the propagation channel's characteristics change considerably with time and must be continuously tracked by the adaptive equalizer and combiner.

The adaptive equalizers used in telephone data modems to correct for the dispersion incurred in telephone voice channel have traditionally used LMS or related approximate gradient search algorithms because they are robust, they require a relative minimum of hardware (or microcode cycles), and they converge rapidly enough for most traditional modem applications [Bingham, 1988]. However, there is considerable interest in equalizers that adapt very rapidly. One such application is the case where a central computer must poll many distant processors on a so-called multidrop circuit. The time required to equalize each modem (about half a second) can in fact be longer than the time required to transfer the needed data. Algorithms such as RLS and "fast" RLS can provide dramatically improved convergence speeds in such cases [Falconer and Ljung, 1978] [Satorius and Alexander, 1979]. Because of this improvement in efficiency, it may become cost-effective to use the more complicated RLS-type algorithms. Another application where RLS has been successfully employed is in HF data modems where the propagation channel changes too rapidly for a gradient-based algorithm to track the channel.

10

Design Example:
Modeling the Propagation Path
for a Digital Television Signal

> • *Precis: There are many practical engineering circumstances in which the input-output relationship of a system must be determined. In this chapter we examine a particular example—that of developing a propagation model from operating data for terrestrial digital broadcast television signals.*

10.1 BACKGROUND

The use of digital broadcast in the television industry has become popular for transmission of high-quality video entertainment to the consumer. Factors unique to this market environment tended to bias many of the engineering choices defining transmission:

- *Flexibility*—To assure longevity, the structure was expected to accommodate possible future changes and expansions in service format;
- *RF regulation*—The transmitted spectrum had to be compatible with current 6-MHz channel allocations inherited from traditional TV broadcast, defining requirements on bitstream structure, compression, and modulation format; and
- *Consumer appeal*—For economic viability, the implementation of receiver functions must minimize complexity and cost to encourage a large consumer base.

Our discussion in this chapter focuses on the last aspect. In particular, defining a robust and cost-effective receiver implementation requires an accurate understanding of propagation effects. For the TV band, effects that degrade traditional analog broadcasts in familiar ways have an entirely different impact on digital transmissions. Rather than causing a gradual degradation in image quality, problems such as marginal signal strength (snow and ignition noise), reflections (ghosting), and Doppler returns (wavy fluctuating image), often completely disrupt digital demodulation, either blanking or freezing the image. A critical goal of the receiver becomes

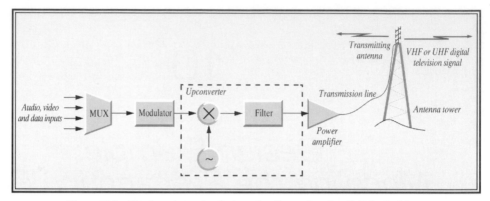

Figure 10.1 The key elements of a broadcasting system for digital television.

to mitigate such common channel effects to the point that reception provides the flawless image that the consumer has come to expect from digital multimedia.

   To understand the nature of this problem, consider Figure 10.1, which illustrates the key elements of a simple terrestrial system for broadcasting digital television signals. One or more streams of digitized television and other data are combined into a serial form and then passed to modulator and upconversion elements, properly formatting the signal for RF transmission. This modulated signal is amplified and fed to the antenna, which is typically located on a tower or vantage point that illuminates the surrounding service areas. Coverage may range from the immediate near-field to many tens of kilometers. The signal reaching each receiver is weaker in power level than the transmitted signal due to "R-squared" losses. But, as discussed in Chapters 1 and 9, often the receiver's signal has also been filtered as a result of both the reflective multipath propagation encountered in transit and the effects of the electronics in both transmitter and receiver.

   The effects of this filtering are sufficiently severe that the demodulator in the receiver virtually always requires an adaptive equalizer of the type discussed in Chapter 9. Important questions facing the designer of such a demodulator center on the sophistication of the equalizer:

- What must its temporal extent be?
- How fast must it find the proper solution from arbitrary initialization?
- How much time variation in the propagation characteristics of the transmission channel must it be able to "track"?

When designing a receiver, particularly one for commercial application such as broadcast television, there is an important tradeoff to be considered and resolved. The equalizer must be complex enough to handle the wide range of channels that receiver owners might encounter, while being simple enough to be economically viable. These questions cannot be answered properly without knowledge of the characteristics of those channels.

Thus, our objective in this chapter is to develop a method for modeling the propagation characteristics of a radio frequency transmission system. Given this model, the issues identified above can be addressed and an appropriate receiver design determined.

10.2 THE BASIC APPROACH

The approach to channel modeling that we use here is drawn from the block diagram in Figure 1.9 of Chapter 1. We assume that the modulator's output is applied to a linear and possibly slowly time-varying filter, and that the output of this filter is applied directly to the demodulator's input. Thus, the filter includes (1) the effects of the transmitter's electronics, (2) the receiver's front-end electronics, and (3) the propagation channel itself. We also assume that independent noise is present at the receiver's input, additively degrading the received signal. We attempt to model this lumped system with an FIR digital filter. Specifically, we find the pulse response for such a digital filter so that its output matches the actual received signal as well as possible. When this occurs, we assert that the filter's pulse response models the actual system and can be used to make the design assessments outlined above.

This approach is shown in Figure 10.2. The modulator output is applied both to the television power amplifier and to the digital modeling filter. The input to the demodulator, after surviving transmission, propagation, and reception effects, is compared with the digital filter's output. We presume here that the filter's coefficients,

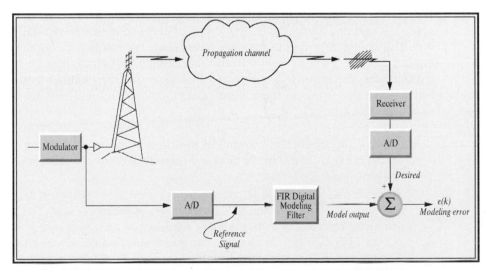

Figure 10.2   Modeling an RF transmission system using an FIR digital filter.

that is, its pulse response, can be chosen to make the difference between the two as small as the received noise permits. When this is done, we claim that the pulse response constitutes the real system's model.

There are many methods available for determining the proper coefficients; in fact, this problem, termed *system identification*, is a very rich technical field in its own right (as pointed out in Chapter 5 with reference to Ljung and Soderstrom [1983], Ljung [1987], and Soderstrom and Stoica [1989]). For the purposes of this example, however, we begin with the use of a straightforward method that has already been addressed in this text—the method of least squares discussed at length in Chapter 3. Using this approach, we collect data records of the received signal at the demodulator's input, plus data records at the modulator's output (i.e., the digital modeling filter's input) and compute the filter pulse response that minimizes the squared difference between the two. Mathematically, we seek $\mathbf{W}_{opt}$, which satisfies

$$\mathbf{W}_{opt} = R^{-1}\mathbf{P}, \tag{10.2.1}$$

where $\mathbf{P}$ and R are as defined in equations (3.2.8) and (3.2.9). This pulse response constitutes the desired model of the modulator-to-demodulator system of interest, at least during the time interval when the data records were taken. In general the modeling process must be repeated often enough that the slow time variation in the channel is captured in the sequence of models that is produced. The rate at which this must be done, and the associated computational impact, are directly proportional to the rate of the channel's time variation.

10.3 A MORE ADVANCED APPROACH

There are a number of practical details that must be addressed to make the technical approach outlined above work, but it can be done in a relatively straightforward way. The biggest impediment to its use, however, is the fact that the modeling filter's input must be obtained directly from the modulator's output, a quite impractical requirement, particularly if one would like to model the channel from locations widely separated from the transmitter (and modulator) itself. There are three ways to address this problem:

1. Capture the modulator's output at the transmitter at the same moment that data is being captured in the field and then store them later for processing and analysis.
2. Transmit a sequence known *a priori* to the modeling processor, allowing it to compute its solution in the field at the point of measurement. The use of this sequence, referred to as the *training sequence* or *pilot sequence* in Chapter 9, is very effective, but its use has the disadvantage that revenue-bearing signals must be halted while the training sequence is transmitted. This is reasonable if the channel modeling is being done before the broadcasting system is ever built or operated commercially, but it becomes quite unreasonable

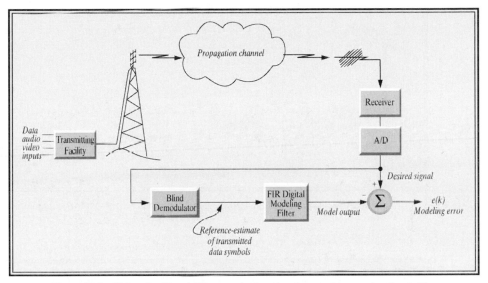

Figure 10.3   Using the Gooch-Harp method to develop a reference signal suitable for the realtime modeling of a digital signal's propagation channel.

if the channel modeling is to be conducted while commercial operation is underway.[1]

3. Use blind modeling during normal operation. To avoid the shortcomings of the first two approaches, we consider here the scheme suggested by Gooch and Harp, [Gooch and Harp, 1988], which is shown in Figure 10.3. This somewhat counterintuitive method relies on the use of a "blind demodulator," of the type described in Chapter 9, to produce a high-quality estimate of the modulator's output from the received signal. These recovered "symbols" can then be applied to the modeling filter's input in lieu of a known reference transmission. The modeling filter's output is compared with a version of the received signal that has been delayed sufficiently to match delays associated with the blind demodulator. Gooch and Harp used the LMS algorithm to drive the modeling error to its minimum level and thus develop the pulse response model. Other methods, including least-squares and (fast) recursive least-squares (RLS), could be used as well.

10.4 EXAMPLE

The process is best illustrated by using actual digital broadcast examples. To characterize broadcast impairments, measurements were made of actual U.S. digital television transmissions in the San Francisco area, an urban environment whose terrain is

---

[1]Invariant content inherent in the transmission, such as framing patterns, may be of limited use in this context.

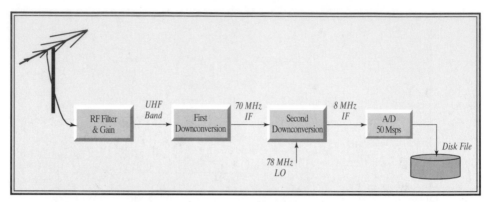

Figure 10.4 Equipment configuration for digital television channel characterization.

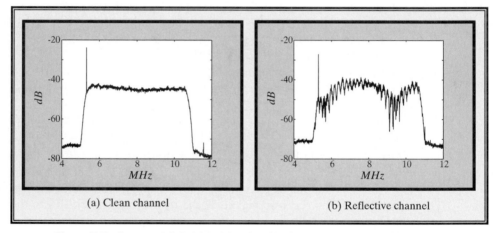

Figure 10.5 Spectra of digital television signal in different reflection environments.

known for its unusual reflective effects on TV reception.[2] The basic setup is depicted in Figure 10.4: The signal from a conventional antenna was downconverted to a first intermediate frequency (IF) at 70 MHz, then translated to a second IF of 8 MHz. The resulting 6-MHz signal was captured in 40 msec snapshots at a 50 MHz sampling rate and stored to disk file.

Power spectra of two different tests are seen in Figure 10.5. In the U.S., digital television is currently transmitted using a somewhat unusual format, an 8-level real-valued pulse amplitude modulation (PAM) with upper vestigial sideband pulse

[2]The authors gratefully acknowledge the support of the ABC affiliate, station KGO, in supporting the data collection.

shaping [ATSC 1995].[3] For these cases, the original signal was centered at 533 MHz (channel 24). Note that downconversion preserves the propagation effects seen at the original radio frequency.

Figure 10.5(a) shows the spectrum with near-ideal reception, i.e., flat across about 5.4 MHz and centered in its 6-MHz channel allocation. The symbol rate is about 10.76 MHz, but because the modulation involves real values, the signal can be sent in about half that bandwidth. In this case, a "square-root Nyquist" pulse filter isolates the upper sideband of the spectrum. Its carefully defined transition band passes a "vestige" of the lower sideband that complements distortion of the upper. The modulation carrier is provided to establish a phase reference to the receiver, and is located about 310 kHz above the lower channel edge on the shoulder of the transition band.

In Figure 10.5(b), the signal shown has been subjected to typical multipath effects, manifested as rippling in the frequency domain, whose period is determined by differential path delay. The complexity of the rippling pattern is a crude indication of the reflection density. In this case we see a relatively simple characteristic involving two disparate ripple patterns across the band. The tighter fine-structure periodicity corresponds to about a 5 μsec delay path, interacting with a second ray of about a 250 nsec path delay, that defines the spectrum's "envelope." This would indicate a reflection field with differential path lengths on the order of 1.5 km down to 75 m. In this environment, reflections are expected to result from planar surfaces of nearby structures, as well as return from gross terrain illumination. Note that in most cases, the spectral characteristics are considerably more complicated than those illustrated by Figure 10.5(b), involving a wide range of delay times and attentuation factors.

Recall that the modeling process depicted in Figure 10.3 involves a blind demodulation. While the specifics of the DTV modulation structure offer certain advantages in this operation, the basic process follows the discussion given in Chapter 9. Specific steps include:

- *Signal isolation*—Given the position of the signal (8 MHz in this example), it is translated in complex form to center at 0 Hz. A lowpass filter then eliminates any adjacent signal energy.

- *Resampling*—The input sampling rate of 50 MHz is next converted to a $T/2$ rate suitable for blind equalization. In this case the symbol rate of 21.524 MHz (the exact value given in MHz is 6156/286) is derived with a net resampling by interpolating the rate up by 3078, followed by decimation by 7150.

- *Phase synchronization*—The presence of the carrier component in DTV greatly simplifies carrier phase synchronization of the demodulator. In this case, the carrier is isolated from the adjacent modulation energy and used to lock a digital local oscillator in phase and frequency. Its output is used to translate the carrier position exactly to 0 Hz.

---

[3] At the time of publication, this 8-VSB format has been adopted for North and South America and parts of Asia. The OFDM system, a "multicarrier" format, has been adopted in Europe and Australia.

- *Sideband recovery*—At this point the lower sideband is recovered by simply discarding the imaginary part of the signal.
- *Blind equalization*—Basic pulse timing and integrity are restored by means of a blind equalizer, such as that described in Chapter 6, using the constant modulus algorithm. Recall that its robust behavior even in the presence of envelope variations makes the algorithm ideal for digital modulation environments.
- *Decision-direction equalization*—Once the CMA converges, the final step in blind recovery involves a switch to decision direction to drive the equalizer convergence in the classic mean-square sense. The output symbol decisions represent the best estimate of the actual transmitted data.

The resulting real-valued signal, available at the symbol rate, can be depicted in the "strip chart" time plot form seen in Figure 10.6. This is the real-valued analogy to the constellation pictures seen in Chapter 6, with each symbol shown as a spot at its point along a time axis. Note that we see a "condensation" into eight values, appearing as vague horizontal bars. A figure of merit equivalent to an equalized SNR can be estimated from dispersion of the bars. For the eight-level signal shown here, we can begin to see definition of the bar structure when this error power falls below 18 dB beneath the signal power.

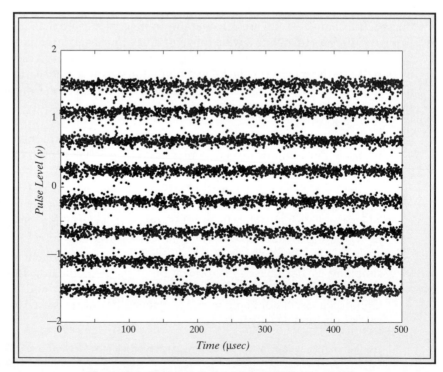

Figure 10.6   Bar constellation for digital television signal.

It should be noted that blind recovery in the modeling context is somewhat less demanding than equalization required for quality broadcast reception. That is, equalization required to achieve the low error rate necessary for consumer acceptance is challenging, given the range of multipath effects encountered. This situation has fostered a number of robust algorithmic innovations, many of which are currently held proprietary. However, modeling in the manner described here can tolerate error losses in the 1% range and still provide accurate characterization of the system's end-to-end propagation effects.

Once equalization has provided a reasonably accurate representation of the transmitted data, the symbols can be used in the manner described in Section 10.3. The recovered symbols become the input to a filter that models the linear impulse response of the unknown channel. At this point, the model may be generated in a variety of ways using a range of structures. Furthermore, it may be driven adaptively, allowing it to track channel changes, or may be derived numerically from the appropriate normal equations using the data record available.

For simplicity in this example, we used a simple FIR structure satisfying the least-squares match to the channel output. For the channel giving rise to the spectrum shown in Figure 10.5(b), the model filter has the finite impulse response shown in Figure 10.7. Figure 10.7(a) shows the raw impulse response, and Figure 10.7(b) shows an energy-based smoothing intended to identify reflection strength. Note that the dominant delay paths responsible for the rippling spectral features are clearly visible.

10.5 ADDITIONAL CONSIDERATIONS

Clearly, some care is in order when configuring the modeling process. In particular, the order of both equalizer filter and modeling filter enter into the viability of the solution. The degree of the modeling filter naturally must be sufficient to span the significant portions of the channel's time response. In this example, a delay span of 5 μsec for a signal at 10 Msymbols/sec calls for a model with some 50 available coefficients. In practice, one allows excess degrees of freedom to accommodate the indeterminant time reference as well as excess delay paths.

On the other hand, specification of the modeling equalizer is another matter. At first appearance, there is an element of circularity in the whole concept: The goal is to construct an equalizer appropriate for a digital receiver, by using a derived estimate of the channel's time behavior. In the modeling approach just demonstrated, that channel model is directly dependent on an equalizer that can recover transmitted symbols, whose design was the original objective.

In reality, practical factors make this circular process viable. As mentioned, the equalizer's performance used for the modeling operation need only be marginal, producing a symbol error rate under a few percent; for that reason the equalizer impulse response may be kept artificially short. However, in true off-line implementations, the equalizer complexity is of little concern, and its length may be chosen with worst case in mind. At any rate, specification of the modeling equalizer requires only a first-order understanding of the channel effects, rather than the detailed quantitative

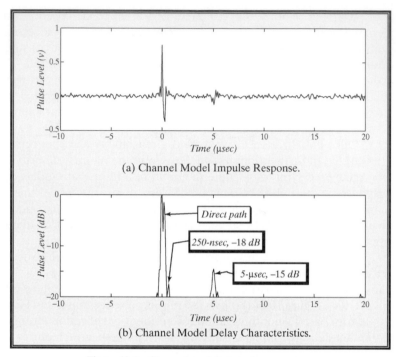

(a) Channel Model Impulse Response.

(b) Channel Model Delay Characteristics.

Figure 10.7   Channel model's impulse response.

characterization necessary for a functional receiver. In particular, an intuitive feeling of the span of reflective delay often provides sufficient information for the modeling equalizer. A rule-of-thumb calls for an equalizer impulse response that spans several times the longest delay path among larger impulse response coefficients, as explained in the next section.

It must be noted that in some situations the modeling process may have to accommodate time variation in the channel. Mobility of source, receiver, or reflectors may translate into variability of the channel, and at times it is the rate and extent of those variations that may be of interest. For example, in the DTV case one scenario of great interest deals with "indoor" channel effects, i.e., the channel seen by an antenna integral to the receiver unit. To provide reliable reception, the receiver (hence the adaptive equalizer) must be able to compensate for nearby reflectors, which most certainly will include people in motion within the room. The design of a viable equalizer hinges on the rate at which the channel changes in response to such motion, i.e., on accurate modeling of the channel as a time-varying impulse response.

Pursuing this example, consider a person moving at typical indoor rates on the order of several meters per second, i.e. something under 10 wavelengths/sec in the UHF band. Motion at this rate, radial to the antenna, could generate variation in a reflective path with periodicity as short as a hundred milliseconds; adequate tracking of the "rise time" might call for an adaptive time constant for the various components of under 20 msec, i.e., on the order of 100,000 symbols. To capture and characterize this effect in a quantitative sense, the modeling process described above would likewise have to track the rate of change. As described in earlier chapters, this tracking requirement would impact the design and implementation of both the blind equalizer and the channel modeling filter.

10.6 USING THE CHANNEL MODEL TO INFLUENCE THE EQUALIZER'S DESIGN

Recall that the objectives of a mathematical modeling process can take many forms, sometimes establishing a basis for understanding the physical factors defining a system's response, other times providing parameters for design of a control strategy. The thrust of this chapter has been focused on modeling to provide a quantitative basis for designing an equalizer in a communications system. Once a model is available that characterizes propagation effects, the requirements for an equalizer's design can be determined. The important factors in the design include (1) the number of coefficients, (2) receiver response time in terms of adaptive step size, and (3) the bulk delay or "cursor position."

The role of the first two factors has been covered in earlier discussions. Specifically, longer FIR filters may improve performance at the cost of implementational complexity and convergence time. Convergence rate is controlled by the adaptive step size, trading off agility at the expense of performance loss due to coefficient jitter (misadjustment noise). The third factor, bulk delay, is somewhat unique to the equalization scenario and is often a degree of freedom necessary to mitigate strong reflectors in the presence of main-path attenuation.

Given the model characteristics, design of the equalizer may be done in a number of ways, using any of several architectures and techniques described in Chapters 4, 5, and 6.[4] Note that while the final implementation may call for an adaptive filter for all of the usual reasons, studying design sensitivities need not be done as such. In fact, one may often choose numerical solution to the normal equations where practical to reduce some of the ambiguities due to convergence rate and coefficient misadjustment of a recursive/adaptive solution.

In the case of an equalizer specification, the designer is often interested in quantifying the expected equalizer performance as a function of the three parameters given above. The traditional performance measure in such cases takes the form of the expected error rate in recovering symbols at the output of the equalizer. Thus, to characterize behavior of a specific configuration, one might compute the optimal least

---

[4] As mentioned, there are several innovative architectures purported to address extreme multipath effects; for purposes of this discussion, we concentrate on the simple FIR structure.

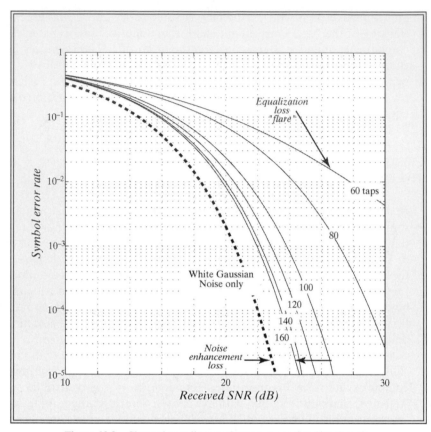

Figure 10.8 Channel equalizer performance, varying filter length.

squares solution and its residual mean-squared error, interpreted as the source of symbol decision errors. Then, repeated for a range of input SNR levels, the predicted SER values define a performance curve for that design configuration.

Figure 10.8 depicts the equalizer performance for our example channel with the $T/2$- or fractionally spaced linear equalizer. Note that as a baseline of comparison, the left-most curve labeled "white noise only" shows ideal performance expected in the absence of any intersymbol interference. The top-most curve in the figure indicates the performance expected for under-equalization, i.e., too few taps. In such cases, for even larger SNR the top curve tends to flatten out or flare away from the ideal curve; effectively, for low noise conditions, the residual intersymbol interference dominates symbol degradation and the error rate.

On the other hand, when properly specified, a $T/2$-spaced linear equalizer provides a curve that tracks the white gaussian noise (WGN) baseline in shape. However, note that depending on the channel's spectral impairments, the equalizer will exhibit some degree of noise enhancement. In other words, in compensating the spectral response of the channel, the equalizer tends to shape the incoming flat noise component in ways that worsen its effect at the output. So, while the SER curve approaches the proper shape, it is displaced some number of decibels to the right of the ideal.

In this example, it would appear that an equalizer of some 150 taps provides performance degraded from the ideal by a bit under 2 dB. A designer could confidently promote that structure as suitable for an adaptive implementation; at convergence one would expect its performance to approximate the derived curve. Given this length specification, rules for convergence/tracking rate and misadjustment degradation can be used to determine an appropriate step-size.

In addition to examining length sensitivity for a design, we can also test behavior with respect to bulk delay. Figure 10.9 shows the SER curves for a fixed equalizer length (100 taps), but ranging the delay from a very low value of 4 up through 50. For the first value, the receiver is given a duration of only 4 samples to make a symbol decision. For this channel model, we see that very low values give unacceptable performance; for a delay of 4 samples (i.e., two symbols), the curve is very flat and does not drop below an 80% SER. However, for a filter of 100 taps we see that a delay of 50 samples (25 symbols) can be excessive, and that the lesser value of 20 actually performs about a 1-1/2 dB better. Adjusting the delay in this manner effectively shifts the time origin and provides more degrees for freedom for the negative-going section of the impulse response at the expense of the positive-time span. In a design scenario of this type it may be appropriate to determine the most effective use of taps by empirically testing performance in this manner. Again, note for a proper range of delays, performance will tend to parallel the ideal curve with a displacement loss.

The solution of the fractionally spaced normal equations may be subject to numerical effects that are aggravated by poor matrix condition number, i.e., spectral disparities in the received signal [Gitlin et al., 1992]. For this reason, design of extremely long equalizers by this means may be inaccurate. In such cases, it may be necessary to use inversion techniques that exploit the block Toeplitz structure of the matrix [Robinson and Treitel, 1980].

10.7 THE DIFFERENCE BETWEEN THE FILTERING PROBLEM AND SYSTEM IDENTIFICATION

In our discussion of the modeling problem, we have purposely posed the structure in the form of the adaptive filtering scenario, i.e., a given input to be filtered to match a desired component. However, it must be noted that while structurally the operations are similar, philosophically adaptive filtering and system identification are considerably different. In the case of the adaptive filter, it is the degree of similarity in the two signal components, the desired and filter output, that is critical.

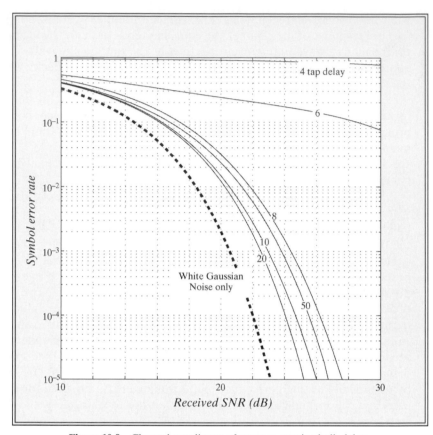

Figure 10.9   Channel equalizer performance, varying bulk delay.

That is, the level of the mean squared error determines the quality of the filtering operation.

In the case of modeling, however, it is the accuracy of the model parameterization that is important. In the case of the FIR structure that we have chosen, deviation in the filter coefficients, not output, determines the quality of the model. As illustrated by our example, these values determine the matrix elements in the design equation, and must be accurate to be of value in the design process, be it an equalizer or controller. The impact of various parameter inaccuracies depends on the ultimate use to which the identified model is to be put, e.g., designing an equalizer or a feedback controller. The challenge is to predict effectively the future output of the "identified" physical system under an excitation scenario different from the one used to determine the parameter estimates.

This distinction between filtering and modeling may seem artificial; after all, the output error is directly determined by the coefficient error. However, with under-specification of the identifier order, the output error is also impacted by correlation of the input samples applied to the filter. In the absence of input correlation (i.e., a stimulus signal with a flat spectrum), the residual mean-squared error is proportional to the sum-squared coefficient error; with input correlation, it is not. This can result in a large sum-squared coefficient error not reflected in mean-squared output prediction error.

That raises a credibilty question: Because one really has little control over the input excitation in a blind modeling situation, to what degree does the resulting impulse response represent the actual channel? While the issue of inaccuracy in the coefficients is a legitimate question and under some circumstances may jeopardize the model's value, in most practical cases the results will be adequate, provided that some reasonable spectral distribution is maintained over the portion of the band of interest. After all, a gap in the spectrum of the input represents an ill-conditioning that gives rise to non-uniqueness of the model, i.e., a mode unobservable under that condition. In digital communications scenarios, transmitter coding usually provides an excitation that is spectrally flat across the band of interest.

10.8 FINAL COMMENTS

As a final observation, the idea of channel characterization has long been used in communications and control applications. Until recently, many of the techniques were limited to off-line analysis and relatively stationary conditions. With advances in digital signal processing, we see real-time applications beyond the example shown in this chapter, e.g., "channel probing" in such areas as mobile telephony and high-rate voice channel modems.

11

Design Example: Enhancing Signal Reception Quality Using an Array of Antennas

- *Precis: Intelligently combining the outputs of many antennas or sensors can improve the quality of the resultant signal by increasing its signal-to-noise ratio, by reducing the effects of interference, or both. This intelligent combination is often accomplished with multichannel digital filters driven by adaptive algorithms.*

11.1 THE PROBLEM

Many situations occur in the design of communications and sensing systems where the signal of interest to the user can be received at many locations and where it might be advantageous to combine a number of them to produce a system output of higher quality than any of the individual received signals. An example of this, radio astronomy, was discussed in Section 1.4. In that section it was shown that the objective of high signal sensitivity could be achieved with a large number of smaller antennas if only a mechanism could be found to combine the antenna outputs coherently. We explore this problem in this chapter, first by examining a very simple example and then expanding it to more complicated and realistic situations.

11.2 A SIMPLIFIED VERSION OF THE PROBLEM AND A SOLUTION

Suppose that we are interested in tracking a distant space probe using an array of antennas such as those shown in Figure 1.11 in Chapter 1. We begin by assuming that the space probe is emitting a sinusoidal signal at a radio frequency f_0 that is known or at least predictable back on earth, and that the general direction of the probe is known so that the antennas can be aimed within the accuracy limits of their steering machinery. We desire to combine the outputs of the antennas to improve the signal-to-noise ratio of the resultant signal, thereby maximizing the distance to which the space probe can be accurately tracked.

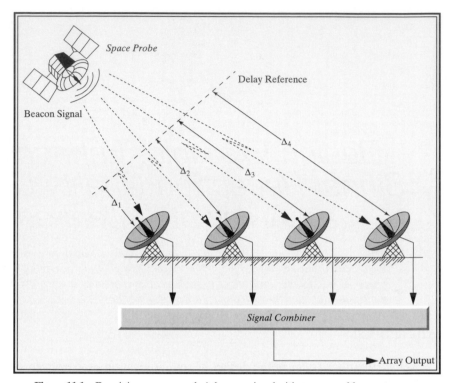

Figure 11.1   Receiving a space probe's beacon signal with an array of four antennas. Note the time differences in which the signal arrives at each of the antennas.

Unfortunately, as we discussed in Section 1.4, it is not a simple matter to combine the outputs of the antennas. Figure 11.1 illustrates the problem. In this case four antennas are shown, each receiving its version of the beacon signal transmitted by the space probe. Because the probe is not directly overhead, the amount of time required for the beacon signal to reach each antenna is different from the others. This difference in arrival time translates directly into a phase shift in each received signal. Simply adding together signals that have been phase-shifted arbitrarily from each other results in a much poorer resultant signal than had the shifting not occurred. Our objective then is to design a signal processing structure which can recover this lost performance.

Figure 11.2 shows such a structure. The output of each antenna is phase-shifted by the appropriate amount, say θ_n for the nth antenna, and then added together to produce the array's output. If each phase shift is chosen to exactly compensate for the shift induced by the differential delay and any implementation imperfections, then all of the antenna outputs will be in phase with each other and direct addition will produce the highest possible signal quality.

Possibly the earliest example of such a system is the Multiple Unit Steerable Array (MUSA) shown in Figure 11.3. It consisted of six array elements, each a large

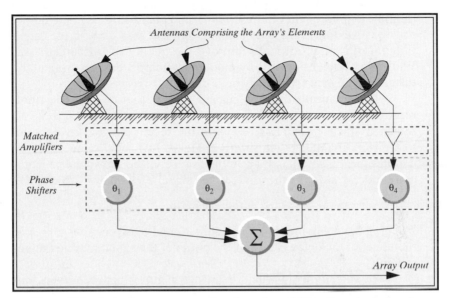

Figure 11.2 A simple antenna array based on phase-shifting the output of each array element.

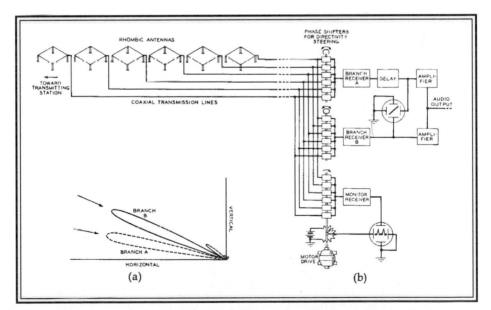

Figure 11.3 The "Multiple Unit Steerable Array", a six-element phased-array antenna built by the Bell Laboratories to optimize the reception of high-frequency (HF) transatlantic telephone signals. © *1937 AT&T. All rights reserved. Reprinted with permission.*

rhombic high-frequency radio antenna, and phase-shifters implemented with motor-driven capacitors [Friis and Feldman, 1937]. It was built in the late 1930s by Bell Laboratories in an effort to improve the quality of transatlantic radiotelephony. While very straightforward by modern standards, this experimental design was at the cutting edge of technology in its day.

Mathematically the problem and solution that we have described so far can be represented as follows. The beacon signal has been assumed to be a sinusoid with radian frequency $\omega_0 = 2\pi f_0$. Each of the received signals is delayed with respect to a given reference point, shown in Figure 11.1, by the time interval Δ_n, where n denotes the nth antenna. If all antennas receive the sinusoidal beacon with the same amplitude, A say, then the nth received signal is given by

$$\bar{x}_n(t) = A \cos\{\omega_0(t + \Delta_n)\}. \tag{11.2.1}$$

Defining the delay-induced phase-shift ϕ_n by the expression $\phi_n = \Delta_n \omega_0$ we see that the effect of the delay is to shift the phase of the signal received at antenna n by ϕ_n radians.

The antenna array structure shown in Figure 11.2 produces an output $y(t)$ where $y(t)$ is given by

$$y(t) = \sum_{n=1}^{N} S\{\theta_n, \bar{x}_n(t)\}, \tag{11.2.2}$$

where the operator $S\{a, b\}$ rotates the signal b by the angle a radians. Making the appropriate substitutions for $\bar{x}_n(t)$ and S, we find that

$$y(t) = \sum_{n=1}^{N} S\{\theta_n, A \cos(\omega_0 t + \phi_n)\}$$

$$= \sum_{n=1}^{N} A \cos(\omega_0 t + \phi_n - \theta_n). \tag{11.2.3}$$

If somehow the control variable θ_n could be chosen to equal the delay-induced phase shift $\phi_n (= \Delta_n \omega_0)$ for each of the n antenna elements, then the array output $y(t)$ becomes

$$y(t) = \sum_{n=1}^{N} A \cos\{\omega_0 t\} = NA \cos\{\omega_0 t\}, \tag{11.2.4}$$

its maximum possible amplitude level. This obviously then is the set of choices that we desire to make.

How might these compensating phase shifts be automatically chosen? If the array elements and their electronics were perfectly calibrated, and if the exact angle of the space probe from the antennas were known, then the phase shifts ϕ_n could be computed ahead of time and updated predictably. In many practical cases, how-ever, one or more of these assumptions is untrue or too expensive to achieve. It would therefore be desirable to have a mechanism by which the proper phase shifts could

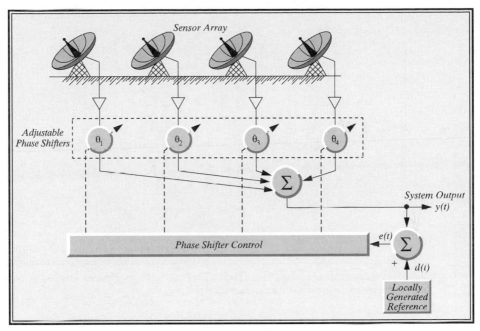

Figure 11.4   Adaptive compensating phase shifts permits operation in a time varying environment and with an uncalibrated array.

be found and then updated as the space probe moves through the sky. One approach to accomplishing this objective is shown in Figure 11.4.

As in Figure 11.2, the antenna outputs in Figure 11.4 are phase-shifted and then combined to produce the resultant, the system output $y(t)$. The system output is compared with $d(t)$, a locally produced version of the beacon signal being sent by the spacecraft. The difference, the error signal $e(t)$, is to be used to select the proper value for each phase shift. When these values are found, the system output and the locally generated reference are as close to each other as they can be.

A system of the type just described is often termed a *phased array antenna* and a variety of methods have been developed to find and update the best choices for the phase shifters [Monzingo and Miller, 1980] [Widrow and Stearns, 1985] [Compton, 1988]. We address this issue further in Section 11.4.3.

11.3 MORE COMPLICATED FILTERS TO DEAL WITH MORE COMPLICATED SIGNALS

11.3.1 The Adaptive Linear Combiner

In the development of the adaptive structure shown in Figure 11.4, we assumed that the only differences between the signals received at the different antennas are the phase shifts induced by the path length differences. Implicitly, we assumed that

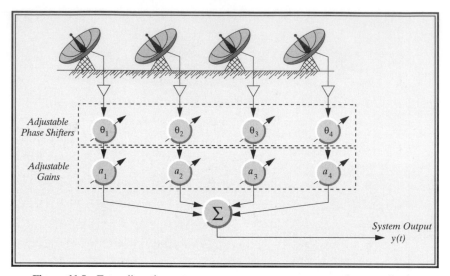

Figure 11.5 Extending the antenna array concept to accommodate amplitude matching errors and differences in received noise levels.

only noise and the beacon signal were present at the antenna inputs and that the noise impinging on each of the antennas was of equal power and statistically independent of that seen at all others. In practice none of these assumptions is true. The signals are not received with the same power levels, particularly if the array elements are geographically dispersed. The noise, for a variety of reasons, may not have the same power at each antenna. Furthermore, implementation shortcomings can ruin the assumptions. The amplifiers used at each antenna do not have precisely the same gain, nor do the antennas, and the cable lengths are not the same. If these degradations are small enough, then the "phase-shift only" design shown in Figures 11.2 and 11.4 can function adequately. The MUSA seen in Figure 11.3 and the large number of phased-array radars in operational service attest to that fact. However, there are many practical cases in which these degradations are large enough to render the phase-shift-only design ineffective. The first step in dealing with this shortcoming can be taken by permitting each of the phase-shifters to introduce amplitude scaling as well. Each antenna output is therefore scaled and/or phase shifted before being added together with the others. Such a structure is shown in Figure 11.5.

To make the mathematical description simpler, we assume from this point that the antenna signals have been sampled with A/D convertors and that complex-valued representations of each have been produced using techniques described in Chapter 7. This version of the sensor and processing system is shown in Figure 11.6. We call the complex, sampled output of the nth antenna $x_n(k)$. With this assumption the desired adjustment of both amplitude and phase of each of the antenna output signals can be achieved by multiplying it by a complex-valued weighting scalar.

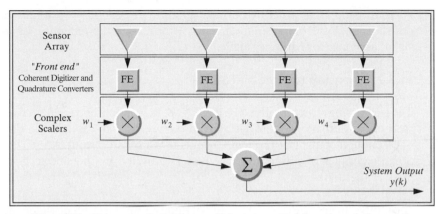

Figure 11.6 Using complex scaling coefficients to control the gain and phase shift applied to the output of each sensor.

We designate the weighting coefficient for the nth antenna as w_n. With these assumptions, the complex-valued array output $y(k)$ becomes

$$y(k) = \sum_{n=1}^{N} w_n x_n(k). \tag{11.3.1}$$

We can make the notation even simpler by defining $\mathbf{W}$ as the complex-valued vector of the weights w_n and $\mathbf{X}(k)$ as the complex-valued vector of the sampled array element outputs. The array output can therefore be written compactly as

$$y(k) = \mathbf{W}^t \mathbf{X}(k). \tag{11.3.2}$$

The structure shown in Figure 11.6 and represented mathematically in (11.3.2) is often termed the *linear combiner* (as was done in Section 2.1) because the output $y(k)$ is linear in both the coefficients and the antenna outputs. The adaptive version is known as the *adaptive linear combiner* (ALC) [Widrow and Stearns, 1985].

The fact that the system output $y(k)$ is a linear combination of input signals should immediately suggest that all of the adaptive filtering machinery developed in Chapters 2 through 7 can be immediately applied. That is, in fact, true. Before pursuing that, however, we first must confirm that the introduction of amplitude scaling permits the freedom needed to solve the problems that we identified. Specifically, we note that

- Gain imbalances induced by differences in signal levels, antenna gains, amplifier gains, and cable losses can all be compensated by picking the right amplitude $\{w_n\}$, and
- Inequalities in the level of noise received by each antenna can be addressed by using the weighting coefficient to lower the gain for antennas with higher noise levels.

As it turns out, this structure permits yet another benefit—the ability to receive the desired signal well while simultaneously suppressing the reception of an interfering signal arriving from another angle.

11.3.2 Extension to Time and Space

The processing structure illustrated in Figure 11.6 is an improvement over the "phase shift only" design of Figure 11.2 but in many practical cases it still does not introduce enough control of the input signals to attain an output of the desired quality. Some examples of problems inadequately handled by the simple linear combiner include the following:

- Introducing the desired degree of delay compensation in wideband signals, i.e. phase shifting alone is sufficient for sinusoidal beacon signals but not for broadband ones,
- Compensating for spectral shaping of the signals by the propagation medium or the receiving electronics,
- Compensating for noise with nonwhite power spectra, and
- Selectively discriminating against interferers which are in the same direction as the signal of interest but on a different frequency.

System designers encountering one or more of these practical problems have often augmented the simple linear combiner of Figure 11.6 with the "space/time" architecture shown in Figure 11.7. Instead of simple multiplication by a single weighting coefficient, each antenna's output is applied to a finite-pulse-response filter of order P. The filter outputs are summed to produce the system output $y(k)$. Instead of N weighting coefficients there are now NP, with the complex-valued coefficient w_{np} multiplying the pth-delayed version of the signal from sensor n. The fact that the structure is now capable of a measure of temporal as well as spatial filtering permits it to address each of the issues identified in the list above. For example, the need to perform delay compensation of up to P time samples for a wideband received signal is easily accommodated with the temporal delay lines in this space/time combiner.

Note in passing that, in the limit when $P = 0$, there is no temporal filtering and the architecture reduces to the linear combiner of Figure 11.6. Note conversely, however, that when P is greater than zero and $n = 1$, the processor becomes a single FIR filter accepting its input from a degenerate array consisting of only one element.

Mathematically this spatial-temporal processor has a representation much like that in (11.3.2). Suppose we define the coefficient vector $\mathbf{W}$ partitioned as

$$\mathbf{W} = [w_{11} \ldots w_{1P} \vdots w_{21} \ldots w_{2P} \vdots \ldots \vdots w_{N1} \ldots w_{NP}]^t \qquad (11.3.3)$$

and $\mathbf{X}(k)$ in the corresponding fashion as

$$\mathbf{X}(k) = [x_1(k) \ldots x_1(k - P) \vdots \ldots \vdots x_N(k) \ldots x_N(k - P)]^t. \qquad (11.3.4)$$

With these definitions the array output $y(k)$ once again can be expressed as

$$y(k) = \mathbf{W}^t \mathbf{X}(k). \tag{11.3.5}$$

11.4 ADDING ADAPTIVITY TO SPATIAL
AND SPATIO-TEMPORAL PROCESSORS

11.4.1 The Need for Adaptivity

From a theoretical perspective, the spatial/temporal processor shown in Figure 11.7 and encapsulated mathematically in (11.3.5) achieves our stated objective. It can accept the outputs of N sensors and coherently combine them to produce a system output with quality higher than any of the inputs. Further, assuming the coefficients w_{np} are chosen properly, the structure can "null out" interfering signals impinging on the array, it can compensate for imperfections in the array's implementation, and it can equalize the effects of propagation on the received signals. What could make it better then? In many (but not all) practical cases, the answer to this question is

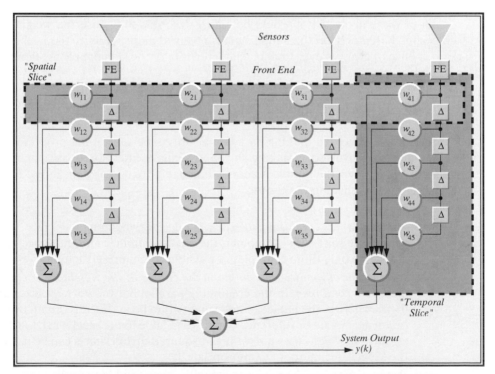

Figure 11.7   Replacing the individual scaling coefficients in the linear combiner with digital filters to produce a "space/time processor."

to make the choice of the weighting coefficients adaptive. The reasons for this are exactly the same as those discussed in Chapter 1 for purely time-domain adaptive filters. They include the following:

- Many of the characteristics of the signal of interest and its propagation path to the array are unknown *a priori*. One such characteristic often initially unknown in a receiving array is the direction from which the signal of interest to the user is arriving.
- Similarly the characteristics of signals not of interest to the user, such as noise and interference, must also be known to configure the array's response with the optimal choice of weighting coefficients.
- Even if initially known or measured, these same characteristics usually change with time, forcing the calculation of a new set of weights to maintain near-optimal performance.
- The characteristics of the receiving system itself must be known to compute optimal values of the weighting coefficients. In a nonadaptive array this knowledge must be gained by careful construction of the array, a calibration process, or both.

All of these imply that it would be highly desirable to choose the weighting coefficients based only on the actual signals received and to modify them as needed in response to changes over time in characteristics of the signal, propagation medium, interference, and the receiving system.

11.4.2 System Level Choices

The design choices in making an adaptive space- or space-time processor directly parallel those involved in making an adaptive digital filter. These are summarized in Figure 11.8, which the nimble reader will recognize to be an extension of Figure 2.1. In brief, the designer must choose:

- *Structure of the combining network*. While overwhelmingly the most common, the "phase shift only" combiner, the linear combiner and the space-time processor are only three examples of possible combining structures.
- *Assessment of quality used to guide the choice of the weighting coefficients in the signal combiner*. In the continuing parallel between array processing and digital filtering, the choice of how quality is to be assessed is driven by whether or not a template or reference signal is available to the receiver (i.e., a "training signal"), in which case sum- or mean-squared-error criteria can be used. If not, the "blind" techniques are appropriate.
- *Adaptation rules*. The means to actually choose and then update the weighting coefficients must be defined.

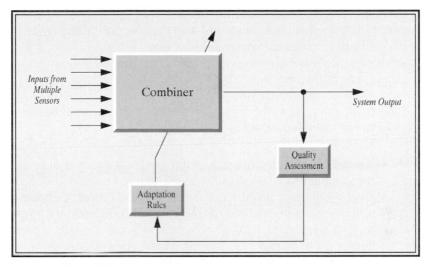

Figure 11.8   The general structure of an adaptive receiving array.

Implicit in these choices are issues associated with implementation. While most mirror those encountered in the practical implementation of adaptive filters discussed in Chapter 7, some issues appear disproportionately in the design of antenna arrays. The principal reason for this is that historically the bandwidths over which an antenna array needed to operate were much larger than those that could be supported with digital implementations. As a result, considerable portions of some adaptive arrays were built with analog components, including the quality assessment and the coefficient updating mechanism [Monzingo and Miller, 1980]. Further, adaptation algorithms were developed to accommodate the fact that in some implementations it is not possible to sample or sense the coefficient inputs. When this is true (i.e., the **X** vector is not available to the algorithm), then the least-sum-squared and least-mean-squared techniques of Chapter 4 cannot be directly used. Even though semiconductor performance has improved enormously over the past decades, sampling rates and processing speeds are still outstripped by the bandwidths of communications and radio astonomy signals. Thus the design of purely and partially analog implementations of array processors can be expected to continue.

11.4.3 A Simple Design Example

To provide an example of how the design process might proceed, we now revisit the problem of tracking a deep space probe for the purpose of receiving its onboard telemetry and sensor data. We assume for the purpose of this example that a known template or training signal is being sent whenever data or telemetry is not, and further that the quality of the reception is good enough that high-quality data decisions can be sent back to the adaptive processor whenever data or telemetry is being sent. We assume that the bandwidth of the telemetry signal is about 1 MHz, permitting the use of a fully digital implementation, and that the rate of change of the propagation channel and interference environment is slow enough that accurate updating of the array's coefficients every second is sufficiently fast to obtain the full performance gain of which the receiving array is capable.

Many design approaches could be used to meet these requirements. We pursue a logical one here, but with no implication that others might not perform as well or be better in special circumstances.

- **Array Design**—The first step in the design of the overall system is to identify the antennas to be used and to verify that collectively they have the ability to receive the space probe's signal with sufficient signal-to-noise ratio to be able to recover the transmitted telemetry and data. The adaptive processor cannot recover signals not actually present at the sensor inputs. This step defines the number of sensors N.

- **Processor structure**—In reviewing the capabilities of each of the structures defined earlier in this chapter, we choose here the space/time (a.k.a. "multi-channel digital filter") design in Figure 11.8 because the signal is "wideband" when compared to the digitization frequency, since we anticipate broad- and narrowband interference, and because we desire to have the maximum possible tolerance of implementation imperfections.

- **Processor "depth" P**—The required "depth" of the processor P in (11.3.3) and (11.3.4) depends on a number of factors which the designer must evaluate, including: (i) the amount of equalization to be afforded the signal of interest, (ii) the number of interferers to be expected, and whether they are wide- or narrowband, and (iii) the ratio of the signal's bandwidth to the sampling rate.

- **Quality assessment method**—Since the probe has been assumed to send a pilot or training when data or telemetry is not being sent, there is no need to use a "blind" performance criteria. We therefore choose the low risk and highly robust approach shown in Figure 11.9 and typical of that used in dial-up telephone modems (see Figure 6.4). The array processor's output $y(k)$ is subtracted from a locally produced version of the pilot or training signal $d_1(k)$ when it is being transmitted and from the demodulator's estimate of the telemetry or data $d_2(k)$ when it is being transmitted. The difference signal, is termed, as always, the error $e(k)$ and its summed or mean square reflects the degree of agreement between the processor's output and the two references.

- **Updating scheme**—With the decision to use a squared error performance criteria, the last key decision is how the coefficients should be updated. The most important issue in making this choice is the speed with which the coefficients must be updated. In general, practical problems fall into one of two classes. In the first the system is sufficiently dynamic that the coefficients must be updated as rapidly as possible to maintain a reasonable level of system-level

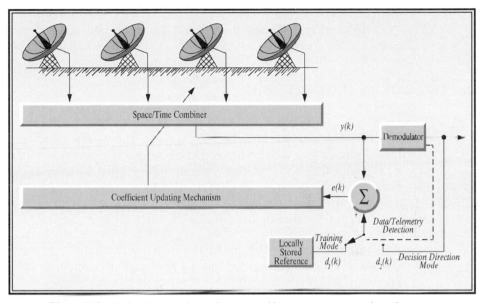

Figure 11.9   A simple example—using a space/time processor to receive telemetry from a space probe.

performance. This is the domain in which the "recursive least-squares" techniques of Section 4.3 or the accelerated gradient-descent techniques of Section 4.2.6 can be usefully applied.

In the other class of practical problems, the dynamics of the system are slow enough that high-quality updates can be made without requiring highly efficient use of the data. In these cases two methods are commonly used:

- Block computation of a solution to the optimal summed-squared error problem. When the data quality is good and the required update rate is low, then "blocks" of data can be used which are much smaller than the total number available between those updates. This reduces the computation burden considerably.
- LMS-based approximate-gradient-descent. This is not as data-efficient as least-squares techniques but has the advantage of a very simple implementation.

Because the input sampling rate must exceed the 1 MHz bandwidth of the signal and the required update rate is once per second, it would appear that this example falls into the second class. We assume this to be the case here. Further, based on its ease of implementation, we complete our high-level design by electing to use LMS, perhaps with a small amount of coefficient leakage (see Section 4.2.7) to add even more robustness to the system.

With the appropriate definitions for y, d, e, $\mathbf{W}$ and $\mathbf{X}(k)$ developed in support of (11.3.5), we see that LMS (and "leaky LMS") can be applied directly as described in Chapter 4 to this example.

11.5 APPLICATIONS AND EXTENSIONS

We have focused so far on the use of adaptive processors to intelligently combine signals provided by a number of different sensors. This is only one of a variety of interrelated applications in this wide and fascinating technical field. With no serious attempt at completeness we list here some of these related topic areas. All of these have been and continue to be of great theoretical and practical interest. All have the same theoretical underpinnings, but the underlying assumptions and practical objectives serve to distinguish them from each other.

- **Aperture combining**—This is the common name for the type of processing discussed in this chapter so far because antennas are commonly referred to as *apertures* by theoreticians.
- **Electronic beam steering**—In this case, the processor's coefficients are selected to steer the receiving beam of the antenna array without having to move the antennas themselves, e.g., in phased array radars.
- **Diversity reception**—This is the use of the adaptive procesor in a multi-input receiving system to compensate for the propagation-induced degradation impacting each of the individually received signals. When the multiple signals come from spatially separated sensors, termed *spatial diversity*, this is simply the dual of aperture combining. It is also possible, however, to combine signals operating at different frequencies (frequency diversity) or on different polarizations (polarization diversity). Some communications systems employ a combination of these techniques to attain the signal quality desired by the ultimate user.

    In addition to the two-channel troposcatter processing system discussed in Section 9.3, another example of diversity combining can be found in modern cellular telephone systems. A service provider accommodates connection with users' wireless telephones by partitioning the region of coverage into nonoverlapping cells, often depicted as the hexagonal pattern shown in the inset on Figure 11.10. The RF contact with the individual subscriber is handled by a transmitter and receiver at *base stations* distributed within this pattern. To minimize equipment, real estate, and deployment costs, base stations are placed at a corner, i.e. at the intersection of three cells. By proper arrangement about the corner's 120° symmetry, the base station antennas can illuminate (and receive from) the three neighboring cells. Shading in the figure's hexagonal pattern indicates placement of one such base station with its three illuminated sectors.

    The photo in Figure 11.10 shows the antenna arrangement typical for a base station location, seen routinely in urban areas and along transportation

Figure 11.10   The cellular base station antenna: Spatial diversity reception within each of three 120° sectors.

corridors. This photograph shows the tower and its three antenna sets, oriented at 120° to serve the three sectors. Each set has three elements; the center one transmits to the mobile users, and the two end elements, along with their supporting electronics, form a two-channel spatial diversity receiving system for the signals coming from the mobile users.

- **Interference reduction**—This refers to the use of the coefficients to null interference being received from a direction or at a frequency different from the one used by the desired signal while still receiving the desired signal with high quality.

- **Direction-finding**—In this class of problem the coefficients of the array are used to determine the direction from which a signal is arriving.

There is a rich literature regarding the theory and practice of multichannel processing. The reader is encouraged to seek out tutorial works such as Paulraj and Papadias [1997].

12

Epilog

The purpose of this book was to deal with adaptive filtering from many perspectives, including research, development, and design. This was done in the following way:

1. *Establishing the proper context for adaptive processing*—Chapters 1 and 8 through 11 were centered on real applications of adaptive processing. These chapters discussed the trade-offs and concerns surrounding the motivation for an adaptive solution, enabling the engineer to answer the following questions: When does the addition of an adaptive filter make sense? What types of performance gains can be expected?

2. *Determining the means by which satisfactory parameter adjustments can be made*—Chapters 2 through 6 were devoted to the development of many of the common adaptive techniques currently in use and under study.

3. *Determining the expected properties of such adaptive filters*—In Chapter 3, the concepts of optimality, convergence, and average behavior were discussed, along with the factors that determine convergence rate and performance. Chapters 4, 5, and 6 used these concepts to examine different classes of filters and algorithms.

4. *Exploring for possible extensions*—By building on the "classical" least-squares approaches of Chapter 3 and 4, Chapters 5 and 6 presented more recently developed means of filter adjustment. In Chapter 5, the alternative to the finite-impulse-response (FIR) structures of Chapter 4 was the infinite-impulse-response (IIR) structure. Key tools in this development were stability theory and the search and minimization procedures common for adaptive FIR filters. Connection was made between the statistical averaging analysis of Chapters 3

and 4 and the analysis of Chapter 5. Chapter 6 addressed the alternative performance function definition of property restoral. The formations of Chapters 4 and 5, which relied on the presence of a desired signal for sample-by-sample prediction error generation, were shown to be only one special case of the more general property restoral concept. At this time the development, analysis, and refinement of such extensions form a major component of the ongoing research effort in adaptive filter theory.

5. *Using this theory in practice*—Given a filter structure and a bandwidth requirement, there are a variety of implementation alternatives available. Chapter 7 discussed many of the practical aspects of digital designs, as well as providing a more general overview of implementational tradeoffs.

In summary, each of these points was considered in the applications introduced in Chapter 1 and then resolved for the same applications in Chapters 8 through 11. In each case, the practical concerns and objectives influenced the choices made in filter configuration, adaptive algorithm selection, and hardware or software realization. The background needed to perform these selections was provided by the intervening chapters of this book, which presented extensible fundamentals of the theory and design of adaptive filters.

Appendix A

Adaptive Filtering in MATLAB

For the practicing engineer, the MATLAB environment satisfies two very important aspects of digital signal processing development. First, in the context of batch processing it offers a high degree of performance efficiency in common filtering and transform operations. At the same time, the environment and language provide a convenient means of prototyping and evaluating processing algorithms, integrated closely with statistical and graphical tools. In fact, throughout this text many of the assertions have been illustrated using MATLAB-generated graphics.

In this appendix, we present some of the techniques appropriate for software implementation of adaptive filtering techniques. By way of illustration, scripts for the generation of certain figures appearing in the text are provided as a starting point for those developing related implementations.

A.1 STRUCTURAL NOTES

Under most circumstances, a MATLAB implementation involves memory-based access to the record of input data. That is, data samples to be processed will often be read as a block from its disk file. Occasionally, when the application involves huge amounts of data, it may be necessary to partition the disk file into subblocks, processing with suitable overlap to provide filtering continuity across the block boundaries. For simplicity in this discussion we assume the former situation.

As a starting point, consider the basic filtering/update operation as might be implemented in MATLAB. The following excerpt given in Figure A.1 focuses on the LMS algorithm, (4.2.5)–(4.2.7), but serves as a fundamental framework for related

```
%   For the following segment, assume the variables are defined as:
%       w     = row vector of adaptive filter coefficients
%       ntaps = number of adaptive coefficients
%       x     = row array of input data values to filter
%       d     = row array of desired data values
%       nsize = number of samples in the input and desired array
%       mu    = appropriate scalar step size
%
%   The filter output will be stored in the row array y
%

y=zeros(1,nsize);               %(1) Reserve and initialize output array

for k=ntaps:nsize,              %(2) Update over all data values
    y(k)=w*x(k:-1:k-1)';        %(3) Form filter output sample
    e=d(k)-y;                   %(4) Error: desired - output
    w=w+mu*e*x(k:-1:k-1);       %(5) Update weight vector
end
```

Figure A.1   The basic update loop.

adaptation as well. This sample illustrates a specific implementation that makes use of the block processing efficiencies offered by the MATLAB language. Three items are worth noting about this structure.

- Note that the native convolutional procedures available in MATLAB (e.g., "*filter*") are not suitable in this context; because adaptation results in time variation of the coefficients, such functions are inappropriate.
- The computation and storage of the output samples, y, is best done by defining and initializing the destination array before entering the iterative stage, as in line (1). The alternative approach of appending each new output sample to the current array, so that it grows to its ultimate length, is very inefficient. While this approach is attractive in that it does not require *a priori* knowledge of data block lengths, the overhead associated with dynamic memory allocation causes the execution time to grow rapidly with the vector's length and can severely bog down throughput.
- Lastly, note the "in place" reference to the input data in lines (3) and (5). That is, when the convolutional calculation forming the output samples is expressed as a vector inner product, reversal of the data samples can be done using the indexing flexibility allowed by MATLAB. In this case, we can reverse the data simply by running the indices backward over the appropriate range.

Given this framework, many of the related iterative algorithms discussed in this text can be implemented by simply substituting for line (4), i.e., the error definition. For example, for the "sign-error" LMS algorithm, we would simply substitute the line

```
    e = sign(d(k)-y);                    %Sign error LMS
```

for line (4) in Figure A.1; the Constant Modulus algorithm as embodied in (6.4.8)–(6.4.9) would call for the line

```
    e = y(k) * (A^2 - abs(y(k))^2);    %Constant modulus error
```

A.2 EXAMPLES

In this section, we present complete MATLAB scripts used to generate three figures appearing in the text: the output of the adaptive hum canceller given in Figure 8.2, and two comparing LMS and RLS performance as depicted in Figure 4.5. Note that the code given is intended to provide a starting point for adaptive implementations. Many of the specific details are present by virtue of the figure presentation, and may well be inappropriate for actual processing tasks. Furthermore, little attention has been focused on optimization aspects in these code segments; again, the reader should be prepared to tailor the script for the requirements of the specific application.

A.2.1 Figure 8.2: LMS Hum Canceller

```
%
%    Simulated hum cancellation, generating Fig 8.2
%


%-------------------------------------------------------------------------
%
%    Simulated input signal:
%


%
%    Set up pulse cycle of 1 sec at 500 Hz
%
cycle=zeros(1,500);
y=[1 2 3 4 5 6 7 8 9 10 9 8 7 6 5 4 3 2 1 0]/4; %Ramping segment
t=[0:1:40];                              %Local use time axis
a=(.05*(t-20).*(t-20)-20)/50;            %Parabolic recovery segment
cycle(1:61)=2*[y a];                     %Place pulse in 1-sec cycle
cyc=filter([1 1 1 1 1], [1], cycle);     %Smooth the corners


%
%    Set up 1 sec of 60-cycle hum
%
```

```
t=[1:500]/500;                            %Overall time axis at 500 Hz
inter=100*cos(2*pi*60*t);                 %Tone interference at 60 Hz


%
%   Form primary signal, i.e. five pulse cycles, plus interference and WGN
%
x=inter+cyc;                              %One cycle
[idum, nsize]=size(x);                    %Number values in cycle
x=[ x x x x x]+randn(1,nsize*5);          %Concatenate five cycles
[idum, nsize]=size(x);                    %Overall vector size


%
%   Form reference signal, out of phase 60 Hz, 5 seconds
%
b=sin(2*pi*60*t);                         %One pulse period
r=[b b b b b];                            %Append to make five copies


%-----------------------------------------------------------------------------
%
%   Adaptive cancelling:

%
%   Initialization
%
w=[0 0];                                  %Two real weights
mu=0;                                     %Freeze adaptation at first
out=zeros(1,nsize);                       %Reserve output array


%
%   Update recursion over all data
%
for k=2:nsize,                            %Adapt over full five sec
    y=w*r(k:-1:k-1)';                     %Filter output: from reference

    if k >200,                            %Start adapting at 0.4 sec
        mu=.015;                          %Set active stepsize
    end

    err=x(k)-y;                           %Error: primary - reference
    out(k)=err;                           %Canceller output = error
    w=w+mu*err*r(k:-1:k-1);               %Update weight vector
end


%-----------------------------------------------------------------------------
%
%   Output picture
```

```
figure(1)                              %Plot the resulting output
t=[0:1:nsize-1]/500;                   %Time scale
subplot(211)                           %Long plot aspect ratio
plot(t,out,'k')                        %Plot canceller output, b&w
axis([0 5 -100 100])                   %Scale it
grid on                                %Reference grid

print pix8-2.eps -deps                 %Capture it
```

A.2.2 Figure 4.5a: Learning Curve for LMS Line Canceller

```
%
%    Ensemble averaging of LMS performance curves, generating Fig 4.5a
%

%--------------------------------------------------------------------------
%
%    Set up structure for the run
%
clear all                              %Clean up everything
close all

N=32;                                  %Filter order
npts=100;                              %Time duration
ntrials=100;                           %Ensemble size
t=[1:npts+N];                          %Time span
f=[0:1:N-1];                           %Frequency steps
wave=zeros(2,npts+1);                  %Averaging storage
                                       % for averaging 2-bins history

%
%    Tone parameters
%
a=4;                                   %Off frequency f1 in input
b=3;                                   %Input tone at f2 that cancels
c=2;                                   %Desired tone at f2
f1=5/N;                                %Frequency of non-cancelling tone
f2=9/N;                                %Frequency of cancelling tone

v1=exp(-i*2*pi*f*f1);                  %DFT coefficient vector, f1
v2=exp(-i*2*pi*f*f2);                  %DFT coefficient vector, f2

d=c*cos(2*pi*t'*f2);                   %Desired tone defined
mu=.00078;                             %LMS step size

%--------------------------------------------------------------------------
%
```

```
%    Outer loop, once per ensemble member
%
for m=1:ntrials,
    r1=rand(1,1)*2*pi;                      %Randomize phase on two inputs
    r2=rand(1,1)*2*pi;
    n=randn([npts+N,1])*sqrt(.16);          %Record of random noise
    x=a*cos(2*pi*t'*f1+r1)+b*cos(2*pi*t'*f2+r2)+n; %Composite input record
    w=real((v1+v2)'*c/b/N);                 %Initial weights, bin level .5
    whold=zeros(2,npts);                    %Initialize 2-bin evolution

    %
    %    Inner iteration loop
    %
    for k=1:npts+1;
        y=w'*x(k+N-1:-1:k);                 %Output calculation
        e=d(k+N-1)-y;                       %Error
        w=w+mu*e*x(k+N-1:-1:k);             %Update

        whold(1,k)=abs(v1*w);               %Save bin gain, both frequencies
        whold(2,k)=abs(v2*w);
    end

    whold=abs(whold*b/c);                   %Normalize gain, known final value
    wave=wave+whold;                        %Accumulate current weights

    %
    %    Plot individual members in grey
    %
    h=plot([.1,1:npts]',whold(1,:));        %Frequency f1 curve
    set(h,{'Color'},{[.9 .9 .9]})           %Light grey
    set(h,'LineWidth',.1)                   %Narrow line
    hold on

    h=plot([.1,1:npts]',whold(2,:));        %Frequency f2 curve
    set(h,{'Color'},{[.9 .9 .9]})           %Light grey
    set(h,'LineWidth',.1)                   %Narrow line

    if mod(m,10) == 0,
        fprintf('%3i\r',m)                  %Counter display
    end
end


%-----------------------------------------------------------------------
%
%    Finish up by plotting average curves
%
```

```
h=plot([0:npts]',wave(1,:)/ntrials);      %Average of frequency 1 ensemble
set(h,{'Color'},{[0 0 0]})                %Black
set(h,'LineWidth',2.5)                     %Broad line

h=plot([0:npts]',wave(2,:)/ntrials);      %Average of frequency 2 ensemble
set(h,{'Color'},{[0 0 0]})                %Black
set(h,'LineWidth',2.5)                     %Broad line
grid                                       %Grid
axis([0 npts 0 1.4])                       %With proper scale


%-----------------------------------------------------------------------
%
%    Print it
%
print figpix.eps -depsc
```

A.2.3 Figure 4.5b: Learning Curve for RLS Line Canceller

```
%
%    Ensemble averaging of RLS performance curves, generating Fig 4.5b
%


%-----------------------------------------------------------------------
%
%    Set up structure for the run
%
%
clear all                                  %Clean up everything
close all

N=32;                                      %Filter order
npts=100;                                  %Time duration
ntrials=100;                               %Ensemble size
t=[1:npts+N];                              %Time span
f=[0:1:N-1];                               %Frequency steps
wave=zeros(2,npts+1);                      %Averaging storage
                                           %  for averaging 2-bins history

%
%    Tone parameters
%
a=4;                                       %Off frequency f1 in input
b=3;                                       %Input tone at f2 that cancels
c=2;                                       %Desired tone at f2
f1=5/N;                                    %Frequency of non-cancelling tone
f2=9/N;                                    %Frequency of cancelling tone
```

```
v1=exp(-i*2*pi*f*f1);                     %DFT coefficient vector, f1
v2=exp(-i*2*pi*f*f2);                     %DFT coefficient vector, f2

d=c*cos(2*pi*t'*f2);                      %Desired tone defined
eta=10000;                                %Initialization of Rinv matrix
rho=1;                                    %RLS forgetting factor


%-------------------------------------------------------------------------
%
%   Outer loop for each ensemble member
%
for m=1:ntrials,
    r1=rand(1,1)*2*pi;                    %Randomize phase on two inputs
    r2=rand(1,1)*2*pi;
    n=randn([npts+N,1])*sqrt(.16);        %Record of random noise
    x=a*cos(2*pi*t'*f1+r1)+b*cos(2*pi*t'*f2+r2)+n; %Composite input record
    w=real((v1+v2)'*c/b/N);               %Initial weights, bin level .5
    whold=zeros(2,npts);                  %Initialize 2-bin evolution
    Rinv=eta*eye(N);                      %Initialization of Rinv matrix

    %
    %   Inner iteration loop
    %
    for k=1:npts+1;
        y0=w'*x(k+N-1:-1:k);              %Apriori output
        e0=d(k+N-1)-y0;                   %Apriori error
        Z=Rinv*x(k+N-1:-1:k);            %Filtered input
        q=x(k+N-1:-1:k)'*Z;              %Power estimate
        v=1/(rho+q);
        Ztilda=v*Z;
        w=w+e0*Z*v;                       %Update equation
        Rinv=(Rinv-Z*Z'*v)/rho;          %And correlation inverse

        whold(1,k)=abs(v1*w);             %Save bin gain, both frequencies
        whold(2,k)=abs(v2*w);
        ehold(k)=abs(e0);                 %And apriori error
    end

    whold=abs(whold*b/c);                 %Normalize gain, known final value
    wave=wave+whold;                      %Accumulate current weights

    %
    % Plot individual members in grey
    %
    h=plot([.1,1:npts]',whold(1,:));      %Frequency f1 curve
    set(h,{'Color'},{[.9 .9 .9]})         %Light grey
```

```
    set(h,'LineWidth',.1)                  %Narrow line
    hold on

    h=plot([.1,1:npts]',whold(2,:));       %Frequency f2 curve
    set(h,{'Color'},{[.9 .9 .9]})          %Light grey
    set(h,'LineWidth',.1)                  %Narrow line

    if mod(m,10) == 0,
        fprintf('%3i\r',m)                 %Counter display
    end

end

%---------------------------------------------------------------------------
%
%   Finish up by plotting average curves
%

h=plot([0:npts]',wave(1,:)/ntrials);       %Average of frequency 1 ensemble
set(h,{'Color'},{[0 0 0]})                 %Black
set(h,'LineWidth',2.5)                     %Broad line

h=plot([0:npts]',wave(2,:)/ntrials);       %Average of frequency 2 ensemble
set(h,{'Color'},{[0 0 0]})                 %Black
set(h,'LineWidth',2.5)                     %Broad line
grid                                       %Grid
axis([0 npts 0 1.4])                       %With proper scale

%---------------------------------------------------------------------------
%
%   Print it
%
print figpix.eps -depsc
```

Bibliography

B. AGEE, "The Least-Squares CMA: A New Technique for Rapid Correction of Constant Modulus Signals," *Proc. 1986 IEEE Int. Conf. on Acoustics, Speech, and Signal Processing*, Tokyo, Japan, pp. 953–956, 1986.

A. E. ALBERT AND L. A. GARDNER, *Stochastic Approximation and Non-Linear Regression*, MIT Press, 1967.

S. T. ALEXANDER, *Adaptive Signal Processing Theory and Applications*, Springer-Verlag, 1986.

B. D. O. ANDERSON AND C. R. JOHNSON, JR., "Exponential Convergence of Adaptive Identification and Control Algorithms," *Automatica*, vol. 18, pp. 1–13, January 1982a.

B. D. O. ANDERSON AND C. R. JOHNSON, JR., "On Reduced-Order Adaptive Output Error Identification and Adaptive IIR Filtering," *IEEE Trans. on Automat. Control*, vol. AC-27, pp. 927–933, August 1982b.

B. D. O. ANDERSON AND R. M. JOHNSTONE, "Adaptive Systems and Time-Varying Plants," *Int. J. Control*, vol. 37, pp. 367–377, 1983.

B. D. O. ANDERSON, R. R. BITMEAD, C. R. JOHNSON, JR., P. V. KOKOTOVIC, R. L. KOSUT, I. M. Y. MAREELS, L. PRALY, AND B. D. RIEDLE, *Stability of Adaptive Systems: Passivity and Averaging Analysis*, MIT Press, 1986.

ADVANCED TELEVISION SYSTEMS COMMITTEE (ATSC), "Digital Television Standard Document A/53," September 1995 (and "Amendment No. 1," March 2000).

J. BELLAMY, *Digital Telephony*, 2nd ed., Wiley, Chapter 2, 1991.

M. G. BELLANGER AND J. L. DAGUET, "TDM-FDM Transmultiplexer: Digital Polyphase and FFT," *IEEE Trans. on Communications*, vol. COM-22, pp. 1199–1205, September 1974.

S. BELLINI, "Bussgang Techniques for Blind Deconvolution and Equalization" in *Blind Deconvolution*, Simon Haykin, editor, pp. 8–59, Prentice-Hall, 1994.

P. A. BELLO, "Characterization of Randomly Time-Invariant Linear Channels," *IEEE Trans. on Communication Syst.*, vol. CS-11, pp. 360–393, December 1963.

A. BENVENISTE, M. GOURSAT, AND G. RUGET, "Robust Identification of a Nonminimum Phase System: Blind Adjustment of a Linear Equalizer in Data Communications," *IEEE Trans. on Automatic Control*, vol. AC-25, pp. 385–399, June 1980.

A. BENVENISTE, M. MÉTIVIER, AND P. PRIOURET, *Adaptive Algorithms and Stochastic Approximations*, Springer-Verlag, 1990.

N. J. BERSHAD AND P. L. FEINTUCH, "The Recursive LMS Filter: A Line Enhancer Application and Analytical Model for Mean Weight Behavior," *IEEE Trans. on Acoustics, Speech, and Signal Processing*, vol. ASSP-28, pp. 652–660, December 1980.

J. A. C. BINGHAM, *The Theory and Practice of Modem Design*, Wiley Interscience, 1988.

R. R. BITMEAD AND C. R. JOHNSON, JR., "Discrete Averaging Principles and Robust Adaptive Identification" in *Control and Dynamic Systems: Advances in Theory and Applications, Vol. 25: System Identification and Adaptive Control, Part 1 of 3*, ed. C. T. Leondes, pp. 237–271, 1987.

C. S. BURRUS AND T. W. PARKS, *DFT/FFT and Convolution Algorithms*, Wiley Interscience, 1985.

J. A. CADZOW, "Recursive Digital Filter Synthesis via Gradient Based Algorithms," *IEEE Trans. on Acoustics, Speech, and Signal Processing*, vol. ASSP-24, pp. 349–355, October 1976.

C. CARAISCOS AND B. LIU, "A Roundoff Error Analysis of the LMS Adaptive Algorithm," *IEEE Trans. on Acoustics, Speech, and Signal Processing*, vol. ASSP-32, pp. 34–41, February 1984.

J.-F. CARDOSO, "Blind Signal Separation: Statistical Principles," *Proc. IEEE*, vol. 86, pp. 2009–2025, October 1998.

A. B. CARLSON, *Communication Systems*, McGraw-Hill, 1975.

R. A. CASAS, T. J. ENDRES, A. TOUZNI, C. R. JOHNSON, JR., AND J. R. TREICHLER, "Current Approaches to Blind Decision Feedback Equalization" in *Signal Processing Advances in Communications, Part I: Trends in Blind Channel Estimation and Equalization*, G. Giannakis, Y. Hua, P. Stoica, and L. Tong, ed., Prentice-Hall, pp. 367–415, 2001.

J. CHANG AND J. R. GLOVER, JR., "The Feedback Adaptive Line Enhancer: A Constrained IIR Adaptive Filter," *IEEE Trans. on Signal Processing*, vol. 41, pp. 3161–3166, November 1993.

J. M. CIOFFI AND T. KAILATH, "Fast, Recursive-Least-Squares Transversal Filters for Adaptive Filtering," *IEEE Trans. on Acoustics, Speech, and Signal Processing*, vol. ASSP-32, pp. 304–337, April 1984.

R. T. COMPTON, JR., *Adaptive Antennas: Concepts and Performance* Prentice-Hall, 1988.

J. E. COUSSEAU, "Adaptive IIR Filtering: Available Results," *IEEE Circuits and Systems Society Newsletter*, vol. 10, September/October 1999.

S. DASGUPTA AND C. R. JOHNSON, JR., "Some Comments on the Behavior of Sign-Sign Adaptive Identifiers," *Systems and Control Letters*, pp. 75–82, April 1986.

M. DENTINO, J. McCOOL, AND B. WIDROW, "Adaptive Filtering in the Frequency Domain," *Proc. IEEE*, vol. 66, pp. 1658–1659, December 1978.

Z. DING, R. A. KENNEDY, B. D. O. ANDERSON, AND C. R. JOHNSON, JR., "Ill-Convergence of Godard Blind Equalizers in Data Communication Systems," *IEEE Transactions on Communications*, vol. 39, pp. 1313–1327, September 1991.

D. L. DONOHO, "On Minimum Entropy Deconvolution" in *Applied Time Series Analysis II*, D. Findley, editor, pp. 565–608, Academic, 1981.

S. C. DOUGLAS, A. CHICHOCKI, AND S. AMARI, "Self-Whitening Algorithms for Adaptive Equalization and Deconvolution," *IEEE Trans. on Signal Processing*, vol. 47, pp. 1161–1165, April 1999.

D. D. FALCONER AND L. LJUNG, "Application of Fast Kalman Estimation to Adaptive Equalization," *IEEE Trans. on Communications*, vol. COM-26, pp. 1439–1446, October 1978.

P. L. FEINTUCH, "An Adaptive Recursive LMS Filter," *Proc. IEEE*, vol. 64, pp. 1622–1624, November 1976.

E. R. FERRARA, "Fast Implementation of the LMS Adaptive Filter," *IEEE Trans. on Acoustics, Speech, and Signal Processing*, vol. ASSP-28, pp. 474–475, August 1980.

E. R. FERRARA AND B. WIDROW, "The Time-Sequenced Adaptive Filter," *IEEE Trans. on Acoustics, Speech, and Signal Processing*, vol. ASSP-29, pp. 679–683, June 1981.

G. J. FOSCHINI, "Equalizing Without Altering or Detecting Data (Digital Radio Signals)," *AT & T Technical Journal*, vol. 64, pp. 1885–1911, October 1985.

U. FORSSÉN, "Simple Derivation of Adaptive Algorithm for Arbitrary Filter Structures," *Electronics Letters*, October 11, 1990.

S. L. FREENEY, "TDM/FDM Translation as an Application of Digital Signal Processing," *IEEE Communications Magazine*, vol. 18, pp. 5–15, January 1980.

B. FRIEDLANDER, "System Identification Techniques for Adaptive Signal Processing," *IEEE Trans. on Acoustics, Speech, and Signal Processing*, vol. ASSP-30, pp. 240–246, April 1982.

H.T. FRIIS AND C.B. FELDMAN, "A Multiple Unit Steerable Array for Short-wave Reception," *Bell System Technical Journal*, vol. 16, pp. 337–419, 1937.

A. GERSHO, "Adaptive Equalization of Highly Dispersive Channels for Data Transmission," *Bell System Tech. Journal*, vol. 48, pp. 55–70, January 1969.

A. GERSHO, "Adaptive Filtering with Binary Reinforcement," *IEEE Trans. on Information Theory*, vol. IT-30, pp. 191–199, March 1984.

J. D. GIBSON, "Adaptive Prediction in Speech Differential Encoding Systems," *Proc. IEEE*, vol. 68, pp. 488–525, April 1980.

R. D. GITLIN, H. C. MEADORS, AND S. B. WEINSTEIN, "The Tap-Leakage Algorithm: An Algorithm for the Stable Operation of a Digitally Implemented, Fractionally Spaced, Adaptive Equalizer," *Bell Syst. Tech. Journal*, vol. 61, pp. 1817–1840, October 1982.

R. D. GITLIN, J. F. HAYES, AND S. B. WEINSTEIN, *Data Communications Principles*, Plenum Press 1992.

J. R. GLOVER, "Adaptive Noise Cancelling Applied to Sinusoidal Interference," *IEEE Trans. on Acoustics, Speech, and Signal Processing*, vol. ASSP-25, pp. 484–491, December 1977.

D. N. GODARD, "Self-Recovering Equalization and Carrier Tracking in Two-Dimensional Data Communication Systems," *IEEE Trans. on Communications*, vol. COM-28, pp. 1867–1875, November 1980.

B. GOLD AND C. M. RADER, *Digital Processing of Signals*, McGraw-Hill, Chapter 8, 1969.

R. P. GOOCH AND J. C. HARP, "Blind Channel Identification Using the Constant Modulus Algorithm," *Proc. 1988 IEEE Int. Conf. on Communications*, Philadelphia, PA, pp. 75–79, 1988.

G. C. GOODWIN AND K. S. SIN, *Adaptive Filtering, Prediction, and Control*, Prentice-Hall, 1984.

R. M. GRAY, "On the Asymptotic Eigenvalue Distribution of Toeplitz Matrices," *IEEE Trans. on Info. Thy.*, vol. IT-18, pp. 725–730, November 1972.

A. H. GRAY AND J. D. MARKEL, "Digital Lattice and Ladder Filter Synthesis," *IEEE Trans. on Audio and Electroacoustics*, vol. AU-21, pp. 491–500, December 1973.

L. J. GRIFFITHS, "A Simple Adaptive Algorithm for Real Time Processing in Antenna Arrays," *Proc. IEEE*, vol. 57, pp. 1696–1704, October 1967.

M. L. HONIG AND D. G. MESSERSCHMITT, *Adaptive Filters: Structures, Algorithms, and Applications*, Kluwer Academic, 1984.

S. HORVATH, JR., "A New Adaptive Recursive LMS Filter," in *Digital Signal Processing* (ed. V. Cappellini and A. G. Constantinides), Academic Press, pp. 21–26, 1980.

N. S. JAYANT AND P. NOLL, *Digital Coding of Waveforms: Principles and Applications to Speech and Video*, Prentice-Hall, 1984.

F. JIANG, H. TSUJI, H. OHMORI, AND A. SANO, "Adaptation for Active Noise Control," *IEEE Control Systems Magazine*, vol. 17, pp. 36–47, December 1997.

C. R. JOHNSON, JR., "A Convergence Proof for a Hyperstable Adaptive Recursive Filter," *IEEE Trans. on Info. Thy.*, vol. IT-25, pp. 745–749, November 1979.

C. R. JOHNSON, JR., "Adaptive IIR Filtering: Current Results and Open Issues," *IEEE Trans. on Information Theory*, vol. 30, pp. 237–250, March 1984.

C. R. JOHNSON, JR. AND M. G. LARIMORE, "Comments on and Additions to 'An Adaptive Recursive LMS Filter'," *Proc. IEEE*, vol. 65, pp. 1399–1401, September 1977.

C. R. JOHNSON, JR., M. G. LARIMORE, J. R. TREICHLER, AND B. D. O. ANDERSON, "SHARF Convergence Properties," *IEEE Trans. on Acoustics, Speech, and Signal Processing*, vol. ASSP-29, pp. 659–670, June 1981.

C. R. JOHNSON, JR., P. SCHNITER, T. J. ENDRES, J. D. BEHM, D. R. BROWN, AND R. A. CASAS, "Blind Equalization Using the Constant Modulus Criterion: A Review," *Proc. IEEE*, vol. 86, pp. 1927–1950, October 1998.

C. R. JOHNSON, JR., P. SCHNITER, I. FIJALKOW, L. TONG, J. D. BEHM, M. G. LARIMORE, D. R. BROWN, R. A. CASAS, T. J. ENDRES, S. LAMBOTHARAN, A. TOUZNI, H. H. ZENG, M. GREEN, AND J. R. TREICHLER, "The Core of FSE-CMA Behavior Theory" in *Unsupervised Adaptive Filtering, vol. II: Blind Deconvolution*, Simon Haykin, editor, pp. 13–112, Wiley, 2000.

M. S. KACZMERZ, "ANGENÄHERTE AUSLÖSUNG VON SYSTEMEN LINEARER GLEICHUNGEN," *Academie Polonaise des Sciences et des Lettres*, Bull. A, vol. 3, pp. 355–357, 1937.

T. KAILATH, *Linear Systems*, Prentice-Hall, 1980.

K. KNOPP, *Infinite Sequences and Series*, Dover, 1956.

I. D. LANDAU, "Unbiased Recursive Identification Using Model Reference Adaptive Techniques," *IEEE Trans. on Automat. Control*, vol. AC-21, pp. 194–202, April 1976.

M. G. LARIMORE AND M. J. GOODMAN, "Implementation of the Constant Modulus Algorithm at RF Bandwidths," *Proc. 19th Asilomar Conf. on Circuits, Sys., and Computers*, Pacific Grove, CA, November 1985.

M. G. LARIMORE, J. R. TREICHLER, AND C. R. JOHNSON, JR., "SHARF: An Algorithm for Adapting IIR Digital Filters," *IEEE Trans. on Acoustics, Speech, and Signal Processing*, vol. ASSP-28, pp. 428–440, August 1980.

D. A. LAWRENCE AND C. R. JOHNSON, JR., "Recursive Parameter Identification Algorithm Stability Analysis Via Pi-Sharing," *IEEE Trans. on Automat. Control*, vol. AC-31, pp. 16–24, January 1986.

J. C. LIBERTI AND T. S. RAPPAPORT, *Smart Antennas for Wireless Communications: IS-95 and Third Generation CDMA Applications*, Prentice-Hall, 1999.

L. LJUNG, "On Positive Real Functions and the Convergence of Some Recursive Schemes," *IEEE Trans. on Automat. Control*, vol. AC-22, pp. 539–551, August 1977.

L. LJUNG, *System Identification: Theory for the User*, Prentice Hall, 1987.

L. LJUNG, M. MORF, AND D. FALCONER, "Fast Calculation of Gain Matrices for Recursive Estimation Schemes," *Int. J. Control*, vol. 27, pp. 1–19, 1978.

L. LJUNG AND T. SÖDERSTRÖM, *Theory and Practice of Recursive Identification*, MIT Press, 1983.

R. W. LUCKY, J. SALZ, AND E. J. WELDON, JR., *Principles of Data Communications*, McGraw-Hill, Chapter 3, 1968.

O. MACCHI, *Adaptive Processing: The Least Mean Squares Approach with Applications in Transmission*, Wiley, 1995.

O. MACCHI AND E. EWEDA, "Convergence Analysis of Self-Adaptive Equalizers," *IEEE Trans. on Info. Theory*, vol. IT-30, pp. 161–176, March 1984.

I. MAREELS AND J. W. POLDERMAN, *Adaptive Systems: An Introduction*, Birkhäuser, 1996.

J. L. MELSA AND A. P. SAGE, *An Introduction to Probability and Stochastic Processes*, Prentice-Hall, 1973.

J. M. MENDEL, *Discrete Techniques of Parmaeter Estimation: The Equation Error Formulation*, Marcel Dekker, 1973.

L. B. MILSTEIN, "Interference Rejection Techniques in Spread Spectrum Communications," *Proc. IEEE*, vol. 76, pp. 657–671, June 1988.

P. MONSON, "Feedback Equalization for Fading Dispersive Channels," *IEEE Trans. on Info. Thy.*, vol. IT-17, pp. 54–64, January 1971.

R. A. MONZINGO AND T. W. MILLER, *Introduction to Adaptive Arrays*, Wiley-Interscience, 1980.

M. J. NARASIMHA AND A. M. PETERSON, "Design of a 24-Channel Transmultiplexer," *IEEE Trans. on Acoustics, Speech, and Signal Processing*, vol. ASSP-27, pp. 752–762, December 1979.

M. NAYERI AND W. K. JENKINS, "Alternate Realizations of Adaptive IIR Filters and Properties of their Error Surfaces," *IEEE Trans. Circuits and Systems*, vol. 36, pp. 485–496, April 1989.

P. A. NELSON AND S. J. ELLIOTT, *Active Control of Sound*, Academic Press, 1992.

B. NOBLE AND J. W. DANIEL, *Applied Linear Algebra*, Prentice-Hall, 1977.

F. F. E. OWEN, *PCM and Digital Transmission Systems*, McGraw-Hill, 1982.

M. D. PAEZ AND T. H. GLISSON, "Minimum Mean Squared-Error Quantization in Speech," *IEEE Trans. on Communications*, vol. COM-20, pp. 225–230, April 1972.

D. PARIKH AND N. AHMED, "On an Adaptive Algorithm for IIR Filters," *Proc. IEEE*, vol. 65, pp. 585–587, May 1978.

D. PARIKH, N. AHMED, AND S. STEARNS, "An Adaptive Lattice Algorithm for Recursive Filters," *IEEE Trans. on Acoustics, Speech, and Signal Processing*, vol. ASSP-28, pp. 110–111, February 1980.

A. J. PAULRAJ AND C. B. PAPADIAS, "Space-Time Processing for Wireless Communications," *IEEE Signal Processing Magazine*, vol. 14, pp. 49–83, November 1997.

V. M. POPOV, *Hyperstability of Control Systems*, Springer-Verlag, 1973.

L. R. RABINER AND B. GOLD, *Theory and Application of Digital Signal Processing*, Prentice-Hall, 1975.

L. R. RABINER AND R. W. SCHAFER, *Digital Processing of Speech Signals*, Prentice-Hall, 1978.

B. RAFAELY AND S. J. ELLIOTT, "A Computationally Efficient Frequency-Domain LMS Algorithm with Constraints on the Adaptive Filter," *IEEE Trans. on Signal Processing*, vol. 48, pp. 1649–1655, June 2000.

T. S. RAPPAPORT, *Wireless Communications Principles and Practice*, Prentice-Hall, 1996.

P. A. REGALIA, *Adaptive IIR Filtering in Signal Processing and Control*, Marcel Dekker, 1995.

E. A. ROBINSON AND S. TREITEL, *Geophysical Signal Analysis*, Prentice Hall, 1980.

J. A. RODRIGUEZ-FONOLLOSA AND E. MASGRAU, "Simplified Gradient Calculation in Adaptive IIR Lattice Filters," *IEEE Trans. on Signal Processing*, vol. 39, pp. 1702–1705, July 1991.

U. L. ROHDE AND T. T. N. BUCHER, *Communications Receivers: Principles and Design*, McGraw-Hill, 1988.

J. SALZ, "Optimum Mean-Square Decision Feedback Equalization," *Bell System Tech. Journal*, vol. 50, no. 8, pp. 1341–1373, October 1973.

E. H. SATORIUS AND S. T. ALEXANDER, "Channel Equalization Using Adaptive Lattice Algorithms," *IEEE Trans. on Communications*, vol. COM-27, pp. 899–905, June 1979.

W. A. SETHARES AND C. R. JOHNSON, JR., "A Comparison of Two Quantized State Adaptive Algorithms," *IEEE Trans. on Acoustics, Speech, and Signal Processing*, vol. 37, pp. 138–143, January 1989.

W. A. SETHARES, I. M. Y. MAREELS, B. D. O. ANDERSON, C. R. JOHNSON, JR., AND R. R. BITMEAD, "Excitation Conditions for Signed-Regressor Least Mean Squares Adaptation," *IEEE Trans. on Circuits and Systems*, vol. 35, pp. 613–624, June 1988.

W. A. SETHARES, B. D. O. ANDERSON, AND C. R. JOHNSON, JR., "Adaptive Algorithms with Filtered Regressor and Filtered Error," *Mathematics of Control, Signals, and Systems*, vol. 2, pp. 381–403, 1989.

J. J. SHYNK, "Adaptive IIR Filtering Using Parallel-Form Realizations," *IEEE Trans. on Acoustics, Speech, and Signal Processing*, vol. 37, pp. 519–533, April 1989a.

J. J. SHYNK, "Adaptive IIR Filtering," *IEEE Signal Processing Magazine*, vol. 6, pp. 4–21, April 1989b.

J. J. SHYNK, "Frequency-Domain and Multirate Adaptive Filtering," *IEEE Signal Processing Magazine*, vol. 9, pp. 14–37, January 1992.

J. J. SHYNK AND R. P. GOOCH, "Frequency-Domain Adaptive Pole-Zero Filtering," *Proc. IEEE*, vol. 73, pp. 1526–1528, October 1985.

T. SÖDERSTRÖM, L. LJUNG, AND I. GUSTAVSSON, "A Theoretical Analysis of Recursive Identification Methods," *Automatica*, vol. 14, pp. 231–244, May 1978.

T. SÖDERSTRÖM AND P. STOICA, *System Identification*, Prentice Hall, 1989.

V. SOLO, "The Convergence of AML," *IEEE Trans. on Automat. Control*, vol. AC-24, pp. 958–962, December 1979.

V. SOLO AND X. KONG, *Adaptive Signal Processing Algorithms: Stability and Performance*, Prentice-Hall, 1995.

T. STARR, J. M. CIOFFI, AND P. J. SILVERMAN, *Understanding Digital Subscriber Line Technology*, Prentice-Hall, 1999.

S. D. STEARNS, G. R. ELLIOTT, AND N. AHMED, "On Adaptive Recursive Filtering," *Proc. 10th Asilomar Conf. on Circuits, Sys., and Computers*, Pacific Grove, CA, pp. 5–10, November 1976.

K. E. STEIGLITZ AND L. E. MCBRIDE, "A Technique for the Identification of Linear Systems," *IEEE Trans. on Automatic Control*, vol. 10, pp. 461–464, October 1965.

M. J. TANT, *The White Noise Book*, White Crescent Press, 1974.

M. TOMIZUKA, "Parallel MRAS without Compensation Block," *IEEE Trans. on Automat. Control*, vol. AC-27, pp. 505–506, April 1982.

J. R. TREICHLER, "Transient and Convergent Behavior of the Adaptive Line Enhancer," *IEEE Trans. on Acoustics, Speech, and Signal Processing*, vol. ASSP-27, pp. 53–62, February 1979.

J. R. TREICHLER, "Observability and Its Effect on the Design of ML and MAP Joint Estimators," *IEEE Trans. on Information Theory*, vol. IT-26, pp. 498–503, July 1980.

J. R. TREICHLER, "Adaptive Algorithms for Infinite Impulse Response Filters" in *Adaptive Filters*, eds. C. F. N. Cowan and P. M. Grant, Prentice-Hall, 1985.

J. R. TREICHLER AND B. G. AGEE, "A New Approach to Multipath Correction of Constant Modulus Signals," *IEEE Trans. on Acoustics, Speech, and Signal Processing*, vol. ASSP-31, pp. 459–472, April 1983.

J. TREICHLER AND J. BOHANON, "Blind Demodulation of High-order QAM Signals in the Presence of Cross-Pole Interference," *Proc. 1998 IEEE Int. Conf. on Circuits and Systems*, Monterey, CA, June 1998.

J. R. TREICHLER AND M. G. LARIMORE, "New Processing Techniques Based on the Constant Modulus Adaptive Algorithm," *IEEE Trans. on Acoustics, Speech, and Signal Processing*, vol. ASSP-33, pp. 420–431, April 1985a.

J. R. TREICHLER AND M. G. LARIMORE, "The Tone Capture Properties of CMA-Based Interference Suppressors," *IEEE Trans. on Acoustics, Speech, and Signal Processing*, vol. ASSP-33, pp. 946–958, August 1985b.

J. R. TREICHLER, I. FIJALKOW, AND C. R. JOHNSON, JR., "Fractionally Spaced Equalizers: How Long Should They Really Be?" *IEEE Signal Processing Magazine*, vol. 13, pp. 65–81, May 1996.

J. R. TREICHLER, M. G. LARIMORE, AND J. C. HARP, "Practical Blind Demodulators for High-Order QAM Signals," *Proc. IEEE*, vol. 86, pp. 1907–1926, October 1998.

J. R. TREICHLER, M. G. LARIMORE, AND C. R. JOHNSON, JR., "Voiceband Modems: A Signal Processing Success Story," *IEEE Signal Processing Magazine*, vol. 16, pp. 21–25, March 1999.

S. A. TRETTER, *Introduction to Discrete Time Signal Processing*, Wiley, Chapter 2, 1976.

S. A. WHITE, "An Adaptive Recursive Filter," *Proc. 9th Asilomar Conf. on Circuits, Sys., and Computers*, Pacific Grove, CA, pp. 21–25, November 1975.

B. WIDROW, "Statistical Analysis of Amplitude-Quantized Sampled-Data Systems," *AIEE Trans. (Applications and Industry)*, vol. 81, pp. 555–568, January 1961.

B. WIDROW AND M. HOFF, JR., "Adaptive Switching Circuits," *IRE WESCON Conv. Record*, pt. 4, pp. 96–104, 1960.

B. WIDROW AND J. M. MCCOOL, "A Comparison of Adaptive Algorithms Based on the Methods of Steepest Descent and Random Search," *IEEE Trans. of Antennas and Propagation*, vol. AP-24, No. 5, pp. 615–636, September 1976.

B. WIDROW AND S. STEARNS, *Adaptive Signal Processing*, Prentice Hall, 1985.

B. WIDROW, J. M. MCCOOL, AND M. BALL, "The Complex LMS Algorithm," *Proc. IEEE*, vol. 63, pp. 719–720, April 1975a.

B. WIDROW, J. R. GLOVER, JR., J. M. MCCOOL, J. KAUNITZ, C. S. WILLIAMS, R. H. HEARN, J. R. ZEIDLER, E. DONG, JR., AND R. C. GOODLIN, "Adaptive Noise Cancelling: Principles and Applications," *Proc. IEEE*, vol. 63, pp. 1692–1716, December 1975b.

B. WIDROW, J. M. MCCOOL, M. G. LARIMORE, AND C. R. JOHNSON, JR., "Stationary and Non-stationary Learning Characteristics of the LMS Adaptive Filter," *Proc. IEEE*, vol. 64, pp. 1151–1162, August 1976.

G. A. WILLIAMSON, B. D. O. ANDERSON, AND C. R. JOHNSON, JR., "On the Local Stability Properties of Adaptive Parameter Estimators with Composite Errors and Split Algorithms," *IEEE Trans. on Automatic Control*, vol. 36, pp. 463–473, April 1991a.

G. A. WILLIAMSON, C. R. JOHNSON, JR., AND B. D. O. ANDERSON, "Locally Robust Identification of Linear Systems Containing Unknown Gain Elements with Application to Adapted IIR Lattice Models," *Automatica*, vol. 27, pp. 783–798, September 1991b.

E. S. YAM AND M. D. REDMAN, "Development of a 60-Channel FDM-TDM Transmultiplexer," *COMSAT Technical Review*, vol. 13, pp. 1–56, Spring 1983.

C. L. ZAHM, "Application of Adaptive Arrays to Suppress Strong Jammers in the Presence of Weak Signals," *IEEE Trans. on Aerospace and Electronic Systems*, vol. AES-9, No. 2, pp. 260–271, March 1973.

J. R. ZEIDLER, E. H. SATORIUS, D. M. CHABRIES, AND H. T. WEXLER, "Adaptive Enhancement of Multiple Sinusoids in Uncorrelated Noise," *IEEE Trans. on Acoustics, Speech, and Signal Processing*, vol. ASSP-26, pp. 240–254, June 1978.

Index